Pocket
French–English
English–French
Dictionary

Published 2020 by Geddes & Grosset,
an imprint of The Gresham Publishing Company,
31, Six Harmony Row,
Glasgow, G51 3BA, Scotland

www.geddesandgrosset.com
Contact us at info@geddesandgrosset.com
Find us on facebook/pages/geddesandgrosset
© 1998 Geddes & Grosset

First published 1998
Reprinted 1999 (twice), 2000 (three printings),
2001, 2002 (twice), 2003, 2004,
2005 (twice), 2006, 2009, 2016 (revised), 2020

ISBN: 978 1 910965 36 8

Printed and bound in the EU

WEBSTER'S **WORD POWER** ✔

Pocket
French–English
English–French
Dictionary

GEDDES & GROSSET

	Abbreviations	**Abréviations**
abrev	abbreviation	abréviation
adj	adjective	adjectif
adv	adverb	adverbe
art	article	articule
auto	automobile	automobile
aux	auxiliary	auxiliaire
bot	botany	botanique
com	commerce	commerce
comput	computers	informatique
conj	conjunction	conjonction
f	feminine noun	substantif fémenin
fam	colloquial term	expression familière
fig	figurative	figuré
gr	grammar	grammaire
law	law term	jurisprudence
ling	linguistics	linguistique
m	masculine noun	substantif masculin
mar	marine term	vocabulaire marin
mat, math	mathematics	matémathiques
med	medicine	médicine
mil	military term	vocabulaire militaire
mus	music	musique
n	noun	substantif
pl	plural	pluriel
pn	pronoun	pronom
pp	past participle	participe passé
prep	preposition	préposition
rail	railway	chemin de fer
sl	slang	argot
vi	intransitive verb	verbe intransitif
vr	reflexive verb	verbe réfléchi
vt	transitive verb	verbe transitif
zool	zoology	zoologie

French–English Dictionary

A

à *prép* (in)to; at; on; by, per: —**aller ~ l'école** to go to school.

abaisser *vt* to lower.

abandon *m* abandonment, desertion.

abandonner *vt* to abandon, leave.

abattement *m* despondency; exhaustion.

abattoir *m* abattoir, slaughterhouse.

abattu *adj* despondent; exhausted.

abbaye *f* abbey.

abcès *m* abscess.

abdomen *m* abdomen.

abeille *f* bee.

aberration *f* aberration.

abîmer *vt* spoil, damage.

abolir *vt* to abolish.

abolition *f* abolition.

abondamment *adv* abundantly.

abondance *f* abundance.

abondant *adj* abundant, plentiful.

abonder *vi* to be abundant *ou* plentiful.

abonné *m*, **-ée** *f*: —*adj* subscriber.

abonnement *m* subscription.

abonner s'~ *vr* to subscribe, take out a subscription (*à* to).

abord *m*: —**d'~** first (of all).

aborder *vt* to approach.

aboutir *vi* to succeed.

aboutissement *m* outcome; success.

abréger *vt* to shorten; abridge.

abréviation *f* abbreviation.

abri *m* shelter.

abriter *vt* to shelter: —**s'~** *vr* to shelter.

abrupt *adj* abrupt: —**~ement** *adv* abruptly.

absence *f* absence.

absent *adj* absent.

absenter (s') *vr* to leave, go out.

absolu *adj* absolute: —**~ment** *adv* absolutely: —*m* absolute.

absorbant *adj* absorbent.

absorber *vt* to absorb.

absorption *f* absorption.

abstinence *f* abstinence.

abstrait *adj* abstract.

absurde *adj* absurd: —**~ment** *adv* absurdly.

absurdité *f* absurdity.

abus *m* abuse.

abuser *vt* **~ de** to exploit; abuse.

académie *f* academy.

accélérateur *m* accelerator.

accélération *f* acceleration.

accélérer *vi* to speed up, accelerate.

accent *m* accent.

accentuer *vt* to accentuate.

acceptable *adj* acceptable.

accepter *vt* to accept.

accès *m* access.

accessible *adj* accessible.

accident *m* accident.

accidentel *adj* accidental: — **~le-ment** *adv* accidentally.

accommodant *adj* accommodating.

accommoder *vt* to prepare; adapt.

accompagner *vt* to accompany.

accomplir *vt* to do, accomplish.

accomplissement *m* accomplishment.

accord *m* agreement: — **d'~!** okay!, all right!: — **être d'~** to agree.

accorder *vt* to give: — **s'~** *vr* to agree.

accoucher *vi* to give birth.

accrocher *vt* to hang up (*à* on).

accroissement *m* increase.

accroître *vt* to increase.

accueil *m* welcome, reception.

accueillir *vt* to welcome.

accumuler *vt* to accumulate.

accusation *f* accusation.

accusé *m*, **-ée** *f* accused, defendant.

accuser *vt* to accuse.

achat *m* purchase.

acheter *vt* to buy.

acheteur *m*, **-euse** *f* buyer.

achèvement *m* completion.

achever *vt* to finish; complete.

acide *adj* acidic: — *m* acid.

acier *m* steel.

acoustique *adj* acoustic: — *f* acoustics.

acquérir *vt* to buy, purchase.

acrobate *mf* acrobat.

acte *m* act; deed.

acteur *m* **actrice** *f* actor.

actif *adj* active.

action *f* act, action; share.

activement *adv* actively.

activer *vt* to speed up.

activité *f* activity.

actualité *f*: — **l'~** current events.

actuel *adj* current, present: — **~lement** *adv* currently.

adaptable *adj* adaptable.

adaptation *f* adaptation.

adapter *vt* to adapt (*à* to): — **s'~** *vr* to adapt (*à* to).

addition *f* addition; bill.

adéquat *adj* suitable, appropriate.

adhérer *vi* to adhere, stick.

adhésif *adj* adhesive.

adjectif *m* adjective.

admettre *vt* to admit; accept; assume.

administrer *vt* to run; administer.

admirable *adj* admirable: — **-ment** *adv* admirably, brilliantly.

admiration *f* admiration.

admirer *vt* to admire.

adolescence *f* adolescence.

adolescent *m*, **-e** *f* adolescent.

adopter *vt* to adopt.

adorer *vt* to adore, worship.

adrénaline *f* adrenalin.

adresse *f* address; skill.

adresser *vt* to address; send.

adroit *adj* deft, skilful: — **-ement** *adv* deftly, skilfully.

adulte *mf* adult, grown-up: — *adj* adult, full-grown.

adversité *f* adversity.

aérodrome *m* aerodrome, airfield.

aéroport *m* airport.

affable *adj* affable.

affaiblir *vt* to weaken: — **s'~** *vr* to weaken, grow weaker.

affaire *f* matter.

affamé *adj* starving.

affamer *vt* to starve.

affection *f* affection.

affectueusement *adv* affectionately.

affectueux *adj* affectionate.

affermir *vt* to strengthen.

affiche *f* poster.

affiner *vt* to refine.

affirmatif *adj* affirmative.

affirmation *f* assertion.

affirmer *vt* to assert.

affluent *m* tributary.

affoler *vt* to throw into a panic:—**s'~** *vr* to get into a panic.

affréter *vt* to charter.

affreux *adj* horrible; awful.

afin *prép*:—**~ de** (in order) to:—**~ que** in order that.

africain *adj*, *mf* African.

Afrique *f* Africa.

âge *m* age:—**quel ~ as-tu?** how old are you?

âgé *adj* old:—**~ de 10 ans** 10 years old.

agence *f* agency; branch; offices.

agenda *m* diary.

agenouiller (s') *vr* to kneel (down).

agent *m* agent; policeman.

agglomération *f* town, urban area.

aggraver *vt* to make worse; increase.

agile *adj* agile, nimble:—**~ment** *adv* nimbly.

agilité *f* agility.

agir *vi* to act.

agitation *f* agitation.

agiter *vt* to shake; wave:—**s'~** *vr* to move about; fidget.

agneau *m* lamb.

agrandir *vt* to make bigger; to widen; to expand.

agrandissement *m* enlargement.

agréable *adj* agreeable, pleasant.

agressif *adj* aggressive.

agression *f* attack.

agriculteur *m* farmer.

agriculture *f* agriculture, farming.

ahuri *adj* stunned; stupefied.

aide *f* help; aid;

aider *vt* to help.

aigle *m* eagle.

aigre *adj* sour, bitter:—**~ment** *adv* sourly.

aigu *adj* (*f* **aiguë**) shrill; acute.

aiguille *f* needle.

ail *m* garlic.

ailleurs *adv* elsewhere:—**partout ~** everywhere else:—**nulle part ~** nowhere else:—**d'~** moreover; by the way.

aimable *adj* kind:—**~ment** *adv* kindly.

aimant *m* magnet.

aimer *vt* to love.

aîné *m*, **aînée** *f* eldest child:—*adj* elder; eldest.

ainsi *adv* so, thus.

air *m* air:—**avoir l'~ content** to look happy.

aire *f* area.

aisé *adj* easy; well-off:—**~ment** *adv* easily.

ajouter *vt* to add.

ajuster *vt* to adjust.

alarme *f* alarm.

alarmer *vt* to alarm:—**s'~** *vr* to get alarmed (*de* at, about).

album *m* album.

alcool *m* alcohol.

alentours *mpl* surroundings, neighbourhood.

alerte *adj* alert; agile:—*f* alarm, alert.

alerter *vt* to alert; notify; warn.

algue *f* seaweed.

aligner *vt* to align, line up.

aliment *m* food.

alimenter *vt* to feed:—**s'~** *vr* to eat.

alinéa *m* paragraph.

allée *f* avenue; path.

alléger *vt* to make lighter; alleviate.

aller *vi* to go:—**comment allez-vous?**

how are you?:—**allons-y** let's go:—
s'en aller to go away, leave:—*m* single ticket.

allergie *f* allergy.

alliance *f* alliance; marriage; wedding
ring.

allô *excl* hello!

allocation *f* allocation; allowance.

allouer *vt* to allocate.

allumer *vt* to light; turn *ou* switch on.

allumette *f* match.

allure *f* speed; look.

alors *adv* then:—**~ que** while; whereas.

alphabet *m* alphabet.

alpiniste *mf* mountaineer.

altérer *vt* to change, alter.

alternatif *adj* alternate.

alternative *f* alternative.

altitude *f* altitude, height.

amabilité *f* kindness.

amaigrir *vt* to make thin.

amant *m* lover.

amas *m* pile, heap.

amasser *vt* to amass, pile up.

amateur *m* amateur; connaisseur.

ambassade *f* embassy.

ambassadeur *m*, **-drice** *f* ambassador.

ambiance *f* atmosphere.

ambigu *adj*, *f* **ambiguë** ambiguous.

ambitieux *adj* ambitious.

ambition *f* ambition.

ambulance *f* ambulance.

âme *f* soul.

amélioration *f* improvement.

améliorer *vt* to improve:—**s'~** *vr* to
improve.

aménagement *m* fitting out; adjustment; development.

aménager *vt* to fit out; adjust; develop.

amener *vt* to bring.

amer *adj* bitter.

Américain *m*, **-e** *f* American.

américain *adj* American.

Amérique *f* America.

ameublement *m* furniture.

ami *m*, **-ie** *f* friend.

amical *adj* friendly:—**~ement** *adv* in a
friendly manner.

amitié *f* friendship.

amnistie *f* amnesty.

amoindrir *vt* to weaken; reduce.

amorcer *vt* to bait; begin.

amortir *vt* to soften; deaden.

amour *m* love.

amoureux *adj* in love (*de* with).

amovible *adj* detachable.

amphibie *adj* amphibious.

ample *adj* roomy; wide.

ampleur *f* fullness; range.

amplifier *vt* to increase; amplify.

amusant *adj* amusing.

amuser *vt* to amuse.

an *m* year:—**avoir vingt ~s** to be 20
(years old).

analogie *f* analogy.

analphabète *adj* illiterate.

analyse *f* analysis; test.

analyser *vt* to analyse.

analyste *mf* analyst; psychoanalyst.

ananas *m* pineapple.

anarchie *f* anarchy.

anatomie *f* anatomy.

ancestral *adj* ancestral.

ancêtre *m* ancestor.

ancien *adj* old; former:—**~nement** *adv*
formerly.

ancre *f* anchor.

âne *m* ass, donkey.

anecdote *f* anecdote.

anesthésie *f* anaesthetic; anaesthesia.

ange *m* angel.

Anglais *m*, **-e** *f* Englishman; English-woman.

anglais *adj* English:—*m* (*ling*) English.

angle *m* angle; corner.

Angleterre *f* England.

anglophone *adj* English-speaking:—*mf* English speaker.

angoisse *f* anguish.

animal *m* animal.

animation *f* animation.

animé *adj* busy; lively.

animosité *f* animosity.

anneau *m* ring.

année *f* year:—**les ~s soixante** the Sixties.

annexe *f* annexe:—*adj* subsidiary.

annexer *vt* to annex; append.

anniversaire *m* birthday:—**joyeux ~!** happy birthday!

annonce *f* advertisement; announcement.

annoncer *vt* to announce (*à* to).

annuaire *m* telephone directory, phone book.

annuel *adj* annual:—**~lement** *adv* annually.

annuler *vt* to cancel; nullify.

anomalie *f* anomaly.

anonyme *adj* anonymous; impersonal:—**~ment** *adv* anonymously.

anorexique *adj*, *mf* anorexic.

anormal *adj* abnormal:—**~ement** *adv* abnormally.

antagonisme *m* antagonism.

antenne *f* (*rad*, *tv*) aerial; (*zool*) feeler.

antérieur *adj* earlier, previous.

anthologie *f* anthology.

anticancéreux *adj* cancer.

anticipation *f* anticipation.

anticonceptionnel *adj* contraceptive.

anticyclone *m* anticyclone.

antidote *m* antidote.

antigel *m* antifreeze.

antipathie *f* antipathy.

antipathique *adj* unpleasant.

antique *adj* ancient.

antiquité *f* antiquity; antique.

antirouille *adj invar* rustproof.

antisocial *adj* antisocial.

antithèse *f* antithesis.

antonyme *m* antonym.

anxiété *f* anxiety.

anxieux *adj* anxious.

août *m* August.

apaisant *adj* soothing.

apaiser *vt* to calm (down); relieve.

apathie *f* apathy.

apathique *adj* apathetic.

apercevoir *vt* to see; catch a glimpse of.

apéritif *m* aperitif.

apeuré *adj* frightened.

aphone *adj* voiceless, hoarse.

aphrodisiaque *adj*, *m* aphrodisiac.

apitoyer *vt* to move to pity:—**s'~** *vr* to feel pity (*sur* for).

aplanir *vt* to level (out); smooth away.

aplati *adj* flat.

apolitique *adj* apolitical; non-political.

apologie *f* apology.

apostrophe *f* apostrophe.

apparaître *vi* to appear.

appareil *m* device; appliance; (tele)phone;—**~-photo** camera.

apparence *f* appearance.

apparent *adj* apparent.

appartement *m* flat, apartment.

appartenir *vi*:—**~ à** to belong to.

appauvrir *vt* to impoverish:—**s'~** *vr* to grow poorer.

appel *m* call; appeal.

appeler *vt* to call:—**s'~** *vr* **je m'appelle Léon** my name is Leon.

appellation *f* appellation; name.

appétissant *adj* appetising.

appétit *m* appetite (*de* for).

applaudir *vt vi* to applaud.

application *f* application; use.

appliquer *vt* to apply:—**s'~** *vr* to apply oneself.

apporter *vt* to bring.

appréciation *f* estimation, assessment

apprécier *vt* to assess; appreciate.

appréhender *vt* to apprehend; to dread.

appréhension *f* apprehension.

apprendre *vt* to learn:—**~ à lire** to learn to read:—**~ à lire à un enfant** to teach a child to read.

apprenti *m*, **-ie** *f* apprentice.

apprentissage *m* apprenticeship.

approbation *f* approval.

approche *f* approach.

approcher *vt* to move near; approach:—**s'~** *vr* to approach.

approuver *vt* to approve of.

approvisionner *vt* to supply:—**s'~** *vr* to stock up (*de*, *en* with).

approximatif *adj* approximate.

appui *m* support.

appuyer *vt* to support *vi* to press:—*vr* **s'~ sur** to lean on.

âpre *adj* bitter:—**~ment** *adv* bitter-ly.

après *prép* after:—**après tout** after all:—**d'~ elle** according to her.

après-midi *m/f invar* afternoon.

apte *adj* capable (*à* of).

aptitude *f* aptitude:—ability.

aquatique *adj* aquatic.

araignée *f* spider.

arbitraire *adj* arbitrary:—**~ment** *adv* arbitrarily.

arbitre *m* arbiter; referee.

arbitrer *vt* to arbitrate; referee.

arbre *m* tree.

arc *m* bow; arc; arch.

arc-en-ciel *m*, *pl* **arcs-en-ciel** rainbow.

arche *f* arche.

archéologie *f* archaeology.

archipel *m* archipelago.

architecte *mf* architect.

architecture *f* architecture.

archiver *vt* to file, archive.

archives *fpl* archives, records.

ardu *adj* difficult.

argent *m* silver; money.

argument *m* argument.

argumenter *vi* to argue (*sur* about).

aride *adj* arid.

aristocrate *mf* aristocrat.

aristocratie *f* aristocracy.

arithmétique *f* arithmetic:—*adj* arithmetical.

arme *f* arm, weapon.

armée *f* army.

armer *vt* to arm:—**s'~** *vr* to arm oneself.

armoire *f* cupboard; wardrobe.

aromatique *adj* aromatic.

arôme *m* aroma; flavour.

arqué *adj* curved, arched.

arracher *vt* to pull (out); to tear off.

arrangement *m* arrangement.

arranger *vt* to arrange:—**s'~** *vr* to come to an arrangement.

arrêt *m* stopping; stop (button).

arrêter *vt* to stop:—**s'~** *vr* to stop.

arrière *m invar* back:—**en ~** back-(wards):—**à l'~** at the back:—*adj invar* back, rear.

arrière-plan *m* background.

arrivant *m*, **-e** *f* newcomer.

arrivée *f* arrival, coming.

arriver *vi* to arrive, come.

arrogant *adj* arrogant.

arrondir *vt* to make round; to round off.

arrondissement *m* district.
arsenal *m* arsenal.
art *m* art.
artère *f* artery; road.
article *m* article.
articuler *vt* to articulate.
artificiel *adj* artificial:—**~lement** *adv* artificially.
artisan *m* artisan, craftsman.
artisanat *m* craft industry.
artiste *mf* artist.
artistique *adj* artistic:—**~ment** *adv* artistically.
ascenseur *m* lift, elevator.
ascension *f* ascent.
asiatique *adj* Asian.
asile *m* refuge; asylum.
aspect *m* appearance, look.
asphyxier *vt* to asphyxiate, suffocate.
aspirateur *m* vacuum cleaner.
aspirine *f* aspirin.
assaillant *m* assailant.
assaillir *vt* to assail.
assainir *vt* to clean up; to purify.
assaisonner *vt* to season.
assassin *m* murderer; assassin.
assassiner *vt* to assassinate.
assaut *m* assault, attack.
assemblage *m* assembly; assembling.
assemblée *f* meeting.
assembler *vt* to assemble:—**s'~** *vr* to assemble.
asseoir (s') *vr* to sit down.
assertion *f* assertion.
asservissement *m* enslavement; slavery.
assez *adv* enough; quite, rather:—**avoir ~ d'argent** to have enough money:—**~ bien** quite well.
assidu *adj* assiduous; regular.
assiette *f* plate.
assigner *vt* to assign.

assimiler *vt* to assimilate.
assis *adj* seated, sitting (down).
assistant(e) *m(f)* assistant.
assister *vt* to attend; to assist.
association *f* association.
associé(e) *m(f)* associate, partner.
assombrir *vt* to darken:—**s'~** to darken.
assommer *vt* to stun.
assortir *vt* to match:—**s'~** *vr* to go well together.
assoupir (s') *vr* to doze off.
assourdir *vt* to deafen; to muffle.
assourdissant *adj* deafening.
assouvir *vt* to satisfy.
assumer *vt* to assume.
assurance *f* (self-)assurance; assurance; insurance (policy).
assuré *m*, **-e** *f* assured:—*adj* assured.
assurer *vt* to assure:—**s'~** *vr* to insure oneself.
asthme *m* asthma.
astre *m* star.
astreignant *adj* demanding.
astreindre *vt* to force, compel.
astrologie *f* astrology.
astrologue *m* astrologer.
astronaute *m* astronaut.
astronome *m* astronomer.
astronomie *f* astronomy.
astuce *f* shrewdness; (clever) trick; pun.
astucieux *adj* astute.
athée *mf* atheist:—*adj* atheistic.
athlète *mf* athlete.
athlétisme *m* athletics.
atlas *m* atlas.
atmosphère *f* atmosphere.
atome *m* atom.
atomique *adj* atomic.

atout *m* trump; advantage, asset.

atroce *adj* atrocious; dreadful.

atrocité *f* atrocity.

attaché *m*, **-e** *f* attaché; assistant.

attacher *vt* to tie together; tie up; fasten; attach (*à* to).

attaque *f* attack.

attaquer *vt* to attack; tackle.

attarder (s') *vr* to linger.

atteindre *vt* to reach; affect; contact.

atteinte *f* attack (*à* on): —**hors d'~** beyond *ou* out of reach.

attendre *vt* to wait: —**s'~** *vr* : —**s'~ à qch** to expect something.

attendrir *vt* to fill with pity: —**s'~** *vr* to be moved (*sur* by).

attendrissant *adj* touching, moving.

attendu *adj* expected; long-awaited.

attentat *m* attack (*contre* on); murder attempt.

attente *f* wait; expectation.

attention *f* attention; care.

attentionné *adj* considerate, thoughtful (*pour* towards).

atténuer *vt* to alleviate; ease.

atterrir *vi* to land, touch down.

atterrissage *m* landing, touch down.

attester *vt* to testify to.

attirant *adj* attractive.

attirer *vt* to attract.

attitude *f* attitude; bearing.

attrait *m* attraction, appeal.

attraper *vt* to catch.

attribuer *vt* to attribute; award.

attribut *m* attribute.

attribution *f* attribution.

attrister *vt* to sadden.

au = à le.

aube *f* dawn, daybreak.

auberge *f* inn: —**~ de jeunesse** youth hostel.

aucun *adj* no; not any; any: —**~ement** *adv* in no way: —*pron* none; not any; any (one): —**~ d'entre eux** none of them.

audacieux *adj* audacious, bold; daring.

audience *f* audience; hearing.

auditeur *m*, **-trice** *f* listener; auditor.

auditoire *m* audience.

augmentation *f* increase, rise (*de* in); increasing(*de* of).

augmenter *vt* to increase, raise.

aujourd'hui *adv* today.

auparavant *adv* before, previously; before, first.

auprès *prép* **~ de** next to; compared (with).

auquel = à lequel.

aurore *f* dawn, first light.

aussi *adv* too, also; so: —**nous ~** us too: —**une ~ belle journée** such a beautiful day.

aussitôt *adv* immediately: —**~ dit, ~ fait** no sooner said than done: —**~ que** as soon as.

autant *adv* as much; as many; so much; such; so many; such a lot of; the same: —**~ que je sache** as far as I know: —**~ que possible** as much as possible.

autel *m* altar.

auteur *m* author.

authentique *adj* authentic: —**~ment** *adv* authentically.

auto-école *f* driving school.

auto-stop *m* hitchhiking: —**faire de l'~** to hitchhike.

auto-stoppeur *m*, **-euse** *f* hitchhiker.

autobiographie *f* autobiography.

autocar *m* coach.

autodéfense *f* self-defence.

autodidacte *mf* self-taught.

automatique *adj* automatic: — ~**ment** *adv* automatically.

automne *m* autumn.

automobile *f* motor car.

automobiliste *mf* motorist.

autonome *adj* autonomous.

autopsie *f* autopsy, post-mortem (examination).

autorisation *f* authorisation, permission; permit.

autoriser *vt* to authorise, give permission for.

autorité *f* authority.

autoroute *f* motorway.

autour *prép* ~ **de** (a)round: — *adv* (a) round.

autre *adj* other: — ~ **chose** something else *ou* different: — ~ **part** somewhere else: — **d'** ~ **part** on the other hand: — *pn* another.

autrefois *adv* in the past, in days gone by.

autrement *adv* differently; otherwise: — **je n'ai pas pu faire ~** I couldn't do differently *ou* otherwise.

aux = **à les**.

auxiliaire *adj* auxiliary: — *m* auxiliary: — *mf* assistant.

avalanche *f* avalanche.

avaler *vt* to swallow.

avance *f* advance; lead: — **arriver en ~** to arrive early: — **payer d'** ~ to pay in advance.

avancer *vt* to move forward: — **s'** ~ *vr* to advance, move forward: — *vi* move forward, advance; make progress.

avant *prép* before: — ~ **peu** shortly:

— ~ **tout** above all: — *adv* before: — **en** ~ in front, ahead: — *m* front; bow; forward.

avant-bras *m invar* forearm.

avant-hier *adv* the day before yesterday.

avantage *m* advantage.

avantageux *adj* profitable, worthwhile; attractive; flattering.

avarie *f* damage.

avec *prép* with; to.

avenir *m* future.

aventure *f* adventure; venture; experience.

avenue *f* avenue.

avérer (s') *vr* to turn out, prove to be.

aversion *f* aversion.

avertir *vt* to warn; inform.

avertissement *m* warning.

aveugle *adj* blind: — *mf* blind person.

aveuglement *m* blindness.

aveugler *vt* to blind.

aviation *f* flying; aviation.

avide *adj* greedy; eager.

avion *m* (air)plane, aircraft.

avis *m* opinion.

avisé *adj* wise, sensible.

aviser *vt* to advise: — **s'** ~ *vr* **s'aviser de** to realise suddenly.

avoir *vt* to have: — **il y a** there is/are: — **il y a deux mois** two months ago: — **qu'as-tu?** what's the matter?: — *m* resources; credit.

avortement *m* abortion.

avoué *m* solicitor.

avril *m* April.

axe *m* axis; axle; main road.

B

babiole f trinket, trifle.

bac m ferry.

badge m badge.

bagage m luggage.

bagarre f fight, brawl.

bagatelle f trinket; trifling sum.

bague f ring.

baguette f stick; loaf of French bread.

baie f (geog) bay.

baigner vt vi to bathe: —**se ~** vr to have a bathe, swim.

baignoire f bathtub.

bâiller vi to yawn.

bain m bath; bathe, swim.

baiser m kiss: —vt to kiss.

baisse f fall, drop.

baisser vi to fall, drop vt to lower.

bal m dance.

balai m broom, brush.

balance f balance; scales.

balançoire f swing; seesaw.

balayer vt to sweep, brush.

balbutier vt to stammer, mumble.

balcon m balcony.

baleine f whale.

balle f bullet; ball.

ballon m ball; balloon.

balustrade f balustrade; handrail.

bambou m bamboo.

banal adj banal, trite: —**~ement** adv tritely.

banane f banana.

bancaire adj banking, bank.

bandage m bandage.

bande f band; tape.

bandeau m headband; blindfold.

bander vt to bandage; stretch.

bandit m bandit.

banlieue f suburbs.

bannière f banner.

bannir vt to banish.

banque f bank; banking.

banquette f seat, stool.

banquier m banker.

baptiser vt to baptise.

bar m bar.

barbare adj barbarian; barbaric.

barbe f beard.

barème m list, schedule.

baril m barrel, cask.

baromètre m barometer.

barque f small boat.

barre f bar, rod.

barrer vt to bar, block.

barricader vt to barricade: —**se ~** vr to barricade o.s.

barrière f barrier; fence.

bas adj low, base: —n stocking; sock.

bascule f weighing machine, scales.

base f base; basis.

baser vt to base: —**se baser sur** vr to depend on, rely on.

basse f (mus) bass; shoal, reef.

bassesse f meanness; vulgarity.

bassin m pond, pool; dock.

bataille f battle.

batailler vi to battle.

bateau m boat, ship.

bâtiment m building.

bâtir vt to build.

bâton m stick, staff.

batte f bat; beating.

batterie *f* battery.

battre *vt* to beat, defeat.

baume *m* balm, balsam.

bavard *m*, **-e** *f* chatterbox:—*adj* talkative, loquacious.

bavardage *m* chatting, gossiping.

bavarder *vi* to chat, gossip.

bazar *m* bazaar; general store.

béat *adj* blessed; complacent.

béatitude *f* beatitude; bliss.

beau, *f* **belle** *adj* beautiful, lovely.

beaucoup *adv* a lot, a great deal:— ~ **de monde** a lot of people.

beauté *f* beauty, loveliness.

beaux-arts *m pl* fine art.

bébé *m* baby.

bec *m* beak, bill.

bégayer *vi* to stammer, stutter.

beige *adj* beige:—*m* beige.

bêler *vi* to bleat.

Belge *mf* Belgian.

belge *adj* Belgian.

Belgique *f* Belgium.

belligérant *m*, **-ante** *f* belligerent:—*adj* belligerent.

bénédiction *f* benediction, blessing.

bénéfice *m* profit; benefit.

bénéficier *vi* to benefit; enjoy.

bénin, *f* **bénigne** *adj* benign; harmless.

bénir *vt* to bless.

bénit *adj* consecrated, holy.

béquille *f* crutch; prop.

berceau *m* cradle.

bercer *vt* to rock, cradle.

béret *m* beret.

berge *f* riverbank; barge.

berger *m* shepherd, **-ère** *f* shepherdess.

besogne *f* work; job.

besoin *m* need; want:—**avoir** ~ **de** to need.

bête *adj* stupid, silly:—~**ment** *adv* stupidly, foolishly:—*f* animal.

bêtise *f* stupidity, foolishness.

béton *m* concrete.

beurre *m* butter.

biberon *m* baby's bottle.

bible *f* bible.

bibliographie *f* bibliography.

bibliothécaire *mf* librarian.

bibliothèque *f* library; bookcase.

bicyclette *f* bicycle.

bidon *m* tin, can; flask.

bien *adv* well; properly; very:—*n* property, estate.

bien-être *m* well-being.

bienfaiteur *m* benefactor, **-trice** *f* benefactress.

bienheureux *adj* blessed; lucky; happy.

bientôt *adv* soon.

bienvenu *adj* welcome.

bière *f* beer; coffin.

bifteck *m* steak.

bigot *adj* bigoted.

bijou *m* jewel.

bijouterie *f* jewellery.

bilan *m* balance sheet; assessment.

bilingue *adj* bilingual.

billet *m* ticket; note.

billetterie *f* cash dispenser.

billion *m* billion.

binaire *adj* binary.

biodégradable *adj* biodegradable.

biographie *f* biography.

biologie *f* biology.

biologiste *mf* biologist.

bipède *m* biped.

biscuit *m* cake; biscuit.

bisexuel *adj* bisexual.

bissextile *adj* bissextile, leap (year).

bitumer *vt* to asphalt, tarmac.

bizarre *adj* bizarre, strange:—~**ment** *adv* strangely, oddly.

blague *f* joke, trick.

blaguer *vi* to joke.

blagueur *m*, **-euse** *f* joker, wag:—*adj* jokey, teasing.

blaireau *m* badger.

blâme *m* blame, rebuke.

blâmer *vt* to blame, rebuke.

blanc *adj*, *f* **blanche** white:—*m* white; blank:—*mf* white person:—*f* minim.

blancheur *f* whiteness.

blanchir *vi* to turn white:—*vt* to whiten.

blanchisserie *f* laundry.

blasphème *m* blasphemy.

blé *m* wheat.

blêmir *vi* to turn pale.

blessé *adj* injured, wounded.

blesser *vt* to injure, wound.

bleu *adj* blue:—*n* blue; bruise.

bleuir *vi* to turn blue:—*vt* to make blue.

bloc *m* block, group, unit.

blogue *m* blog.

blond *adj* blond, fair.

blondir *vi* to turn blond, turn golden:—*vt* to bleach.

bloquer *vt* to block, blockade.

blouse *f* blouse; overall.

bœuf *m* ox, bullock.

boire *vt* to drink:—*vi* to drink, tipple.

bois *m* wood.

boisson *f* drink.

boîte *f* box.

boiter *vi* to limp.

boiteux *adj* lame.

bol *m* bowl.

bombarder *vt* to bombard, bomb.

bombe *f* bomb.

bon *adj*, *f* **bonne** good:—*m* slip, coupon, bond.

bonbon *m* sweet, candy.

bond *m* leap; bounce.

bondir *vi* to jump, leap; to bounce.

bonheur *m* happiness; luck.

bonhomme *m*, *pl* **bonshommes** chap, fellow.

bonifier *vt* to improve:—**se ~** *vr* to improve.

bonjour *m* hello, good morning.

bonsoir *m* good evening.

bonté *f* goodness, kindness.

bord *m* side, edge.

border *vt* to edge, border.

borner *vt* to restrict, limit.

botanique *f* botany:—*adj* botanical.

botaniste *f* botanist.

botte *f* boot.

bouche *f* mouth.

bouché *adj* cloudy, overcast.

bouche-à-bouche *m* kiss of life.

bouchée *f* mouthful.

boucher *vt* to butcher:—*m*, **-ère** *f* butcher.

boucherie *f* butcher's; butchery.

bouchon *m* cork.

boudeur *adj* sullen, sulky.

boudin *m* pudding.

boue *f* mud.

bouée *f* buoy.

bouger *vi* to move:—*vt* to move, shift.

bougie *f* candle.

bouillir *vi* to boil.

bouilloire *f* kettle.

boulanger *m*, **-ère** *f* baker.

boulangerie *f* bakery.

boule *f* ball, bowl.

boulevard *m* boulevard.

bouleversement *m* confusion, disruption.

bouleverser *vt* to confuse, disrupt.

boulon *m* bolt.

bourdon *m* bumblebee.

bourdonner *vi* to buzz, hum.

bourg *m* market-town.

bourgeois *m*, **-e** *f* bourgeois, middle-class person:—*adj* bourgeois, middle-class.

bourse *f* purse; stock exchange.

boursier *m*, **-ière** *f* broker; speculator.

bousculer *vt* to jostle, hustle.

bout *m* end; piece, scrap.

bouteille *f* bottle.

boutique *f* shop, store.

bouton *m* button.

boutonner *vt* to button.

boxe *f* boxing.

boxer *vi* to box.

boycotter *vt* to boycott.

bracelet *m* bracelet.

braguette *f* fly (trousers).

brancher *vt* to connect, link.

bras *m* arm.

brasse *f* breaststroke.

brasser *vt* to brew; to mix.

brasserie *f* bar; brewery.

brave *adj* brave, courageous.

braver *vt* to brave, defy.

brèche *f* breach, gap.

bredouiller *vi* to stammer, mumble.

bref *adj*, *f* **brève** brief, concise:—**en ~** *adv* in short.

brevet *m* licence, patent.

bric-à-brac *m* bric-a-brac.

bricolage *m* DIY, odd jobs.

bricoler *vi* to do odd jobs.

bride *f* bridle.

brider *vt* to restrain, restrict.

brièveté *f* brevity.

brillant *adj* brilliant, shining.

briller *vi* to shine.

brique *f* brick, slab.

brise *f* breeze.

briser *vt* to smash, shatter.

broche *f* brooch.

brochure *f* brochure, pamphlet.

bronze *m* bronze.

bronzer *vi* to get a tan.

brosse *f* brush.

brosser *vt* to brush.

brouette *f* wheelbarrow.

brouillard *m* fog, mist.

brouter *vt vi* to graze.

bruine *f* drizzle.

bruit *m* noise, sound.

bruitage *m* sound-effects.

brûler *vt vi* to burn.

brûlure *f* burn.

brume *f* haze, mist.

brun *m* dark-haired man, **brune** *f* brunette:—*adj* brown.

brusque *adj* brusque, abrupt.

brut *adj* crude, raw.

brutal *adj* brutal, rough.

brutalité *f* brutality.

brute *f* brute; animal.

bruyant *adj* noisy.

bûche *f* log.

bûcheron(ne) *m(f)* woodcutter, lumberjack.

budget *m* budget.

buée *f* condensation; steam.

buffet *m* sideboard, buffet.

bulbe *m* bulb.

bulletin *m* bulletin.

bureau *m* office; desk.

bureaucrate *mf* bureaucrat.

bus *m* bus.

buste *m* bust, chest.

but *m* objective, goal.

buvable *adj* drinkable.

buvette *f* refreshment-room.

buveur *m*, **-euse** *f* drinker.

C

ça *pron* that; it:— **~ va?** How goes it?:— **~ alors!** you don't say!

cabaret *m* cabaret; tavern.

cabine *f* cabin, cab; cockpit.

cabinet *m* surgery; office, study.

câble *m* cable.

cacahouète *f* peanut.

cacao *m* cocoa.

caché *adj* hidden, secluded.

cacher *vt* to hide, conceal.

cadavre *m* corpse.

cadeau *m* present.

cadenasser *vt* to padlock.

cadet *m*, **-ette** *f* youngest child.

cadre *m* frame; context; scope.

caduc *adj f* **caduque** null and void; obsolete.

café *m* coffee.

cafétéria *f* cafeteria.

cafetière *f* coffeepot.

cage *f* cage.

cahier *m* notebook.

caillou *m* stone; pebble.

caisse *f* box; till; fund.

caissier *m*, **-ière** *f* cashier.

calcul *m* sum, calculation.

calculatrice, calculette *f* calculator.

calculer *vt* to calculate, reckon:— *vi* to budget carefully.

caleçon *m* shorts, pants.

calendrier *m* calendar.

calibre *m* calibre, bore.

calmant *m* tranquilliser, sedative:— *adj* tranquillising.

calme *m* calm, stillness:— *adj* calm, still.

calmer *vt* calm, soothe, pacify.

calorie *f* calorie.

camarade *mf* companion, friend.

camaraderie *f* camaraderie, friendship.

cambrioler *vt* to burgle.

caméra *f* camera.

camion *m* lorry.

camionneur *m* lorry driver, trucker.

camouflage *m* camouflage.

camp *m* camp.

campagnard *m* countryman, **-e** *f* countrywoman:— *adj* country, rustic.

campagne *f* country, countryside.

camper *vi* to camp.

canal *m* canal, channel.

canapé *m* sofa, settee.

cancer *m* cancer.

cancéreux *adj* cancerous.

candidat *m*, **-e** *f* candidate.

candide *adj* frank, ingenuous.

canne *f* cane, rod.

canoë *m* canoe.

canon *m* cannon, gun.

cantatrice *f* singer.

cantine *f* canteen.

caoutchouc *m* rubber.

cap *f* cape; course.

capable *adj* capable, competent.

capacité *f* capacity.

capitaine *m* captain.

capital *adj* capital, cardinal, major:— *m* capital, stock.

capitale *f* capital (letter, city).

capitaliste *mf* capitalist.

capituler *vt* to capitulate.

capoter *vt* to capsize, overturn.

caprice *m* caprice, whim.

capricieux *adj* capricious.

capsule *f* capsule.

captif *m*, **-ve** *f* captive:—*adj* captive.

captiver *vt* to captivate, enthrall.

captivité *f* captivity.

capture *f* capture.

capturer *vt* to capture.

car *conj* for; because:—*m* bus; van.

caractère *m* character, disposition.

caractériser *vt* to characterise.

caractérisque *f* characteristic, feature:
   —*adj* characteristic.

carat *m* carat.

caravane *f* caravan.

carbone *m* carbon.

carburant *m* motor-fuel.

cardiaque *adj* cardiac.

carence *f* deficiency; insolvency.

caressant *adj* affectionate.

caresse *f* caress.

caresser *vt* to caress, fondle.

cargaison *f* cargo, freight.

caricature *f* caricature.

caricaturer *vt* to caricature.

caritatif *adj* charitable.

carnaval *m* carnival.

carnet *m* notebook; logbook.

carnivore *mf* carnivore:—*adj* carnivorous.

carotte *f* carrot.

carreau *m* tile; pane.

carrefour *m* crossroads.

carrière *f* career.

carrosserie *f* bodywork, coachwork.

carte *f* card; map.

cartilage *m* cartilage.

carton *m* cardboard.

cartonner *vt* to bind (book).

cas *m* case; circumstance.

cascade *f* waterfall.

case *f* square; box.

casier *m* compartment; filing cabinet.

casino *m* casino.

casque *m* helmet.

cassant *adj* brittle.

casse-croûte *m invar* snack.

casser *vt* to break:—**se ~** *vr* to break.

casserole *f* saucepan.

cassette *f* cassette; cash-box.

catalogue *m* catalogue.

cataloguer *vt* to catalogue.

catastrophe *f* catastrophe.

catastrophique *adj* catastrophic.

catégorie *f* category.

catégorique *adj* categorical.

cathédrale *f* cathedral.

catholique *adj* Catholic.

cauchemar *m* nightmare.

cause *f* cause, reason.

causer *vt* to cause; to chat:—*vi* to talk, chat.

cavalerie *f* cavalry.

cavalier *m*, **-ière** *f* rider.

cave *f* cellar.

caverne *f* cave, cavern.

cavité *f* cavity.

ce *adj* **cet** (*bef. vowel and mute h*), *f* **cette**, *pl* **ces** this, these:—**cet homme -là** that man:—*pron:*—**c'est le facteur** it's the postman:—**~ sont mes lunettes** these are my glasses.

ceci *pron* this.

céder *vi* to give in:—*vt* to give up, transfer.

ceinture *f* belt, girdle.

cela *pron* that:—*emphasis* **qui ~?** who (do you mean)?:—**comment ~?** how (do you mean)?.

célèbre *adj* famous.

célébrer *vt* to celebrate.

célébrité *f* fame, celebrity.

célibataire *mf* single person:—*adj* single, unmarried.

cellule f cell, unit.

celluloïde m celluloid.

celui pron, f **celle** this one, pl **ceux** these ones.

cendre f ash.

censure f censorship.

cent adj a hundred:—**tu as ~ fois raison** you are absolutely right:—m a hundred:—**~ pour ~** per cent.

centenaire m centenarian:—adj a hundred years old.

centigrade m centigrade.

centigramme m centigram.

centime m centime.

centimètre m centimetre.

central adj central.

centre m centre.

cependant conj however.

cercle m circle, ring.

céréale f cereal.

cérébral adj cerebral.

cérémonie f ceremony.

certain adj certain, sure:—**~s** pn some, certain.

certificat m certificate.

certifier vt to certify; to guarantee.

certitude f certainty, certitude.

cervelle f brain.

cesser f to cease, stop.

cessez-le-feu m cease-fire.

cet adj f **cette** see **ce**.

ceux see **ce**.

chacun pron each one:—**~e d'entre elles** each of them.

chagrin m sorrow, chagrin.

chaîne f chain.

chair f flesh.

chaise f chair.

châlet m chalet.

chaleur f heat.

chaleureux adj warm, cordial.

chambre f room.

chameau m camel.

champ m field.

champignon m mushroom.

champion m, **-onne** f champion.

championnat m championship.

chance f luck.

chanceler vi to stagger, totter.

chanceux adj lucky, fortunate.

changement m change, changing.

changer vi to change:—vt to change.

chanson f song.

chantage m blackmail.

chanter vi, vt to sing.

chanteur m, **-euse** f singer.

chantier m building site.

chaos m chaos.

chapeau m hat.

chapelle f chapel.

chapitre m chapter.

chaque adj each.

charbon m coal.

charge f load; responsibility.

charger vt to load:—**se ~ de** to take responsibility for, attend to.

charisme m charisma.

charitable adj charitable, kind.

charité f charity.

charme m charm.

charmer vt to charm, beguile.

charpente f structure, framework.

charpentier m carpenter.

charrue f plough.

chasse-neige m invar snowplough.

chasser vt to hunt, chase.

châssis m chassis.

chat m, **chatte** f cat.

château m castle, château.

châtiment m chastisement, punishment.

chaud adj warm, hot.

chaudière f boiler.

chauffage *m* heating.

chauffer *vi* to heat: — *vt* to heat up.

chauffeur *m* driver.

chaumière *f* cottage.

chaussée *f* road, street.

chaussette *f* sock.

chaussure *f* shoe.

chauve-souris *f* bat.

chef *m* head, boss; chef.

chef-d'œuvre *m* masterpiece.

chemin *m* way, road: — ~ **de fer** railway.

cheminée *f* chimney.

chemise *f* shirt.

chêne *m* oak.

chèque *m* cheque.

chéquier *m* chequebook.

cher *adj f* **chère** dear, expensive.

chercher *vt* to look for.

chéri *m*, **-ie** *f* darling: — *adj* cherished.

cheval *m* horse.

cheveu *m* hair.

cheville *f* ankle.

chèvre *f* goat.

chez *prép* at home: — **je rentre ~ moi** I'm going home.

chic *m* style, stylishness.

chien *m*, **chienne** *f* dog.

chiffre *m* figure.

chimie *f* chemistry.

chimiste *mf* chemist.

chimpanzé *m* chimpanzee.

chirurgie *f* surgery.

chirurgien *m* surgeon.

choc *m* shock, crash.

chocolat *m* chocolate.

choir *vi* to fall.

choisir *vt* to choose.

choix *m* choice.

chômage *m* unemployment.

chômeur *m*, **-euse** *f* unemployed person.

choquer *vt* to shock.

chose *f* thing, matter, object.

chou *m* cabbage.

chouette *f* owl.

chrétien *m*, **-ienne** *f* Christian, *adj* Christian.

christianisme *m* Christianity.

chronologie *f* chronology.

chuchoter *vi* to whisper.

chuinter *vi* to hiss.

chute *f* fall, drop.

chuter *vi* to fall.

ci *adv*: — **ces fleurs-ci** these flowers: — **ci-joint** enclosed.

cible *f* target.

cicatrice *f* scar.

cidre *m* cider.

ciel *m*, *pl* **cieux, ciels** sky.

cierge *m* candle.

cigare *m* cigar.

cigarette *f* cigarette.

cil *m* eyelash.

ciment *m* cement.

cimetière *m* cemetery.

cinéma *m* cinema.

cingler *vt* to lash, sting.

cinq *m* five.

cinquante *m* fifty.

cinquième *mf* fifth, *adj* fifth.

cirage *m* polish.

circonférence *f* circumference.

circonspect *adj* circumspect.

circonstance *f* circumstance.

circuit *m* circuit, tour.

circulaire *adj* circular.

circulation *f* circulation; traffic.

circuler *vi* to circulate, move.

cirer *vt* to polish.

cirque *m* circus.

ciseau *m* chisel; scissor(s).

citadelle *f* citadel.

citadin(e) *m(f)* city dweller:—*adj* town, urban.

citation *f* citation, summons.

cité *f* city.

citer *vt* to quote, cite.

citoyen *m*, **-enne** *f* citizen.

citron *m* lemon.

civil *adj* civil:—~**ement** *adv* civilly.

civilisation *f* civilisation.

civiliser *vt* to civilise.

clair *adj* clear, bright:—~**ement** *adv* clearly.

clameur *f* clamour.

clandestin *adj* clandestine.

claque *f* slap, smack.

claquer *vi* to bang, slam.

clarifier *vt* to clarify:—**se** ~ *vr* to become clear.

clarté *f* light, brightness.

classe *f* class, standing.

classer *vt* to file, classify.

classification *f* classification.

classique *adj* classical, standard.

clause *f* clause.

claustrophobie *f* claustrophobia.

clavier *m* keyboard.

clé, clef *f* key.

cliché *m* cliché; negative.

client *m*, **-e** *f* client.

cligner *vi* to blink.

clignoter *vi* to blink, flicker.

climat *m* climate.

climatisation *f* air conditioning.

clinique *f* clinic.

clochard *m*, **-e** *f* down-and-out.

cloche *f* bell.

cloison *f* partition.

clore *vt* to close, conclude.

clou *m* nail.

clouer *vt* to nail.

coalition *f* coalition.

cochon *m*, **-onne** *f* pig.

code *m* code.

cœur *m* heart.

coffre *m* chest:—~**-fort** safe.

cohabitation *f* cohabitation.

cohérent *adj* coherent.

cohésion *f* cohesion.

coiffer *vt* to arrange someone's hair:—**se** ~ *vr* to do one's hair.

coiffeur *m*, **-euse** *f* hairdresser.

coin *m* corner.

coïncidence *f* coincidence.

col *m* neck.

colère *f* anger.

colis *m* parcel.

collaborateur *m*, **-trice** *f* collaborator, colleague.

collaborer *vi* to collaborate.

collection *f* collection.

collectionner *vt* to collect.

collège *m* college, school.

collègue *mf* colleague.

coller *vt* to stick, glue:—*vi* to stick, be sticky.

colline *f* hill.

collision *f* collision.

colonie *f* colony.

coloniser *vt* to colonise.

coloration *f* colouring, staining.

colorier *vt* to colour in.

coma *m* coma.

comateux *adj* comatose.

combat *m* combat, fight.

combattre *vt* to fight:—*vi* to fight.

combien *adv* how much, how many:—~ **de temps** how much time.

combiner *vt* to combine.

combustible *m* fuel.

combustion *f* combustion.

comédie *f* comedy.

comédien *m*, **-ienne** *f* actor, comedian.

comète *f* comet.

comique *adj* comic:—**~ment** *adv* comically:— *m* comedian.

comité *m* committee.

commande *f* command, order.

commander *vt vi* to order, command.

comme *conj* as, like:—**~ ci ~ ça** so-so:—*adv* how.

commémorer *vt* to commemorate.

commencer *vt* to begin:—*vi* to begin, start.

comment *adv* how:—**~ dire?** how shall we say?

commentaire *m* comment; commentary.

commenter *vt* to comment.

commerçant *m*, **-e** *f* merchant, trader.

commerce *m* business, commerce.

commercial *adj* commercial:—**-ement** *adv* commercially.

commercialiser *vt* to market.

commettre *vt* to commit.

commission *f* commission, committee.

commodité *f* convenience.

commun *adj* common, joint.

communal *adj* common, communal.

commune *f* town, district.

communication *f* communication.

communiquer *vt* to communicate, transmit:—*vi* to communicate.

communiste *mf* communist.

compact *adj* compact, dense.

compagne *f* companion.

compagnon *m* companion.

comparable *adj* comparable.

comparaison *f* comparison.

comparer *vt* to compare.

compartiment *m* compartment.

compas *m* compass.

compassion *f* compassion.

compatible *adj* compatible.

compatriote *mf* compatriot.

compensation *f* compensation.

compenser *vt* to compensate; offset.

compétence *f* competence.

compétitif *adj* competitive.

compétitivité *f* competitiveness.

complaisant *adj* kind; complacent.

complément *m* complement; extension.

complet *adj* complete, full.

compléter *vt* to complete.

complexe *adj* complex, complicated.

complication *f* complication.

complice *mf* accomplice.

compliment *m* compliment.

compliquer *vt* to complicate.

comportement *m* behaviour; performance.

comporter *vt* to consist of:—**se ~** *vr* to behave.

composer *vt* to compose, make up:—**se ~** *vr*:—**se ~ de** to be made up of.

compréhensible *adj* comprehensible.

compréhensif *adj* comprehensive, understanding.

comprendre *vt* to understand; consist of.

compression *f* compression; reduction.

comprimer *vt* to compress; to restrain.

compromettre *vt* to compromise.

comptable *mf* accountant.

compter *vt vi* to count.

comptoir *m* counter, bar.

concentration *f* concentration.

concept *m* concept.

conception *f* conception, design.

concerner *vt* to concern, regard.

concert *m* concert.

concession *f* concession; privilege.

concevoir *vt* to imagine, conceive.

concierge *mf* caretaker, concierge.

conciliation *f* conciliation; reconciliation.

concilier *vt* to reconcile; to attract.

concision *f* conciseness, brevity.

conclure *vt* to conclude; to decide.

conclusion *f* conclusion.

concours *m* competition; conjuncture.

concret *adj* concrete, solid.

concubin *m*, **-e** *f* concubine; cohabitant.

concurrence *f* competition.

condamnation *f* condemnation; sentencing.

condamner *vt* to condemn; to sentence.

condensation *f* condensation.

condenser *vt* to condense, compress.

condition *f* condition, term.

conditionner *vt* to condition; to package.

conducteur *m*, **-trice** *f* driver; operator.

conduire *vt vi* to lead; to drive.

conduite *f* conduct; driving; running.

cône *m* cone.

conférence *f* conference.

confession *f* confession.

confiance *f* confidence, trust.

confidence *f* confidence; disclosure.

confidentiel *adj* confidential.

confier *vt* to confide, entrust: **—se ~** *vr* to confide in.

confiner *vt* to confine: **—se ~** to be confined.

confirmer *vt* to confirm: **—se ~** *vr* to be confirmed.

confiserie *f* confectionery.

confiture *f* jam.

conflit *m* conflict, contention.

confondre *vt* to confuse, mingle.

conforme *adj* consistent; true.

conformer *vt* to model: **—se ~** *vr* to conform.

confort *m* comfort.

confortable *adj* comfortable, cosy.

confronter *vt* to confront.

confus *adj* confused, indistinct.

confusion *f* confusion, disorder.

congédier *vt* to dismiss.

congeler *vt* to freeze.

congratuler *vt* to congratulate.

congrégation *f* congregation.

congrès *m* congress, conference.

conjurer *vt* to conspire; to implore.

connaissance *f* knowledge; consciousness.

connaisseur *m*, **-euse** *f* connoisseur; expert.

connaître *vt* to know, be acquainted with.

connecter *vt* to connect.

connexion *f* connection, link.

connu *adj* known; famous.

conquérir *vt* to conquer.

conquête *f* conquest.

conscience *f* consciousness; conscience.

consciencieux *adv* conscientious.

conscient *adj* conscious, aware.

consécutif *adj* consecutive.

conseil *m* advice, counsel.

conseiller *vt* to advise, counsel.

consentir *vi* to consent, acquiesce.

conséquence *f* consequence, result.

conséquent *adj* consequent, logical.

conservateur *m*, **-trice** *f* conservative; curator.

conservation *f* conservation.

conserver *vt* to keep, preserve: **—se ~** *vr* to keep.

considérable *adj* considerable; notable.

considération *f* consideration, respect.

considérer *vt* to consider, regard.

consistance *f* consistency; strength.

consister *vi*: **— en** to consist of.

consolation *f* consolation, solace.

consoler *vt* to console, comfort.

consolider *vt* to consolidate, reinforce.

consommateur *m*, **-trice** *f* consumer.

consommation *f* consumption; accomplishment.

consommer vt to consume, use.
conspirer vi to conspire, plot.
constant adj constant, continuous.
constat m report; acknowledgement.
constater vt to record; to verify.
constellation f constellation, galaxy.
consterner vt to dismay.
constipation f constipation.
constituer vt to constitute, form.
constitution f constitution, formation.
constructeur m, **-trice** f builder, maker.
construction f building, construction.
construire vt to construct, build.
consulat m consulate.
consultant m, **-e** f consultant.
consulter vt to consult, take advice from.
consumer vt to consume, spend.
contact m contact, touch.
contagieux adj contagious, infectious.
contaminer vt to contaminate, pollute.
conte m story, tale.
contempler vt to contemplate, meditate.
contemporain adj contemporary.
contenir vt to contain.
contentement m contentment, satisfaction.
contenter vt to please, satisfy.
contenu m contents, enclosure.
contester vt to contest, dispute.
contexte m context.
continent m continent.
continental adj continental.
continuation f continuation.
continuel adj continual, continuous.
continuer vt to continue, proceed with:—vi to continue, go on.
contour m contour, outline.
contraceptif adj contraceptive.
contracter vt to contract, acquire:—**se ~** vr to contract, shrink.

contradiction f contradiction, discrepancy.
contraindre vt to constrain, compel.
contraire m opposite, contrary:—adj opposite, contrary.
contrarier vt to annoy; to oppose.
contraste m contrast.
contrat m contract, agreement.
contre prép against:—**par ~** on the other hand.
contre-attaquer vi to counter-attack.
contrebande f contraband, smuggling.
contrecœur:—à ~ reluctantly.
contredire vt to contradict, refute.
contrefaire vt to counterfeit, forge.
contrepartie f compensation; consideration.
contresens m nonsense; misunderstanding; mistranslation.
contribuer vt vi to contribute.
contribution f contribution; tax.
contrôler vt to control, check.
contrôleur m, **-euse** f inspector; auditor.
controverse f controversy.
convaincre vt to convince, persuade.
convalescence f convalescence.
convenable adj fitting, suitable:—**~ment** adv suitably, fitly.
convenir vi to agree, accord.
convention f convention, agreement.
conventionnel adj conventional; contractual.
conversation f conversation, talk.
conversion f conversion.
convertir vt to convert:—**se ~** vr to be converted.
conviction f conviction.
convoi m convoy; train.
convoquer vt to convoke, convene.
coopération f cooperation.
coopérative f cooperative.

coopérer *vi* to cooperate, collaborate.

coordination *f* coordination; committee.

copain *m* friend, pal.

copie *f* copy, reproduction.

copier *vt* to copy, reproduce.

copilote *m* co-pilot.

coq *m* cock, rooster.

coquet *adj* stylish, smart.

coquin *m*, **-e** *f* naughty, mischievous.

corail *m* coral.

coran *m* Koran.

corbeille *f* basket.

corde *f* rope; string.

cordial *adj* cordial, warm.

cordialité *f* cordiality, warmth.

cordon *m* cord, string; cordon.

corne *f* horn, antler.

corneille *f* crow.

cornet *m* cornet, cone.

corporatif *adj* corporative, corporate.

corporation *f* corporation, guild.

corps *m* body, corpse.

corpulent *adj* corpulent.

correct *adj* correct, accurate.

correcteur *m*, **-trice** *f* examiner; proof-reader.

correction *f* correction; proofreading.

correspondance *f* correspondence, communication.

correspondre *vi* to correspond, communicate.

corridor *m* corridor, passage.

corriger *vt* to correct.

corroder *vt* to corrode.

corrompre *vt* to corrupt, debase.

corrosion *f* corrosion.

corruption *f* corruption, debasement.

corset *m* corset.

cortège *m* cortège, procession.

cosmétique *m* cosmetic.

cosmique *adj* cosmic.

cosmopolite *adj* cosmopolitan.

cosmos *m* cosmos.

costume *m* costume, dress.

côte *f* coast; rib; slope.

côté *m* side; point.

coteau *m* hill.

coter *vt* to quote; to classify.

coton *m* cotton.

cou *m* neck.

couche *f* layer, coat.

coucher *vt* to put to bed:—**se ~** *vr* to go to bed.

coucou *m* cuckoo.

coude *m* elbow.

coudre *vt vi* to sew.

couler *vi* to flow, run.

couleur *f* colour, shade.

coulisser *vi* to slide, run.

couloir *m* corridor, passage.

coup *m* blow; shot:—**tout à ~** suddenly:—**après ~** afterwards, after the event:—**~ de feu** shot:—**jeter un ~ d'œil** to glance.

coupable *mf* culprit:—*adj* guilty.

coupe *f* cut; cutting.

couper *vt* to cut, slice.

couple *m* couple, pair.

coupon *m* coupon, voucher, ticket.

cour *f* court, yard, courtyard.

courage *m* courage, daring.

courageux *adj* courageous.

courant *adj* current; present:—*m* stream, current.

courbe *f* curve; contour.

courber *vt* to curve, bend.

coureur *m*, **-euse** *f* runner.

courir *vi* to run, race.

couronne *f* crown, wreath.

courriel *m* email.

courrier *m* mail, post.

cours *m* course; flow; path.

course *f* running; race; flight; journey.
coursier *m*, **-ière** *f* courier, messenger.
court *adj* short, brief.
court-circuiter *vt* to short-circuit.
courtier *m*, **-ière** *f* broker, agent.
courtois *adj* courteous.
cousin *m*, **-e** *f* cousin.
coussin *m* cushion, pillow.
coût *m* cost, charge.
couteau *m* knife.
coûter *vi, vt* to cost.
coûteux *adj* costly, expensive.
coutume *f* custom, habit.
couvent *m* convent.
couvercle *m* lid, cap.
couvert *m* shelter; cover; pretext:—*adj* covered; secret.
couverture *f* blanket; cover; roofing.
couvrir *vt* to cover.
crabe *m* crab.
cracher *vt* to spit.
craie *f* chalk.
craindre *vt* to fear.
crampe *f* cramp.
crâne *m* cranium, skull.
crapaud *m* toad.
craquement *m* crack, creaking, snap.
craquer *vi* to creak, squeak, crack.
cratère *m* crater.
cravate *f* tie.
créateur *m*, **-trice** *f* creator, author.
création *f* creation.
créature *f* creature.
crèche *f* creche; crib.
crédible *adj* credible.
crédit *m* credit, trust.
crédule *adj* credulous, gullible.
créer *vt* to create, produce.
crème *f* cream.
crémerie *f* dairy.
crêpe *f* pancake:—*m* crepe.

crépiter *vi* to crackle; to rattle.
crépuscule *m* twilight, dusk.
crête *f* crest, comb.
crétin *m*, **-e** *f* cretin, idiot.
creuser *vi* to dig, burrow:—*vt* to dig, hollow.
crevaison *f* puncture, flat.
crever *vt* to burst; to gouge:—*vi* to burst; to split.
cri *m* cry, howl, yell.
crible *m* riddle, sieve.
crier *vi* to cry, shout.
crime *m* crime, offence.
criminel *m*, **elle** *f* criminal:—*adj* criminal.
crise *f* crisis, attack.
cristal *m* crystal, glassware.
cristalliser *vt* to crystallise.
critère *m* criterion, standard.
critique *adj* critical, censorious:—*f* criticism; critique.
critiquer *vt* to criticise, censure.
crochet *m* hook, clip.
crocodile *m* crocodile.
croire *vt* to believe, think.
croiser *vt* to cross; to fold:—**se ~** *vr* to cross, intersect.
croisière *f* cruise.
croissance *f* growth, increase.
croître *vi* to grow, rise.
croix *f* cross.
croquer *vt* to crunch, munch.
croquette *f* croquette.
croquis *m* sketch, outline.
croustiller *vi* to be crusty, crispy.
croûte *f* crust.
croyance *f* belief.
croyant *adj* believing.
cru *adj* raw, uncooked:—*m* vineyard; wine.
cruauté *f* cruelty, inhumanity.
crucial *adj* crucial, decisive.

crucifix *m* crucifix.
crudité *f* crudity, coarseness.
cruel *adj* cruel.
crypter *vt* to encode, scramble.
cube *m* cube, block.
cueillir *vt* to pick, gather.
cuiller, cuillère *f* spoon, spoonful.
cuir *m* leather, hide.
cuire *vi* to cook.
cuisine *f* kitchen; cookery.
cuisiner *vt vi* to cook.
cuisinier *m*, **-ière** *f* cook.
cuisse *f* thigh.
cuisson *f* cooking, baking.
cuit *adj* cooked.
cul-de-sac *m* blind alley, cul-de-sac.
culminer *vi* to culminate, tower.
culotte *f* knickers; underpants; shorts.
culpabiliser *vt* to make someone feel guilty.
culte *m* cult, veneration.

cultivateur *m*, **-trice** *f* farmer.
cultiver *vt* to cultivate:—**se ~** *vr* to improve oneself
culture *f* culture; cultivation.
culturel *adj* cultural.
cumuler *vt* to accumulate.
cupide *adj* greedy.
cure *f* cure; treatment.
curé *m* parish priest, parson.
curieux *adj* curious, inquisitive.
cuvette *f* basin, bowl.
cycle *m* cycle; stage.
cyclique *adj* cyclical.
cyclisme *m* cycling.
cycliste *mf* cyclist.
cyclone *m* cyclone.
cygne *m* swan.
cylindre *m* cylinder.
cynique *adj* cynical:—**~ment** *adv* cynically.
cynisme *m* cynicism.

D

dactylographe *mf* typist.
dactylographier *vt* to type.
dame *f* lady.
damier *m* draughtboard.
danger *m* danger, risk.
dangereux *adj* dangerous, risky.
dans *prép* in; into.
danse *f* dance; dancing.
danser *vi* to dance.
danseur *m*, **-euse** *f* dancer.
dard *m* dart; sting.
date *f* date.
dater *vt* to date.

dauphin *m* dolphin.
davantage *adv* more.
de *prép* of; from:—**deux ~ plus** two more:—**~ art** some, any.
dé *m* die; thimble.
débâcle *f* disaster; collapse.
débarquer *vt* to land, unship:—*vi* to disembark, land.
débarrasser *vt* to clear, rid.
débat *m* debate; dispute, contest.
débattre *vi* to debate, discuss.
débile *adj* weak, feeble.
débilitant *adj* debilitating, weakening.

débiteur *m*, **-trice** *f* debtor.

débloquer *vt* to release, unlock.

déboiser *vt* to deforest.

débordant *adj* exuberant, overflowing.

déborder *vi* to overflow; to outflank.

debout *adv* upright, standing:—**être ~** to stand.

débris *m* debris, waste.

début *m* beginning, outset.

débuter *vi* to start, begin:—*vt* to lead, start.

décadence *f* decadence, decline.

décadent *adj* decadent.

décaféiné *adj* decaffeinated.

décaler *vt* to stagger; to shift.

décathlon *m* decathlon.

décéder *vi* to die.

déceler *vt* to detect; to disclose.

décembre *m* December.

décence *f* decency.

décennie *f* decade.

décent *adj* decent, proper.

décentraliser *vt* to decentralise.

déception *f* disappointment; deceit.

décès *m* death, decease.

décevoir *vt* to disappoint; to deceive.

déchaîner *vt* to unleash.

décharge *f* discharge; receipt.

décharger *vt* to unload, discharge.

déchet *m* loss, waste.

déchiffrer *vt* to decipher, decode.

déchirer *vt* to tear, rip.

décibel *m* decibel.

décidé *adj* decided; determined.

décimal *adj* decimal.

décision *f* decision.

déclarer *vt* to declare, announce.

déclencher *vt* to release, set off.

décliner *vi* to decline, refuse.

décollage *m* take-off, lift-off.

décoller *vi* to unpaste.

décolleté *adj* low-cut.

décomposer *vt* to decompose; to break up.

décompte *m* discount; deduction.

décongeler *vt* to thaw, defrost.

déconnecter *vt* to disconnect.

décontenancé *adj* embarrassed; disconcerted.

décor *m* scenery; setting.

décorateur *m*, **-trice** *f* decorator; set designer.

décoration *f* decoration, embellishment.

décorer *vt* to decorate, adorn.

découper *vt* to carve, cut up.

décourageant *adj* discouraging, disheartening.

décourager *vt* discourage, dishearten.

découvert *adj* uncovered; open.

découverte *f* discovery.

découvrir *vt* to discover.

décréter *vt* to decree, enact.

décrire *vt* to describe.

décroître *vi* to decrease, diminish.

déçu *adj* disappointed.

dédaigner *vt* to disdain, scorn.

dédaigneux *adj* disdainful, scornful.

dedans *adv* inside, indoors:—*m* inside:—**au ~** inside.

dédier *vt* to consecrate, dedicate to.

dédommager *vt* to compensate, indemnify.

déduction *f* deduction.

déduire *vt* to deduct; to deduce.

défaire *vt* to undo, dismantle.

défaite *m* defeat, overthrow.

défaut *m* defect, fault.

défavorable *adj* unfavourable.

défection *f* defection.

défectueux *adj* defective, faulty.

défendeur *m*, **-deresse** *f* defendant.

défendre *vt* to defend, protect; to prohibit.

défense *f* defence; prohibition.

défi *m* defiance; challenge.

déficience *f* deficiency.

déficit *m* deficit, shortfall.

défier *vt* to challenge, defy.

défiler *vi* to parade, march; (*comput*) scroll.

définir *vt* to define, specify.

définitif *adj* definitive, final.

définition *f* definition.

déformation *f* deformation, distortion.

déformer *vt* to deform.

défouler *vt* to unwind, relax.

défunt *m*, **-e** *f* deceased:—*adj* late, deceased.

dégagement *m* freeing, clearance.

dégager *vt* to free, clear:—**se ~** *vr* to free oneself.

dégât *m* havoc, damage.

dégel *m* thaw.

dégénérer *vi* to degenerate, decline.

dégoût *m* disgust, distaste.

dégradation *f* degradation, debasement.

dégrader *vt* to degrade, debase.

degré *m* degree; grade.

déguiser *vt* to disguise:—**se ~** *vr* to disguise oneself.

dégustation *f* tasting, sampling.

dehors *adv* outside, outdoors:—**en ~ de** outside; apart from:—*m* outside, exterior.

déjà *adv* already.

déjeuner *vi* to lunch:—*m* lunch.

delà *adv*:—**au ~ de** beyond:—**par ~** beyond.

délai *m* delay; respite; time limit.

délaisser *vt* to abandon, quit.

délasser *vt* to refresh, relax:—**se ~** *vr* to rest, relax.

délayer *vt* to thin; to drag out.

délectation *f* delectation, delight.

délégation *f* delegation.

délégué *m*, **-e** *f* delegate:—*adj* delegated.

déléguer *vt* to delegate.

délibéré *adj* deliberate; resolute.

délicat *adj* delicate, dainty.

délicieux *adj* delicious, delightful.

délimiter *vt* to delimit, demarcate.

délinquant *m*, **-e** *f* delinquent, offender:—*adj* delinquent.

délire *m* delirium, frenzy.

délirer *vi* to be delirious.

délit *m* offence, misdemeanour.

délivrer *vt* to deliver; to release.

déloyal *adj* disloyal, unfaithful.

delta *m* delta.

demain *adv* tomorrow.

demande *f* request, petition; question.

demander *vt* to ask, request:—**se ~** *vr* to wonder.

démaquiller *vt* to remove make-up.

démarche *f* bearing; gait, walk.

déménager *vi* to move house.

dément *adj* mad, insane, crazy.

démentir *vt* to deny, refute.

demeure *f* residence, dwelling place.

demeurer *vi* to live at, reside, stay.

demi *adj* half:—**à ~** halfway:—*m* half.

demi-cercle *m* semicircle.

demi-douzaine *f* half-dozen.

demi-heure *f* half hour.

demi-lune *f* half-moon.

démilitariser *vt* to demilitarise.

démission *f* resignation.

démissionner *vi* to resign.

démocrate *mf* democrat.

démocratie *f* democracy.

démocratique *adj* democratic.

démodé *adj* old-fashioned, out-of-date.

demoiselle *f* young lady.

démolir *vt* to demolish, knock down.

démolition *f* demolition.

démonstration *f* demonstration; proof.

démonter *vt* to dismantle, take down, dismount.

démontrer *vt* demonstrate; to prove.

démoraliser *vt* to demoralise.

déni *m* denial, refusal.

dénier *vt* to deny, disclaim.

dénigrer *vt* to denigrate, disparage.

dénombrer *vt* to number, enumerate.

dénomination *f* denomination, designation.

dénoncer *vt* to denounce; to inform against.

dénonciation *f* denunciation.

dénoyauter *vt* to stone (fruit).

dense *adj* dense, thick.

densité *f* density, denseness.

dent *f* tooth.

dentelle *f* lace.

dentifrice *m* toothpaste.

dentiste *mf* dentist.

dénuder *vt* to bare, denude.

dépanner *vt* to repair, fix.

dépanneur *m*, **-euse** *f* breakdown mechanic.

départ *m* departure; start.

département *m* department.

dépasser *vt* to exceed; to go past.

dépêcher *vt* to dispatch, send:—**se ~ vr** to hurry, rush.

dépendant *adj* dependent.

dépendre *vi* to depend on, be dependent on.

dépenser *vt* to expend, spend:—**se ~ vr** to exert oneself.

dépérir *vi* to decline, waste away.

dépit *m* spite; grudge:—**en ~ de** in spite of.

déplacement *m* displacement; removal.

déplacer *vt* to displace; to move:—**se ~ vr** to change residence.

déplaire *vi* to displease; to offend.

déplaisant *adj* disagreeable, unpleasant.

déplorable *adj* deplorable, disgraceful.

déployer *vt* to deploy; to display.

déportation *f* deportation, transportation.

déporter *vt* to deport, transport.

déposer *vt* to lodge, deposit.

dépôt *m* deposit; warehouse.

dépouillement *m* scrutiny, perusal; despoiling.

dépréciation *f* depreciation.

déprécier *vt* to depreciate.

dépression *f* depression, slump; dejection.

déprimant *adj* depressing.

déprimer *vt* to depress; to discourage.

depuis *prép* since, from; after.

déraillement *m* derailment.

dérangement *m* derangement; inconvenience.

déranger *vt* to upset, unsettle.

déraper *vi* to skid, slip.

dérision *f* derision, mockery.

dérisoire *adj* derisory; pathetic.

dériver *vi* to drift.

dernier *adj* last; latest; back:—*m*, **-ière** *f* last one; latter.

dernièrement *adv* recently; lately.

dérober *vt* to steal; to hide:—**se ~ vr** to steal away, escape.

déroger *vi* to derogate; to detract.

déroulement *m* unfolding; progress, development.

dérouler *vt* to unwind, uncoil:—**se ~ vr** to develop; to unfold.

dérouter *vt* to rout, overthrow.

derrière *prép* behind:—*adv*:—**par ~**

by the back: — *m* bottom; back: — **de ~** back, rear.

des *art* = de les: — *see* **un, une**.

dès *prép* from, since: — **~ que** when; as soon as.

désaccord *m* disagreement, discord.

désaffecté *adj* disused.

désagréable *adj* disagreeable, unpleasant.

désagréger *vt* to separate: — **se ~** *vr* to become separated.

désagrément *m* displeasure, annoyance.

désapprobation *f* disapproval.

désapprouver *vt* to disapprove, object.

désarmement *m* disarmament.

désarroi *m* disarray, confusion.

désastre *m* disaster.

désavantage *m* disadvantage; prejudice.

désavantager *vt* to disadvantage, handicap.

descendant *m*, **-e** *f* descendant.

descendre *vi* to descend, go down: — *vt* to take down.

descente *f* descent, way down.

descriptif *adj* descriptive, explanatory.

description *f* description.

désenchantement *m* disenchantment; disillusion.

déséquilibré *adj* unbalanced, unhinged.

désert *m* desert, wilderness: — *adj* deserted.

déserter *vt* to desert.

désespéré *adj* desperate, hopeless.

désespérer *vi* to despair, give up hope.

désespoir *m* despair, despondency.

déshabiller *vt* to undress: — **se ~** *vr* to undress.

déshériter *vt* to disinherit.

désignation *f* designation, nomination; name.

désigner *vt* to designate, indicate.

désillusionner *vt* to disillusion; to disappoint.

désinfectant *m* disinfectant: — *adj* disinfectant.

désintégration *f* disintegration.

désintégrer *vt* to split, break up: — **se ~** *vr* to disintegrate.

désintéressé *adj* disinterested, unselfish.

désir *m* desire, wish, longing.

désirable *adj* desirable.

désirer *vt* to desire, wish, long.

désobéir *vi* to disobey.

désolation *f* desolation; ruin; grief.

désolé *adj* desolate; disconsolate, grieved.

désordonné *adj* untidy; inordinate; reckless.

désordre *m* disorder, confusion, disturbance.

désorienté *adj* disorientated.

désormais *adv* from now on, henceforth.

dessécher *vt* to dry, parch: — **se ~** *vr* to dry out.

dessein *m* design, plan, scheme: — **à ~** intentionally.

desserrer *vt* to unscrew: — **se ~** *vr* to work loose.

dessert *m* dessert, sweet.

dessin *m* drawing, sketch; draft.

dessiner *vt* to draw, sketch; to design.

dessous *adv* under, beneath: — *m* underside, bottom.

dessus *adv* over, above: — *m* **~** top.

destin *m* destiny, fate, doom.

destinataire *mf* addressee, consignee.

destination *f* destination; purpose.

destiner *vt* to determine; to intend, destine, aim.

destruction *f* destruction.

détachable *adj* detachable.

détachement *m* detachment, indifference.

détacher *vt* to detach, unfasten.

détail *m* detail, particular.

détaillant *m*, **-e** *f* retailer.

détailler *vt* to detail; to sell retail.

détecter *vt* to detect.

détecteur *m* detector.

détection *f* detection.

détective *m* detective.

détendre *vt* to release, loosen.

détenir *vt* to detain; to hold.

détente *f* relaxation, easing.

détérioration *f* deterioration.

détériorer *vt* to damage, impair:—**se ~** *vr* to deteriorate, worsen.

détermination *f* determination; resolution.

déterminer *vt* to determine, decide.

détestable *adj* detestable, odious.

détester *vt* to detest, hate.

détonation *f* detonation, explosion.

détour *m* detour; curve; evasion.

détournement *m* diversion, rerouting.

détourner *vt* to divert, reroute.

détresse *f* distress, trouble.

detruire *vt* to destroy, demolish.

dette *f* debt.

deuil *m* mourning, bereavement, grief.

deux *adj* two:—*m* two:—**en moins de ~** in a jiffy.

deuxième *adj* second:—*mf* second.

dévaliser *vt* to burgle; to rifle.

dévaloriser *vt* to depreciate, reduce the value of.

dévaluation *f* devaluation.

devancer *vt* to outstrip, outrun; to precede.

devant *prép* in front of, before:—*adv* in front:—*m* front.

devanture *f* display; shop-front.

développement *m* development; growth; progress.

développer *vt* to develop, expand:—**se ~** *vr* to develop, grow.

devenir *vi* to become, grow.

dévêtir *vt* to undress:—**se ~** *vr* to get undressed.

déviation *f* deviation; diversion.

deviner *vt* to guess; to solve; to foretell.

devise *f* currency.

dévisser *vt* to unscrew, undo.

devoir *m* duty; homework:—*vt* to owe; to have to.

dévorer *vt* to devour, consume.

dévotion *f* devotion, piety.

dextérité *f* dexterity, adroitness.

diabétique *adj* diabetic.

diable *m* devil.

diagnostic *m* diagnosis.

diagnostiquer *vt* to diagnose.

diagonale *f* diagonal.

diagramme *m* diagram; graph.

dialecte *m* dialect.

dialogue *m* dialogue, conversation.

diamant *m* diamond.

diamètre *m* diameter.

dictateur *m*, **-trice** *f* dictator.

dictée *f* dictating; dictation.

dictionnaire *m* dictionary.

diesel *m* diesel.

diète *f* diet.

diététicien *m*, **-ienne** *f* dietician.

dieu *m* god.

diffamer *vt* to defame, slander.

différence *f* difference.

différencier *vt* to differentiate.

différent *adj* different; various.

différer *vt* to differ; to vary.

difficile *adj* difficult; awkward, tricky.

difficulté *f* difficulty; problem.

diffuser *vt* to diffuse, circulate, broadcast.

digérer *vt* to digest.

digestion *f* digestion.

digne *adj* worthy; dignified.

dignité *f* dignity.

dilapider *vt* to squander; to embezzle.

dilemme *m* dilemma.

diluer *vt* to dilute.

dimanche *m* Sunday.

dimension *f* dimension, size.

diminuer *vt* to diminish, reduce:— *vi* to diminish, lessen.

diminutif *m* diminutive.

diminution *f* reduction, lessening.

dîner *vi* to dine:— *m* dinner.

diocèse *m* diocese.

diplomate *m* diplomat.

diplomatie *f* diplomacy.

diplomatique *adj* diplomatic.

diplôme *m* diploma, certificate.

dire *vt* to say; to tell:— **se ~** to say to oneself; to call oneself:— *vr* **se ~ que** to be said that.

direct *adj* direct:— *m* express.

directeur *m*, **-trice** *f* director.

direction *f* direction, management.

diriger *vt* to run, direct:— **se ~** *vr*:— **se ~ vers** to head for, make for.

discerner *vt* to discern, distinguish.

disciple *m* disciple.

discipline *f* discipline.

discorde *f* discord, dissension.

discothèque *f* discotheque.

discours *m* speech, talking.

discréditer *vt* to discredit.

discret *adj* discreet.

discrétion *f* discretion, prudence.

discrimination *f* discrimination.

discriminer *vt* to distinguish; to discriminate.

disculper *vt* to excuse, exonerate.

discussion *f* discussion, debate.

discuter *vi, vt* to discuss, debate.

disgrâce *f* disgrace.

disparaître *vi* to disappear, vanish.

disparité *f* disparity, incongruity.

disparition *f* disappearance; death; extinction.

dispenser *vt* to dispense, exempt.

dispersion *f* dispersal, scattering.

disponible *adj* available; transferable.

disposer *vt* to arrange, dispose.

dispositif *m* device, mechanism.

disposition *f* arrangement, layout.

dispute *f* dispute, argument.

disque *m* disk; record.

disquette *f* diskette.

dissertation *f* dissertation.

dissidence *f* dissidence, dissent.

dissident *m* dissident.

dissimuler *vt* to dissemble, conceal.

dissipation *f* dissipation, waste.

dissiper *vt* to dispel; to dissipate.

dissolution *f* dissolution.

dissoudre *vt* to dissolve.

dissuader *vt* to dissuade.

distance *f* distance, interval.

distant *adj* distant.

distiller *vt* to distil.

distillerie *f* distillery.

distinct *adj* distinct, different.

distinction *f* distinction.

distingué *adj* distinguished.

distinguer *vt* to distinguish; to discern.

distraire *vt* to distract; to amuse:— **se ~** *vr* to enjoy oneself.

distrait *adj* inattentive, absentminded.

distribuer *vt* to distribute.

distribution *f* distribution.

district *m* district.

divaguer *vi* to ramble, rave.

divergence *f* divergence.
diverger *vi* to diverge, differ.
divers *adj* diverse, varied.
diversification *f* diversification.
diversifier *vt* to vary, diversify:—**se ~** *vr* to diversify.
diversité *f* diversity, variety.
divertir *vt* to amuse, entertain:—**se ~** *vr* to amuse oneself.
divertissant *adj* amusing, entertaining.
divin *adj* divine, exquisite.
divinité *f* divinity.
diviser *vt* to divide, split.
division *f* division.
divorce *m* divorce.
divorcer *vi* to get divorced.
dix *adj, m* ten.
dix-huit *adj, m* eighteen.
dix-huitième *adj, mf* eighteenth.
dix-neuf *adj, m* nineteen.
dix-neuvième *adj, mf* nineteenth.
dix-sept *adj, m* seventeen.
dix-septième *adj, mf* seventeenth.
dixième *adj, mf* tenth.
docile *adj* docile, submissive.
docteur *m* doctor.
doctrine *f* doctrine.
document *m* document.
documentaire *adj* documentary.
documentation *f* documentation; information.
documenter *vt* to document.
dogmatique *adj* dogmatic.
doigt *m* finger.
doigté *m* touch; fingering technique.
domaine *m* domain, estate; sphere.
domestique *adj* domestic, household.
domestiquer *vt* to domesticate, tame.
domicile *m* domicile, address.
dominant *adj* dominant, prevailing.
domination *f* domination; to dominion.

dominer *vt* to dominate; to prevail:—**se ~** to control oneself.
dommage *m* damage; harm:—**c'est ~** it's a pity.
dompter *vt* to tame, train.
don *m* gift; talent.
donation *f* donation.
donc *conj* so, therefore, thus:— **pourquoi ~?** why was that?.
donné *adj* given; fixed:—**étant ~** seeing that, in view of.
donnée *f* datum.
donner *vt* to give:—*vi* to knock, beat.
donneur *m*, **-euse** *f* giver, donor; dealer.
dont *pron* whose, of which.
dormir *vi* to sleep, be asleep; to be still.
dortoir *m* dormitory.
dos *m* back; top; ridge.
dose *f* dose; amount; quantity.
dossier *m* dossier, file; case.
douane *f* customs.
douanier *adj* custom(s).
double *adj* double, duplicate, dual:—*m* copy, double.
doubler *vt vi* to double, duplicate.
douceur *f* softness, gentleness.
douche *f* shower.
doucher (se) *vr* to take a shower.
doué *adj* gifted, endowed with.
douleur *f* pain, ache; anguish.
douloureux *adj* painful, grievous.
doute *m* doubt, misgiving:—**sans ~** without doubt.
douter *vi* to doubt, question:—**se ~ que** to suspect that, expect that.
douteux *adj* doubtful, dubious.
doux *adj* (*f* **douce**) soft; sweet; mild.
douzaine *f* dozen.
douze *adj m* twelve.
douzième *adj* twelfth:—*mf* twelfth.
dragon *m* dragon.

dramatique *adj* dramatic.

dramaturge *mf* playwright.

drame *m* drama.

drap *m* sheet.

drapeau *m* flag.

drogue *f* drug.

drogué(e) *m(f)* drug addict:—*adj* drugged.

droguer *vt* to drug, administer drugs.

droit *adj* right; straight; sound; honest:—*adv* straight, straight ahead:— *m* right; law; tax.

droite *f* right side; right (wing); straight line.

droitier *adj* right-handed.

drôle *adj* funny, amusing; peculiar.

du *art* of the.

dû *adj* owed; due:—**~ment** *adv* duly.

dubitatif *adj* doubtful, dubious.

duc *m* duke, **duchesse** *f* duchess.

dune *f* dune.

duo *m* duo; duet.

duper *vt* to dupe, take in.

dupliquer *vt* to duplicate.

dur *adj* hard, tough; difficult.

durable *adj* durable, lasting.

durant *prép* during, for.

durcir *vt vi* to harden:—**se ~** *vr* to become hardened.

durée *f* duration, length.

durer *vi* to last.

duvet *m* down.

dynamique *f* dynamic; dynamics:—*adj* dynamic.

dynamite *f* dynamite.

dynamo *f* dynamo.

dynastie *f* dynasty.

dyslexie *f* dyslexia.

dyslexique *adj* dyslexic.

E

eau *f* water; rain.

eau-de-vie *f* brandy.

éblouir *vt* to dazzle; to fascinate.

ébriété *f* intoxication.

écart *m* distance; interval; discrepancy.

écarter *vt* to separate; to avert; to dismiss.

ecclésiastique *adj* ecclesiastical:—*m* ecclesiastic, clergyman.

échange *m* exchange, barter, trade.

échanger *vt* to exchange.

échantillon *m* sample.

échappement *m* exhaust; release.

échapper *vi* to escape, avoid, elude.

écharpe *f* scarf; arm-sling.

échauffer *vt* to heat, overheat; to excite.

échec *m* failure, defeat.

échelle *f* ladder; scale.

échelonner *vt* to grade; to stagger, set at intervals.

échine *f* backbone, spine.

écho *m* echo; rumour.

échoir *vi* to fall due; to befall.

éclair *m* flash; lightning flash; spark.

éclairage *m* lighting, light.

éclaircir *vt* to lighten, brighten up.

éclairer *vt* to light; clarify, explain.

éclat *m* brightness; splendour.

éclatement *m* explosion, bursting, rupture.

éclipse *f* eclipse.

éclipser *vt* to eclipse, overshadow.

écœurer *vt* to nauseate, disgust.

école *f* school, schooling; sect, doctrine.

écolier *m* schoolgirl, **-ière** *f* schoolgirl.

écologie *f* ecology.

écologiste *mf* ecologist.

économe *adj* thrifty.

économie *f* economy, thrift; economics.

économique *adj* economic.

économiser *vt* to economise, save.

Écossais *m* Scotsman, **-e** *f* Scotswoman.

écossais *adj* Scottish.

Écosse *f* Scotland.

écoulement *m* flow, discharge, outlet.

écouler *vt* to flow, discharge; to sell.

écouter *vt* to listen to, hear.

écran *m* screen.

écraser *vt* to crush; to run over:—**s'**~ *vr* to crash.

écrire *vt* to write; to spell.

écriture *f* writing; handwriting; script.

écrivain *m* writer.

écrouler (s') *vr* to collapse, crumble.

écume *f* foam, froth; scum.

écureuil *m* squirrel.

édifice *m* edifice, building.

édifier *vt* to build, construct; to edify.

éditer *vt* to publish, produce; to edit.

éditeur *m*, **-trice** *f* publisher; editor.

éducation *f* education; upbringing.

éduquer *vt* to educate; to bring up, raise.

effacer *vt* to efface, erase, wipe off.

effaroucher *vt* to frighten; to shock.

effectif *m* staff; size, complement:— *adj* effective, positive.

effectuer *vt* to effect, execute, carry out.

effet *m* effect; bill, note.

efficace *adj* effective; efficient.

efficacité *f* effectiveness, efficiency.

efforcer (s') *vr* to endeavour, do one's best.

effort *m* effort, exertion; stress, strain.

effrayer *vt* to frighten, scare.

effroi *m* terror, dismay.

effronté *adj* shameless, impudent, cheeky.

effroyable *adj* horrifying, appalling.

égal *adj* equal; even, level; equable.

égaler *vt* to equal, match.

égaliser *vt* to equalise; to level out.

égalité *f* equality; equableness; evenness.

égard *m* consideration, respect:—**à l'**~ **de** concerning, regarding.

égarer *vt* to mislead, lead astray:—**s'**~ *vr* to get lost.

église *f* church.

égoïsme *m* selfishness, egoism.

égoïste *mf* egotist:—*adj* egotistic.

éjecter *vt* to eject, throw out.

élaborer *vt* to elaborate, develop.

élan *m* surge, momentum, speed; spirit, elan.

élargir *vt* to widen, stretch:—**s'**~ *vr* to get wider.

élastique *adj* elastic; flexible:—*m* elastic, elastic band.

élection *f* election; choice.

électorat *m* electorate; constituency; franchise.

électricité *f* electricity.

électrique *adj* electric.

électroménager *m* household appliance.

élégance *f* elegance, stylishness.

élégant *adj* elegant, stylish.

élémentaire *adj* elementary; basic.

éléphant *m* elephant.

élève *mf* pupil, student.

élever *vt* to bring up, raise:—**s'**~ *vr* to rise, go up.

éligible *adj* eligible.

élimination *f* elimination.

éliminer *vt* to eliminate, discard.

élire *vt* to elect.

élite *f* elite.

elle *pron* she; it; her:—**~-même** herself.

élocution *f* elocution, diction.

éloigné *adj* distant, remote.

éloigner *vt* to move away:—**s'~** *vr* to go away.

éloquent *adj* eloquent.

émancipation *f* emancipation, liberation.

émanciper *vt* to emancipate:—**s'~** *vr* to become emancipated.

emballer *vt* to pack up, wrap up.

embarcation *f* boat, craft.

embargo *m* embargo.

embarquer *vt* to embark:—*vi* to embark.

embarras *m* embarrassment, confusion; trouble.

embarrasser *vt* to embarrass; to hamper.

embaucher *vt* to take on, hire.

embellir *vt* to beautify, make more attractive.

emblème *m* symbol, emblem.

embouteillage *m* traffic jam; bottling.

embrasser *vt* to kiss, embrace.

embrayage *m* clutch.

embryon *m* embryo.

embuscade *f* ambush.

émerger *vi* to emerge; to stand out.

émerveiller *vt* to astonish, amaze:— **s'~** *vr* to marvel at.

émettre *vt* to send out, emit, transmit.

émeute *f* riot.

émigration *f* emigration.

émigrer *vi* to emigrate.

éminent *adj* eminent, distinguished.

émission *f* sending out; transmission; broadcast; emission.

emménager *vi* to move in.

emmener *vt* to take away; to lead.

émoi *m* agitation, emotion.

émotion *f* emotion; commotion.

émouvoir *vt* to move, upset:—**s'~** *vr* to be moved.

empaqueter *vt* to parcel up, pack.

emparer (s') *vr* to seize, grab; to take possession of.

empêcher *vt* to prevent, stop.

empereur *m* emperor.

empiler *vt* to pile up, stack.

empire *m* empire; influence, ascendancy.

empirer *vi* to get worse, deteriorate.

emplacement *m* site, location.

emploi *m* use; job, employment.

employé *m*, **-e** *f* employee.

employer *vt* to use, spend; to employ.

employeur *m*, **euse** *f* employer.

empoisonner *vt* to poison.

emporter *vt* to take; to carry off.

emprisonner *vt* to imprison, trap.

emprunter *vt* to borrow; to assume; to derive.

ému *adj* moved, touched, excited.

en *prép* in; to; by; on:—**~ tant que** as:—*pn* from there; of it, of them:— **je n'~ veux plus** I don't want any more.

encadrer *vt* to frame; to train; to surround.

encaisser *vt* to collect, receive; to cash.

enceinte *f* pregnant.

encercler *vt* to encircle, surround.

enchaînement *m* linking; link; sequence.

enchaîner *vt* to chain.

enchanté *adj* enchanted, delighted.

enchanter *vt* to enchant, delight.

enclave *f* enclave.

encombrer *vt* to clutter, obstruct.

encore *adv* still; only; again; more:— ~ **que** even though.

encouragement *m* encouragement.

encourager *vt* to encourage; to incite.

encre *f* ink.

encyclopédie *f* encyclopaedia.

endetter (s') *vr* to get into debt.

endommager *vt* to damage.

endormir *vt* to put to sleep:—**s'~** *vr* to fall asleep.

endosser *vt* to put on; to shoulder; to endorse.

endroit *m* place.

enduit *m* coating.

endurance *f* endurance, stamina.

endurcir *vt* to harden:—**s'~** *vr* to become hardened.

endurer *vt* to endure, bear.

énergie *f* energy; spirit, vigour.

énergique *adj* energetic, vigorous.

énerver *vt* to irritate, annoy:—**s'~** *vr* to get worked up.

enfance *f* childhood; infancy.

enfant *mf* child; native.

enfer *m* hell.

enfermer *vt* to lock up; to confine.

enfin *adv* at last; in short; after all.

enflammer *vt* to set on fire:—**s'~** *vr* to ignite.

enfler *vi* to swell up, inflate.

enfuir (s') *vr* to run away, flee.

engagement *m* agreement, commitment.

engager *vt* to bind; to involve:—**s'~** *vr* to undertake to.

engin *m* machine; instrument; contraption.

engourdi *adj* numb; dull.

engraisser *vi* to get fatter.

énigme *f* enigma, riddle.

enivrer *vt* to intoxicate, make drunk:— **s'~** *vr* to get drunk.

enlever *vt* to remove; to abduct.

enneigé *adj* snowy, snowbound.

ennemi(e) *m(f)* enemy.

ennui *m* boredom, tedium, weariness.

ennuyer *vt* to bore, bother:—**s'~** *vr* to get bored.

énorme *adj* enormous, huge.

enquête *f* inquiry, investigation; survey.

enquêter *vi* to hold an inquiry; to investigate.

enraciner *vt* to implant, root.

enregistrer *vt* to record; to register.

enrichir *vt* to enrich, expand:—**s'~** *vr* to get rich.

enrober *vt* to wrap, cover, coat.

enrôler *vt* to enlist, enrol.

enrouler *vt* to roll up, wind up.

enseignant(e) *m(f)* teacher.

enseignement *m* education, training, instruction.

enseigner *vt* to teach.

ensemble *adv* together, at the same time:—*m* unity; whole.

ensoleillé *adj* sunny.

ensuite *adv* then, next, afterwards.

entasser *vt* to pile up, heap up.

entendement *m* understanding, comprehension.

entendre *vt* to hear; to intend, mean; to understand:—**s'~** *vr* to agree; to know how to.

entendu *adj* agreed:—**bien ~** of course.

enterrer *vt* to bury, inter.

entêté *adj* stubborn, obstinate.

enthousiasme *m* enthusiasm.

enthousiaste *adj* enthusiastic:—*mf* enthusiast.

entier *adj* entire, whole; intact.

entité *f* entity.

entourer *vt* to surround, frame, encircle:—*vr*:—**s'~ de** to surround oneself with.

entraider (s') *vr* to help one another.

entrain *m* spirit, liveliness.

entraîner *vt* to drag; to lead; to train:—**s'~** *vr* to train oneself.

entraîneur *m* trainer, coach.

entre *prép* between, among, into.

entrée *f* entry, entrance; insertion:—**d'~ de jeu** from the outset.

entremêler *vt* to intermingle, intermix.

entrepôt *m* warehouse, bonded warehouse.

entreprendre *vt* to embark upon, undertake.

entrepreneur *m*, **-euse** *f* contractor; entrepreneur.

entreprise *f* company; venture, business.

entrer *vi* to enter, go in.

entretemps *adv* meanwhile.

entretenir *vt* to maintain, look after; to speak with.

entretien *m* upkeep, maintenance; conversation.

entrevue *f* meeting, interview.

énumérer *vt* to enumerate, list.

envahir *vt* to invade, overrun.

enveloppe *f* envelope; covering; exterior.

envelopper *vt* to envelop; to wrap up; to veil.

envers *prép* towards, to:—*m*:—**à l'~** inside out, upside down.

envie *f* desire, longing, inclination; envy.

envier *vt* to envy.

environ *adv* about, around:—**-s** *mpl* vicinity, neighbourhood.

environnement *m* environment.

environnemental *adj* environmental.

environner *vt* to surround, encircle.

envisager *vt* to view, envisage.

envoi *m* dispatch, remittance; kick-off.

envoyer *vt* to send, dispatch; hurl, fire.

épais *adj* thick; deep.

épaissir *vi* to thicken:—*vt*; **s'~** *vr* to get thicker.

épanouir *vt* to brighten; to open out:—**s'~** *vr* to bloom.

épargner *vt* to save; to spare.

épaule *f* shoulder.

épeler *vt* to spell.

éperdu *adj* distraught, overcome.

épice *m* spice.

épicier *m*, **-ière** *f* grocer.

épidémie *f* epidemic.

épier *vt* to spy on.

épine *f* spine; thorn; quill.

épingle *f* pin.

épiscopal *adj* episcopal.

épisode *m* episode.

épitaphe *f* epitaph.

éponge *f* sponge.

éponger *vt* to sponge, mop.

époque *f* time, epoch, age, period.

épouser *vt* to marry, wed; espouse.

épouvanter *vt* to terrify, appall.

époux *m*, **épouse** *f* spouse.

éprendre(s') *vr* to fall in love with.

épreuve *f* test; ordeal, trial; proof.

éprouver *vt* to feel, experience.

épuisement *m* exhaustion.

épuiser *vt* to exhaust, wear out.

épurer *vt* to purify, refine.

équateur *m* equator.

équation *f* equation.

équilibre *m* balance, equilibrium; harmony.

équilibrer *vt* to balance.

équipe *f* team, crew, gang, staff.

équipement *m* equipment; fitting out, fittings.

équiper *vt* to equip, fit out.

équitable *adj* equitable, fair.

équivalence *f* equivalence.

équivalent *adj* equivalent, same:—*m* equivalent.

équivoque *adj* equivocal, questionable.

ère *f* era.

érection *f* erection; establishment.

ergot *m* spur; lug.

ermite *m* hermit.

éroder *vt* to erode.

érotique *adj* erotic.

errer *vi* to wander, roam.

erreur *f* error, mistake, fault.

érudition *f* erudition, learning.

éruption *f* eruption.

escalade *f* climbing; escalation.

escalader *vt* to climb, scale.

escalier *m* stairs, steps.

escargot *m* snail.

esclavage *m* slavery, bondage.

esclave *mf* slave.

escompte *m* discount.

escompter *vt* to discount.

escorte *f* escort; retinue.

escorter *vt* to escort.

espace *m* space, interval.

espacer *vt* to space out.

espèce *f* sort, kind; species.

espérance *f* hope, expectation.

espérer *vt* to hope.

espion *m*, **-onne** *f* spy.

espionner *vt* to spy.

espoir *m* hope.

esprit *m* mind, intellect; spirit; wit.

esquisse *f* sketch, outline.

esquisser *vt* to sketch, outline.

esquiver *vt* to dodge; to shirk.

essai *m* test, trial; attempt; essay.

essayer *vt* to test, try, try on.

essence *f* petrol; essential oil.

essentiel *adj* essential, basic.

essieu *m* axle.

essuyer *vt* to wipe, mop:—**s'~** *vr* to wipe oneself.

est *m* east.

esthéticien(ne) *m(f)* beautician.

estimation *f* valuation; estimation, reckoning.

estimer *vt* to value, assess, estimate.

estival *adj* summer.

estivant *m*, **-e** *f* holidaymaker, summer visitor.

estomac *m* stomach.

et *conj* and.

établi *adj* established:—*m* workbench.

établir *vt* to establish **s'~** *vr* to become established.

établissement *m* establishing, building; establishment.

étage *m* floor, storey; stage, level.

étanche *adj* waterproof.

étang *m* pond.

étape *f* stage, leg; staging point.

état *m* state, condition; statement.

étayer *vt* to prop up, support.

été *m* summer.

éteindre *vt* to put out, extinguish.

étendre *vt* to spread, extend:—**s'~** *vr* to spread; to stretch out.

étendue *f* expanse, area; duration.

éternel *adj* eternal, everlasting.

éternité *f* eternity; ages.

éternuer *vi* to sneeze.

éthnique *adj* ethnic.

ethnologie *f* ethnology.

étinceler *vi* to sparkle, gleam.

étincelle *f* spark; gleam, glimmer.

étiquette *f* label, ticket; etiquette.

étoffe *f* material, fabric; stuff.

étoile *f* star.

étonnement *m* surprise, astonishment.

étonner *vt* to astonish, surprise:—**s'~** *vr* to be astonished.

étouffer *vt* to suffocate:—**s'~** *vr* to be suffocated, to swelter.

étourdi *adj* absentminded.

étourdir *vt* to stun, daze; to deafen.

étourdissement *m* blackout, dizzy spell.

étrange *adj* strange, funny.

étranger *m*, **-ère** *f* foreigner, stranger, alien:—*adj* foreign, strange, unknown.

étrangeté *f* strangeness, oddness.

étrangler *vt* to strangle, stifle:—**s'~** *vr* to strangle oneself, choke.

être *vi* to be:—**c'est-à-dire** namely, that is to say:—*m* being, person, soul.

étreindre *vt* to embrace, hug; to seize.

étroit *adj* narrow; strict.

étude *f* study; survey; office.

étudier *vt* to study, examine.

étymologie *f* etymology.

eu = *p.p.* **avoir** had.

eucalyptus *m* eucharist.

eucharistie *f* euphoria.

européen *m*, **-enne** *f* European:—*adj* European.

euthanasie *f* euthanasia.

eux *pron* they, them:—**c'est à ~** it's up to them; it's theirs:—**~-mêmes** themselves.

évacuer *vt* to evacuate, clear.

évader (s') *vr* to escape.

évaluation *f* evaluation, appraisal.

évaluer *vt* to evaluate, appraise.

évanouir (s') *vr* to faint, pass out.

évanouissement *m* faint, blackout.

évaporation *f* evaporation.

évaporer (s') *vr* to evaporate.

évasion *f* escape; escapism.

éveiller *vt* to waken, arouse:—**s'~** *vr* to wake up.

événement *m* event, incident.

éventualité *f* eventuality, possibility.

éventuel *adj* possible.

évêque *m* bishop.

évidence *f* evidence, proof.

évident *adj* obvious, evident.

évier *m* sink.

éviter *vt* to avoid; to spare.

évoluer *vi* to evolve, develop.

évolution *f* evolution, development.

évoquer *vt* to evoke, recall.

exacerber *vt* to exacerbate, aggravate.

exact *adj* exact, accurate.

exagération *f* exaggeration.

exagéré *adj* exaggerated, excessive.

exagérer *vt* to exaggerate.

examen *m* examination, survey, investigation.

examiner *vt* to examine, survey.

exaspérer *vt* to exasperate.

excellent *adj* excellent.

exceller *vi* to excel.

excentrique *adj* eccentric.

excepté *adj* apart, aside:—*prép* except, but for.

exception *f* exception, derogation.

exceptionnel *adj* exceptional.

excès *m* excess, surplus.

excitant *m* stimulant:—*adj* exciting, stimulating.

exciter *vt* to excite, stimulate:—**s'~** *vr* to get excited.

exclamation *f* exclamation.

exclamer (s') *vr* to exclaim.

exclure *vt* to exclude, oust, expel.

exclusif *adj* exclusive.

exclusion *f* exclusion, suspension.

excursion *f* excursion, trip.

excuse *f* excuse, pretext.

excuser *vt* to excuse, forgive:—**s'~** *vr* to apologise for.

exécuter *vt* to execute, carry out, perform; to produce.

exécution *f* execution, carrying out, performance.

exemple *m* example, model, instance.

exercer *vt* to exercise, perform, fulfil:—**s'~** *vr* to practise.

exercice *m* exercise, practice, use; financial year.

exhaustif *adj* exhaustive.

exhiber *vt* to exhibit, show.

exhibition *f* exhibition, show; display.

exhorter *vt* to exhort, urge.

exiger *vt* to demand, require.

exiler *vt* to exile, banish:—**s'~** *vr* to go into exile.

existence *f* existence, life.

exister *vi* to exist; to be.

exonérer *vt* to exempt.

exotique *adj* exotic.

expansion *f* expansion, development.

expectative *f* expectation, hope.

expédier *vt* to send, dispatch; to dispose of.

expédition *f* dispatch; consignment.

expérience *f* experience; experiment.

expérimental *adj* experimental.

expérimentation *f* experimentation.

expérimenter *vt* to test; to experiment with.

expert *adj* expert, skilled in:—*m* expert; connoisseur; assessor.

expertise *f* expertise; expert appraisal.

explicatif *adj* explanatory.

explication *f* explanation, analysis.

explicite *adj* explicit.

expliquer *vt* to explain, account for; to analyse.

exploitation *f* working; exploitation; concern.

exploiter *vt* to work, exploit; run, operate.

explorer *vt* to explore.

exploser *vi* to explode.

explosion *f* explosion.

exportation *f* export, exportation.

exporter *vt* to export.

exposer *vt* to display; to expose.

exposition *f* display; exposition; exposure.

express *adj* fast:—*m* fast train.

expression *f* expression.

exprimer *vt* to express, voice:—**s'~** *vr* to express oneself.

expropriation *f* expropriation.

expulser *vt* to expel; to evict.

exquis *adj* exquisite.

extase *f* ecstasy; rapture.

extension *f* extension; stretching; expansion.

exténuer *vt* to exhaust:—**s'~** *vr* to exhaust oneself.

extérieur *m* exterior, outside:—*adj* outer, external, exterior.

exterminer *vt* exterminate.

externe *adj* external, outer.

extinction *f* extinction, extinguishing.

extradition *f* extradition.

extraire *vt* to extract; to mine.

extraordinaire *adj* extraordinary.

extravagant *adj* extravagant, wild.

extraverti *m*, **-e** *f* extrovert:—*adj* extrovert.

extrême *adj* extreme.

extrémiste *mf*, *adj* extremist.

exubérance *f* exuberance.

exubérant *adj* exuberant.

F

fable *f* fable, story, tale.

fabricant *m*, **-ante** *f* manufacturer, maker.

fabrique *f* factory.

fabriquer *vt* to manufacture; to forge; to fabricate.

façade *f* façade, front.

face *f* face, side, surface, aspect:—**en ~** opposite:—**~ à** facing.

fâcher *vt* to anger; to grieve:—**se ~** *vr* to get angry.

fâcheux *adj* deplorable, regrettable.

facile *adj* easy; facile.

facilité *f* easiness, ease; ability; facility.

faciliter *vt* to make easier, facilitate.

façon *f* way, fashion; make; imitation:—**de toute ~** at any rate.

façonner *vt* to shape, fashion.

facteur *m* postman.

facture *f* bill, invoice; construction, technique.

facturer *vt* to invoice, charge for.

faculté *f* faculty; power, ability; right.

fade *adj* insipid, bland, dull.

faible *adj* weak, feeble; slight, poor.

faiblesse *f* weakness, feebleness, faintness.

faillir *vi* to come close to; to fail:—**j'ai failli tomber** I almost fell.

faim *f* hunger; appetite; famine.

faire *vt* to do; to make:—**rien à ~!** nothing doing!:—**s'en ~** to worry.

faisable *adj* feasible.

fait *m* event; fact; act.

falaise *f* cliff.

falloir *vi* to be necessary:—**il faut que tu partes** you must leave.

falsifier *vt* to falsify, alter.

familial *adj* family, domestic.

familiariser *vt* to familiarise:—**se ~** *vr* to familiarise oneself.

familiarité *f* familiarity.

familier *adj* familiar; colloquial; informal.

famille *f* family.

famine *f* famine.

fanatique *adj* fanatic:—*mf* fanatic.

faner *vt* to fade:—**se ~** *vr* to wither, fade.

fantaisie *f* whim, extravagance; imagination.

fantastique *adj* fantastic.

fantôme *m* ghost, phantom.

farce *f* joke, prank; farce.

farcir *vt* to stuff, cram.

fardeau *m* load, burden.

farine *f* flour.

farouche *adj* shy, timid; unsociable.

fascination *f* fascination.

fasciner *vt* to fascinate, bewitch.

fasciste *mf*, *adj* fascist.

fastidieux *adj* tedious, boring.

fatal *adj* fatal, deadly; fateful.

fatalité *f* fatality; inevitability.

fatigue *f* fatigue, tiredness.

fatiguer *vt* to tire; to overwork, strain:—**se ~** *vr* to get tired.

faubourg *m* suburb.

faune *f* wildlife, fauna.

faussaire *mf* forger.

fausser *vt* to distort, alter; to warp.

faute *f* mistake, foul, fault:—**~ de mieux** for lack of anything better.

fauteuil *m* armchair.

fautif *m*, **-ive** *f* culprit:—*adj* at fault.

faux *adj* false, forged, fake; wrong; bogus.

faux-semblant *m* sham, pretence.

faveur *f* favour.

favorable *adj* favourable, sympathetic.

favori *m*, **-ite** *f* favourite:—*adj* favourite.

favoriser *vt* to favour, further.

fécond *adj* fertile; prolific, fruitful; creative.

féconder *vt* to impregnate; to fertilise, pollinate.

fédéral *adj* federal.

fédération *f* federation.

feindre *vt* to feign, pretend.

fêlé *adj* cracked, hare-brained.

félicitation *f* congratulation.

féliciter *vt* to congratulate.

femelle *f* female.

féminin *adj* feminine, female.

féministe *mf adj* feminist.

féminité *f* femininity.

femme *f* woman; wife.

fendre *vt* to split, cleave, crack:—**se ~** *vr* to crack.

fenêtre *f* window.

fente *f* crack, fissure; slot.

fer *m* iron, point, blade:—**~ à cheval** horseshoe.

férié *adj* holiday.

ferme *adj* firm, steady; definite:—*f* farm.

ferment *m* ferment, leaven.

fermentation *f* fermentation, fermenting.

fermer *vt* to close; block; turn off:—**se ~** *vr* to close, shut up; to close one's mind to.

fermeté *f* firmness, steadiness.

fermier *m*, **-ière** *f* farmer.

féroce *adj* ferocious, savage.

férocité *f* ferocity, fierceness.

ferroviaire *adj* railway.

fertile *adj* fertile, productive.

fertilité *f* fertility.

fervent *adj* fervent, ardent.

festin *m* feast.

festival *m* festival.

fête *f* feast, holiday.

fêter *vt* to celebrate, fête.

feu *m* fire; light; hearth:—**en ~** on fire.

feuille *f* leaf; (*comput*) *m* **~ de calcul** spreadsheet.

feuilleter *vt* to leaf through.

fiable *adj* reliable; dependable.

fiancer (se) *vr* to become engaged.

fiasco *m* fiasco.

fibre *f* fibre.

ficelle *f* string; stick (bread).

fiche *f* card; sheet; certificate.

ficher *vt* to file, put on file.

fictif *adj* fictitious; imaginary.

fiction *f* imagination, fiction.

fidèle *adj* faithful, loyal.

fidélité *f* fidelity, loyalty.

fier *adj* proud, haughty; noble.

fier (se) *vr* to trust, rely on.

fierté *f* pride; arrogance.

fièvre *f* fever, temperature; excitement.

figuratif *adj* figurative, representational.

figure *f* face; figure; illustration, diagram.

figurer *vt* to represent:—*vi* to appear, feature:—**se ~** *vr* to imagine.

fil *m* thread; wire; cord:—**~ de fer** wire; **sans ~** *adj* wireless communication.

file *f* line, queue:—**à la ~** in line, in succession.

filer *vt* to spin.

filière *f* path; procedures; network.
fille *f* daughter, girl.
fillette *f* (small) girl.
film *m* film, picture.
filmer *vt* to film.
fils *m* son.
filtre *m* filter.
fin *f* end, finish:—*adj* thin, fine; delicate.
final *adj* final.
finance *f* finance.
financer *vt* to finance.
financier *m*, **-ière** *f* financier.
finesse *f* fineness; neatness.
fini *adj* finished, over, complete.
finir *vt* to finish, complete:—*vi* to finish, end; to die.
fissure *f* crack, fissure.
fixe *adj* fixed, permanent, set:—**~ment** *adv* fixedly, steadily.
fixer *vt* to fix; to arrange.
flacon *m* bottle, flask.
flagrant *adj* flagrant, blatant.
flair *m* sense of smell, nose; intuition.
flambeau *m* torch; candlestick.
flamme *f* flame; fervour; ardour.
flanc *m* flank, side.
flâner *vi* to stroll; to lounge about.
flatter *vt* to flatter, gratify.
flatterie *f* flattery.
flèche *f* arrow.
fléchir *vi* to bend, yield, weaken:—*vt* to bend, sway.
fleur *f* flower.
fleurir *vi* to blossom, flower:—*vt* to decorate with flowers.
fleuve *m* river.
flexibilité *f* flexibility.
flexible *adj* flexible, pliant.
flocon *m* fleck, flake.
flore *f* flora.
flot *m* stream, flood; floodtide; wave.

flotte *f* fleet; rain.
flotter *vi* to float; to drift; to wander; to waver.
fluctuation *f* fluctuation.
fluide *adj* fluid, flowing.
flux *m* flood; flow; flux.
foi *f* faith, trust.
foie *m* liver.
foin *m* hay.
foire *f* fair, trade fair.
fois *f* time, occasion.
folie *f* madness, insanity; extravagance.
foncé *adj* dark, deep (colours).
fonction *f* post, duty; function.
fonctionnaire *mf* civil servant.
fonctionner *vi* to work, function, operate.
fond *m* bottom, back:—**au ~** basically, in fact:—**à ~** thoroughly, in depth.
fondamental *adj* fundamental, basic.
fondamentaliste *mf*:—*adj* fundamentalist.
fondateur *m*, **-trice** *f* founder.
fondation *f* foundation.
fonder *vt* to found; to base.
fondre *vi* to melt:—*vt* to melt; to cast.
fonds *m* business; fund; money; stock.
fontaine *f* fountain, spring.
football *m* football, soccer.
force *f* strength, force, violence, energy.
forcé *adj* forced; emergency:—**~ment** *adv* inevitably.
forcer *vt* to force:—*vi* to overdo:—**se ~** *vr* to force oneself to.
forêt *f* forest.
forger *vt* to forge, form, mould.
formalité *f* formality.
formation *f* formation; training.
forme *f* form, shape; mould; fitness.
formel *adj* definite, positive; formal.

former *vt* to form; to train:—**se ~** *vr* to form; to train oneself

formidable *adj* tremendous:—**~ment** *adv* tremendously.

formulaire *m* form.

formule *f* formula; phrase; system.

formuler *vt* to formulate; express.

fort *adj* strong; high; loud; pronounced:—*adv* loudly; greatly; most:—*m* fort; strong point, forte.

fortifier *vt* to fortify, strengthen:—**se ~** *vr* to grow stronger.

fortuit *adj* fortuitous, chance.

fortune *f* fortune, luck.

fosse *f* pit; grave.

fou *adj*, *f* **folle** mad, wild; tremendous; erratic.

foudre *f* lightning, thunderbolt.

foudroyer *vt* to strike (lightning).

fouiller *vt* to search, scour.

foulard *m* scarf.

foule *f* crowd; masses, heaps.

four *m* oven; furnace; fiasco.

fourgon *m* coach, wagon, van.

fourmi *f* ant.

fourmiller *vi* to swarm, teem.

fournir *vt* to supply, provide.

fournisseur *m*, **-euse** *f* purveyor, supplier.

fourrer *vt* to stuff; to line.

fourrure *f* coat, fur.

foyer *m* home; fireplace; focus.

fracas *m* crash; roar, din.

fraction *f* fraction, part.

fracture *f* fracture.

fragile *adj* fragile, delicate.

fragment *m* fragment.

fragmenter *vt* to break up:—**se ~** *vr* to fragment.

fraîcheur *f* freshness, coolness.

frais *mpl* expenses:—*adj*, *f* **fraîche** fresh, cool.

franc *adj*, *f* **franche** frank, open.

Français *m* Frenchman, **-e** *f* Frenchwoman.

français *adj* French:—*m* French.

France *f* France.

franchir *vt* to clear, get over, cross.

francophone *mf* French-speaker, *adj* French-speaking.

frange *f* fringe; threshold.

frapper *vt* to hit; to strike down:—*vi* to strike, knock.

fraternel *adj* fraternal.

fraternité *f* fraternity.

fraude *f* fraud, cheating.

frein *m* brake; check.

freiner *vi* to brake, slow down:—*vt* to slow down; to curb, check.

frémir *vi* to quiver, tremble.

frénétique *adj* frenetic.

fréquence *f* frequency.

fréquent *adj* frequent.

frère *m* brother.

friand *adj* partial to, fond of.

frigidaire *m* refrigerator.

frire *vt* to fry.

frisé *adj* curly, curly-haired.

frisson *m* shiver, shudder.

frissonner *vi* to shudder, tremble, shiver.

frite *f* chip.

frivole *adj* frivolous, shallow.

frivolité *f* frivolity.

froid *adj* cold, cool:—*m* cold; coolness; refrigeration.

froideur *f* coldness, chilliness.

fromage *m* cheese.

front *m* forehead; face; front.

frontière *f* border, frontier.

frotter *vt* to rub, scrape.

fructueux *adj* fruitful, profitable.

frugal *adj* frugal.

frugalité *f* frugality.
fruit *m* fruit, result.
frustration *f* frustration.
frustrer *vt* to frustrate, deprive.
fugitif *m*, **-ive** *f* fugitive:—*adj* fugitive, runaway.
fuir *vi* to avoid; to flee; to leak.
fuite *f* flight, escape; leak.
fumé *adj* smoked.
fumée *f* smoke; vapour.
fumer *vi* to smoke, steam, give off smoke:—*vt* to smoke.
fumeur *m*, **-euse** *f* smoker.
funérailles *fpl* funeral.
funéraire *adj* funeral, funerary.

fureur *f* fury; violence.
furieux *adj* furious, violent.
furtif *adj* furtive; stealthy.
fusée *f* rocket, missile.
fusil *m* rifle, gun.
fusiller *vt* to shoot.
fusion *f* fusion; melting; merger; blending.
fusionner *vt* to merge, combine.
futile *adj* futile.
futilité *f* futility.
futur *adj* future:—*m* intended, fiancé; future.
fuyard *m*, **-e** *f*:—*adj* runaway.

G

gâcher *vt* to mix; to waste.
gachette *f* trigger.
gadget *m* gadget; gimmick.
gage *m* security; pledge; proof.
gagnant *m*, **-e** *f* winner:—*adj* winning.
gagner *vt* to earn, to win:—*vi* to win.
gai *adj* cheerful, happy, gay.
gain *m* earnings; gain, profit, benefit; saving.
gala *m* official reception; gala.
galant *adj* gallant, courteous.
galaxie *f* galaxy.
galerie *f* gallery; tunnel.
galet *m* pebble.
Gallois *m* Welshman, **-e** *f* Welshwoman.
gallois *adj* Welsh:—*m* Welsh.
galop *m* gallop; canter.
galoper *vi* to gallop; to run wild.
gamin *m*, **-e** *f* kid, street urchin.
gamme *f* range; scale.

gant *m* glove.
gap *m* gap; difference, discrepancy.
garage *m* garage.
garagiste *mf* garage owner.
garantie *f* guarantee, surety.
garantir *vt* to guarantee, secure.
garçon *m* boy; assistant; waiter.
garde *f* custody; guard; surveillance:—*m* guard, warder.
garde-boue *m* mudguard.
garder *vt* to look after; to stay in; to keep on.
garde-robe *f* wardrobe.
gardien *m*, **-ienne** *f* guard, guardian, warden; protector.
gare *f* rail station; basin; depot.
gargouiller *vi* to gurgle; to rumble.
garnir *vt* to fit with; to trim, decorate.
garnison *f* (*mil*) garrison.
gaspiller *vt* to waste, squander.

gastronomie *f* gastronomy.

gâté *adj* ruined; spoiled.

gâteau *m* cake.

gâter *vt* to ruin; to spoil:—**se ~** *vr* to go bad, go off.

gauche *adj* left; awkward, clumsy:—*f* left; left wing.

gaucher *adj* left-handed.

gaz *m invar* gas; fizz; wind.

gazeux *adj* gaseous; fizzy.

gazon *m* lawn; turf.

géant *m* giant, **-e** *f* giantess.

gel *m* frost; gel.

geler *vi* to freeze, be frozen:—*vt* to freeze.

gémir *vi* to groan, moan.

gendarme *m* policeman; gendarme.

gendarmerie *f* police force, constabulary.

gêne *f* discomfort; trouble:—**être sans ~** to be inconsiderate.

généalogie *f* genealogy.

gêner *vt* to bother; to hinder; to make uneasy.

général *adj* general, broad; common:—*m* general.

généralisation *f* generalisation.

généraliser *vt* to generalise:—**se ~** *vr* to become widespread.

générateur *m* generator.

génération *f* generation.

générer *vt* to generate

généreux *adj* generous; noble; magnanimous.

générosité *f* generosity; nobility; magnanimity.

génétique *adj* genetic.

génie *m* genius; spirit; genie.

genou *m* knee.

genre *m* kind, type; gender; genre.

gens *mpl* people, folk.

gentil *adj*, *f* **gentille** kind; good; pleasant.

géographie *f* geography.

géographique *adj* geographic.

géologie *f* geology.

géométrie *f* geometry.

géométrique *adj* geometric.

gérant *m*, **-e** *f* manager.

gérer *vt* to manage, administer.

germe *m* germ; seed.

geste *m* gesture; act, deed.

gesticuler *vi* to gesticulate.

gestion *f* management, administration.

ghetto *m* ghetto.

gicler *vi* to spurt, squirt.

gifler *vt* to slap, smack.

gilet *m* waistcoat.

girafe *f* giraffe.

gisement *m* deposit; mine; pool.

gîte *m* shelter; home; self-catering holiday cottage.

givre *m* frost, rime.

glace *f* ice; ice cream; mirror.

glacer *vt* to freeze; to chill; to glaze.

glaçon *m* icicle; ice cube.

glande *f* gland.

glaner *vt* to glean.

glissement *m* sliding; gliding; downturn, downswing.

glisser *vi* to slide, slip, skid.

global *adj* global, overall:—**~ement** *adv* globally.

globe *m* globe, sphere; earth.

gloire *f* glory; distinction; celebrity.

glorieux *adj* glorious.

glorifier *vt* to glory, honour:—**se ~** *vr* to glory in; to boast.

glossaire *m* glossary.

gluant *adj* sticky, gummy.

gobelet *m* beaker, tumbler.

golf *m* golf.

golfeur *m*, **-euse** *f* golfer.

gomme *f* gum; rubber, eraser.

gommer *vt* to rub out; to gum.

gonflable *adj* inflatable.

gonfler *vt* to pump up, inflate:—**se ~** *vr* to swell; to be puffed up.

gorge *f* throat.

gothique *m*, *adj* Gothic.

goudronner *vt* to tar.

goulu *adj* greedy, gluttonous.

goupille *f* pin.

gourde *f* gourd; flask.

gourmand *adj* greedy.

gourmet *m* gourmet.

goût *m* taste; liking; style.

goûter *vt* to taste; to appreciate:—*vi* to have a snack; to taste good:—*m* snack.

goutte *f* drop; gout.

gouvernail *m* rudder; helm.

gouvernement *m* government.

gouverner *vt* to govern, rule; to control; to steer.

grâce *f* grace; favour; mercy; pardon:—**~ à** thanks to.

gracieux *adj* gracious.

grade *m* rank; grade; degree.

graduel *adj* gradual; progressive.

graduer *vt* to step up; to graduate.

grain *m* grain, seed; bead.

graisse *f* grease, fat.

grammaire *f* grammar.

grammatical *adj* grammatical.

gramme *m* gram.

grand *adj* big; tall; great; leading:—**pas ~-chose** not up too much.

grand-mère *f* grandmother.

grand-parents *mpl* grandparents

grand-père *m* grandfather.

grandeur *f* size; greatness; magnitude.

grandir *vi* to grow bigger, increase:—*vt* to magnify; to exaggerate.

graphique *m* graph:—*adj* graphic.

gras *adj f* **grasse** fatty; fat; greasy; crude.

gratification *f* gratuity; bonus.

gratis *adv* free, gratis.

gratitude *f* gratitude, gratefulness.

gratuit *adj* free, gratuitous.

grave *adj* grave, solemn.

graver *vt* to engrave, imprint.

gravitation *f* gravitation.

gravité *f* gravity.

gravure *f* engraving, carving.

gré *m* liking, taste:—**au ~ de** depending on, at the mercy of:—**savoir ~** to be grateful.

greffer *vt* to transplant, graft.

grêle *f* hail.

grelotter *vi* to shiver.

grenier *m* attic, garret.

grenouille *f* frog.

grève *f* strike; shore.

griffe *f* claw.

griffer *vt* to scratch.

griffonner *vt* to scribble, jot down.

grillade *f* grill.

grille *f* railings; gate; grill.

grille-pain *m invar* toaster.

griller *vt* to toast, scorch; to put bars on:—*vi* to toast, grill.

grimace *f* grimace.

grimper *vi* to climb up.

grippe *f* flu, influenza.

gris *adj* grey.

griser *vt* to intoxicate:—**se ~** *vr* to get drunk.

grogner *vi* to grumble, moan.

grommeler *vi* to mutter; to grumble:—*vt* to mutter.

gronder *vt* to scold:—*vi* to rumble, growl.

gros *adj*, *f* **grosse** big; fat; serious;

coarse:—**en** ~ in bulk:—*m* bulk; wholesale; fat man.

grossesse *f* pregnancy.

grosseur *f* thickness; weight; fatness.

grossir *vi* to get fatter; to swell, grow:—*vt* to magnify; to exaggerate.

grossiste *mf* wholesaler.

grotesque *adj* grotesque, ludicrous

groupe *m* group; party; cluster.

grouper *vt* to group together; to bulk:—**se** ~ *vr* to gather.

grue *f* crane.

guépard *m* cheetah.

guêpe *f* wasp.

guère *adv* hardly, scarcely.

guérir *vi* to get better; to heal:—*vt* to cure, heal:—**se** ~ *vr* to get better; to recover from.

guérison *f* recovery; curing.

guerre *f* war; warfare.

guerrier *m*, **-ière** *f* warrior.

guetter *vt* to watch; to lie in wait for.

gueule *f* mouth; face; muzzle.

guichet *m* counter; ticket office, booking office.

guichetier *m*, **-ière** *f* counter clerk.

guide *m* guide.

guider *vt* to guide:—**se** ~ *vr* to be guided by.

guidon *m* handlebars.

guillotine *f* guillotine.

guise *f* manner, way:—**en** ~ **de** by way of:—**à ta** ~ as you please.

guitare *f* guitar.

guitariste *mf* guitarist.

gymnastique *f* gymnastics.

gynécologue, gynécologiste *mf* gynaecologist.

H

habile *adj* skilful, skilled.

habiliter *vt* to qualify; to authorise.

habiller *vt* to dress, clothe:—**s'** ~ *vr* to get dressed.

habitant(e) *m(f)* inhabitant; occupant; dweller.

habitation *f* dwelling; residence; house.

habiter *vi* to live:—*vt* to live in; to occupy.

habitude *f* habit, custom, routine.

habituel *adj* usual, customary.

habituer *vt* to accustom; to teach:—**s'** ~ *vr* to get used to.

hache *f* axe, hatchet.

haie *f* hedge.

haine *f* hatred.

haïr *vt* to hate, detest.

hâle *m* tan, sunburn.

haleine *f* breath, breathing.

haleter *vi* to pant, gasp for breath.

hall *m* hall, foyer.

halle *f* covered market; hall.

hallucination *f* hallucination.

halte *f* stop, break; stopping place.

hameçon *m* fish-hook.

hanche *f* hip; haunch.

handicap *m* handicap.

hanter *vt* to haunt.

harceler *vt* to harass; to pester; to plague.

hardi *adj* bold, daring; brazen.

hargne *f* spite.

haricot *m* bean.

harmonie *f* harmony; wind section.

harmoniser *vt* to harmonise:—**s'~** *vr* to be in harmony.

harpe *f* harp.

hasard *m* chance; accident; hazard; risk.

hasardeux *adj* hazardous, risky.

hâte *f* haste; impatience.

hâter *vt* to hasten; to quicken:—**se ~** *vr* to hurry.

hâtif *adj* precocious; early; hasty.

hausse *f* rise, increase.

hausser *vt* to raise; to heighten.

haut *adj* high, tall; upper; superior.

haut-parleur *m* loudspeaker.

hauteur *f* height; elevation; haughtiness; bearing.

hebdomadaire *adj*:—*m* weekly.

hélice *f* propeller; helix.

hélicoptère *m* helicopter.

hémisphère *m* hemisphere.

hémophile *adj* haemophiliac.

herbe *f* grass:—**en ~** under grass.

herboriste *mf* herbalist.

héréditaire *adj* hereditary.

hérédité *f* heredity; heritage; right of inheritance.

hérisser *vt* to bristle; to spike.

hérisson *m* hedgehog.

héritage *m* inheritance; heritage; heritage, legacy.

hériter *vi* to inherit.

héritier *m* heir, **-ière** *f* heiress.

hermétique *adj* hermetic.

hernie *f* hernia, rupture.

héroïne *f* heroine; heroin.

héroïque *adj* heroic.

héroïsme *m* heroism.

héros *m* hero.

hésitation *f* hesitation.

hésiter *vi* to hesitate.

hétérosexuel *adj* heterosexual.

heure *f* hour; time of day:—**de bonne ~** early.

heureux *adv* lucky; happy.

heurter *vt* to strike, hit; to jostle.

hibernation *f* hibernation.

hibou *m* owl.

hier *adv* yesterday.

hilarité *f* hilarity, laughter.

hippopotame *m* hippopotamus.

hirondelle *f* swallow.

hisser *vt* to hoist, haul up.

histoire *f* history; story; business:—**~ de dire** just to say.

historien *m*, **-ienne** *f* historian.

historique *adj* historic; historical.

hiver *m* winter.

hivernal *adj* winter; wintry.

hocher *vt* to nod; to shake one's head.

homard *m* lobster.

homicide *m* homicide

homme *m* man.

homogène *adj* homogeneous.

homologuer *vt* to ratify; to approve.

homosexuel(le) *m(f)* homosexual.

honnête *adj* honest; decent; honourable.

honnêteté *f* honesty, decency.

honneur *m* honour; integrity; credit:—**en l'~ de** in honour of.

honorable *adj* honourable; reputable.

honorer *vt* to honour; to esteem.

honte *f* shame, disgrace.

honteux *adj* shameful; disgraceful.

hôpital *m* hospital.

horaire *m* timetable:—*adj* hourly.

horizon *m* horizon.

horizontal *adj* horizontal.

horloge *f* clock.

hormone *f* hormone.

horreur *f* horror.
horrible *adj* horrible; dreadful.
horrifier *vt* to horrify.
hors *prép* outside; beyond; save; except.
hors-d'œuvre *m invar* hors d'œuvre, starter.
hospice *m* home, asylum; hospice.
hospitalier *adj* hospital; hospitable.
hospitaliser *vt* to hospitalise.
hospitalité *f* hospitality.
hostile *adj* hostile.
hostilité *f* hostility.
hôte *m*, **hôtesse** *f* host; landlord.
hôtel *m* hotel.
hôtelier *m*, **-ière** *f* hotelier:—*adj* hotel.
houle *f* swell.
huer *vt* to boo.
huile *f* oil; petroleum.
huit *adj*, *m* eight.
huitième *adj* eighth:—*mf* eighth.
huître *f* oyster.
humain *adj* human; humane:—*m* human.
humanitaire *adj* humanitarian.
humanité *f* humanity.
humble *adj* humble; modest.

humeur *f* mood, humour; temper.
humide *adj* humid.
humidité *f* humidity.
humilier *vt* to humiliate.
humilité *f* humility.
humour *m* humour.
hurler *vi*:—*vt* to roar, yell.
hutte *f* hut.
hybride *adj m* hybrid.
hydraulique *adj* hydraulic.
hygiène *f* hygienics; hygiene.
hygiénique *adj* hygienic.
hymne *m* hymn.
hypermarché *m* hypermarket.
hypnose *f* hypnosis
hypnotiser *vt* to hypnotise.
hypocondriaque *mf adj* hypochondriac.
hypocrisie *f* hypocrisy.
hypocrite *mf* hypocrite:—*adj* hypocritical.
hypothèque *f* mortgage.
hypothéquer *vt* to mortgage.
hypothèse *f* hypothesis; assumption.
hypothétique *adj* hypothetical.
hystérie *f* hysteria.
hystérique *mf* hysterical:—*adj* hysteric.

I

iceberg *m* iceberg.
icône *f* icon.
idéal *adj*:—*m* ideal.
idée *f* idea.
identifier *vt* to identify:—**s'~** *vr* to identify with.
identique *adj* identical.
identité *f* identity; similarity.

idiot *m*, **-e** *f* idiot, fool:—*adj* idiotic, stupid.
ignorance *f* ignorance.
ignorant *adj* ignorant; unacquainted; uninformed.
ignorer *vt* to be ignorant of; to be unaware of; to ignore.
il *pron* he, it.

île *f* island, isle.

illégal *adj* illegal; unlawful.

illégitime *adj* illegitimate; unwarranted.

illicite *adj* illicit.

illogique *adj* illogical.

illusion *f* illusion

illustration *f* illustration.

illustrer *vt* to illustrate.

image *f* image, picture; reflection.

imagination *f* imagination.

imaginer *vt* to imagine; to suppose.

imbécile *mf* idiot, imbecile:—*adj* stupid, idiotic.

imitation *f* imitation; mimicry; forgery.

imiter *vt* to imitate.

immatriculation *f* registration.

immédiat *adj* immediate; instant.

immense *adj* immense, boundless.

immeuble *m* building; block of flats; real estate.

immigrant *m*, **-e** *f* immigrant.

immigration *f* immigration.

imminent *adj* imminent, impending.

immobilier *adj* property:—*m* property business.

immobiliser *vt* to immobilise; to bring to a standstill.

immoral *adj* immoral.

immortel *adj* immortal.

immunité *f* immunity.

impair *adj* odd, uneven.

imparfait *adj* imperfect.

impartial *adj* impartial.

impartialité *f* impartiality.

impassible *adj* impassive.

impatience *f* impatience.

impatient *adj* impatient.

imperceptible *adj* imperceptible.

impersonnel *adj* impersonal.

impertinence *f* impertinence.

impertinent *adj* impertinent.

imperturbable *adj* unshakeable; imperturbable.

impétueux *adj* impetuous.

impitoyable *adj* merciless, pitiless.

implacable *adj* implacable.

implantation *f* implantation; establishment; introduction.

implanter *vt* to introduce; to establish; to implant.

implication *f* implication; involvement.

implicite *adj* implicit.

impliquer *vt* to imply; to necessitate; to implicate.

impoli *adj* impolite, rude.

impolitesse *f* impoliteness, rudeness.

importance *f* importance, significance; size.

important *adj* important, significant; sizeable.

importation *f* import, importation.

importer *vt* to import:—*vi* to matter:— **n'importe qui** anybody:—**n'importe quoi** anything.

imposer *vt* to impose, lay down.

impossibilité *f* impossibility.

impossible *adj* impossible.

impôt *m* tax, duty.

imprégner *vt* impregnate; to permeate; to imbue.

impression *f* feeling, impression.

impressioniste *mf*:—*adj* impressionist.

impressionner *vt* to impress; to upset.

imprévisible *adj* unforeseeable; unpredictable.

imprévu *adj* unforeseen, unexpected.

imprimer *vt* to print.

imprimeur *m* printer.

improbable *adj* improbable, unlikely.

improviser *vt* to improvise.

imprudent *adj* careless, imprudent.

impudence *f* impudence; shamelessness.

impuissant *adj* powerless, helpless.

impulsif *adj* impulsive.

inacceptable *adj* unacceptable.

inaccessible *adj* inaccessible.

inactif *adj* inactive, idle.

inactivité *f* inactivity.

inadmissible *adj* inadmissible.

inanimé *adj* inanimate; unconscious.

inaperçu *adj* unnoticed.

inattendu *adj* unexpected, unforeseen.

incapable *adj* incapable; incompetent.

incapacité *f* incompetence; disability.

incarcérer *vt* to incarcerate.

incendie *m* fire, blaze.

incertain *adj* uncertain, unsure.

incessant *adj* incessant, ceaseless.

incident *m* incident, point of law.

inciter *vt* to incite, urge.

inclure *vt* to include; to insert.

incommoder *vt* to disturb, bother.

incomparable *adj* incomparable.

incompatible *adj* incompatible.

incompréhensible *adj* incomprehensible.

inconfortable *adj* uncomfortable; awkward.

incongru *adj* unseemly; incongruous.

inconnu *m*, **-e** *f* stranger, unknown person:—*m* unknown:—*adj* unknown.

inconscience *f* unconsciousness; thoughtlessness.

inconscient *adj* unconscious; thoughtless, reckless:—*m* subconscious, unconscious.

inconsidéré *adj* inconsiderate; thoughtless.

incontestable *adj* incontestable, unquestionable.

inconvénient *m* drawback, inconvenience.

incorporer *vt* to incorporate, integrate.

incorrect *adj* faulty, incorrect.

incroyable *adj* incredible; unbelievable.

indécis *adj* indecisive; unsettled; undefined.

indéfini *adj* undefined; indefinite:— ~**ment** *adv* indefinitely.

indemne *adj* unharmed, unhurt.

indemnité *f* compensation; indemnity.

indéniable *adj* undeniable, indisputable.

indépendant *adj* independent.

indéterminé *adj* undetermined; unspecified.

index *m* index; index finger.

indication *f* indication; piece of information; instruction.

indice *m* indication; clue; sign.

indifférent *adj* indifferent; immaterial.

indigène *mf* native; local:—*adj* indigenous, native.

indigestion *f* indigestion.

indigne *adj* unworthy; undeserving.

indiquer *vt* to indicate, point out; to tell.

indirect *adj* indirect; circumstantial; collateral.

indiscret *adj* indiscreet; inquisitive.

indispensable *adj* indispensable; essential.

indisponible *adj* unavailable.

individu *m* individual.

individuel *adj* individual.

indulgent *adj* indulgent; lenient.

industrie *f* industry; dexterity, ingenuity.

industriel *m*, **-elle** *f* industrialist, manufacturer:—*adj* industrial.

inédit *adj* unpublished; original.
inefficace *adj* ineffective; inefficient.
inégal *adj* unequal; uneven; irregular.
inépuisable *adj* inexhaustible.
inertie *f* inertia, apathy.
inévitable *adj* inevitable, unavoidable.
inexact *adj* inexact, inaccurate.
inexplicable *adj* inexplicable.
infaillible *adj* infallible.
infantile *adj* infantile, childish.
infecter *vt* to infect; to contaminate:—
s'~ *vr* to become infected.
infection *f* infection.
inférieur *adj* inferior; lower.
infériorité *f* inferiority.
infester *vt* to infest; overrun.
infidèle *adj* unfaithful, disloyal.
infini *adj* infinite; interminable.
infirme *adj* feeble; crippled, disabled.
infirmier *m*, **-ière** *f* nurse.
infirmité *f* disability; infirmity.
inflation *f* inflation.
inflexible *adj* inflexible, rigid.
influence *f* influence.
influencer *vt* to influence, sway.
information *f* piece of information; information; inquiry.
informatique *f* computing; data processing:—*adj* computer.
informer *vt* to inform, tell.
ingénieur *m* engineer.
ingénieux *adj* ingenious, clever.
ingénu *adj* ingenuous, naive.
ingrédient *m* ingredient; component.
initial *adj* initial.
initiative *f* initiative; enterprise.
initier *vt* to initiate.
injecter *vt* to inject.
injure *f* injury; insult.
injuste *adj* unjust, unfair.
injustice *f* injustice.

inné *adj* innate, inborn.
innocence *f* innocence.
innocent *m*, **-e** *f* innocent person; simpleton:—*adj* innocent.
innovation *f* innovation.
inondation *f* inundation.
inouï *adj* unprecedented, unheard of.
inquiet *adj* worried, anxious, uneasy.
inscription *f* inscription; registration; matriculation.
inscrire *vt* to inscribe; to register:—
s'~ *vr* to join.
insecte *m* insect.
insensible *adj* insensible, insensitive.
insérer *vt* to insert.
insinuer *vt* to insinuate, imply.
insipide *adj* insipid, tasteless.
insister *vi* to insist, be insistent; to stress.
insolent *adj* insolent; brazen.
insomnie *f* insomnia.
insoutenable *adj* unbearable; untenable.
inspecter *vt* to inspect, examine.
inspection *f* inspection.
inspiration *f* inspiration; suggestion.
inspirer *vt* to inspire; to breathe in.
instable *adj* unstable; unsettled.
installation *f* installation; installing.
installer *vt* to install; to fit out.
instant *m* moment, instant.
instinct *m* instinct.
instinctif *adj* instinctive.
institut *m* institute; school.
institution *f* institution; establishment.
instruction *f* instruction; education; inquiry.
instruire *vt* to instruct; to teach; to conduct an inquiry.
instrument *m* instrument, implement.
insuffisant *adj* insufficient, inadequate.
insulte *f* insult.

insulter *vt* to insult, affront.

insupportable *adj* unbearable, intolerable.

intact *adj* intact.

intégral *adj* integral, complete.

intégrer *vt* to integrate:—**s'~** *vr* to become integrated; to fit in.

intégrité *f* integrity.

intellectuel *m*, **-uelle** *f* intellectual:—*adj* intellectual, mental.

intelligence *f* intelligence; understanding.

intelligent *adj* intelligent.

intelligible *adj* intelligible.

intense *adj* intense; severe.

intensifier *vt* to intensify:—**s'~** *vr* to intensify.

intensité *f* intensity; severity.

intention *f* intention; purpose, intent.

intercepter *vt* to intercept.

interdire *vt* to forbid, ban, prohibit.

intéressant *adj* interesting; attractive, worthwhile.

intéresser *vt* to interest; to affect:—**s'~** *vr*:—**s'~ à** to be interested in.

intérêt *m* interest; significance, importance.

interférence *f* interference; conjunction.

intérieur *adj* interior, internal, inland.

interlocuteur *m*, **-trice** *f* interlocutor, speaker.

intermittent *adj* intermittent, sporadic.

international *adj* international.

interne *adj* internal:—*mf* boarder; house doctor.

Internet *m* internet.

interprète *mf* interpreter.

interpréter *vt* to interpret; to perform.

interrogation *f* interrogation, questioning; question.

interroger *vt* to question; to interrogate:—**s'~** *vr* to wonder.

interrompre *vt* to interrupt, break.

interruption *f* interruption, break.

intervalle *m* interval; space, distance.

intervenir *vi* to intervene; to take part in.

intervention *f* intervention; operation.

intime *adj* intimate; private:—*mf* close friend.

intimider *vt* to intimidate.

intimité *f* intimacy; privacy.

intolérance *f* intolerance.

intolérant *adj* intolerant.

intrépide *adj* intrepid, fearless.

introduction *f* introduction; launching; institution.

introduire *vt* to introduce, insert; to present.

introverti *m*, **-e** *f* introvert:—*adj* introverted.

intuitif *adj* intuitive.

intuition *f* intuition.

inutile *adj* useless; unavailing; pointless.

invalide *adj* disabled; invalid.

invariable *adj* invariable; unvarying.

invasion *f* invasion.

inventer *vt* to invent; to devise; to make up.

invention *f* invention; inventiveness.

inverse *adj* opposite:—*m* opposite, reverse.

inversion *f* inversion; reversal.

investissement *m* investment; investing.

invincible *adj* invincible, indomitable.

invisible *adj* invisible; unseen.

invitation *f* invitation.

inviter *vt* to invite, ask.

involontaire *adj* involuntary; unintentional.

invoquer *vt* to invoke; to call up; to plead.
invraisemblable *adj* unlikely, improbable.
invulnérable *adj* invulnerable.
Irlandais *m* Irishman, **-e** *f* Irishwoman
irlandais *adj* Irish.
Irlande *f* Ireland.
ironique *adj* ironic:—**~ment** *adv* ironically.
irrationnel *adj* irrational.
irréel *adj* unreal.
irrégularité *f* irregularity; variation; unevenness.

irrégulier *adj* irregular; varying; uneven.
irremplaçable *adj* irreplaceable.
irrésistible *adj* irresistible:—**~ment** *adv* irresistibly.
irresponsable *adj* irresponsible
irrigation *f* irrigation.
irriter *vt* to irritate; to provoke.
isoler *vt* to isolate; to insulate.
issue *f* outlet; solution; outcome.
ivre *adj* drunk, inebriated.
ivrogne *mf* drunkard.

J

jadis *adv* formerly, long ago.
jalousie *f* jealousy, envy.
jaloux *adj* jealous, envious.
jamais *adv* never, not ever:—**à ~** for ever.
jambe *f* leg.
jambon *m* ham.
janvier *m* January.
jardin *m* garden.
jardinier *m*, **-ière** *f* gardener.
jargon *m* jargon, slang; gibberish.
jaune *adj* yellow:—*m* yellow.
jaunir *vi* to yellow, turn yellow:—*vt* to make yellow.
jazz *m* jazz.
je, j' *pron* I.
jetable *adj* disposable.
jetée *f* pier.
jeter *vt* to throw.
jeton *m* token; counter.
jeu *m* play; game; gambling:—**~ de mots** pun.
jeudi *m* Thursday.

jeune *adj* young:—*m* youth, young man:—*f* young girl.
jeûne *m* fast.
jeunesse *f* youth, youthfulness.
joaillerie *f* jewelling; jewellery.
joie *f* joy, happiness; pleasure.
joindre *vt* to join, link.
jointure *f* joint (*anat*).
joli *adj* pretty; good, handsome.
jonction *f* junction.
joue *f* cheek.
jouer *vi* to play; to gamble; to act.
jouet *m* toy.
joueur *m*, **-euse** *f* player; gambler.
jouir *vi* to enjoy; to delight in.
jouissance *f* enjoyment; use.
jour *m* day; daylight:—**tous les ~s** every day:—**à ~** up to date:—**~ férié** public holiday:—**mise à ~** updating; update.
journal *m* newspaper; bulletin:—**~ télévisé** television news.
journaliste *mf* journalist.

journée *f* day; day's work.
jovial *adj* jovial, jolly.
joyau *m* jewel, gem.
joyeux *adj* joyful.
judaïsme *m* Judaism.
judiciaire *adj* judicial, legal.
judicieux *adj* judicious.
juge *m* judge.
jugement *m* judgment.
juger *vt* to judge; to decide; to consider.
juif *m* Jewish man, **juive** *f* Jewish woman:—*adj* Jewish.
juillet *m* July.
juin *m* June.
jumeau *m*, **-elle** *f* twin:—*adj* twin; double.
jumelle(s) *f(pl)* binoculars.

jungle *f* jungle.
jupe *f* skirt.
jurer *vt* to swear, pledge.
juridiction *f* jurisdiction; court of law.
juridique *adj* legal, juridical.
jury *m* jury; board of examiners.
jus *m* juice.
jusque, jusqu' *prép* to, as far as; until.
juste *adj* just, fair; exact; sound.
justesse *f* accuracy; aptness; soundness.
justice *f* justice, fairness.
justification *f* justification; proof.
justifier *vt* to justify, prove.
juteux *adj* juicy; lucrative.
juvénile *adj* young, youthful.

K

kaléidoscope *m* kaleidoscope.
kangourou *m* kangaroo.
karaté *m* karate.
képi *m* kepi.
kermesse *f* fair; bazaar.
kidnapper *vt* to kidnap, abduct.
kidnappeur *m*, **-euse** *f* kidnapper.

kilogramme *m* kilogramme.
kilomètre *m* kilometre.
kiosque *m* kiosk, stall.
klaxon *m* horn.
klaxonner *vi* to sound one's horn.
koala *m* koala.

L

la *art pn see* **le**.
là *adv* there; over there; then:—**par ~** that way;**~-dedans** inside, in there:—**~-dessous**, under there:—**~-dessus** on that; thereupon:—**~-haut** up there:—**celui-~** that one.
label *m* label; seal.

labeur *m* labour, toil.
laborantin(e) *m(f)* laboratory assistant.
laboratoire *m* laboratory.
lac *m* lake.
lacer *vt* to lace up; to tie up.
lâche *adj* slack; lax; cowardly.
lâcher *vt* to loosen; to release.

laid *adj* ugly, unsightly.

laideur *f* ugliness, unsightliness.

laine *f* wool.

laisser *vt* to leave; to let: — **~ tomber** to drop.

laisser-passer *m invar* pass, permit.

lait *m* milk

laitue *f* lettuce.

lame *f* blade; strip; metal plate.

lamentable *adj* lamentable, distressing.

lamenter (se) *vr* to lament, bewail.

lampe *f* lamp, light; bulb.

lance *f* lance, spear.

lancement *m* launching; starting up; throwing.

lancer *vt* to throw; to launch.

langage *m* language, speech.

langoureux *adj* languid, languorous.

langouste *f* spiny lobster.

langue *f* tongue; language.

langueur *f* languor.

lanterne *f* lantern; lamp.

lapin *m*, **-e** *f* rabbit.

large *adj* wide; generous; lax; great.

largeur *f* width, breadth.

larme *f* tear.

las *adj*, *f* **lasse** weary, tired.

lasser *vt* to tire: — **se ~** *vr* to grow tired of.

latéral *adj* lateral, side.

latin *adj* Latin: — *m* Latin.

latitude *f* latitude; margin.

lavabo *m* washbasin.

lavage *m* washing; bathing.

laver *vt* to wash; to cleanse: — **se ~** *vr* to wash oneself.

laxatif *adj* laxative: — *m* laxative.

le *art*, *f* **la**, *devant voyelle* **l'**, *pl* **les** the: — *pron* him, her, them.

leçon *f* lesson; reading; class.

lecteur *m*, **-trice** *f* reader.

lecture *f* reading; perusal.

légal *adj* legal, lawful.

légalité *f* legality, lawfulness.

légendaire *adj* legendary.

légende *f* legend; inscription.

léger *adj* light; inconsiderate.

légèreté *f* lightness; thoughtlessness.

législatif *adj* legislative: — *m* legislature.

législation *f* legislation, laws.

légitime *adj* legitimate, lawful.

légitimité *f* legitimacy.

légume *m* vegetable.

lendemain *m* next day, day after.

lent *adj* slow; tardy; sluggish.

lenteur *f* slowness.

lequel *pron*, *f* **laquelle**, *pl* **lesquels**, **lesquelles** who, whom, which.

leste *adj* nimble, agile: — **~ment** *adv* nimbly.

léthargie *f* lethargy.

léthargique *adj* lethargic.

lettre *f* letter, note; literature: — **suivre à la ~** to carry out to the letter.

leur *pron* them: — **le ~**, **la ~**, **les ~s** theirs.

lever *vt* to lift, raise; to levy: — **se ~** *vr* to get up.

levier *m* lever.

lèvre *f* lip.

lexique *m* vocabulary, lexis.

lézard *m* lizard.

liaison *f* connection; liaison, link.

libéral *adj* liberal: — *m* liberal.

libération *f* release, liberation.

libérer *vt* to release; to liberate.

liberté *f* liberty, freedom.

libraire *mf* bookseller.

librairie *f* bookshop; bookselling.

libre *adj* free; independent.

licence *f* degree; permit; licentiousness.

licenciement *m* redundancy; dismissal.

licencier *vt* to make redundant; to dismiss.

lien *m* bond; link, connection; tie.

lier *vt* to bind; to link:—**se ~** *vr*:—**se ~ avec** to make friends.

lieu *m* place; occasion:—**avoir ~** to take place:—**au ~ de** instead of.

lièvre *m* hare.

ligne *f* line; row; range; (*comput*) **en ~** *adj* online.

lignée *f* lineage; offspring.

ligue *f* league.

lime *f* file.

limitation *f* limitation, restriction.

limite *f* boundary, limit:—**à la ~** ultimately.

limiter *vt* to limit, restrict.

limonade *f* lemonade.

limpide *adj* limpid, clear.

linéaire *adj* linear.

linge *m* linen; washing.

lingerie *f* linen room; underwear, lingerie.

linguiste *mf* linguist.

lion *m* lion, **lionne** *f* lioness

liquéfier *vt* to liquefy:—**se ~** *vr* to liquefy.

liqueur *f* liqueur; liquid.

liquide *m* liquid.

liquider *vt* to wind up; to eliminate

lire *vt* to read.

lisible *adj* legible; readable.

lisse *adj* smooth, glossy.

lisser *vt* to smooth, gloss.

liste *f* list; schedule.

lit *m* bed; layer.

litige *m* lawsuit; dispute.

litre *m* litre.

littéral *adj* literal.

littérature *f* literature; writing.

littoral *m* coast:—*adj* coastal.

livraison *f* delivery; number, issue.

livre *m* book:—*f* pound (weight, currency).

livrer *vt* to deliver, hand over; to give away.

livreur *m* delivery man, **-euse** *f* delivery woman.

local *adj* local.

localité *f* locality; town.

locataire *mf* tenant; lodger.

location *f* renting; lease, leasing.

loge *f* lodge; dressing room; box.

logement *m* housing; accommodation.

loger *vt* to accommodate; to billet:—*vi* to live in.

logiciel *m* software.

logique *f* logic:—*adj* logical.

logo *m* logo.

loi *f* law; act, statute; rule.

loin *adv* far, a long way:—*m* distance; background:—**au ~** in the distance:—**de ~** from a distance.

lointain *adj* distant, remote:—*m* distance; background

loisir *m* leisure, spare time.

long *adj*, *f* **longue** long, lengthy.

longévité *f* longevity.

longitude *f* longitude.

longtemps *adv* for a long time.

longueur *f* length.

loquace *adj* loquacious, talkative.

lors *adv* then **~ de** at the time of:—**dès ~** from that time.

lorsque *conj* when.

lot *m* prize; lot; portion.

loterie *f* lottery; raffle.

lotion *f* lotion.

louange *f* praise, commendation.

louer *vt* to rent, lease; to book.

loup *m* wolf.

lourd *adj* heavy; sultry.

lourdeur *f* heaviness.

loyal *adj* loyal, faithful.

loyauté *f* loyalty

loyer *m* rent.

lucide *adj* lucid, clear.

lucidité *f* lucidity, clearness.

lueur *f* glimmer, gleam; glimpse.

lugubre *adj* lugubrious, gloomy.

lui *pron* him, her, it:—**c'est à ~** it is his:—**~-même** himself, herself, itself.

luire *vt* to shine, gleam.

lumière *f* light; daylight; lamp; insight.

lumineux *adj* luminous; illuminated.

lunaire *adj* lunar, moon.

lundi *m* Monday.

lune *f* moon.

lunette *f* telescope; sight:—**~s** glasses.

lutte *f* struggle; contest; strife.

lutter *vi* to struggle, fight.

luxe *m* luxury, excess.

luxueux *adj* luxurious.

lycée *m* secondary school.

lyncher *vt* to lynch.

lyre *f* lyre.

lyrique *adj* lyric.

lyrisme *m* lyricism.

M

mâcher *vt* to chew.

machinal *adj* mechanical, automatic.

machine *f* machine; engine; apparatus.

machinerie *f* machinery, plant.

mâchoire *f* jaw.

maçon *m* builder, mason.

madame *f* Madam; Mrs; lady.

mademoiselle *f* Miss; young lady.

magasin *m* shop, store; warehouse.

magazine *m* magazine.

magicien(ne) *m(f)* magician.

magie *f* magic

magistrat *m* magistrate.

magnanime *adj* magnanimous.

magnétique *adj* magnetic.

magnétophone *m* tape recorder.

magnifique *adj* magnificent; sumptuous.

mai *m* May.

maigre *adj* thin; meagre, scarce.

maigrir *vi* to get thinner; to waste away.

maillot *m* jersey; leotard.

main *f* hand:—**avoir la ~** to have the lead.

main-d'œuvre *f* workforce.

maintenance *f* maintenance, servicing.

maintenant *adv* now:—**à partir de ~** from now on.

maintenir *vt* to keep.

maintien *m* maintenance; preservation; keeping up.

maire *m* mayor, **-esse** *f* mayoress.

mais *conj* but.

maison *f* house; home; building; premises.

maître *m*, **-esse** *f* master; ruler; lord; proprietor.

maîtresse *f* mistress; teacher

maîtrise *f* mastery; control; expertise.

majoritaire *adj* majority.

majorité *f* majority.

mal *adv* wrong, badly:—*m* evil, wrong; harm; pain.

malade *adj* sick, ill; diseased:—*mf* invalid, sick person.

maladie *f* illness; malady, complaint; disorder.

maladroit *adj* clumsy, awkward.

malchanceux *adj* unlucky, unfortunate.

mâle *m* male:—*adj* male; manly, virile.

malentendu *m* misunderstanding.

malgré *prép* in spite of; despite.

malheur *m* misfortune; calamity.

malheureux *adj* unfortunate; unlucky; unhappy.

malhonnête *adj* dishonest, crooked; uncivil.

malicieux *adj* malicious, spiteful; mischievous.

malnutrition *f* malnutrition.

malsain *adj* unhealthy, unwholesome; immoral.

maltraiter *vt* to abuse; to handle roughly.

malveillant *adj* malevolent, spiteful.

maman *f* mother, mummy, mum.

mammifère *m* mammal.

manche *f* sleeve; game, round:—*m* handle, shaft.

mangeable *adj* edible.

manger *vt* to eat; to consume, squander.

maniable *adj* handy, workable.

manier *vt* to handle; to manipulate.

manière *f* manner, way, style.

manifeste *adj* manifest, evident, obvious:—*m* manifesto.

manifester *vt* to display, make known; to demonstrate.

manipulation *f* handling; manipulation.

manipuler *vt* to handle; to manipulate

manœuvre *f* manoeuvre, operation; scheme:—*m* labourer.

manœuvrer *vt* to manoeuvre:—*vi* to manoeuvre, move.

manque *m* lack, shortage; shortcoming, deficiency.

manquer *vt* to miss; to fail; to be absent.

manteau *m* coat; mantle, blanket; cloak.

manuel *m* manual, handbook:—*adj* manual.

manufacture *f* factory; manufacture.

manufacturier *m*, **-ière** *f* factory owner; manufacturer:—*adj* manufacturing.

manuscrit *m* manuscript; typescript:—*adj* handwritten.

maquillage *m* make-up.

marathon *m* marathon.

marbre *m* marble; marble statue.

marchand(e) *m*(*f*) merchant:—*adj* market, trade.

marchandise *f* merchandise, commodity; goods.

marche *f* walk; journey; progress; movement:—**mettre en ~** to start up; to turn on.

marché *m* market; transaction, contract.

marcher *vi* to walk, march; to progress; to work.

mardi *m* Tuesday.

marée *f* tide.

marge *f* margin; latitude, freedom; mark-up.

marginal *adj* marginal.

mari *m* husband.

mariage *m* marriage.

marié *m* bridegroom:—*adj* married.

marier *vt* to marry; blend, harmonise: —**se ~** *vr* to get married.

marin *m* sailor.

marine *f* navy; seascape; marine.

maritime *adj* maritime; seaboard.

marque *f* mark, sign; brand; make.

marquer *vt* to mark; to note down; to score.

mars *m* March.
marteau *m* hammer; knocker.
masculin *adj* masculine.
masque *m* mask; facade; front.
massage *m* massage.
masse *f* mass, heap; bulk; mob.
masser *vt* to mass, assemble; to massage.
masseur *m* masseur, **euse** *f* masseuse.
massif *adj* massive, solid, heavy:—*m* massif; clump.
match *m* match; game.
matelas *m* mattress.
matérialiser (se) ~ *vr* to materialise.
matériaux *mpl* material, materials.
matériel *adj* material, physical; practical.
maternel *adj* maternal, motherly.
maternité *f* motherhood; pregnancy; maternity hospital.
mathématicien(ne) *m(f)* mathematician.
mathématique *adj* mathematical:—*f* mathematics.
matière *f* material, matter; subject:— ~ **première** raw material.
matin *m* morning; dawn.
matrice *f* womb; mould; matrix.
maturité *f* maturity; prime.
maussade *adj* sulky, sullen.
mauvais *adj* bad; wicked; faulty; hurtful; poor.
maximum *m* maximum.
me, m' *pn* me; myself.
mécanicien(ne) *m(f)* mechanic; engineer.
mécanique *f* mechanics:—*adj* mechanical.
méchant *adj* spiteful; wicked; mischievous.
méconnu *adj* unrecognised; misunderstood.

mécontentement *m* discontent; displeasure.
médecin *m* doctor, physician.
médecine *f* medicine.
médias *mpl* the media.
médias sociaux *mpl* social media.
médical *adj* medical.
médiocre *adj* mediocre; indifferent.
méditation *f* meditation.
méditer *vi* to meditate:—*vt* to contemplate, have in mind.
méfier (se) *vr* to mistrust, distrust; to be suspicious.
meilleur *adj* better, preferable:—**le ~, la ~e** the best.
mélancolique *adj* melancholy; melancholic.
mélange *m* mixture.
mélanger *vt* to mix, blend; to muddle.
mêler *vt* to mix; to combine:—**se ~** *vr* to mix, mingle.
mélodie *f* melody, tune.
membre *m* member; limb.
même *adv* even:—**tout de ~** nevertheless, all the same:—*adj* same, identical:—*pn*:—**le/la ~, les ~s** the same one(s).
mémoire *f* memory:—*m* memorandum, report.
mémorable *adj* memorable.
menace *f* threat; intimidation; danger.
menacer *vt* to threaten, menace; to impend.
ménage *m* housework, housekeeping; household.
ménager *vt* treat with caution; manage; arrange:—*adj* household, domestic.
ménagère *f* housewife.
mendiant(e) *m(f)* beggar, mendicant.
mener *vt* to lead, guide; to steer; to manage.

ménopause *f* menopause.

mensonge *m* lie, falsehood; error, illusion.

menstruation *f* menstruation.

mental *adj* mental.

menteur *m*, **-euse** *f* liar:—*adj* lying, deceitful.

mention *f* mention; comment; grade.

mentionner *vt* to mention.

mentir *vi* to lie, tell lies; to be deceptive.

menton *m* chin.

menu *m* menu; meal:—*adj* slender, thin; petty, minor.

mépriser *vt* to scorn, despise.

mer *f* sea; tide.

merci *m* thank you:—*f* mercy:—**sans ~** merciless.

mercredi *m* Wednesday.

mère *f* mother.

méridien *m* meridian; midday.

mériter *vt* to deserve, merit.

merveilleux *adj* marvellous, wonderful.

message *m* message.

messager *m*, **-ère** *f* messenger.

messe *f* mass.

mesure *f* measure; gauge; measurement:—**au fur et à ~** as; one by one:—**dans la mesure où** insofar as:—**en ~** in time.

mesurer *vt* to measure; to assess; to limit:—**se ~ vr** to try one's strength.

métal *m* metal.

métaphore *f* metaphor.

météore *m* meteor.

météoroloque, météorologiste *mf* meteorologist.

méthode *f* method, way.

méthodique *adj* methodical.

métier *m* job; occupation:—**~ à tisser** weaving loom.

mètre *m* metre.

métro *m* underground, metro.

métropole *f* metropolis.

mettre *vt* to put, place; to put on:—**~ en marche** to start up:—**se ~ à** to begin to:—**se ~ en route** to start off.

meuble *m* piece of furniture.

meurtrier *m* murderer, **-ière** *f* murderess.

mi- *adj* half:—**à ~chemin** halfway:—**~clos** half-closed:—**à ~jambe** up to the knees:—**à ~voix** in a low voice.

miauler *vi* to mew.

micro-onde *f* microwave:—*m* **micro-ondes** microwave oven.

micro-ordinateur *m* microcomputer.

microbe *m* germ, microbe.

microfilm *m* microfilm.

microphone *m* microphone.

microscope *m* microscope.

midi *m* midday, noon.

miel *m* honey.

mien *pron*, *f* **mienne**:—**le ~, la mienne, les ~s, les miennes** mine, my own.

mieux *m* improvement:—**le ~** the best:—**de ~ en ~** better and better.

migraine *f* headache; migraine.

migrateur *m* migrant.

migration *f* migration.

milieu *m* middle, centre; medium; environment.

militaire *m* serviceman:—*adj* military, army.

militant(e) *m(f)* *adj* militant.

militer *vi* to militate; to be a militant.

mille *m* *adj* one thousand.

milliard *m* thousand million; milliard.

millième *m* *adj* thousandth.

millier *m* thousand.

million *m* million.

millionnaire *adj* millionaire; worth millions:—*mf* millionaire.

mime *m* mime:—*mf* mimic.

mimer *vt* to mime; to mimic, imitate.

mince *adj* thin, slender; meagre, trivial.

mincir *vi* to get slimmer, get thinner.

mine *f* expression; appearance; mine:—**avoir bonne ~** to look good.

minéral *adj* mineral; inorganic:—*m* mineral.

mineur(e) *m(f)* minor:—*adj* minor:—*m* miner.

mini-jupe *f* miniskirt.

miniature *f* miniature.

minimal *adj* minimal, minimum.

minimum *m* minimum.

ministère *m* ministry; agency.

ministre *m* minister; clergyman.

minorité *f* minority.

minuit *m* midnight.

minute *f* minute, moment.

minutieux *adj* meticulous; minute.

miracle *m* miracle, wonder.

miraculeux *adj* miraculous.

mirage *m* mirage.

miroir *m* mirror, reflection.

mise *f* putting, placing; stake; deposit; investment:—**~ en scène** production, staging:—**~ en liberté** release:—**~ en ordre** ordering, arrangement:—**~ en œuvre** implementation.

misérable *adj* miserable; destitute; pitiable.

misère *f* misery; poverty; destitution.

mission *f* mission, assignment.

missionnaire *m* missionary.

mitigé *adj* mitigated; lukewarm.

mitoyen *adj* common; semi-detached.

mixer *vt* to mix; to blend.

mixte *adj* mixed; joint; combined.

mobile *adj* moving; movable:—*m* motive; moving body.

mobilier *m* furniture.

mobilité *f* mobility.

mode *f* fashion; custom:—*m* form, mode; way.

modèle *m* model; pattern; design; example.

modeler *vt* to model; to shape.

modem *m* modem.

modération *f* moderation; diminution.

modéré *adj* moderate

modérer *vt* to moderate.

moderne *adj* modern, up-to-date.

moderniser *vt* to modernise.

modeste *adj* modest, simple; unassuming.

modestie *f* modesty.

modification *f* modification, alteration.

modifier *vt* to modify, alter.

moelle *f* marrow; core.

mœurs *fpl* morals; customs.

moi *pn* me, I:—**c'est à ~** it is mine, it is my turn:—**~-même** myself.

mois *m* month.

moisson *f* harvest.

moissonner *vt* to reap, mow.

moite *adj* moist, damp.

moitié *f* half.

molécule *f* molecule.

moment *m* moment, instant, while; time; opportunity.

momentané *adj* momentary; brief.

mon *pron*, *f* **ma**, *pl* **mes** my.

monastère *m* monastery.

mondain *adj* worldly, mundane; society, fashionable.

monde *m* world, earth; society, company.

mondial *adj* world, worldwide.

moniteur *m*, **-trice** *f* instructor, coach; supervisor.

monnaie f currency; coin; change.

monopole f monopoly.

monopoliser vt to monopolise.

monotone adj monotonous.

monsieur m sir, gentleman, Mr, pl **messieurs** gentlemen, Messrs.

monstre m monster.

mont m mountain; mount.

montage m assembly; setting up; editing.

montagne f mountain.

montagneux adj mountainous.

montée f climb, climbing; ascent; rise.

monter vi to go up, ascend; get into (vehicle): —vt to go up; to carry/bring up.

montre f watch.

montrer vt to show, point to; prove.

monument m monument, memorial.

moquer (se) vr to make fun, jeer, laugh at.

moqueur m, **-euse** f mocker, scoffer: —adj mocking.

moral adj moral, ethical; intellectual.

moralité f morals, morality.

morceau m piece, morsel, fragment; extract.

mordre vt to bite, gnaw; to grip.

morose adj sullen, morose.

mort m dead man, **-e** f dead woman: —adj dead: —f death.

mortalité f mortality; death rate.

mortel adj mortal; fatal.

mortuaire adj mortuary; funeral.

mosquée f mosque.

mot m word; saying: —**~s croisés** crossword.

moteur m engine, motor: —adj motor, driving.

motif m motive, grounds; motif, design.

motivation f motivation.

motiver vt to justify; to motivate.

moto f motorbike.

mou adj (f **molle**) soft; gentle; muffled.

mouche f fly.

moucher (se) vr to blow one's nose.

mouchoir m handkerchief.

moudre vt to mill, grind.

mouiller vt to wet; to water down: —**se ~** vr to get wet.

moule m mould: —f mussel.

mouler vt to mould; to model.

moulin m mill.

mourir vi to die.

mousser vi to froth, foam

mousseux adj sparkling; frothy: —m sparkling wine.

moustache f moustache; whiskers.

moustique m mosquito.

mouton m sheep; mutton.

mouvement m movement, motion; animation.

mouvoir vt to drive, power: —**se ~** vr to move.

moyen m means; way: —adj average, medium, moderate: —**~ âge** Middle Ages.

moyenne f average.

muet(te) m(f) mute: —adj dumb; silent, mute.

multicolore adj multicoloured.

multiple adj numerous, multiple: —m multiple.

multiplication f multiplication.

multiplier (se) vr to multiply, increase.

municipal adj municipal; local.

municipalité f town, municipality.

munir vt to provide, equip with: —**se ~** vr to equip oneself.

mur m wall.

mûr *adj* ripe, mature; worn out.

mûrir *vi* to ripen, mature.

murmure *m* murmur; muttering; grumbling.

murmurer *vi* to murmur.

muscle *m* muscle.

musculaire *adj* muscular.

musée *m* art gallery, museum.

musicien(ne) *m(f)* musician:—*adj* musical.

musique *f* music.

musulman(e) *m(f) adj* Muslim.

muter *vt* to transfer, move.

myope *mf* short-sighted person:—*adj* short-sighted.

myopie *f* short-sightedness, myopia.

mystère *m* mystery.

mystérieux *adj* mysterious.

mystifier *vt* to mystify; to hoax.

mystique *adj* mystical:—*mf* mystic.

mythe *m* myth.

mythique *adj* mythical.

mythologie *f* mythology.

N

nager *vi* to swim.

nageur *m*, **-euse** *f* swimmer; rower.

naissance *f* birth, extraction; dawn, beginning.

naître *vi* to be born; to arise, spring up.

naïveté *f* naïvety, artlessness, gullibility.

narcotique *m* drug, narcotic:—*adj* narcotic.

narrateur *m*, **-trice** *f* narrator.

nasal *adj* nasal.

natalité *f* birth rate.

nation *f* nation.

national *adj* national; domestic.

nationaliste *mf* nationalist:—*adj* nationalist.

nationalité *f* nationality.

nature *f* nature; kind, sort; temperament.

naturel *adj* natural; bodily; native; unsophisticated:—**~lement** *adv* naturally; of course.

nautique *adj* nautical.

navigation *f* sailing, navigation.

navire *m* ship, vessel.

ne *adv* no, not.

né *adj* born

néanmoins *adv* nevertheless.

nécessaire *adj* necessary; requisite; indispensable.

nécessité *f* necessity; need; inevitability.

nécessiter *vt* to require, necessitate.

négatif *adj* negative.

négligent *adj* negligent, careless; nonchalant.

négliger *vt* to neglect; to be negligent about.

négociation *f* negotiation.

négocier *vi* to negotiate; to trade:—*vt* to negotiate.

neige *f* snow.

neiger *vi* to snow, be snowing.

nerf *m* nerve.

nerveux *adj* nervous; vigorous; excitable.

net *adj, f* **nette** clean; clear; plain; sharp; net.

nettoyage *m* cleaning; clearing up.

nettoyer *vt* to clean; to ruin, clean out.

neuf *adj* nine:— *m* nine.

neutre *adj* neutral; neuter.

neuvième *adj* ninth:— *mf* ninth.

neveu *m* nephew.

nez *m* nose; flair:— **avoir du ~** to have flair.

niais *adj* silly, simple, inane.

nid *m* nest; den; berth.

nièce *f* niece.

nier *vt* to deny; to repudiate.

niveau *m* level; standard; par; gauge.

noble *adj* noble, dignified.

noce *f* wedding, wedding feast; marriage ceremony.

nocif *adj* noxious, harmful.

nocturne *adj* nocturnal, night.

Noël *m* Christmas.

nœud *m* knot, bow; crux.

noir *adj* black; dark:— *m* black; darkness; black man.

noircir *vt* to blacken; to dirty:— **se ~** *vr* to darken, grow black.

noix *f* walnut

nom *m* name; fame; noun.

nombre *m* number, quantity.

nombreux *adj* numerous, frequent.

nommer *vt* to appoint; nominate.

non *adv* no; not.

non-sens *m* nonsense.

nonchalant *adj* nonchalant.

nord *m* north, northerly (wind)

normal *adj* normal, usual; standard-sized.

norme *f* norm; standard.

nostalgique *adj* nostalgic.

notable *adj* notable; noteworthy.

note *f* note; minute; mark; bill.

noter *vt* to note down; to notice; to mark.

notice *f* note; directions; instructions.

notion *f* notion, idea.

notoire *adj* notorious; well-known, acknowledged.

notre *adj* (*pl* **nos**) ours, our own.

nôtre *poss pn:—* **le ~, la ~, les ~s** ours, our own.

nouer *vt* to tie, knot.

nourrir *vt* to feed, provide for; to stoke:— **se ~** *vr* to feed o.s.

nourriture *f* food; sustenance.

nous *pron* we; us:— **c'est à ~** it's ours; it's our turn:— **~-mêmes** ourselves.

nouveau *adj* new; recent; additional.

nouvelle *f* piece of news; short story.

novembre *m* November.

novice *mf* novice, beginner.

noyer *vt* to drown; to flood:— **se ~** *vr* to drown.

nu *adj* naked, nude; plain, unadorned.

nuage *m* cloud.

nucléaire *adj* nuclear:— *m* nuclear energy.

nudité *f* nakedness, nudity.

nuire *vi* to harm, injure; to prejudice.

nuisible *adj* harmful; noxious.

nuit *f* night, darkness.

nul *adj* no; nil; null and void:— **~lement** *adv* not at all.

numérique *adj* numerical; digital.

numéro *m* number; issue.

numéroter *vt* to number.

nylon *m* nylon.

O

obéir *vt* to obey, be obedient; to comply.

obéissant *adj* obedient.

obèse *adj* obese.

objecter *vt* to object.

objectif *adj* objective, unbiased:—*m* objective, target.

objection *f* objection.

objet *m* object, thing; purpose; matter.

obligation *f* obligation, duty; bond.

obligatoire *adj* obligatory, compulsory.

obliger *vt* to oblige, require; to bind.

oblitérer *vt* to obliterate; to cancel (stamp)

obscène *adj* obscene.

obscur *adj* obscure, dark, gloomy.

obscurcir *vt* to darken; to obscure:—**s'~** *vr* to get dark.

obscurité *f* obscurity; darkness.

observation *f* observation; remark.

observatoire *m* observatory.

observer *vt* to observe.

obsession *f* obsession.

obstacle *m* obstacle, hindrance.

obstination *f* obstinacy, stubbornness.

obstiné *adj* obstinate, stubborn.

obstiner (s') *vr* to insist, persist.

obtenir *vt* to obtain.

occasion *f* occasion, opportunity; bargain.

occidental *adj* western.

occupant *m*, **-e** *f* occupant, occupier.

occupation *f* occupation; occupancy.

occuper *vt* to occupy:—**s'~** *vr* to keep busy.

océan *m* ocean.

octobre *m* October.

odeur *f* smell, odour.

odieux *adj* hateful, obnoxious.

odorat *m* smell (sense).

œil *m* (*pl* **yeux**) eye; look; bud.

œuf *m* egg.

œuvre *f* work; action, deed; production.

offense *f* offence; injury.

offenser *vt* to offend:—**s'~** *vr* to take offence.

offensif *adj* offensive.

office *m* office; duty; function.

officiel *adj* official.

officier *m* officer.

officieux *adj* officious; unofficial.

offre *f* offer, tender, bid.

offrir *vt* to offer.

oie *f* goose.

oignon *m* onion; bulb.

oiseau *m* bird.

oisif *adj* idle.

oisiveté *f* idleness.

olive *f* olive.

olivier *m* olive tree.

olympique *adj* Olympic.

ombre *f* shade, shadow.

omelette *f* omelette.

omettre *vt* to omit.

omission *f* omission.

omniprésent *adj* omnipresent.

on *pn* one; someone, anyone.

once *f* ounce.

oncle *m* uncle.

onde *f* wave.

onduler *vi* to undulate; to ripple.

onéreux *adj* onerous; costly.

ongle *m* nail; claw, talon; hoof.

onze *adj* eleven: — *m* eleven.

onzième *adj* eleventh: — *mf* eleventh.

opaque *adj* opaque; impenetrable.

opéra *m* opera.

opération *f* operation, performance.

opérationnel *adj* operational.

opérer *vt* to operate.

opiniâtre *adj* stubborn; persistent.

opinion *f* opinion, view.

opportun *adj* timely, opportune.

opposant *m*, **-e** *f* opponent: — *adj* opposing.

opposé *adj* opposite: — *m* opposite: — **à l'~** contrary to.

opposer *vt* to oppose.

opposition *f* opposition; conflict.

oppresser *vt* to oppress, weigh down.

oppressif *adj* oppressive.

optimiste *mf* optimist: — *adj* optimistic.

option *f* option, choice.

optionnel *adj* optional.

opulent *adj* opulent, wealthy.

or *m* gold: — *conj* now.

orage *m* storm.

orageux *adj* stormy.

oral *adj* oral, verbal.

orange *f* orange: — *adj* orange.

orateur *m*, **-trice** *f* orator.

orbite *f* orbit; socket; sphere.

orchestre *m* orchestra.

ordinaire *adj* ordinary: — *m* usual routine: — **d'~, à l'~** ordinarily, usually.

ordinateur *m* computer.

ordonner *vt* to order.

ordre *m* order, command; class.

ordure *f* filth; rubbish.

oreille *f* ear; hearing.

oreiller *m* pillow.

organe *m* organ; instrument; medium.

organique *adj* organic.

organisateur *m*, **-trice** *f* organiser.

organisation *f* organisation.

organiser *vt* to organise, arrange.

orgueil *m* pride, arrogance.

orgueilleux *adj* proud, arrogant.

orient *m* orient, east.

oriental *adj* eastern, oriental.

orienter *vt* to orientate.

original *adj* original, novel: — *m* original.

originalité *f* originality.

origine *f* origin: — **à l'~** originally.

originel *adj* original, primitive.

orner *vt* to adorn, decorate.

orphelin *m*, **-e** *f* orphan.

orteil *m* toe.

orthodoxe *adj* orthodox: — *mf* orthodox.

os *m* bone.

oser *vt* to dare.

ossature *f* skeleton; framework.

ostensible *adj* open, conspicuous.

otage *m* hostage.

ôter *vt* to take away.

ou *conj* or.

où *adv* where, in which; *pron* where.

oubli *m* forgetfulness; oblivion.

oublier *vt* to forget.

ouest *m* west; *adj* west.

oui *adv* yes.

ouïe *f* hearing.

ouragan *m* hurricane, whirlwind.

ours *m*, **-e** *f* bear.

outil *m* tool, implement.

outillage *m* (set of) tools; equipment.

outiller *vt* to equip; to provide with tools.

outrage *m* outrage, insult, wrong.

outre *prép* as well as, besides: — **en ~** moreover.

ouvert *adj* open; exposed; frank.
ouverture *f* opening.
ouvrable *adj* working, business.
ouvrage *m* work; piece of work.

ouvrier *m*, **-ière** *f* worker:—*adj* labour.
ouvrir *vt* to open; to unlock; to broach.
oxygène *m* oxygen.
ozone *f* ozone.

P

pacifier *vt* to pacify.
pacifique *adj* peaceful.
pacte *m* pact, treaty.
page *f* page; passage.
paiement *m* payment
païen(ne) *m(f)* pagan:—*adj* pagan.
paille *f* straw.
pain *m* bread; loaf; bar
pair *adj* even:—*m* peer; par.
paire *f* pair
paisible *adj* peaceful; calm.
paix *f* peace; stillness.
palais *m* palace.
pâle *adj* pale, pallid.
pâleur *f* paleness, pallor.
pâlir *vi* to turn pale; to dim; to fade.
pallier *vt* to palliate; to offset.
palme *f* palm leaf; palm.
palmier *m* palm tree.
palpable *adj* palpable.
palper *vt* to feel, touch; to palpate.
palpiter *vi* to palpitate; to beat; to race.
panache *m* panache; gallantry
pancarte *f* sign, notice; placard.
panda *m* panda.
panique *f* panic.
paniquer *vi* to panic.
panne *f* breakdown; fault.
panneau *m* panel; sign, notice.
pansement *m* dressing, bandage.
panser *vt* to dress, bandage.
pantalon *m* trousers.

pantomime *f* pantomime; mime.
pantoufle *f* slipper.
papa *m* dad; daddy.
pape *m* pope.
papeterie *f* stationery.
papier *m* paper.
papillon *m* butterfly.
Pâques *fpl* Easter.
paquet *m* packet, pack.
par *prép* by, with, through; from; along:— **~-ci, ~-là** here and there.
parachever *vt* to perfect; to complete.
parachute *m* parachute.
parade *f* parade, show; parry.
paradis *m* paradise; gallery.
paradoxal *adj* paradoxical.
paradoxe *m* paradox.
paragraphe *m* paragraph.
paraître *vi* to appear; to seem.
parallèle *adj* parallel.
paralyser *vt* to paralyse.
paralysie *f* paralysis.
paranoïaque *adj* paranoid.
parapluie *m* umbrella.
parasite *m* parasite, sponger.
parasol *m* parasol; sunshade.
parc *m* park; grounds; depot.
parce que *conj* because
parcelle *f* particle; parcel.
parcourir *vt* to travel through.
pardon *m* pardon, forgiveness.
pardonner *vt* to pardon.

pare-brise *m invar* windscreen.

pare-chocs *m invar* bumper.

pareil(le) *m(f)* equal; match:—*adj* like, similar; identical.

parent(e) *m(f)* relative, relation; (*pl*) parents.

parental *adj* parental.

parenté *f* relationship, kinship.

paresse *f* laziness.

paresseux *adj* lazy.

parfaire *vt* to perfect.

parfait *adj* perfect, flawless.

parfois *adv* sometimes.

parfumer *vt* to perfume.

pari *m* bet, wager.

parier *vt* to bet, wager.

parking *m* car park; parking.

parlement *m* Parliament.

parlementaire *adj* parliamentary:—*mf* MP.

parler *vi* to talk, speak:—*vt* to speak.

parmi *prép* among.

paroi *f* wall; surface.

parole *f* word; speech; voice; lyrics.

parquer *vt* to park.

parrain *m* godfather; patron.

parrainer *vt* to sponsor, propose.

part *f* part; share; portion:—**prendre ~ à** to participate in:—**autre ~** elsewhere:—**nulle ~** nowhere.

partage *m* sharing, distribution.

partager *vt* to divide up.

partenaire *mf* partner.

parti *m* party; match.

partial *adj* partial, biased.

participant(e) *m(f)* participant, member.

participation *f* participation.

participer *vi* to participate.

particulier *adj* particular, specific:—*m* person, private individual.

partie *f* part; subject; party.

partiel *adj* part, partial.

partir *vi* to leave.

partisan(e) *m(f)* partisan.

partout *adv* everywhere.

parvenir *vi*:—**~ à** to reach.

pas *m* step; pace:—*adv* no, not.

passable *adj* passable, tolerable.

passage *m* passage; transit.

passager *m*, **-ère** *f* passenger:—*adj* passing, transitory.

passant(e) *m(f)* passer-by.

passe *f* pass; permit; channel.

passé *m* past.

passe-temps *m invar* pastime

passeport *m* passport.

passer *vi* to pass:—**se ~ vr** to take place.

passion *f* passion.

passionné *adj* passionate.

passionner (se) *vr* to be fascinated by, have a passion for.

passivité *f* passivity.

paternel *adj* paternal, fatherly.

paternité *f* paternity; fatherhood.

pathétique *adj* pathetic.

patience *f* patience.

patient *adj* patient.

patin *m* skate.

patiner *vi* to skate; to slip; to spin.

patineur *m*, **-euse** *f* skater.

pâtisserie *f* cake shop, confectioner's.

pâtissier *m*, **-ière** *f* pastry cook, confectioner.

patrie *f* homeland, country.

patriotisme *m* patriotism.

patron(ne) *m(f)* owner, boss.

patronner *vt* to patronise.

patte *f* leg, paw, foot.

paume *f* palm.

paupière *f* eyelid.

pause *f* pause; half-time.

pauvre *adj* poor; indigent: —*mf* pauper.

paye *f* pay, wages.

payer *vt* to pay.

pays *m* country; region.

paysage *m* landscape; scenery.

paysan *m* countryman, **-anne** *f* country-woman.

péage *m* toll; tollgate.

peau *f* skin; hide, pelt.

pêche *f* peach; fishing.

pécher *vi* to sin.

pêcher *vt* to fish; to catch.

pécheur *m*, **-eresse** *f* sinner

pêcheur *m* fisherman.

pédale *f* pedal; treadle.

pédaler *vi* to pedal.

pédestre *adj* pedestrian.

peigne *m* comb.

peigner (se) *vr* to comb one's hair.

peindre *vt* to paint.

peine *f* effort; pain; punishment.

peiner *vi* to toil; to struggle.

peintre *m* painter.

peinture *f* painting; paintwork.

peler *vi* to peel.

pèlerinage *m* pilgrimage.

peloton *m* pack; platoon.

pelouse *f* lawn.

pénaliser *vt* to penalise.

pencher *vi* to lean: —**se ~** *vr* to bend down.

pendant *prép* during; for: —**~ que** while.

pendre *vi* to hang.

pendule *f* clock: —*m* pendulum.

pénétrer *vi* to enter, penetrate: —*vt* to penetrate.

pénible *adj* hard, tiresome.

péninsule *f* peninsula.

pénis *m* penis.

pénitencier *m* prison, penitentiary.

pensée *f* thought.

penser *vt* to think, suppose, believe: —*vi* to think.

pension *f* pension; boarding house.

pensionnaire *mf* boarder; lodger.

pente *f* slope; gradient.

Pentecôte *f* Pentecost.

pépère *m* granddad, grandpa.

percée *f* opening, breach.

perception *f* perception.

percer *vt* to pierce.

percevoir *vt* to perceive; to collect.

percussion *f* percussion.

percuter *vt* to strike.

perdant(e) *m(f)* loser.

perdre *vt* to lose.

père *m* father; sire.

perfection *f* perfection.

perfectionnement *m* perfection.

perfectionner *vt* to perfect.

perfectionniste *mf* perfectionist: —*adj* perfectionist.

performance *f* performance.

performant *adj* high-performance

péril *m* peril, danger.

périmètre *m* perimeter.

période *f* period; epoch, era.

périodique *adj* periodic.

péripétie *f* event, episode.

périphérie *f* periphery.

périphérique *adj* peripheral

périple *m* voyage; journey.

périr *vi* to perish, die.

permanence *f* permanence.

permanent *adj* permanent.

perméable *adj* permeable.

permettre *vt* to allow, permit.

permis *adj* permitted: —*m* permit, licence.

permission *f* permission; leave.

permuter *vt* to permutate.

perpendiculaire *adj* perpendicular.
perpétuel *adj* perpetual.
perpétuité *f* perpetuity.
perplexe *adj* perplexed, confused.
perplexité *f* perplexity, confusion.
perquisition *f* search.
perroquet *m* parrot.
persécuter *vt* to persecute.
persécution *f* persecution.
persévérance *f* perseverance.
persévérer *vi* to persevere; to persist in.
persil *m* parsley.
persistance *f* persistence.
persister *vi* to persist, keep up.
personnage *m* character, individual.
personnalité *f* personality.
personne *f* person; self; appearance:— **en ~** in person:—*pron* anyone, anybody; nobody.
personnel *adj* personal.
perspective *f* perspective; view; angle.
perspicace *adj* perspicacious.
persuader *vt* to persuade; to convince.
persuasion *f* persuasion; conviction.
perte *f* loss, losing; ruin.
pertinent *adj* pertinent.
perturber *vt* to disrupt, disturb.
pervers *adj* perverse; perverted.
perversité *f* perversity.
pesanteur *f* gravity; heaviness.
peser *vt* to weigh.
pessimisme *m* pessimism.
pessismiste *mf* pessimist:—*adj* pessimistic.
peste *f* pest, nuisance; plague.
petit *adj* small, tiny; slim; young.
petit-fils *m* grandson.
petite-fille *f* granddaughter.
petitesse *f* smallness; meanness.
pétition *f* petition.
petits-enfants *mpl* grandchildren.

pétrifié *adj* petrified.
pétrole *m* oil, petroleum.
peu *adv* little, not much, few:—**un petit ~** a little bit:—**quelque ~** a little:—**pour ~ que** however little:—**~ de** little, few.
peuple *m* people, nation; crowd.
peupler *vt* to populate, stock; to plant.
peur *f* fear, terror, apprehension:— **avoir ~** to be afraid.
peut-être *adv* perhaps.
phare *m* lighthouse; headlight.
pharmaceutique *adj* pharmaceutical.
pharmacie *f* pharmacy; pharmacology.
pharmacien(ne) *m(f)* pharmacist.
phase *f* phase, stage.
phénoménal *adj* phenomenal.
phénomène *m* phenomenon.
philosophe *mf* philosopher.
philosophie *f* philosophy.
philosophique *adj* philosophical.
phobie *f* phobia.
phonétique *f* phonetics:—*adj* phonetic.
photo *f* photo.
photocopie *f* photocopy.
photogénique *adj* photogenic.
photographe *mf* photograph.
photographie *f* photography.
photographier *vt* to photograph.
phrase *f* sentence; phrase.
physicien(ne) *m(f)* physicist.
physiologique *adj* physiological.
physionomie *f* countenance, physiognomy.
physiothérapie *f* physiotherapy.
physique *f* physics:—*adj* physical.
pianiste *mf* pianist.
piano *m* piano.
pic *m* peak.
pictural *adj* pictorial.
pièce *f* piece; room; document.

pied *m* foot; **à ~** on foot.
piège *m* trap; pit; snare.
piéger *vt* to trap, set a trap.
pierre *f* stone.
piété *f* piety.
piéton *m* pedestrian.
pieu *m* post, stake, pile.
pieux *adj* pious, devout.
pigment *m* pigment.
pile *f* pile; battery.
piler *vt* to crush, pound.
pilier *m* pillar.
pilote *m* pilot; driver.
piloter *vt* to pilot, fly; to drive.
pilule *f* pill.
piment *m* pepper.
pin *m* pine.
pinceau *m* brush, paintbrush.
pincer *vt* to pinch.
pingouin *m* penguin.
pinte *f* pint.
piolet *m* ice axe.
pionnier *m* pioneer.
pipe *f* pipe.
pique-nique *m* picnic.
pique-niquer *vi* to picnic.
piquer *vt* to sting.
piqûre *f* prick; sting; bite.
pirate *m* pirate.
pire *adj* worse:—**le ~** the worst.
pis-aller *m invar* last resort, stopgap.
piscine *f* swimming pool.
piste *f* track; clue.
pistolet *m* pistol, gun.
piteux *adj* pitiful, pathetic.
pitié *f* pity, mercy.
pittoresque *adj* picturesque.
pivoter *vi* to revolve, pivot.
placard *m* poster, notice.
place *f* place; square; seat:—**à la ~ de** instead of.

placer *vt* to place; to invest.
placide *adj* placid, calm.
plafond *m* ceiling; roof.
plage *f* beach.
plaider *vt* to plead.
plaie *f* wound, cut.
plaignant(e) *m(f)* plaintiff.
plaindre *vt* to pity:—**se ~** *vr* to complain.
plaine *f* plain.
plainte *f* complaint.
plaire *vi* to please:—**se ~** *vr* to enjoy.
plaisant *adj* pleasant, agreeable.
plaisanter *vi* to joke, jest.
plaisir *m* pleasure.
plan *m* plan; plane, level.
planche *f* plank, board.
plancher *m* floor.
planer *vi* to glide, soar.
planète *f* planet.
planeur *m* glider.
planifier *vt* to plan.
plante *f* plant.
planter *vt* to plant.
plaque *f* sheet, plate; plaque.
plastique *m* plastic:—*adj* plastic.
plat *adj* flat; straight; dull:—*m* plate; course.
plateau *m* tray; turntable; plateau.
plâtre *m* plaster.
plâtrer *vt* to plaster.
plébiscite *m* plebiscite.
plein *adj* full; entire.
pleur *m* tear, sob:—**en ~s** in tears.
pleurer *vi* to cry, weep.
pleuvoir *vi* to rain.
pli *m* fold; crease; envelope.
pliant *adj* collapsible, folding.
plier *vt* to fold; to bend.
plissement *m* creasing, folding.
plisser *vt* to pleat, fold.

plomb *m* lead; sinker; fuse.

plomber *vt* to weight; to fill.

plomberie *f* plumbing.

plongée *f* diving, dive.

plongeon *m* dive.

plonger *vi* to dive; to plunge.

plongeur *m*, **-euse** *f* diver.

pluie *f* rain; shower.

plume *f* feather.

plupart *f* most; majority.

pluriel *m* plural: — *adj* plural.

plus *adv* more, most: — ~ **grand que** bigger than: — **de ~ en ~** more and more: — **de ~** moreover: — **non ~** neither, not either.

plusieurs *adj* several.

plutôt *adv* rather, quite, fairly.

pluvieux *adj* rainy, wet.

pneu *m* tyre.

pneumonie *f* pneumonia.

poche *f* pocket; pouch; bag.

poêle *m* stove: — *f* frying pan.

poème *m* poem.

poète *m* poet.

poids *m* weight, influence.

poignée *f* handful: — ~ **de mains** handshake.

poil *m* hair; bristle.

poinçon *m* hallmark.

poinçonner *vt* to hallmark.

poing *m* fist: — **coup de ~** punch.

point *m* point; full stop: — **mettre au ~** to finalise; to perfect: — **être sur le ~ de** to be about to: — **à ~** medium, just right: — ~ **de vue** point of view.

pointe *f* point, head; spike: — **sur la ~ des pieds** on tiptoe.

pointu *adj* pointed, sharp.

poire *f* pear.

poireau *m* leek.

pois *m* pea.

poison *m* poison.

poisson *m* fish.

poitrine *f* chest, breast; bosom.

poivre *m* pepper.

poivrer *vt* to pepper.

polaire *adj* polar.

pôle *m* pole; centre.

polémique *f* controversy: — *adj* controversial.

poli *adj* polite; polished, smooth.

police *f* police.

policier *m* policeman, **-ière** *f* policewoman.

polir *vt* to polish; to refine.

politesse *f* politeness, courtesy.

politicien(ne) *m(f)* politician.

politique *f* politics; policy: — *adj* political.

politiser *vt* to politicise.

polluer *vt* to pollute.

pollution *f* pollution.

polyglotte *adj* polyglot: — *mf* polyglot.

pomme de terre *f* potato.

pomme *f* apple.

pompe *f* pump.

pomper *vt* to pump.

pompeux *adj* pompous; pretentious.

pompier *m* fireman.

poncer *vt* to sand down, rub down.

ponctualité *f* punctuality.

ponctuel *adj* punctual.

ponctuer *vt* to punctuate.

pondre *vt* to lay; to produce.

pont *m* bridge; deck; axle.

ponton *m* pontoon; landing stage.

populaire *adj* popular.

popularité *f* popularity.

population *f* population.

porc *m* pig; pork.

porche *m* porch.

pore *m* pore.

poreux *adj* porous.

port *m* port; pass; wearing.

portatif *adj* portable.

porte *f* door; gate; threshold.

porte-avions *m invar* aircraft carrier.

porte-clefs, porte-clés *m invar* key ring.

porte-parole *m invar* spokesperson.

portée *f* reach, range; significance:—**à la ~ de** within reach:—**hors de ~** out of reach.

portefeuille *m* wallet; portfolio.

porter *vt* to carry; to take; to wear.

porteur *m*, **-euse** *f* porter; carrier:—*adj* booster; strong, buoyant.

portière *f* door.

portion *f* portion, share.

portrait *m* portrait.

pose *f* pose, posture; setting.

poser *vt* to put; to install:—**se ~** *vr* to land, settle.

positif *adj* positive, definite.

position *f* position; situation; state; stance.

positionner *vt* to position, locate.

posséder *vt* to possess.

possesseur *m* possessor, owner.

possession *f* possession.

possibilité *f* possibility; potential.

possible *adj* possible; potential:—*m* **faire son ~** to do one's best.

postal *adj* postal, mail.

poste *f* post office, post:—*m* position; job.

poster *vt* to post, mail; to position.

postérieur *adj* subsequent.

postérité *f* posterity; descendants.

postier *m*, **-ière** *f* post office worker.

postuler *vt* to apply for; to postulate.

posture *f* posture, position.

pot *m* jar; pot; can.

pot-de-vin *m* bribe.

potable *adj* drinkable; passable.

potage *m* soup.

poteau *m* post, stake.

potentiel *adj* potential:—*m* potential

poterie *f* pottery.

potier *m* potter.

poubelle *f* dustbin.

pouce *m* thumb; big toe; inch.

poudre *f* powder, dust.

poudrer *vt* to powder.

poule *f* hen, fowl.

poulet *m* chicken.

pouls *m* pulse.

poumon *m* lung.

poupon *m* baby.

pouponnière *f* creche

pour *prép* for; to; in favour of; in order:—**~ que** in order that.

pourboire *m* tip.

pourcentage *m* percentage.

pourparlers *mpl* talks, negotiations.

pourquoi *adv* why:—**~ pas?** why not?:—*m* reason, question.

pourri *adj* rotten.

pourrir *vi* to rot.

pourriture *f* rot, rottenness.

poursuite *f* pursuit; prosecution.

poursuivre *vt* to pursue; to prosecute.

pourtant *adv* however, yet, nevertheless.

pourvoir *vt* to provide, equip.

pourvu *conj*:—**~ que** provided that.

poussée *f* pressure; thrust.

pousser *vt* to push:—*vi* to push; to grow.

poussière *f* dust.

poussiéreux *adj* dusty.

pouvoir *vi* can, be able; may:—*m* power; authority.

pragmatique *adj* pragmatic.

prairie *f* meadow, prairie.

praticable *adj* practicable; passable.
pratique *f* practice; exercise; observance:—*adj* practical.
pratiquer *vt* to practise, exercise; to carry out.
pré *m* meadow.
préalable *adj* preliminary.
préavis *m* notice, advance warning.
précaire *adj* precarious.
précaution *f* precaution; care.
précédent *adj* previous:—*m* precedent.
précéder *vt* to precede.
prêcher *vt* to preach.
précieux *adj* precious.
précipice *m* precipice.
précipitation *f* haste, violent hurry.
précipiter *vt* to hasten, precipitate.
précis *adj* precise, exact.
préciser *vt* to specify:—**se ~** *vr* to become clear.
précision *f* precision.
précoce *adj* precocious.
précurseur *m* precursor.
prédateur *m* predator.
prédécesseur *m* predecessor.
prédiction *f* prediction.
prédire *vt* to predict, foretell.
prédominance *f* predominance.
prédominer *vi* to predominate.
préfabriqué *adj* prefabricated.
préférable *adj* preferable.
préféré(e) *m(f)* favourite.
préférence *f* preference.
préférer *vt* to prefer.
préjudice *m* loss; damage.
préjudiciable *adj* prejudicial.
préjudicier *vt* to be prejudicial.
préjugé *m* prejudice.
préliminaire *m* preliminary:—*adj* preliminary.
prématuré *adj* premature.

préméditation *f* premeditation.
premier *m* first:—*adj* first; primary.
prémonition *f* premonition.
prénatal *adj* prenatal.
prendre *vt* to take:—**se ~** *vr* to consider oneself.
prénom *m* first name, forename.
préoccuper *vt* to preoccupy:—**se ~** *vr* to concern oneself.
préparation *f* preparation.
préparer *vt* to prepare.
prérogative *f* prerogative.
près *adv* near; almost:—**de ~** closely:—**à peu ~** just about.
prescrire *vt* to prescribe.
présence *f* presence.
présent *m* present:—*adj* present:—*m* present:—**à ~** just now.
présentation *f* presentation; introduction.
présenter *vt* to introduce; to present.
préservatif *m* condom.
préserver *vt* to preserve.
présidence *f* presidency.
président(e) *m(f)* president.
présider *vt* to preside, chair.
présomption *f* presumption.
présomptueux *adj* presumptuous.
presque *adv* almost.
presse *f* press.
pressentiment *m* presentiment.
pressentir *vt* to have a presentiment of.
presser *vt* to press; to hurry up:—**se ~** *vr* to hurry.
pression *f* pressure.
pressoir *m* press (wine, cider)
prestation *f* benefit; payment.
prestige *m* prestige.
présumer *vt* to presume.
prêt *adj* ready; prepared:—*m* loan.
prêt-à-porter *m* ready-to-wear.

prétendant(e) *m(f)* candidate.

prétendre *vt* to claim; to want; to intend.

prétendu *adj* so-called, supposed.

prétentieux *adj* pretentious.

prétention *f* pretension, claim.

prêter *vt* to lend; to attribute.

prétexte *m* pretext, excuse.

prêtre *m* priest.

preuve *f* proof, evidence.

prévaloir *vi* to prevail.

prévenant *adj* considerate.

prévenir *vt* to prevent; to warn.

prévention *f* prevention.

prévisible *adj* foreseeable.

prévision *f* prediction; forecast.

prévoir *vt* to anticipate; to plan.

prévoyance *f* foresight.

prévoyant *adj* provident.

prévu *adj* provided for.

prier *vi* to pray.

prière *f* prayer; entreaty.

primaire *adj* primary.

primate *m* primate.

prime *f* premium, subsidy.

primer *vi* to dominate:—*vt* to outdo.

primitif *adj* primitive.

primordial *adj* primordial.

prince *m* prince.

princesse *f* princess.

principal *m* principal:—*adj* main, principal.

principe *m* principle; origin.

printanier *adj* spring.

printemps *m* spring.

prioritaire *adj* priority.

priorité *f* priority.

prise *f* hold, grip; catch; plug; dose —~ **de sang** blood sample:—~ **de courant** plug, power point:—~ **de conscience** awareness, realisation.

prison *f* prison; jail.

prisonnier *m*, **-ière** *f* prisoner:—*adj* captive.

privation *f* deprivation.

privatiser *vt* to privatise.

privé *adj* private; unofficial.

priver *vt* to deprive.

privilège *m* privilege.

privilégié *adj* privileged, favoured.

privilégier *vt* to favour.

prix *m* price, cost; prize.

probabilité *f* probability.

probable *adj* probable, likely.

problématique *adj* problematical.

problème *m* problem, issue.

procédé *m* process; behaviour.

procéder *vi* to proceed.

procédure *f* procedure; proceedings.

procès *m* proceedings; lawsuit.

procès-verbal *m* minutes; report.

procession *f* procession.

prochain *adj* next; imminent:—*m* neighbour.

proche *adj* nearby; close.

proclamation *f* proclamation.

proclamer *vt* to proclaim, declare.

procurer *vt* to procure.

procureur *m* prosecutor.

prodigieux *adj* prodigious.

producteur *m*, **-trice** *f* producer.

productif *adj* productive.

production *f* production.

productivité *f* productivity.

produire *vt* to produce.

produit *m* product; yield.

profane *adj* secular, profane.

professeur *m* teacher, professor.

profession *f* profession; occupation.

professionnel(le) *m(f)* professional; skilled worker:—*adj* professional.

profil *m* profile, outline.

profiler *vt* to profile.

profit *m* profit; advantage.

profitable *adj* profitable.

profiter *vi* to profit.

profond *adj* deep, profound.

profondeur *f* depth; profundity.

profusion *f* profusion.

programme *m* programme.

programmer *vt* to programme; to schedule.

progrès *m* progress; improvement; advance.

progresser *vi* to progress; to advance.

progression *f* progress

prohiber *vt* to prohibit, ban.

proie *f* prey, victim.

projection *f* projection, casting.

projet *m* plan; draft.

projeter *vt* to plan; to cast, project.

prolétaire *mf* proletarian.

prolifération *f* proliferation.

proliférer *vi* to proliferate.

prolongement *m* continuation, extension.

prolonger *vt* to prolong.

promenade *f* walk, stroll.

promener (se) *vr* to go for a walk.

promeneur *m*, **-euse** *f* walker.

promesse *f* promise.

promettre *vt* to promise.

promotion *f* promotion.

promouvoir *vt* to promote.

prompt *adj* prompt.

prononcer *vt* to pronounce.

prononciation *f* pronunciation.

pronostic *m* forecast; prognosis.

pronostiquer *vt* to forecast, prognosticate.

propagande *f* propaganda.

propagation *f* propagation.

propager *vt* to propagate.

prophète *m* prophet.

prophétique *adj* prophetic.

prophétiser *vt* to prophesy.

propice *adj* propitious.

proportion *f* proportion, ratio.

proportionnel *adj* proportional.

propos *m* talk, remarks; intention:—**à ~ de** about, on the subject of.

proposer *vt* to propose.

proposition *f* proposition.

propre *adj* clean; own; suitable.

propreté *f* cleanliness; tidiness.

propriétaire *mf* owner; landlord.

propriété *f* ownership; suitability.

propulser *vt* to propel, power.

propulsion *f* propulsion.

prorogation *f* prorogation.

proroger *vt* to prorogue.

proscrire *vt* to proscribe.

prose *f* prose.

prospecter *vt* to prospect.

prospecteur *m*, **-trice** *f* prospector.

prospectus *m* leaflet; prospectus.

prospère *adj* prosperous.

prospérer *vi* to prosper, flourish.

prospérité *f* prosperity.

prostituée *f* prostitute.

prostitution *f* prostitution.

protagoniste *m* protagonist

protection *f* protection.

protéger *vt* to protect.

protestant(e) *m(f)* Protestant:—*adj* Protestant.

protestation *f* protest.

protester *vi* to protest; to affirm.

prototype *m* prototype.

prouesse *f* prowess.

prouver *vt* to prove; to demonstrate.

provenir *vi* to come from.

proverbe *m* proverb.

province *f* province.

provincial *adj* provincial
provision *f* provision; supply.
provisoire *adj* provisional, temporary.
provocation *f* provocation.
provoquer *vt* to provoke; to cause.
proximité *f* proximity.
prudence *f* prudence, care.
prudent *adj* prudent, careful.
pseudonyme *m* pseudonym.
psychanalyser *vt* to psychoanalyse
psychanalyste *mf* psychoanalyst.
psychiatre *mf* psychiatrist
psychiatrie *f* psychiatry.
psychique *adj* psychic.
psychisme *m* psyche, mind.
psychologie *f* psychology.
psychologique *adj* psychological.
psychologue *mf* psychologist: — *adj* psychological.
psychosomatique *adj* psychosomatic.
puberté *f* puberty.
public *adj*, *f* **publique** public: — *m* public, audience.
publicité *f* publicity.
publier *vt* to publish.
puce *f* flea.

pudique *adj* modest; chaste.
puer *vi* to stink: — *vt* to stink.
puéril *adj* puerile, childish.
puérilité *f* puerility, childishness.
puis *adv* then, next.
puisque *conj* since; as.
puissance *f* power, strength.
puissant *adj* powerful.
puits *m* well; shaft.
pulmonaire *adj* pulmonary, lung.
pulsation *f* pulsation.
pulvériser *vt* to pulverise; to powder.
punir *vt* to punish.
punition *f* punishment.
pupille *f* pupil; ward.
pupitre *m* desk; console.
pur *adj* pure; neat.
pureté *f* purity, pureness.
purifier *vt* to purify, cleanse.
puritain(e) *m(f)* *adj* puritan.
pur-sang *m invar* thoroughbred.
putréfier *vt* to putrefy, rot.
pyjama *m* pyjamas.
pylône *m* pylon.
pyramide *f* pyramid.

Q

quai *m* quay, wharf; platform.
qualificatif *adj* qualifying.
qualification *f* qualification.
qualifier *vt* to describe; to qualify.
qualitatif *adj* qualitative.
qualité *f* quality; skill; position.
quand *conj* when, while.
quant *prép*: — **~ à lui** as for him/it.
quantifier *vt* to quantify.
quantitatif *adj* quantitative.

quantité *f* quantity, amount.
quarante *adj*, *m inv* forty.
quarantième *adj*, *mf* fortieth.
quart *m* quarter; watch.
quartier *m* district; quarter.
quasi *adv* almost, nearly.
quatorze *adj m* fourteen.
quatorzième *adj mf* fourteenth.
quatre *adj m* four.
quatre-vingt(s) *adj m* eighty.

quatre-vingt-dix *adj m* ninety.
quatre-vingtième *adj mf* eightieth.
quatrième *adj mf* fourth.
que *conj* that; than;—*pron* that; whom; what; which.
quel, *f* **quelle** *adj* who, what, which.
quelconque *adj* some, any; least, indifferent.
quelqu'un, *f*-**une** someone *pl* **quelques-uns, -unes** *pron* some.
quelque *adj* some:—~ **part** somewhere.
quelque chose *pron* something.
quelquefois *adv* sometimes
querelle *f* quarrel; row; debate.
quereller (se) *vr* to quarrel.
question *f* question; issue.

questionnaire *m* questionnaire.
questionner *vt* to question.
quête *m* quest, search.
queue *f* tail; stalk; queue.
qui *pn* who, whom; which.
quiconque *pn* whoever, whosoever.
quiétude *f* quiet; peace.
quincaillerie *f* hardware, ironmongery.
quintuple *adj* quintuple:—*m* quintuple.
quintupler *vi* to quintuple.
quinzaine *f* about fifteen; fortnight.
quinze *adj*, *m* fifteen.
quinzième *adj*, *mf* fifteenth.
quitter *vt* to leave.
quoi *pn* what:—~ **que** whatever.
quoique *conj* although, though.
quotidien *adj* daily:—*m* everyday life.

R

rabais *m* reduction, discount.
rabaisser *vt* to humble.
rabattre *vt* to close; to reduce.
rabbin *m* rabbi.
raccommoder *vt* to mend, repair.
raccord *m* join; link; pointing.
raccorder *vt* to link up.
raccourci *m* shortcut.
raccourcir *vt* to shorten.
raccrocher *vt* to ring off, hang up.
race *f* race; stock; breed.
rachat *m* repurchase, purchase.
racheter *vt* to repurchase.
racial *adj* racial.
racine *f* root:—~ **carrée** square root.
raciste *mf* racist:—*adj* racist.
raconter *vt* to tell, recount.
radar *m* radar.
rade *f* harbour, roads.

radiateur *m* radiator; heater.
radiation *f* radiation.
radical *adj* radical.
radieux *adj* radiant, dazzling.
radio *f* radio; X-ray.
radio-taxi *m* radio taxi.
radioactif *adj* radioactive.
radiodiffuser *vt* to broadcast (radio).
radiographie *f* radiography; X-ray photography.
radiologue *mf* radiologist.
radis *m* radish.
radoucir *vt* to soften.
rafale *f* gust, blast; flurry.
raffermir *vt* to harden.
raffinage *m* refining.
raffiné *adj* refined, sophisticated.
raffiner *vt* to refine.
raffoler *vi*:—~ **de** to be crazy about.

rafraîchir *vt* to cool, freshen.
rafraîchissant *adj* refreshing, cooling.
rage *f* rage, fury; mania; rabies.
raid *m* raid; trek.
raide *adj* stiff; steep; broke.
raideur *f* stiffness; steepness.
raidir *vt* to stiffen.
raie *f* line; furrow; scratch.
rail *m* rail; railway.
railler *vt* to scoff at, mock.
raillerie *f* mockery, scoffing.
raisin *m* grape.
raison *f* reason; motive; ratio:—**avoir ~ to** be right:—**en ~ de** because of.
raisonnable *adj* reasonable, sensible.
raisonnement *m* reasoning.
raisonner *vi* to reason; to argue.
rajeunir *vt* to rejuvenate.
rajuster *vt* to readjust.
ralenti *adj* slow:—*m* slow motion:—**au ~** ticking over, idling.
ralentir *vi* to slow down.
ralentissement *m* slowing down.
râler *vi* to groan, moan.
rallier *vt* to rally; to win over.
rallumer *vt* to relight.
ramadan *m* Ramadan.
ramassage *m* gathering.
ramasser *vt* to collect, gather.
rame *f* oar; underground train.
rameau *m* branch.
ramener *vt* to bring back, restore.
ramer *vi* to row.
rameur *m*, **euse** *f* rower.
ramollir (se) *vr* to soften.
ramoner *vt* to sweep.
rampe *f* ramp, slope; gradient.
ramper *vi* to crawl, slither.
rance *adj* rancid, rank.
rançon *f* ransom.
rancune *f* grudge, rancour.

randonnée *f* drive; ride; ramble.
randonneur *m*, **-euse** *f* hiker, rambler.
rang *m* row, line; rank; class.
rangée *f* row, range, tier.
ranger *vt* to arrange.
ranimer *vt* to reanimate.
rapatriement *m* repatriation.
rapatrier *vt* to repatriate.
rapide *adj* rapid, quick.
rapidité *f* rapidity, quickness.
rapiécer *vt* to patch up.
rappel *m* recall; reminder
rappeler *vt* to recall; to remind:—**se ~** *vr* to remember.
rapport *m* report; relation; reference.
rapporter *vt* to report; to bring back.
rapporteur *m*, **-euse** *f* reporter.
rapprochement *m* reconciliation.
rapprocher (se) *vr* to approach; to be reconciled.
raquette *f* racket.
rare *adj* rare; odd.
raréfier (se) *vr* to rarefy.
rareté *f* rarity; scarcity.
ras *adj* close-shaven, shorn.
raser *vt* to shave off; to raze:—**se ~** *vr* to shave.
rasoir *m* razor.
rassemblement *m* assembling; crowd.
rassembler *vt* to rally:—**se ~** *vr* to gather, assemble.
rasseoir (se) *vr* to sit down again.
rassurant *adj* reassuring, comforting.
rassurer *vt* to reassure.
rat *m* rat.
raté *m*, **-e** *f* failure:—*m* misfire.
rater *vt* to miss; to fail:—*vi* to misfire.
ratification *f* ratification.
ratifier *vt* to ratify, confirm.
ration *f* ration, allowance.
rationnel *adj* rational.

rationner *vt* to ration.

rattacher *vt* to refasten; to attach; to link.

rattraper *vt* to catch again; to recover.

rature *f* deletion, erasure.

raturer *vt* to delete, erase.

rauque *adj* hoarse, raucous.

ravage *m* havoc; devestation.

ravager *vt* to ravage; devastate.

ravin *m* ravine, gully.

ravir *vt* to delight.

raviser (se) *vr* to change one's mind.

ravissant *adj* ravishing, delightful.

ravitaillement *m* revictualling.

ravitailler *vt* to revictual.

raviver *vt* to revive.

rayer *vt* to scratch; to cross out.

rayon *m* ray, beam; spoke; shelf.

rayonnement *m* radiance.

rayonner *vi* to radiate, shine.

rayure *f* stripe; streak; groove.

réaccoutumer (se) *vr* to become reaccustomed.

réacteur *m* reactor; jet-engine.

réaction *f* reaction.

réactionnaire *adj* reactionary:—*mf* reactionary.

réagir *vi* to react.

réalisateur *m*, **-trice** *f* director, filmmaker.

réalisation *f* realisation.

réaliser *vt* to realise:—**se ~** *vr* to be realised, come true.

réalisme *m* realism.

réalité *f* reality.

réanimation *f* resuscitation.

réanimer *vt* to reanimate.

réapparaître *vi* to reappear.

rebelle *mf* rebel:—*adj* rebel, rebellious.

rebeller (se) *vr* to rebel.

rébellion *f* rebellion.

reboiser *vt* to reafforest.

rebondir *vi* to rebound.

rebondissement *m* rebound.

rebut *m* scrap; repulse, rebuff.

receler *vt* to harbour.

récent *adj* recent; new.

réceptif *adj* receptive.

réception *f* reception, welcome.

réceptionniste *mf* receptionist.

récession *f* recession.

recette *f* recipe; formula; receipt.

receveur *m*, **-euse** *f* recipient; collector.

recevoir *vt* to receive.

rechange *m* spare.

recharge *f* reloading.

rechargeable *adj* reloadable.

recharger *vt* to reload.

réchauffer *vt* to reheat.

rêche *adj* rough, harsh.

recherche *f* search; research.

rechercher *vt* to seek; to investigate.

rechute *f* relapse; lapse.

récidiver *vi* to reoffend; to recur.

récif *m* reef.

récipient *m* container, receptacle.

réciproque *adj* reciprocal, mutual.

récit *m* account, story.

récitation *f* recitation.

réciter *vt* to recite.

réclamation *f* complaint; claim.

réclamer *vt* to claim.

réclusion *f* reclusion.

récolte *f* harvest; collection.

récolter *vt* to harvest; to collect.

recommandation *f* recommendation.

recommander *vt* to recommend; to register (letter).

recommencement *m* renewal.

recommencer *vi* to begin again.

récompense *f* reward; award.

réconciliation *f* reconciliation.
réconcilier *vt* to reconcile.
réconfort *m* comfort.
réconfortant *adj* comforting; tonic.
réconforter *vt* to comfort.
reconnaissance *f* recognition.
reconnaissant *adj* grateful.
reconnaître *vt* to recognise; to acknowledge; to be grateful.
reconsidérer *vt* to reconsider.
reconstituer *vt* to reconstitute.
reconstitution *f* reconstitution.
reconstruire *vt* to rebuild.
record *m* record.
recourbé *adj* curved, hooked.
recourir *vi* to run again.
recours *m* recourse; appeal.
récréatif *adj* recreative.
récréation *f* recreation.
récrimination *f* recrimination.
récriminer *vi* to recriminate.
recrue *f* recruit.
recrutement *m* recruitment.
recruter *vt* to recruit.
rectangle *m* rectangle.
rectangulaire *adj* rectangular.
rectification *f* rectification.
rectifier *vt* to rectify.
rectiligne *adj* rectilinear.
reçu *pp* recevoir accepted, successful: —*m* receipt.
recueil *m* collection, miscellany.
recueillir *vt* to gather: —**se ~** *vr* to collect one's thoughts.
reculer *vi* to fall back.
récupération *f* recovery.
récupérer *vt* to recover.
recycler *vt* to recycle.
rédacteur *m*, **-trice** *f* editor.
rédaction *f* drafting, drawing up.
rédemption *f* redemption.

redevance *f* rent; tax; fees.
rédiger *vt* to compile; to draft.
redire *vt* to repeat.
redoutable *adj* redoubtable, formidable.
redouter *vt* to dread, fear.
redresser *vt* to rectify; to true.
réduction *f* reduction.
réduire *vt* to reduce.
réduit *adj* reduced: —*m* retreat; recess.
rééducation *f* re-education.
rééduquer *vt* to re-educate.
réel *adj* real, genuine.
réélire *vt* to re-elect.
refaire *vt* to redo; to remake.
réfectoire *m* refectory.
référence *f* reference.
référendum *m* referendum.
réfléchir *vi* to think, reflect.
reflet *m* reflection.
refléter *vt* to reflect, mirror.
réflexe *m* reflex.
réflexion *f* thought, reflection: — ~ **faite** all things considered.
réforme *f* reform.
réformer *vt* to reform.
réfraction *f* refraction.
réfréner *vt* to curb.
réfrigérateur *m* refrigerator.
réfrigérer *vt* to refrigerate.
refroidir *vt* to cool: —*vi* to get cold.
refuge *m* refuge.
réfugié(e) *m(f)* refugee: —*adj* refugee.
réfugier (se) *vr* to take refuge.
refus *m* refusal.
refuser *vt* to refuse.
réfuter *vt* to refute.
regagner *vt* to regain.
régaler *vt* to regale.
regard *m* look; glance.
regarder *vt* to look at.

régénération *f* regeneration.
régénérer *vt* to regenerate, revive.
régie *f* administration.
régime *m* system, régime.
région *f* region, area.
régional *adj* regional.
régir *vt* to govern, rule.
registre *m* register, record.
règle *f* rule; order.
règlement *m* regulation, rules.
réglementation *f* regulations; control.
réglementer *vt* to regulate.
régler *vt* to pay; to regulate.
règne *m* reign.
régner *vi* to reign.
régresser *vi* to regress.
régression *f* regression.
regret *m* regret.
regretter *vt* to regret, be sorry; to miss.
regroupement *m* reassembly
regrouper *vt* to reassemble:—**se ~** *vr* to assemble.
régulariser *vt* to regularise.
régularité *f* regularity.
régulier *adj* regular; consistent.
réhabilitation *f* rehabilitation.
réhabiliter *vt* to rehabilitate.
réhabituer (se) *vr* to reaccustom oneself.
rein *m* kidney.
réincarnation *f* reincarnation.
reine *f* queen.
réinsertion *f* reinsertion.
réintégrer *vt* to reinstate.
réitérer *vt* to reiterate.
rejet *m* rejection.
rejeter *vt* to reject.
rejoindre *vt* to rejoin.
rejouer *vt* to replay.
réjouir *vt* to delight:—**se ~** *vr* to rejoice.

réjouissance *f* rejoicing.
relâche *f* intermission, respite.
relâchement *m* relaxation.
relâcher (se) *vr* to relax; to become lax.
relais *m* relay.
relatif *adj* relative.
relation *f* relation; reference.
relaxation *f* relaxation.
relaxer (se) *vr* to relax.
relayer *vt* to relieve; to relay.
relecture *f* rereading.
reléguer *vt* to relegate.
relève *f* relief.
relevé *m* statement; bill.
relever *vt* to raise again; to rebuild.
relief *m* relief; contours; depth.
relier *vt* to link up; to bind.
religieux *m* monk, **-euse** *f* nun:—*adj* religious.
religion *f* religion.
relire *vt* to reread.
reluire *vi* to gleam, shine.
remaniement *m* recasting; revision.
remanier *vt* to recast; to amend.
remarquable *adj* remarkable.
remarque *f* remark, comment.
remarquer *vt* to remark; to notice.
remboursement *m* reimbursement.
rembourser *vt* to reimburse.
remède *m* remedy, cure.
remédier *vi* **~ à** to remedy, cure.
remerciement *m* thanks; thanking.
remercier *vt* to thank.
remettre *vt* to replace:—**se ~** *vr* to recover.
réminiscence *f* reminiscence.
remise *f* delivery; remittance:—**~ en état** repairing:—**~ à neuf** restoration:—**~ en question** calling into question:—**~ en cause** calling into question.

remmener *vt* to take back.

remonter *vi* to go up again:—*vt* to take up.

remorque *f* trailer; towrope.

remorquer *vt* to tow.

remorqueur *m* tug.

rempart *m* rampart; defence.

remplaçant *m*, **-e** *f* replacement.

remplacer *vt* to replace.

remplir *vt* to fill.

remporter *vt* to take away.

remue-ménage *m invar* commotion; hullabaloo.

remuer *vt* to move; to fidget.

rémunération *f* remuneration.

rémunérer *vt* to remunerate, pay.

renaissance *f* rebirth, Renaissance.

renaître *vi* to be reborn.

renard *m* fox.

rencontre *f* meeting, encounter.

rencontrer *vt* to meet; to find.

rendement *m* yield; output.

rendez-vous *m* appointment; date; meeting place.

rendormir (se) *vr* to go back to sleep.

rendre *vt* to render; to give back:—**se ~** *vr* to surrender.

renfermer *vt* to contain, hold.

renflouer *vt* to refloat.

renforcer *vt* to strengthen.

renfort *m* reinforcement.

renifler *vt* to sniff.

renom *m* renown, fame.

renommée *f* renowned.

renoncement *m* renouncement.

renoncer *vi* to renounce.

renonciation *f* renunciation.

renouer *vt* to tie again.

renouveau *m* spring.

renouveler *vt* to renew.

renouvellement *m* renewal.

rénovation *f* renovation.

rénover *vt* to renovate.

renseignement *m* information.

renseigner *vt* to inform.

rentable *adj* profitable.

rente *f* rent; profit.

rentrer *vi* to re-enter; to return home.

renversement *m* reversal.

renverser *vt* to reverse; to overturn.

renvoi *m* sending back; dismissal.

renvoyer *vt* to send back;to dismiss.

réorganisation *f* reorganisation.

réorganiser *vt* to reorganise.

répandre *vt* to pour out.

répandu *adj* widespread.

réparation *f* repairing; restoration.

réparer *vt* to repair; to restore.

repartir *vi* to set off again.

répartir *vt* to share out.

répartition *f* sharing out.

repas *m* meal.

repeindre *vt* to repaint.

repentir (se) *vr* to repent, rue.

répercussion *f* repercussion.

répercuter (se) *vr* to reverberate; to echo.

repère *m* line, mark.

repérer *vt* to spot, pick out.

répertorier *vt* to itemise; to index.

répéter *vt* to repeat.

répétitif *adj* repetitive.

répétition *f* repetition; rehearsal.

répit *m* respite, rest.

repli *m* fold, coil, meander.

replier *vt* to fold up.

réplique *f* reply, retort.

répliquer *vt* to reply.

répondeur *m* answering machine.

répondre *vt* to answer, reply.

réponse *f* response, reply.

report *m* postponement, deferment.

reporter *vt* to take back:—*m* reporter.

repos *m* rest; landing.

reposer *vt* to put back:—**se ~** *vr* to rest oneself.

repoussant *adj* repulsive; repellent.

repousser *vt* to repel.

reprendre *vt* to retake, recapture.

représentant *m* representative.

représentation *f* representation; performance.

représenter *vt* to represent.

répressif *adj* repressive.

répression *f* repression.

réprimander *vt* to reprimand.

réprimer *vt* to repress.

reprise *f* resumption:—**à plusieurs ~s** several times.

reproche *m* reproach.

reprocher *vt* to reproach, blame.

reproduction *f* reproduction.

reproduire *vt* to reproduce.

reptile *m* reptile.

républicain *m*, **-e** *f* republican:—*adj* republican.

république *f* republic.

répudier *vt* to repudiate.

répugnance *f* repugnance.

répugnant *adj* repugnant.

réputation *f* reputation; character; fame.

réputé *adj* reputable, renowned.

requérir *vt* to request.

requête *f* request.

réquisition *f* requisition.

réseau *m* network, net.

réservation *f* reservation.

réserve *f* reserve; reservation.

réservé *f* reserved.

réserver *vt* to reserve.

réservoir *m* tank; reservoir.

résidence *f* residence.

résidentiel *adj* residential

résider *vi* to reside.

résignation *f* resignation.

résistance *f* resistance.

résistant *adj* resistant.

résister *vi* to resist, withstand.

résolu *adj* resolved, determined.

résolution *f* resolution; solution.

résonner *vi* to resonate.

résoudre *vt* to solve; to resolve.

respect *m* respect, regard.

respectable *adj* respectable.

respecter *vt* to respect.

respectif *adj* respective.

respectueux *adj* respectful.

respiration *f* respiration.

respiratoire *adj* respiratory.

respirer *vi* to breathe, respire.

responsabilité *f* responsibility.

responsable *adj* responsible; liable:— *mf* official, manager.

ressemblance *f* resemblance.

ressembler *vi* to resemble.

ressentiment *m* resentment.

ressentir *vt* to feel, experience.

resserrement *m* contraction.

resserrer *vt* to tighten.

ressort *m* spring.

ressortissant *m*, **-e** *f* national.

ressource *f* resource; resort.

ressusciter *vi* to reawaken.

restant *m* rest, remainder.

restaurant *m* restaurant.

restauration *f* restoration; catering.

restaurer *vt* to restore:—**se ~** *vr* to take refreshment.

reste *m* rest, remainder:—**du ~** besides.

rester *vi* to stay; to be left.

restituer *vt* to return; to refund.

restitution *f* restitution.

restreindre *vt* to restrict.

restrictif *adj* restrictive.

restriction *f* restriction, limitation.

résultat *m* result; profit.

résulter *vi*: — ~ **de** to result from.

résumé *m* summary.

résumer *vt* to sum up.

résurrection *f* resurrection.

rétablir *vt* to re-establish, restore.

rétablissement *m* re-establishment, restoring.

retard *m* lateness; delay.

retardé *adj* backward, slow.

retarder *vt* to delay.

retenir *vt* to hold back, retain.

réticence *f* reticence.

réticent *adj* reticent.

retirer (se) *vr* to retire, withdraw.

rétorquer *vt* to retort.

retour *m* return; recurrence.

retourner *vi* to return, go back.

rétracter *vt* to retract.

retrait *m* retreat; withdrawal.

retraite *f* retreat; retirement.

retraité(e) *m(f)* pensioner: —*adj* retired.

rétrécissement *m* narrowing; shrinking.

rétribuer *vt* to remunerate.

rétribution *f* retribution.

rétroactif *adj* retroactive.

rétroaction *f* retroaction.

rétrograde *adj* reactionary.

rétrograder *vi* to go backward.

rétrospectif *adj* retrospective.

retrouver *vt* to find again; to recover: —**se** ~ *vr* to meet up.

réunifier *vt* to reunify.

réunir (se) *vr* to meet; to assemble.

réussir *vi* to succeed.

réussite *f* success.

revanche *f* revenge: —**en** ~ on the other hand.

rêve *m* dream, dreaming; illusion.

réveil *m* awaking; alarm clock.

réveiller *vt* to wake: —**se** ~ *vr* to awaken.

révélation *f* revelation.

révéler *vt* to reveal.

revendeur *m*, **-euse** *f* retailer.

revendiquer *vt* to claim; to demand.

revendre *vt* to resell

revenir *vi* to come back, reappear.

revenu *m* income, revenue.

rêver *vi* to dream; to muse.

réverbère *m* street lamp.

révérer *vt* to revere.

rêverie *f* reverie, musing.

revers *m* back, reverse.

réversible *adj* reversible.

rêveur *m*, **-euse** *f* dreamer: —*adj* dreamy

revigorer *vt* to invigorate.

revirement *m* reversal; turnaround.

réviser *vt* to review; to revise.

révision *f* revision.

revivre *vt* to relive.

révocation *f* removal; revocation.

revoir *vt* to see again.

révolte *f* revolt, rebellion.

révolter (se) *vr* to rebel, revolt.

révolu *adj* past, bygone.

révolution *f* revolution.

révolutionnaire *mf* revolutionary: —*adj* revolutionary.

révoquer *vt* to revoke.

revue *f* review.

rez-de-chaussée *m invar* ground floor.

rhabiller (se) *vr* to dress again.

rhétorique *f* rhetoric: —*adj* rhetorical.

rhinocéros *m* rhinoceros.

rhum *m* rum.

rhume m cold.

riant adj smiling; cheerful.

riche adj rich, wealthy.

richesse f richness; wealth.

ride f wrinkle; ripple; ridge.

rideau m curtain.

ridicule adj ridiculous.

ridiculiser vt to ridicule.

rien pron nothing:—**de ~** don't mention it:—m nothingness; mere nothing.

rieur adj cheerful; laughing.

rigide adj rigid.

rigidité f rigidity.

rigoureux adj rigorous, harsh.

rigueur f rigour; harshness.

rime f rhyme.

rimer vi to rhyme (with)

rincer vt to rinse out; to rinse.

riposter vi to answer back, retaliate.

rire vi to laugh; to smile:—m laughter, laugh.

risée f laugh; ridicule.

risible adj laughable.

risque m risk, hazard.

risquer vt to risk; to venture.

rivage m shore

rival m, -e f rival:—adj rival.

rivaliser vi to rival.

rivalité f rivalry.

rive f shore, bank.

riverain adj riverside, lakeside.

rivière f river.

riz m rice.

robe f dress; gown:—~ **de chambre** dressing gown.

robinet m tap.

robot m robot.

robuste adj robust.

roc m rock.

rocher m rock, boulder.

roder vt to grind.

rôder vi to roam; to prowl.

rôdeur m, -euse f prowler.

rognon m kidney.

roi m king

rôle m role, character; roll, catalogue.

roman m novel; romance.

romancier m, -ière f novelist.

romantique adj romantic.

rompre vt to break:—vi to break; to burst.

rond m circle, ring; round:—adj round; chubby.

rond-point m roundabout.

ronde f patrol; round; beat.

ronflement m snore, snoring.

ronfler vi to snore.

ronronner vi to purr; to hum.

rose f rose:—adj pink:—m pink.

rosée f dew.

rossignol m nightingale.

rotation f rotation; turnover.

rôti m joint, roast.

rôtir vt to roast.

rôtisserie f rotisserie, steakhouse.

roue f wheel.

rouge adj red:—m red.

rouge-gorge m robin.

rougeur f redness, blushing.

rougir vi to blush, go red:—vt to redden.

rouille f rust.

rouiller vi to rust.

roulement m rotation; movement.

rouler vt to wheel:—vi to drive.

roulotte f caravan.

route f road; way; direction.

routier adj road:—m lorry driver; transport cafe.

routine f routine.

routinier adj humdrum, routine.

roux m, **rousse** f redhead: —adj red, auburn.
royal adj royal, regal.
royaume m kingdom.
ruban m ribbon; tape.
rubis m ruby.
rubrique f column; rubric.
rude adj rough; hard; unrefined.
rudesse f roughness; harshness.
rudiment m rudiment; principle.
rudimentaire adj rudimentary.
rue f street.
ruelle f alley.
rugir vi to roar.

rugissement m roar, roaring.
ruine f ruin; wreck.
ruiner vt to ruin.
ruineux adj ruinous; extravagant.
ruisseau m stream, brook.
ruisseler vi to stream, flow.
rumeur f rumour; murmur.
rupture f break, rupture.
rural adj rural, country.
ruse f cunning, slyness.
rusé adj cunning, crafty.
rustique adj rustic.
rythme m rhythm; rate, speed.
rythmique adj rhythmic.

S

sable m sand.
sablé adj sandy, sanded.
sabotage m sabotage.
saboter vt to sabotage.
saboteur m, **-euse** f saboteur.
sac m bag: — **~ à main** handbag.
saccade f jerk, jolt.
saccharine f saccharin.
sachet m bag; sachet; packet.
sacré adj sacred.
sacrifice m sacrifice.
sacrifier vt to sacrifice.
sacrilège m sacrilege.
sadique adj sadistic: —mf sadist.
safran m saffron.
saga f saga.
sagace adj sagacious, shrewd.
sage adj wise; well-behaved: —m sage, wise man.
sage-femme f midwife.
sagesse f wisdom, sense; good behaviour.

saignant adj bleeding.
saigner vi to bleed.
saillant adj protruding.
saillir vi to gush out; to project.
sain adj healthy; sound; sane.
saint(e) m(f) saint: —adj holy, saintly.
sainteté f saintliness; holiness.
saisie f seizure.
saisir vt to seize.
saison f season.
saisonnier adj seasonal.
salade f salad.
salaire m salary, pay; reward.
salarié(e) m(f) salaried employee: —adj salaried.
sale adj dirty, filthy; obscene.
salé adj salty, salted.
saler vt to salt, add salt.
saleté f dirt; rubbish; obscenity.
salière f saltcellar.
salir vt to make dirty: —**se ~** vr to get dirty.

salive f saliva.

salle f room; hall: — **~ de séjour** living room: — **~ à manger** dining room: — **~ de bain** bathroom.

salon m lounge; exhibition.

salubre adj healthy, salubrious.

saluer vt to greet; to salute.

salut m safety; welfare; salute.

salutation f salutation, greeting.

samedi m Saturday.

sanctifier vt to sanctify, bless.

sanction f sanction; approval.

sanctionner vt to punish; to sanction.

sanctuaire m sanctuary.

sandale f sandal.

sang m blood; race; kindred

sanglant adj bloody, gory.

sanglot m sob.

sangloter vi to sob.

sanguinaire adj sanguinary, bloodthirsty.

sanitaire adj health, sanitary.

sans-abris mf invar homeless person.

santé f health, healthiness.

saper vt to undermine, sap.

sapeur-pompier m fireman.

sapin m fir tree, fir.

sarcasme m sarcasm.

sarcastique adj sarcastic.

sardine f sardine.

sardonique adj sardonic.

satellite m satellite.

satiété f satiety: — **à ~** ad nauseam.

satin m satin.

satire f satire, lampoon.

satirique adj satirical.

satisfaction f satisfaction.

satisfaire vt to satisfy.

satisfaisant adj satisfying.

saturation f saturation.

saturé adj saturated.

saturer vt to saturate.

sauce f sauce, dressing.

saucisse f sausage.

sauf prép save, except; unless: — adj safe, unhurt.

saumon m salmon.

saut m jump, bound; waterfall.

sauter vi to jump; to blow up.

sauvage adj savage; unsociable.

sauvegarde f safeguard; backup.

sauvegarder vt to safeguard.

sauver vt to save.

sauvetage m rescue; salvage.

sauveteur m rescuer.

savant adj learned; expert: — m scientist, scholar.

saveur f flavour; savour.

savoir vt to know; to be able: — m learning, knowledge.

savoir-faire m know-how.

savon m soap.

savonner vt to soap, lather.

savoureux adj tasty, savoury.

scandale m scandal.

scandaleux adj scandalous.

scandaliser vt to scandalise.

scaphandre m diving suit.

sceau m seal.

sceller vt to seal.

scénario m scenario; screenplay.

scénariste mf scriptwriter.

scène f stage; scenery, scene.

scepticisme m scepticism.

sceptique adj sceptical: — mf sceptic.

schéma m diagram, sketch; outline.

schizophrène mf schizophrenic: — adj schizophrenic.

schizophrénie f schizophrenia.

scie f saw; bore.

sciemment adv knowingly, on purpose.

science f science; skill; knowledge.

science-fiction *f* science fiction.

scientifique *adj* scientific.

scintillant *adj* sparkling, glistening.

scintiller *vi* to sparkle, glisten.

scolaire *adj* school; academic.

scolarité *f* schooling.

scooter *m* scooter.

score *m* score.

scout *m* scout, boy scout.

script *m* printing; script.

scrupule *m* scruple, doubt.

scrupuleux *adj* scrupulous.

sculpter *vt* to sculpt; to carve.

sculpteur *m* sculptor.

sculpture *f* sculpture.

se *pron* oneself, himself, herself, itself, themselves.

séance *f* meeting, session; seat.

seau *m* bucket, pail.

sec *adj*, *f* **sèche** dry, arid.

séchage *m* drying; seasoning.

sèche-cheveux *m invar* hair-drier

sécher *vi* to dry.

sécheresse *f* drought.

second *adj* second.

secondaire *adj* secondary.

seconde *f* second.

secouer *vt* to shake, toss.

secourir *vt* to help, assist.

secouriste *mf* first-aid worker.

secours *m* help, assistance; relief; rescue.

secousse *f* jolt, bump.

secret *m* secret:—*adj* secret; discreet.

secrétaire *mf* secretary:—*m* writing desk.

sécrétion *f* secretion.

secte *f* sect.

secteur *m* sector, section.

section *f* section, division; branch.

séculaire *adj* secular.

sécuritaire *adj* security.

sécurité *f* security; safety.

sédatif *m* sedative:—*adj* sedative.

sédiment *m* sediment.

séduction *f* seduction; captivation

séduire *vt* to seduce; to charm, captivate.

segment *m* segment.

segmenter *vt* to segment.

ségrégation *f* segregation.

seigneur *m* lord, nobleman.

sein *m* breast, bosom; womb:—**au ~ de** within.

séisme *m* earthquake, seism.

seize *adj*, *m* sixteen.

seizième *adj*, *mf* sixteenth.

séjour *m* stay, sojourn.

séjourner *vi* to stay, sojourn.

sel *m* salt; wit.

sélectif *adj* selective.

sélection *f* choosing, selection.

sélectionner *vt* to select, pick.

selle *f* saddle.

selon *prép* according to.

semaine *f* week.

semblable *adj* like, similar.

semblant *m* appearance, look.

sembler *vi* to seem, appear.

semence *f* seed.

semer *vt* to sow.

semestre *m* half-year; semester.

semestriel *adj* half-yearly; semest-ral.

séminaire *m* seminary; seminar.

sénat *m* senate.

sénateur *m* senator.

sénile *adj* senile.

sénilité *f* senility.

sens *m* sense; judgement; meaning; direction.

sensation *f* sensation, feeling.

sensationnel *adj* sensational.

sensé *adj* sensible.

sensibiliser *vt* to make sensitive to.

sensibilité *f* sensitivity.

sensible *adj* sensitive; perceptive.

sensualité *f* sensuality.

sensuel *adj* sensual.

sentence *f* sentence.

sentier *m* path, track.

sentiment *m* sentiment; feeling.

sentimental *adj* sentimental.

sentir *vt* to feel; to perceive.

séparation *f* separation.

séparatiste *mf* separatist.

séparer *vt* to separate:—**se ~** *vr* to separate.

sept *adj*, *m* seven.

septembre *m* September

septième *adj*, *mf* seventh.

sépulture *f* sepulture, burial.

séquence *f* sequence.

serein *adj* serene, calm.

sérénité *f* serenity, calmness.

sergent *m* sergeant.

série *f* series.

sérieux *adj* serious.

seringue *f* syringe.

serment *m* oath.

séropositif *adj* HIV positive, seropositive.

serpent *m* serpent, snake.

serpenter *vi* to meander, wind.

serre *f* greenhouse; claw.

serrer *vt* to tighten.

serrure *f* lock.

sérum *m* serum.

servante *f* servant.

serveur *m* waiter, **-euse** *f* waitress.

service *m* service; function.

serviette *f* towel; serviette.

servile *adj* servile, slavish.

servilité *f* servility.

servir *vi* to be of use:—*vt* to serve:—**se ~ de** to make use of.

servitude *f* servitude.

session *f* session, sitting.

seuil *m* threshold.

seul *adj* alone; single.

sévère *adj* severe, austere.

sévérité *f* severity; strictness

sexe *m* sex.

sexiste *mf* sexist:—*adj* sexist.

sexualité *f* sexuality.

sexuel *adj* sexual.

sexy *adj* sexy.

short *m* shorts.

si *adv* so, so much; yes:—*conj* if; whether.

SIDA *m* AIDS.

sidérurgiste *mf* steel worker.

siècle *m* century.

siège *m* seat; head office.

siéger *vi* to sit; to be located.

sien *pron*, *f* **sienne**:—**le ~ his**, its, his own, its own, **la sienne** her, its, her own, its own, **les ~s, les siennes** their, its own.

siffler *vi* to whistle; to hiss.

sigle *m* abbreviation; acronym.

signal *m* signal, sign.

signaler *vt* to signal, indicate.

signature *f* signature; signing.

signe *m* sign; mark.

signer *vt* to sign.

signet *m* bookmark.

significatif *adj* significant.

signification *f* significance.

signifier *vt* to mean, signify.

silence *m* silence.

silencieux *adj* silent; still.

silhouette *f* silhouette.

similaire *adj* similar.

similarité *f* similarity.

simple *adj* simple; mere; single.
simplicité *f* simplicity.
simplification *f* simplification.
simplifier *vt* to simplify.
simulation *f* simulation.
simuler *vt* to simulate.
simultané *adj* simultaneous.
sincère *adj* sincere, honest.
sincérité *f* sincerity, honesty.
singe *m* monkey.
singularité *f* singularity.
singulier *adj* singular, peculiar.
sinistre *m* disaster; accident:—*adj* sinister.
sinistré(e) *m(f)* disaster victim.
sinon *conj* otherwise, if not; except.
sinueux *adj* sinuous, winding.
site *m* setting, beauty spot.
sitôt *adv* as soon:—~ **que** as soon as.
situation *f* situation, position.
situer *vt* to site, situate.
six *adj, m* six.
sixième *adj, mf* sixth.
ski *m* ski, skiing.
skier *vi* to ski.
skieur *m*, **-euse** *f* skier.
slip *m* briefs; panties.
snob *adj* snobbish.
snobisme *m* snobbishness.
sobre *adj* sober, temperate.
sobriété *f* sobriety, temperance.
sociable *adj* sociable; social.
social *adj* social.
socialiste *mf* socialist:—*adj* socialist.
société *f* society; company.
sociologique *adj* sociological.
sociologue *mf* sociologist.
sœur *f* sister; nun.
sofa *m* sofa.
soi *pn* one(self); self:—~-**même** oneself, himself, herself, itself.

soie *f* silk.
soif *f* thirst
soigner *vt* to look after.
soigneux *adj* neat; careful.
soin *m* care.
soir *m* evening; night.
soit *conj* either; or; whether:—*adv* granted; that is to say.
soixante *adj, m* sixty.
soixantième *adj, mf* sixtieth.
sol *m* ground; floor; soil.
soldat *m* soldier
solde *f* pay:—*m* balance.
solder *vt* to pay; to settle.
soleil *m* sun, sunshine; sunflower.
solennel *adj* solemn.
solidarité *f* solidarity.
solide *adj* solid; sound.
solidifier *vt* to solidify.
solitaire *mf* recluse:—*adj* solitary, lone.
solitude *f* solitude; loneliness.
solution *f* solution.
solvable *adj* solvent.
sombre *f* dark; gloomy.
sommaire *m* summary:—*adj* basic, summary.
sommeil *m* sleep; sleepiness.
sommeiller *vi* to slumber.
sommet *m* summit; crest.
somnambule *mf* sleepwalker:—*adj* sleepwalking.
somnifère *m* sleeping pill.
somnoler *vi* to doze.
somptueux *adj* sumptuous, lavish.
son *m* sound:—*adj, f* **sa**; *pl* **ses** his, her, its.
songe *m* dream.
songer *vt* to dream.
sonner *vi* to ring.
sonore *adj* resonant, deep-toned.
sophistiqué *adj* sophisticated.

sordide *adj* sordid, squalid.

sort *m* fate, destiny, lot.

sorte *f* sort, kind.

sortie *f* exit, way out; trip; sortie.

sortir *vi* to go out.

sot *adj* (*f* **sotte**) silly, foolish.

sottise *f* stupidity; stupid remark.

souci *m* worry; concern.

soucier *vr:*—**se ~ de** to care about.

soucieux *adj* concerned, worried.

soudain *adj* sudden, unexpected.

souder *vt* to solder; to weld.

souffle *m* blow, puff; breath.

souffler *vi* to blow; to breathe.

souffrance *f* suffering; pain

souffrir *vi* to suffer.

souhait *m* wish.

souhaiter *vt* to wish for, desire.

soulagement *m* relief.

soulager *vt* to relieve, soothe.

soulever *vt* to lift:—**se ~** *vr* to rise; to revolt.

soulier *m* shoe.

souligner *vt* to underline.

soumettre *vt* to subdue.

soumission *f* submission.

soupape *f* valve.

soupçon *m* suspicion.

soupçonner *vt* to suspect.

soupçonneux *adj* suspicious.

soupe *f* soup.

soupir *m* sigh; gasp.

soupirer *vi* to sigh; to gasp.

souple *adj* supple; pliable.

souplesse *f* suppleness.

source *f* source.

sourcil *m* eyebrow.

sourd(e) *m*(*f*) deaf person:—*adj* deaf; muted.

sourd(e)-muet(te) *m*(*f*) deaf-mute:—*adj* deaf and dumb.

souriant *adj* smiling, cheerful.

sourire *m* smile, grin.

souris *f* mouse; (*comput*) mouse.

sournois *adj* deceitful.

sous *prép* under, beneath, below.

sous-alimenté *adj* undernourished.

sous-développé *adj* underdeveloped.

sous-entendre *vt* to imply.

sous-estimer *vt* to underestimate.

sous-marin *m* submarine:—*adj* underwater.

sous-titre *m* subtitle.

sous-titrer *vt* to subtitle.

sous-traitant *m* subcontractor.

sous-traiter *vt* to subcontract.

souscrire *vi* to subscribe.

soustraction *f* subtraction.

soustraire *vt* to subtract.

soute *f* hold; baggage hold.

soutenir *vt* to sustain.

souterrain *adj* underground.

soutien *m* support.

soutien-gorge *m* bra.

souvenir *m* memory; recollection.

souvenir (se) *vr* to remember.

souvent *adv* often, frequently.

souverain(e) *m*(*f*) sovereign:—*adj* sovereign.

spacieux *adj* spacious, roomy.

spaghettis *mpl* spaghetti.

spasme *m* spasm.

spécial *adj* special.

spécialiser *vt* to specialise.

spécieux *adj* specious.

spécification *f* specification.

spécifier *vt* to specify.

spécifique *adj* specific.

spécimen *m* specimen.

spectacle *m* spectacle, scene.

spectaculaire *adj* spectacular.

spectateur *m*, **-trice** *f* spectator.

spectre m ghost.

spéculateur m, **-trice** f speculator.

spéculer vi to speculate.

sphère f sphere.

spiritualité f spirituality.

spirituel adj witty; spiritual.

splendeur f splendour, brilliance.

splendide adj splendid.

spontané adj spontaneous.

sport m sport.

sportif m sportsman, **-ive** f sportswoman:—adj sports.

square m square.

squelette m skeleton.

stabiliser vt to stabilise.

stabilité f stability.

stable adj stable.

stade m stadium; stage.

stage m training course.

stagiaire mf trainee.

standard adj standard.

star f star.

starter m choke.

station f station; stage.

stationnaire adj stationary.

stationnement m parking.

stationner vi to park.

station-service f service station.

statique adj static.

statistique f statistics:—adj statistical.

statue f statue.

statuer vt to rule.

statut m statute.

statutaire adj statutory.

stencil m stencil.

sténodactylo mf shorthand typist.

sténographie f shorthand.

stéréotype m stereotype.

stérile adj sterile, infertile.

stériliser vt to sterilise.

stérilité f sterility.

stimulant adj stimulating:—m stimulant.

stimulation f stimulation.

stimuler vt to stimulate.

stipuler vt to stipulate.

stock m stock, supply.

stocker vt to stock, stockpile.

stoïque adj stoical.

stop m stop; stop sign.

stopper vt to stop.

store m blind, shade.

stratégie f strategy.

stratégique adj strategic.

stress m stress.

stressant adj stessful.

strict adj strict, severe.

strident adj strident, shrill.

structural adj structural.

structure f structure.

studieux adj studious.

studio m studio; film theatre.

stupéfier vt to stupefy; to astound.

stupeur f amazement; stupor.

stupide adj stupid, foolish.

stupidité f stupidity.

style m style; stylus.

styliste mf designer; stylist.

stylo m pen.

suave adj suave, smooth.

subconscient m subconscious:—adj subconscious.

subir vt to sustain; to undergo.

subit adj sudden.

subjectif adj subjective.

subjectivité f subjectivity.

subjuguer vt to subjugate.

sublime adj sublime.

submerger vt to submerge.

subséquent adj subsequent.

subside m grant.

subsistance f subsistence.

subsister *vi* to subsist.
substance *f* substance.
substantiel *adj* substantial.
substantif *m* noun, substantive.
substituer *vt* to substitute.
substitut *m* substitute.
substitution *f* substitution.
subtil *adj* subtle.
subtilité *f* subtlety.
subvention *f* grant, subsidy.
subventionner *vt* to subsidise.
subversif *adj* subversive.
succéder *vi*: —~ **à** to succeed, follow.
succès *m* success; hit.
successeur *m* successor.
succession *f* succession.
succinct *adj* succinct.
succomber *vi* to succumb.
succulent *adj* succulent, delicious.
sucursale *f* branch.
sucer *vt* to suck.
sucre *m* sugar.
sud *m* south.
suer *vi* to sweat, perspire.
sueur *f* sweat.
suffire *vi* to suffice.
suffisant *adj* sufficient, adequate.
suffoquer *vi* to choke, suffocate.
suffrage *m* suffrage; vote.
suggérer *vt* to suggest.
suggestion *f* suggestion.
suicide *m* suicide.
suicider (se) *vr* to commit suicide.
suite *f* continuation; series:—**tout de** ~ at once:—**et ainsi de** ~ and so on.
suivant *adj* following, next:—*prép* according to.
suivi *m* follow-up.
suivre *vt* to follow:—~ **son cours** to take its course:—**à suivre** to be continued.

sujet *m* subject, topic:—*adj* subject.
super *adj* ultra, super.
superbe *adj* superb.
superficie *f* area, surface.
superficiel *adj* superficial.
superflu *adj* superfluous.
supérieur *adj* upper; superior.
supériorité *f* superiority.
superlatif *m* superlative:—*adj* superlative.
superstitieux *adj* superstitious.
superstition *f* superstition.
superviser *vt* to supervise.
supplanter *vt* to supplant.
supplément *m* supplement.
supplémentaire *adj* supplementary.
support *m* support, prop; stand.
supporter *vt* to support; to endure.
supposer *vt* to suppose.
suppression *f* suppression.
supprimer *vt* to suppress.
suprématie *f* supremacy.
suprême *adj* supreme.
sur *prép* on; over, above; into; out of, from.
sûr *adj* sure, certain; secure:—~ **de soi** self-assured:—**bien** ~ of course.
surabondance *f* overabundance.
suranné *adj* outmoded, outdated.
surcharge *f* surcharge.
surcroît *m* surplus:—**de** ~ in addition.
surdité *f* deafness.
surélever *vt* to raise, heighten.
surestimer *vt* to overestimate.
sûreté *f* safety; guarantee.
surface *f* surface.
surgeler *vt* to deep-freeze.
surgir *vi* to appear; to arise.
surlendemain *m* day after tomorrow.
surmonter *vt* to surmount.
surnaturel *adj* supernatural.

surnom *m* nickname.

surnommer *vt* to nickname.

surpasser *vt* to surpass, outdo.

surplomber *vt* to overhang.

surplus *m* surplus.

surpopulation *f* overpopulation.

surprenant *adj* surprising.

surprendre *vt* to surprise.

surprise *f* surprise.

sursaut *m* start, jump.

sursauter *vi* to start, jump.

surtaxe *f* surcharge.

surtout *adv* especially; above all.

surveillance *f* surveillance.

surveiller *vt* to watch; to supervise.

survenir *vi* to take place, occur.

survie *f* survival.

survivant(e) *m(f)* survivor:—*adj* surviving.

survivre *vi* to survive.

survoler *vt* to fly over.

susceptible *adj* susceptible:—**être ~ de** to be likely to.

susciter *vt* to arouse, incite.

suspect(e) *m(f)* suspect.

suspecter *vt* to suspect.

suspendre *vt* to hang up; to suspend.

suspension *f* suspension.

suspicieux *adj* suspicious.

suspicion *f* suspicion.

susurrer *vt* to whisper.

svelte *adj* svelte, slim.

syllabe *f* syllable.

symbole *m* symbol

symbolique *adj* symbolic; token.

symboliser *vt* to symbolise.

symétrie *f* symmetry.

symétrique *adj* symmetrical.

sympathie *f* liking; sympathy.

sympathique *adj* likeable, nice; friendly.

symphonie *f* symphony.

symptôme *m* symptom.

synagogue *f* synagogue.

synchroniser *vt* to synchronise.

syndical *adj* trade-union.

syndicaliste *mf* trade unionist:—*adj* trade union.

syndicat *m* trade union; association.

synonyme *m* synonym:—*adj* synonymous.

synthèse *f* synthesis.

synthétique *adj* synthetic.

systématique *adj* systematic.

système *m* system.

T

tabac *m* tobacco.

table *f* table:—**~ ronde** round-table conference.

tableau *m* table; chart.

tablette *f* bar; tablet.

tablier *m* apron; overall.

tabouret *m* stool.

tache *f* mark; stain; spot.

tâche *f* task, assignment; work.

tacite *adj* tacit.

taciturne *adj* taciturn, silent.

tact *m* tact.

tactile *adj* tactile.

tactique *f* tactics:—*adj* tactical.

taille *f* height, stature, size.

tailler *vt* to cut; to carve.

taire(se) *vr* to be quiet.

talent *m* talent, ability.

talentueux *adj* talented.

talon *m* heel; crust; spur.

tambour *m* drum; barrel.

tamis *m* sieve; riddle.

tamiser *vt* to sieve; to sift.

tampon *m* stopper, plug; tampon.

tandem *m* tandem; duo.

tandis *conj*: — ~ **que** while; whereas.

tangible *adj* tangible.

tank *m* tank.

tanner *vt* to tan, weather.

tant *adv* so much: — ~ **que** as long as: — ~ **mieux** that's a good job: — ~ **pis** too bad.

tante *f* aunt.

tantôt *adv* sometimes; this afternoon; shortly.

tapage *m* din, uproar, racket.

tape *f* slap.

taper *vt* to beat; to slap; to type.

tapis *m* carpet; rug; cloth.

tapisser *vt* to wallpaper; to cover.

tapisserie *f* tapestry.

taquin *adj* teasing.

taquiner *vt* to tease; to plague.

tard *adv* late.

tarder *vi* to delay, put off; to dally.

tardif *adj* late; tardy.

tarif *m* tariff; price-list.

tarir (se) *vr* to dry up.

tarte *f* tart, flan.

tartre *m* tartar; fur, scale.

tas *m* heap, pile; lot, set.

tasse *f* cup; coffee cup.

tassement *m* settling, sinking.

tasser *vt* to heap up: — **se** ~ *vr* to sink; subside.

tâter *vt* to feel, try.

tatonner *vi* to feel one's way.

tatouer *vt* to tattoo.

taudis *m* hovel, slum.

taureau *m* bull.

taux *m* rate; ratio: — ~ **de change** exchange rate.

taverne *f* tavern.

taxation *f* taxation, taxing.

taxe *f* tax; duty; rate.

taxer *vt* to tax.

taxi *m* taxi.

te *pn* you, yourself.

technicien(ne) *m(f)* technician.

technique *f* technique: — *adj* technical.

technologie *f* technology.

technologique *adj* technological.

teindre *vt* to dye.

teint *m* complexion, colouring.

teinter *vt* to tint; to stain.

teinture *f* dye; dyeing.

tel *adj* such; like, similar: — ~ **quel** such as it is: — **en tant que** ~ as such.

télé *f* TV, telly.

télécommande *f* remote control.

télécopie *f* facsimile transmission; fax.

télégramme *m* telegram; cable.

télégraphier *vt* to telegraph, cable.

télépathie *f* telepathy.

téléphérique *m* cableway; cable-car.

téléphone *m* telephone.

téléphoner *vi* to telephone.

télescope *m* telescope.

télescopique *adj* telescopic.

téléviseur *m* television set.

télévision *f* television.

télex *m* telex.

tellement *adj* so, so much: — ~ **de** so many, so much.

téméraire *adj* rash, reckless.

témoignage *m* testimony.

témoigner *vi* to testify.

témoin *m* witness.

tempérament *m* temperament.

température *f* temperature

tempête *f* tempest.

temple *m* temple.

temporaire *adj* temporary.

temps *m* time; while; tense; beat; weather:—**de ∼ en ∼** from time to time.

tenace *adj* tenacious, stubborn.

ténacité *f* tenacity; stubbornness.

tenaille *f* pincers; tongs.

tendance *f* tendency; trend.

tendancieux *adj* tendentious.

tendon *m* tendon, sinew.

tendre *adj* tender, soft; delicate.

tendresse *f* tenderness; fondness.

tendu *adj* tight; stretched; delicate

ténébreux *adj* dark, gloomy.

teneur *f* terms; content; grade.

tenir *vt* to hold, keep:—**∼ à** to value, care about.

tennis *m* tennis:—**∼ de table** table tennis.

tentation *f* temptation.

tentative *f* attempt, bid.

tente *f* tent.

tenter *vt* to tempt.

tenue *f* holding; deportment; dress, appearance.

terme *m* term; termination, end; word.

terminaison *f* ending.

terminal *adj* terminal:—*m* terminal.

terminer *vt* to finish off:—**se ∼** *vr* to terminate.

terminologie *f* terminology.

terne *adj* colourless; drab.

terrain *m* ground, earth; site; field.

terrasse *f* terrace.

terre *f* earth; ground, land:—**mettre pied à ∼** to land, alight.

terrestre *adj* land; terrestrial.

terreur *f* terror, dread.

terrible *adj* terrible, dreadful; terrific, great.

terrier *m* burrow; earth; terrier.

terrifiant *adj* terrifying, fearsome.

terrifier *vt* to terrify.

territoire *m* territory, area.

territorial *adj* land, territorial.

terroir *m* soil.

terroriser *vt* to terrorise.

terroriste *mf* terrorist:—*adj* terrorist.

test *m* test.

testament *m* will, testament.

tester *vt* to test; to make out one's will.

tête à tête *m* private conversation.

tête *f* head; top; sense:—**tenir ∼** to cope:—**être en ∼** to head.

tétine *f* teat; udder; dummy.

téton *m* breast.

têtu *adj* headstrong, stubborn.

texte *m* text; theme; passage.

textile *adj* textile.

textuel *adj* textual, literal.

texture *f* texture.

thé *m* tea.

théâtral *adj* theatrical, dramatic.

théâtre *m* theatre; drama.

thème *m* theme.

théologie *f* theology.

théorie *f* theory.

théorique *adj* theoretical.

thérapeute *mf* therapist.

thérapie *f* therapy.

thermique *adj* thermal; thermic.

thermomètre *m* thermometer.

thermos *f/m* thermos.

thèse *f* thesis.

thym *m* thyme.

ticket *m* ticket.

tiède *adj* lukewarm, tepid.

tien *poss pn*:—**le ~, la ~ne, les ~(ne)s** yours.

tiers *adj* third:—**~-monde** Third World:—*m* third; third party.

tigre *m* tiger.

timbre *m* stamp; postmark; bell.

timbrer *vt* to stamp; to postmark.

timide *adj* timid, shy.

timidité *f* timidity, shyness.

tintement *m* ringing toll.

tinter *vi* to ring, toll; to chime.

tir *m* shooting; shot:—**~ à l'arc** archery.

tirailler *vt* to tug; to pester.

tire-bouchon *m* corkscrew.

tirelire *f* moneybox.

tirer *vt* to pull; to draw.

tiret *m* dash; hyphen.

tireur *m*, **-euse** *f* gunner; drawer (cheque).

tiroir *m* drawer.

tisser *vt* to weave.

tissu *m* texture, fabric; tissue.

titre *m* title; heading; right; deed:—**à ~ de** by right of.

tituber *vi* to stagger.

titulaire *mf* incumbent, holder:—*adj* titular.

toi *pn* you:—**~-même** yourself:—**c'est à ~** it's yours; it's your turn.

toile *f* cloth; canvas; sheet.

toilette *f* cleaning, grooming:—**faire sa ~** to wash oneself.

toit *m* roof; home.

tolérable *adj* tolerable, bearable.

tolérant *adj* tolerant.

tolérer *vt* to tolerate.

tomate *f* tomato.

tombe *f* tomb; grave.

tomber *vi* to fall:—**laisser ~** to drop.

tome *m* book; volume.

ton *adj*, *f* **ta**, *pl* **tes** your:—*m* tone; pitch; shade.

tondre *vt* to shear; mow.

tonifiant *m* tonic.

tonifier *vt* to tone up.

tonique *adj* tonic; fortifying:—*m* tonic.

tonne *f* ton, tonne.

tonneau *m* barrel, cask.

tonnerre *m* thunder.

topographie *f* topography.

toquade *f* infatuation; fad, craze.

toquer *vi* to tap, rap.

torche *f* torch.

torcher *vt* to wipe, mop up.

torchon *m* cloth; duster.

tordre *vt* to twist, contort.

tordu *adj* twisted, crooked.

torpeur *f* torpor.

torrent *m* torrent.

torrentiel *adj* torrential.

torride *adj* torrid; scorching.

torse *m* chest; torso.

torsion *f* twisting; torsion.

tort *m* fault; wrong; prejudice:—**avoir ~** to be wrong:—**faire du ~** to harm.

tortiller *vt* to twist:—**se ~** *vr* to wriggle.

tortionnaire *mf* torturer.

tortue *f* tortoise.

tortueux *adj* tortuous, winding.

torture *f* torture.

torturer *vt* to torture.

tôt *adv* early; soon:—**au plus ~** as soon as possible:—**plus ~** sooner.

total *adj* total.

totalitaire *adj* totalitarian.

totalité *f* totality.

touche *f* touch.

toucher *vt* to touch.

touffe *f* tuft, clump.

toujours *adv* always; still.

tour *f* tower:—*m* turn, round; circuit; tour; trick:— **~ à ~** by turns.

tourbillon *m* whirlwind.

tourbillonner *vi* to whirl, eddy.

tourisme *m* tourism.

touriste *mf* tourist.

touristique *adj* tourist.

tourment *m* torment, agony.

tourmenter *vt* to torment.

tournant *m* bend; turning point:—*adj* revolving.

tournée *f* tour; round.

tourner *vi* to turn:—**se ~** *vr* to turn round.

tournesol *m* sunflower.

tournevis *m* screwdriver.

tournoi *m* tournament.

tournure *f* turn; turn of phrase.

tousser *vi* to cough.

tout *adj* (*pl* **tous**, **toutes**) all; whole; every:—**~ le monde** everybody:— *pn* everything; all:—*m* whole:—*adv* entirely, quite.

toutefois *adv* however.

toux *f* cough.

toxicomane *mf* drug addict.

toxique *adj* toxic.

trac *m* nerves, stage fright.

tracasser *vt* to worry; to harass.

trace *f* track; outline, trace.

tracer *vt* to trace.

tract *m* leaflet, tract.

tractation *f* transaction.

tracteur *m* tractor.

tradition *f* tradition.

traditionnel *adj* traditional; usual.

traducteur *m*, **-trice** *f* translator.

traduction *f* translation.

traduire *vt* to translate.

trafic *m* traffic; trading.

trafiquer *vi* to traffic, trade.

tragédie *f* tragedy.

tragique *adj* tragic.

trahir *vt* to betray.

trahison *f* betrayal, treason.

train *m* train; pace, rate.

traîneau *m* sleigh, sledge.

traînée *f* trail, track; drag.

traîner *vi* to drag on, lag.

traire *vt* to milk.

trait *m* trait, feature; relation.

traite *f* trade; draft, bill; milking.

traité *m* treaty; treatise, tract.

traitement *m* treatment; salary.

traiter *vt* to treat; to process.

traiteur *m* caterer.

traître *m* traitor.

traîtrise *f* treachery.

trajet *m* distance; course.

tramer *vt* to plot; to weave.

trampoline *m* trampoline.

tranche *f* slice; edge; section.

trancher *vt* to cut, sever.

tranquille *adj* quiet, tranquil.

tranquilliser *vt* to reassure.

tranquillité *f* tranquillity.

transaction *f* transaction.

transatlantique *adj* transatlantic.

transcription *f* transcription.

transcrire *vt* to transcribe.

transe *f* trance.

tranférer *vt* to transfer.

transfert *m* transfer.

transformateur *m* transformer.

transformation *f* transformation.

transformer *vt* to transform.

transfusion *f* transfusion.

transgresser *vt* to transgress.

transgression *f* transgression.

transistor *m* transistor.

transiter *vi* to pass in transit.

transition *f* transition.

transitoire *adj* transitory.
transmettre *vt* to transmit.
transmissible *adj* transmissible.
transmission *f* transmission.
transparence *f* transparency.
transparent *adj* transparent.
transpercer *vt* to pierce.
transplanter *vt* to transplant.
transport *m* carrying; transport.
transporter *vt* to transport
transporteur *m* haulier; carrier.
transposer *vt* to transpose.
transversal *adj* transverse.
trapèze *m* trapeze.
trapéziste *mf* trapeze artist.
trappe *f* trap door.
trappeur *m* trapper.
traquer *vt* to track; to hunt down.
traumatiser *vt* to traumatise.
travail *m pl* **travaux** work, labour.
travailler *vi* to work.
travailleur *m*, **-euse** *f* worker:—*adj* diligent; hard-working.
travers *m* breadth:—**à ~** through, across.
traversée *f* crossing; traverse.
traverser *vt* to cross, traverse.
trébucher *vi* to stumble.
trèfle *m* clover.
treillis *m* trellis; wire mesh.
treize *adj*, *m* thirteen.
treizième *adj*, *mf* thirteenth.
tremblement *m* trembling **~ de terre** earthquake.
trembler *vi* to tremble, shake.
trémousser (se) *vr* to wriggle.
tremper *vt* to soak.
tremplin *m* springboard.
trentaine *f* about thirty.
trente *adj*, *m* thirty.
trentième *adj mf* thirtieth.

trépidant *adj* pulsating, quivering.
trépigner *vi* to stamp one's feet.
très *adv* very; most; very much.
trésor *m* treasure.
trésorier *m*, **-ière** *f* treasurer.
tressaillir *vi* to thrill; to shudder.
tresse *f* plait, braid.
tresser *vt* to plait, braid.
trêve *f* truce; respite.
tri *m* sorting out; grading.
triangle *m* triangle.
triangulaire *adj* triangular.
tribal *adj* tribal.
tribu *f* tribe.
tribunal *m* court, tribunal.
tribune *f* gallery; rostrum.
tribut *m* tribute.
tricher *vi* to cheat.
tricheur *m*, **-euse** *f* cheater.
tricolore *adj* three-coloured, tricolour.
tricoter *vt* to knit.
tridimensionnel *adj* three-dimensional.
trier *vt* to sort out.
trilingue *adj* trilingual.
trimestre *m* quarter; term.
trimestriel *adj* quarterly; three-monthly.
trinquer *vi* to toast; to booze.
trio *m* trio.
triomphal *adj* triumphal.
triomphe *m* triumph, victory.
triompher *vi* to triumph.
triple *adj* triple, treble.
tripler *vi* to triple.
triste *adj* sad, melancholy.
tristesse *f* sadness.
trivial *adj* trivial; crude.
trivialité *f* triviality; crudeness.
troc *m* exchange; barter.
trois *adj*, *m* three.
troisième *adj*, *mf* third.

trombe *f*: — ~ **d'eau** cloudburst.
trompe *f* trumpet; trunk.
tromper *vt* to deceive, trick: — **se** ~ *vr* to be mistaken.
tromperie *f* deception, deceit.
trompette *f* trumpet.
trompeur *adj* deceitful; deceptive.
tronc *m* trunk, shaft.
trône *m* throne.
tronquer *vt* to truncate, curtail.
trop *adv* too; too much: — *m* ~ excess.
trophée *m* trophy.
tropical *adj* tropical.
tropique *m* tropic.
troquer *vt* to barter, swap.
trotter *vi* to trot; to toddle.
trottinette *f* scooter.
trottoir *m* pavement.
trou *m* hole; gap; cavity.
troublant *adj* disturbing.
trouble *adj* unclear, murky: — *m* trouble, disturbance.
troubler *vt* to trouble, disturb.
trouer *vt* to make a hole in.
troupe *f* troupe; troop.
troupeau *m* herd, drove.
trousse *f* case, kit; wallet.
trouver *vt* to find.

truc *m* (*fam*) trick; gadget.
truite *f* trout.
truquage *m* rigging, fiddling.
truquer *vt* to rig, fiddle.
tu *pn* you.
tube *m* tube, pipe; duct.
tuer *vt* to kill.
tuerie *f* slaughter.
tueur *m*, **-euse** *f* killer.
tuile *f* tile.
tulipe *f* tulip.
tumeur *f* tumour.
tumulte *m* tumult, commotion.
tumultueux *adj* tumultuous.
tunnel *m* tunnel.
turbine *f* turbine.
turbulence *f* turbulence.
turbulent *adj* turbulent.
tutelle *f* guardianship.
tuteur *m*, **tutrice** *f* guardian: — *m* stake, prop.
tutoyer *vt* to address someone as *tu*.
tuyau *m* pipe.
type *m* type; model; bloke, chap.
typhon *m* typhoon.
typique *adj* typical.
tyran *m* tyrant.
tyrannique *adj* tyrannical.

U

ulcère *m* ulcer.
ultérieur *adj* subsequent: — ~**ement** *adv* later.
ultimatum *m* ultimatum.
ultime *adj* ultimate, final.
un, une *art* a, an; one — **l'**~ **l'autre, les** ~**s les autres** one another.

unanime *adj* unanimous.
unification *f* unification.
unifier *vt* to unify.
uniforme *adj* uniform.
uniformité *f* uniformity; regularity.
unilatéral *adj* unilateral.
union *f* union.

unique *adj* only, single; unique:— ~**ment** *adv* only, solely, exclusively.

unir *vt* to unite.

unisson *m* unison.

unité *f* unity; unit.

univers *m* universe; world.

universel *adj* universal.

universitaire *adj* university:— *mf* academic.

université *f* university.

urbain *adj* urban, city.

urbanisme *m* town planning.

urgence *f* urgency.

urgent *adj* urgent.

urne *f* ballot box; urn.

usage *m* use; custom.

usager *m* **ère** *f* user.

usé *adj* worn; banal, trite.

user *vt* to use.

usine *f* factory.

ustensile *m* implement; utensil.

usuel *adj* ordinary; everyday:— ~**lement** *adv* ordinarily.

usurper *vt* to usurp.

utérus *m* womb, uterus.

utile *adj* useful.

utilisateur *m*, **-trice** *f* user.

utiliser *vt* to use, utilise.

utilité *f* usefulness; use; profit.

utopie *f* utopia.

utopique *adj* utopian.

V

vacance *f* vacancy:— ~**s** holiday, vacation.

vacancier *m*, **-ière** *f* holidaymaker.

vacant *adj* vacant.

vacarme *m* racket, row.

vaccin *m* vaccine.

vache *f* cow.

vagabond *m*, **-e** *f* tramp, vagabond.

vagin *f* vagina.

vague *adj* vague:— *m* vagueness:— *f* wave.

vaguer *vi* to wander, roam.

vaillant *adj* brave, courageous.

vain *adj* vain; shallow.

vaincre *vt* to defeat, overcome.

vainqueur *m* conqueror, victor.

vaisseau *m* vessel; ship.

vaisselle *f* crockery; dishes.

valable *adj* valid; worthwhile.

valeur *f* value, worth; security.

valider *vt* to validate.

valise *f* suitcase.

vallée *f* valley.

valoir *vt* to be worth.

valser *vi* to waltz.

vandale *mf* vandal.

vanité *f* vanity, conceit.

vaniteux *adj* vain, conceited.

vantard *adj* boastful, bragging.

vanter *vt* to praise, vaunt:— **se** ~ *vr* to boast.

vapeur *f* haze, vapour.

vaporiser *vt* to spray.

variable *adj* variable, changeable.

variation *f* variation, change.

varié *adj* varied; variegated.

varier *vi* to vary.

variété *f* variety, diversity.

vaste *adj* vast, huge.

vaurien(ne) *m(f)* good-for-nothing.

vautrer (se) *vr* to wallow in.
veau *m* calf; veal.
vedette *f* star; leading light.
végétal *adj* vegetable.
végétarien(ne) *m(f)* vegetarian:—*adj*
vegetarian.
végétatif *adj* vegetative.
véhémence *f* vehemence.
véhément *adj* vehement.
véhicule *m* vehicle.
veille *f* wakefulness; watch; eve.
veiller *vi* to stay up, sit up.
veine *f* vein; inspiration; luck.
vélo *m* cycle.
vélodrome *m* velodrome.
velours *m* velvet.
vendange *f* wine harvest; vintage.
vendangeur *m*, **-euse** *f* grape-picker.
vendeur *m*, **-euse** *f* seller, salesperson.
vendre *vt* to sell.
vendredi *m* Friday.
vénéneux *adj* poisonous.
vénérable *adj* venerable.
vénérer *vt* to venerate.
vengeance *f* vengeance.
venger *vt* to avenge.
venin *m* venom.
venir *vi* to come.
vent *m* wind; breath; vanity.
vente *f* sale; selling.
ventre *m* stomach, belly; womb.
ventriloque *mf* ventriloquist.
venue *f* coming.
ver *m* worm; grub.
véracité *f* veracity; truthfulness.
verbal *adj* verbal.
verbe *m* verb; word.
verdict *m* verdict.
verdure *f* greenery, verdure.
verge *f* stick, cane.
verger *m* orchard.

vérification *f* check; verification.
vérifier *vt* to verify; to audit.
véritable *adj* real, genuine.
vérité *f* truth; truthfulness.
vermine *f* vermin.
verni *adj* varnished.
vernis *m* varnish; glaze.
verre *m* glass; lens; drink.
verrou *m* bolt.
verrouiller *vt* to bolt; to lock.
vers *prép* towards; around:—*m* line,
verse.
versatile *adj* versatile.
verser *vt* to pour.
version *f* version.
vert *m* green:—*adj* green.
vertèbre *f* vertebra.
vertical *adj* vertical.
vertu *f* virtue.
vertueux *adj* virtuous.
verve *f* verve, vigour.
veste *f* jacket.
vestiaire *m* cloakroom.
vestibule *m* hall, vestibule.
veston *m* jacket.
vêtement *m* garment.
vêtir (se) *vr* to dress oneself.
veto *m* veto.
veuf *m* widower:—*adj* widowed.
veuve *f* widow:—*adj* widowed.
vexer *vt* to annoy; to hurt.
viable *adj* viable.
viande *f* meat.
vice *m* vice; fault, defect.
victime *f* victim, casualty.
victoire *f* victory.
victorieux *adj* victorious.
vide *adj* empty, vacant:—*m* vacuum.
vidéo *f* video:—*adj invar* video.
vidéocassette *f* videocassette.
vider *vt* to empty.

vie f life: — **être en ~** to be alive.

vieillard m old man.

vieillesse f old age.

vieillir vi to get old.

vierge f virgin: — adj virgin; blank; un-exposed.

vieux adj, f **vieille** old; obsolete.

vif adj lively; quick; eager.

vigilant adj vigilant.

vigne f vine; vineyard.

vigneron m, **-onne** f wine grower.

vignoble m vineyard.

vigoureux adj vigorous.

vigueur f vigour, strength.

vil adj vile; lowly.

villa f villa, detached house.

village m village.

villageois m, **-e** f village, rustic.

ville f town, city.

vin m wine.

vinaigre m vinegar.

vindicatif adj vindictive.

vingt adj, m twenty.

vingtaine f about twenty.

vingtième adj, mf twentieth.

vinicole adj wine, wine-growing.

viol m rape.

violation f violation.

violence f violence; force.

violent adj violent.

violer vt to violate; to rape.

violet adj violet: — m violet.

violeur m rapist.

violon m violin.

violoniste mf violinist.

vipère f viper, adder.

virage m turn, bend.

virer vt to transfer: — vi to turn.

virginité f virginity; purity.

viril adj virile; male, masculine.

virilité f virility; masculinity.

virtuel adj virtual.

virulence f virulence.

virulent adj virulent.

virus m virus.

vis f screw.

visa m stamp, visa.

visage m face; expression.

vis-à-vis prép opposite: — m encoun-ter: — **en ~** opposite each other.

viser vt to aim, target; to visa.

viseur m sights; viewfinder.

visibilité f visibility.

visible adj visible; evident.

vision f eyesight; vision.

visionnaire mf visionary: — adj vision-ary.

visite f visit; inspection; visitor.

visiter vt to visit.

visiteur m, **-euse** f visitor.

visqueux adj viscous, thick.

visser vt to screw on.

visuel adj visual.

vital adj vital.

vitalité f energy, vitality.

vitamine f vitamin.

vite adv quickly, fast.

vitesse f speed, swiftness; gear.

viticulteur m wine grower.

vitrail m stained-glass window.

vitre f pane, window.

vitreux adj glassy, vitreous.

vitrier m glazier.

vitrine f shop window.

vitupérer vi to vituperate.

vivace adj hardy, perennial.

vivacité f vivacity, liveliness.

vivant adj alive, living; lively.

vivement adv quickly; keenly.

vivifiant adj refreshing.

vivifier vt to enliven.

vivre vi to live.

vivres *mpl* victuals, supplies.

vocabulaire *m* vocabulary.

vocal *adj* vocal.

vocation *f* vocation, calling.

vœu *m* vow; wish.

vogue *f* fashion:—**en ~** in fashion.

voici *prép* here is, here are; ago, past.

voie *f* way, road; means:—**~ ferrée** railway.

voilà *prép* there is, there are; ago.

voile *f* sail:—*m* veil.

voiler *vt* to veil.

voir *vt* to see:—**avoir à ~ avec** to have to do with.

voisin *m*, **-e** *f* neighbour:—*adj* neighbouring.

voisinage *m* neighbourhood.

voiture *f* car; carriage; cart.

voix *f* voice; vote.

vol *m* flight:—**à ~ d'oiseau** as the crow flies.

volant *m* steering wheel:—*adj* flying.

volatile *adj* volatile.

volcan *m* volcano.

volcanique *adj* volcanic.

volée *f* flight; volley.

voler *vi* to fly:—*vt* to steal; to rob.

volet *m* shutter; flap, paddle.

voleur *m*, **-euse** *f* thief.

volontaire *adj* voluntary.

volonté *f* will; willpower.

volontiers *adv* willingly.

volubile *adj* voluble.

volume *m* volume.

volumineux *adj* voluminous.

volupté *f* voluptuousness.

voluptueux *adj* voluptuous.

vomir *vi* to vomit.

vorace *adj* voracious.

voracité *f* voracity.

vos = *pl* **votre**.

votant *m*, **-e** *f* voter.

vote *m* vote; voting.

voter *vi* to vote.

votre *adj*, *pl* **vos** your, your own.

vôtre *poss pn*:—**le/la ~**, **les ~s** yours.

vouer *vt* to vow.

vouloir *vt* to want, wish.

voulu *adj* required; deliberate.

vous *pn* you, yourself.

voûte *f* vault.

vouvoyer *vt* to address someone as *vous*.

voyage *m* journey, trip; travelling.

voyager *vi* to travel, journey.

voyageur *m*, **-euse** *f* traveller, passenger.

voyelle *f* vowel.

vrac *adv*:—**en ~** in bulk.

vrai *adj* true, genuine.

vraisemblable *adj* likely, probable.

vrille *f* tendril; spiral.

vu *adj* seen:—*prép* in view of.

vue *f* sight, eyesight.

vulgaire *adj* vulgar.

vulgarité *f* vulgarity, coarseness.

vulnérable *adj* vulnerable.

W X Y Z

wagon *m* wagon, truck.
wagon-restaurant *m* restaurant car.
W.-C. (water-closet) *mpl* lavatory.
week-end *m* weekend.
whisky *m* whisky.

xénophobe *mf* xenophobe:—*adj* xenophobic.
xénophobie *f* xenophobia.
xylophone *m* xylophone.

yacht *m* yacht.
yaourt *m* yoghurt.
yeux = *pl* œil.
yoga *m* yoga
yoghurt *m* = **yaourt**.
yogi *m* yogi.
yucca *m* yucca.

zèle *m* zeal.
zélé *adj* zealous.
zénith *m* zenith.
zéro *m* zero, nought, nothing.
zézayer *vi* to lisp.
zigzag *m* zigzag.
zigzaguer *vi* to zigzag.
zodiaque *m* zodiac.
zone *f* zone, area.
zoo *m* zoo.
zoologie *f* zoology.
zoologiste *mf* zoologist.
zut *interj* damn!, rubbish!

English–French Dictionary

A

a *art* un, une.

abacus *n* abaque, boulier *m*.

abandon *vt* abandonner, laisser.

abash *vt* couvrir de honte.

abate *vt* baisser:— *vi* baisser; se calmer.

abbey *n* abbaye *f*.

abbreviate *vt* abréger.

abbreviation *n* abréviation *f*.

abdicate *vt* abdiquer; renoncer à.

abdomen *n* abdomen *m*.

abduct *vt* kidnapper, enlever.

abeyance *n* suspension *f*.

abhor *vt* abhorrer, exécrer.

abhorrent *adj* exécrable.

abide *vt* supporter, souffrir.

ability *n* capacité, aptitude *f*.

abject *adj* misérable; abject.

able *adj* capable:— **to be ~** pouvoir.

abnegation *n* renoncement *m*.

abnormal *adj* anormal.

abnormality *n* anomalie *f*.

aboard *adv* à bord.

abode *n* domicile *m*.

abolish *vt* abolir, supprimer.

abolition *n* abolition *f*.

abominable *adj* abominable.

aboriginal *adj* aborigène.

abort *vi* avorter.

abortion *n* avortement *m*.

abound *vi* abonder.

about *prep* au sujet de; vers:— *adv* çà et là:— **to be ~ to** être sur le point de.

above *prep* au-dessus de:— *adv* au-dessus:— **~ all** surtout, principalement.

abrasion *n* écorchure *f*.

abrasive *adj* abrasif.

abroad *adv* à l'étranger.

abrupt *adj* abrupt; brusque.

abscess *n* abcès *m*.

absence *n* absence *f*.

absent *adj* absent:— *vi* s'absenter.

absent-minded *adj* distrait.

absolute *adj* absolu.

absolve *vt* absoudre.

absorb *vt* absorber.

absorption *n* absorption *f*.

abstain *vi* s'abstenir.

abstinence *n* abstinence *f*.

abstinent *adj* abstinent.

abstract *adj* abstrait:— *n* abrégé *m*.

abstraction *n* abstraction *f*.

absurd *adj* absurde.

absurdity *n* absurdité *f*.

abundance *n* abondance *f*.

abundant *adj* abondant.

abuse *vt* abuser de:— *n* abus *m*.

abyss *n* abîme *m*.

academic *adj* universitaire; scolaire; théorique.

academy *n* académie *f*.

accelerate *vt* accélérer.

acceleration *n* accélération *f*.

accelerator *n* accélérateur *m*.

accent *n* accent *m*:—*vt* accentuer.

accept *vt* accepter.

acceptable *adj* acceptable.

acceptance *n* acceptation *f*.

access *n* accès *m*.

accessible *adj* accessible.

accident *n* accident *m*.

accidental *adj* accidentel.

acclaim *vt* acclamer.

accommodate *vt* loger; accommoder.

accommodation *n* logement *m*.

accompany *vt* accompagner.

accomplice *n* complice *mf*.

accomplish *vt* accomplir.

accomplishment *n* accomplissement *m*.

accord *n* accord *m*:—**of one's own ~** de son propre chef.

accordance *n*:—**in ~ with** conformément à.

according *prep* selon:—**~ as** selon que: —**~ly** *adv* en conséquence.

accost *vt* accoster.

account *n* compte *m*:—**on no ~** en aucun cas:—**on ~ of** en raison de:—*vt* **to ~ for** expliquer.

accountability *n* responsabilité *f*.

accountancy *n* comptabilité *f*.

accountant *n* comptable *mf*.

accumulate *vt* accumuler:—*vi* s'accumuler.

accumulation *n* accumulation *f*.

accuracy *n* exactitude *f*.

accurate *adj* exact.

accusation *n* accusation *f*.

accuse *vt* accuser.

accused *n* accusé(e) *m(f)*.

accustom *vt* accoutumer.

ace *n* as *m*.

ache *n* douleur *f*:—*vi* faire mal.

achieve *vt* réaliser; obtenir.

achievement *n* réalisation *f*.

acid *adj* acide:—*n* acide *m*.

acknowledge *vt* reconnaître.

acknowledgment *n* reconnaissance *f*.

acoustics *n* acoustique *f*.

acquaint *vt* informer, aviser.

acquaintance *n* connaissance *f*.

acquiesce *vi* acquiescer, consentir.

acquiescent *adj* consentant.

acquire *vt* acquérir.

acquisition *n* acquisition *f*.

acquit *vt* acquitter.

acrimonious *adj* acrimonieux.

across *adv* en travers:—*prep* à travers.

act *vt* jouer:—*vi* agir; jouer la comédie:—*n* acte *m*.

action *n* action *f*.

activate *vt* activer.

active *adj* actif.

activity *n* activité *f*.

actor *n* acteur *m*.

actress *n* actrice *f*.

actual *adj* réel; concret.

acute *adj* aigu; perspicace

ad lib *vt* improviser.

ad nauseam *adv* à satiété.

adamant *adj* inflexible.

adapt *vt* adapter, ajuster.

adaptable *adj* adaptable.

adaptation *n* adaptation *f*.

add *vt* ajouter.

addict *n* intoxiqué *m*, -e *f*.

addiction *n* dépendance *f*.

addition *n* addition *f*.

additional *adj* additionnel.

address *vt* adresser.

adept *adj* adroit.

adequate *adj* adéquat; suffisant.

adhere *vi* adhérer.

adhesion *n* adhésion *f*.

adhesive *adj* adhésif.

adjacent *adj* adjacent, contigu.

adjective *n* adjectif *m*.

adjoin *vi* être contigu.

adjourn *vt* reporter, remettre.

adjournment *n* ajournement *m*.

adjust *vt* ajuster, adapter.

adjustable *adj* ajustable.

adjustment *n* ajustement *m*; réglage *m*.

administer *vt* administrer.

administration *n* administration *f*.

administrative *adj* administratif.

admirable *adj* admirable.

admiral *n* amiral *m*.

admiration *n* admiration *f*.

admire *vt* admirer.

admirer *n* admirateur *m*, -trice *f*.

admission *n* admission, entrée *f*.

admit *vt* admettre: —**to ~ to** reconnaître.

admonish *vt* admonester.

admonition *n* admonestation.

adolescence *n* adolescence *f*.

adopt *vt* adopter.

adoption *n* adoption *f*.

adoptive *adj* adoptif.

adorable *adj* adorable.

adore *vt* adorer.

adorn *vt* orner.

adrift *adv* à la dérive.

adroit *adj* adroit, habile.

adulation *n* adulation *f*.

adult *adj* adulte: —*n* adulte *mf*.

adultery *n* adultère *m*.

advance *vt* avancer: —*vi* avancer: —*n* avance *f*.

advantage *n* avantage *m*: —**to take ~ of** profiter de.

advantageous *adj* avantageux.

a.m. *adv* du matin.

adventure *n* aventure *f*.

adventurous *adj* aventureux.

adversary *n* adversaire *mf*.

adverse *adj* défavorable.

adversity *n* adversité *f*.

advertise *vt* faire de la publicité pour.

advertisement *n* publicité *f*; annonce *f*.

advice *n* conseil *m*; avis *m*.

advise *vt* conseiller; aviser.

advisory *adj* consultatif.

advocacy *n* plaidoyer *m*.

advocate *n* avocat *m*: —*vt* plaider pour.

aerial *n* antenne *f*.

aerobics *npl* aérobic *m*.

aeroplane *n* avion *m*.

aeroplane *n* avion *m*.

aerosol *n* aérosol *m*.

affability *n* affabilité *f*.

affable *adj* affable.

affair *n* affaire *f*.

affect *vt* toucher; affecter.

affection *n* affection *f*.

affectionate *adj* affectueux.

affiliate *vt* affilier.

affinity *n* affinité *f*.

affirm *vt* affirmer, déclarer.

affirmative *adj* affirmatif.

afflict *vt* affliger.

affluent *adj* riche; abondant.

afford *vt* fournir: —**to be able to ~** avoir les moyens d'acheter.

affront *n* affront *m*, injure *f*: —*vt* affronter; insulter.

afloat *adv* à flot.

afraid *adj* apeuré: —**I am ~** j'ai peur.

after *prep* après: —*adv* après: —**~ all** après tout.

afterbirth *n* placenta *m*.

aftermath *n* conséquences *fpl*.

afternoon *n* après-midi *mf*.

afterward(s) *adv* ensuite.

again *adv* à nouveau.

against *prep* contre.

age *n* âge *m*:—*vt* vieillir.

agency *n* agence *f*.

agenda *n* ordre du jour *m*.

agent *n* agent *m*.

aggravate *vt* aggraver; énerver.

aggravation *n* aggravation *f*.

aggression *n* agression *f*.

aggressive *adj* agressif.

aggressor *n* agresseur *m*.

agile *adj* agile; adroit.

agility *n* agilité *f*; adresse *f*.

agitate *vt* agiter.

agitation *n* agitation *f*.

ago *adv*:—**how long ~?** il y a combien de temps?

agony *n* agonie *f*.

agree *vt* convenir:—*vi* être d'accord.

agreeable *adj* agréable.

agreed *adj* convenu:—**~!** *adv* d'accord!

agreement *n* accord *m*.

agricultural *adj* agricole.

agriculture *n* agriculture *f*.

ahead *adv* en avant.

aid *vt* aider, secourir:—*n* aide *f*.

AIDS *n* SIDA *m*.

ailment *n* maladie *f*.

aim *vt* pointer; viser.

air *n* air *m*.

air terminal *n* aérogare *f*.

air-conditioned *adj* climatisé.

air-conditioning *n* climatisation *f*.

aircraft *n* avion *m*.

airiness *n* aération, ventilation *f*.

airlift *n* pont aérien *m*.

airline *n* ligne aérienne *f*.

airmail *n*:—**by ~** par avion.

airport *n* aéroport *m*.

airsick *adj*:—**to be ~** avoir le mal de l'air.

airtight *adj* hermétique.

aisle *n* nef d'église *f*.

ajar *adj* entrouvert.

akin *adj* ressemblant.

alarm bell *n* sonnette d'alarme *f*.

alarm *n* alarme *f*:—*vt* alarmer; inquiéter.

alarmist *n* alarmiste *mf*.

albeit *conj* bien que.

album *n* album *m*.

alcohol *n* alcool *m*.

alcoholic *adj* alcoolisé:—*n* alcoolique *mf*.

ale *n* bière *f*.

alert *adj* vigilant:—*n* alerte *f*.

alertness *n* vigilance *f*.

alien *adj* étranger:—*n* étranger *m*, -ère *f*; extra-terrestre *mf*.

alienate *vt* aliéner.

alight *vi* mettre pied à terre:—*adj* en feu.

alike *adj* semblable, égal:—*adv* de la même façon.

alimentation *n* alimentation *f*.

alive *adj* en vie, vivant; actif.

all *adj* tout:—*adv* totalement:—**~ the same** cependant:—**~ the better** tant mieux:—**not at ~!** pas du tout!:—*n* tout *m*.

allege *vt* alléguer.

allegiance *n* loyauté, fidélité *f*.

allergy *n* allergie *f*.

alley *n* ruelle *f*.

alliance *n* alliance *f*.

allocate *vt* allouer.

allocation *n* allocation *f*.

allot *vt* assigner.

allow *vt* permettre; accorder.

allowance *n* allocation *f*; concession *f*.

allude *vi* faire allusion à.

allure *n* charme, attrait *m*.

allusion *n* allusion *f*.

allusive *adj* allusif.

ally n allié m, -e f: — vt allier.

almost adv presque.

alone adj seul: — adv seul.

along adv le long (de): — ~side à côté.

aloud adj à voix haute.

alphabet n alphabet m.

alphabetical adj alphabétique.

already adv déjà.

also adv aussi.

altar n autel m.

alter vt modifier.

alteration n modification f.

alternate adj alterné: — vt alterner.

alternation n alternance f.

alternative n alternative f: — adj alternatif: — ~ly adv sinon.

although conj bien que, malgré.

altitude n altitude f.

always adv toujours.

amalgamate vt amalgamer; vi s'amalgamer.

amalgamation n amalgamation f.

amass vt accumuler, amasser.

amateur n amateur m.

amaze vt stupéfier.

amazement n stupéfaction f.

ambassador n ambassadeur m.

ambidextrous adj ambidextre.

ambiguity n ambiguïté f.

ambiguous adj ambigu.

ambition n ambition f.

ambitious adj ambitieux.

ambulance n ambulance f.

ambush n embuscade f: — vt tendre une embuscade à.

ameliorate vt améliorer.

amelioration n amélioration f.

amend vt modifier; amender.

amendment n amendement m.

amenities npl commodités fpl.

America n Amérique f.

American adj américain.

amiability n amabilité f.

amiable adj aimable.

amicable adj amical.

amid(st) prep entre, parmi.

ammunition n munitions fpl.

amnesia n amnésie f.

amnesty n amnistie f.

among(st) prep entre, parmi.

amorous adj amoureux.

amount n montant m: — vi se monter.

amphibian n amphibie m.

amplify vt amplifier.

amplitude n amplitude f.

amputate vt amputer.

amputation n amputation f.

amuse vt distraire, divertir.

amusement n distraction f.

amusing adj divertissant.

an art un, une.

anachronism n anachronisme m.

anaemic adj (med) anémique.

anaesthetic n anesthésique m.

analogy n analogie f.

analyse vt analyser.

analysis n analyse f.

analytical adj analytique.

anarchic adj anarchique.

anarchy n anarchie f.

anatomical adj anatomique.

anatomy n anatomie f.

ancestor n ancêtre mf.

anchor n ancre f.

ancient adj ancien, antique

and conj et.

anecdote n anecdote f.

angel n ange m.

anger n colère f: — vt irriter.

angle n angle m: — vi pêcher à la ligne.

angler n pêcheur à la ligne m.

angry adj en colère, irrité.

anguish n angoisse f.
angular adj angulaire.
animal n adj animal m.
animate vt animer:—adj vivant.
animation n animation f.
animosity n animosité f.
ankle n cheville f.
annex vt annexer:—n annexe f.
annihilate vt annihiler, anéantir.
anniversary n anniversaire m.
annotate vt annoter.
annotation n annotation f.
announce vt annoncer.
announcement n annonce f.
annoy vt ennuyer.
annoyance n ennui m.
annual adj annuel
annul vt annuler.
anomaly n anomalie.
anonymity n anonymat m.
anonymous adj anonyme.
another adj un autre:—one ～ l'un l'autre.
answer vt répondre à:—n réponse f.
ant n fourmi f.
antagonise vt provoquer.
antagonism n antagonisme m.
antarctic adj antarctique.
antenna n antenne f.
anterior adj antérieur.
anthem n hymne m.
anthology n anthologie f.
anthropology n anthropologie f.
antibiotic n antibiotique m.
anticipate vt prévoir.
anticipation n attente f.
antidote n antidote m.
antipathy n antipathie f.
antiquarian n antiquaire mf.
antique n antiquité f.
antiquity n antiquité f.

antithesis n antithèse f.
antler n corne f.
anxiety n anxiété f; désir m.
anxious adj anxieux.
any adj pn n'importe quel, n'importe quelle; un, une; tout:—～body quelqu'un; n'importe qui; personne: —～thing quelque chose; n'importe quoi; rien.
apart adv séparément.
apartment n appartement m.
apathetic adj apathique.
apathy n apathie f.
aperture n ouverture f.
apex n sommet m; apex m.
apologise vt excuser.
apology n apologie, défense f.
apostle n apôtre m.
appall vt horrifier, atterrer.
apparatus n appareil m.
apparent adj évident, apparent.
apparition n apparition, vision f.
appeal vi faire appel:—n (law) appel m.
appear vi paraître.
appearance n apparence f.
appellant n (law) appelant m.
append vt annexer.
appetising adj appétissant.
appetite n appétit m.
applaud vt vi applaudir.
applause n applaudissements mpl.
apple n pomme f.
apple tree n pommier m.
appliance n appareil m.
applicable adj applicable.
applicant n candidat m, -e f.
application n application f.
apply vt appliquer:—vi s'adresser.
appoint vt nommer.
appointment n rendez-vous m; nomination f.

apportion vt répartir.

apposite adj adapté.

appraisal n estimation f.

appraise vt évaluer.

appreciate vt apprécier.

appreciation n appréciation f.

appreciative adj reconnaissant.

apprehend vt appréhender.

apprehension n appréhension f.

apprentice n apprenti m.

approach vi approcher (s'): — n approche f.

appropriate adj approprié, adéquat.

approval n approbation f.

approve (of) vt approuver.

approximate adj approximatif.

approximation n approximation f.

April n avril m.

apron n tablier m.

apt adj idéal.

aqualung n scaphandre autonome m.

aquarium n aquarium m.

aquatic adj aquatique.

arable adj arable.

arbiter n arbitre m.

arbitrary adj arbitraire.

arbitrate vt arbitrer.

arbitration n arbitrage m.

arcade n galerie f.

arch n arc m.

archbishopric n archevêché m.

archeological adj archéologique.

archeology n archéologie f.

architect n architecte mf.

architecture n architecture f.

archives npl archives fpl.

arctic adj arctique.

ardent adj ardent.

ardour n ardeur f.

area n région f; domaine m.

argue vi se disputer.

argument n argument m; dispute f.

argumentative adj raisonneur.

arid adj aride.

aridity n aridité f.

arise vi se lever; survenir.

aristocracy n aristocratie f.

aristocrat n aristocrate mf.

arithmetic n arithmétique f.

arm n bras m; arme f: — vt armer: — vi (s')armer.

armament n armement m.

armchair n fauteuil m.

armful n brassée f.

armistice n armistice m.

armour n armure f.

armpit n aisselle f.

army n armée f.

aroma n arôme m.

aromatic adj aromatique.

around prep autour de: — adv autour.

arouse vt éveiller; exciter.

arrange vt arranger, organiser.

arrangement n arrangement m.

array n série f.

arrest n arrestation f: — vt arrêter.

arrival n arrivée f.

arrive vi arriver.

arrogance n arrogance f.

arrogant adj arrogant.

arrow n flèche f.

arsenal n (mil) arsenal m.

art gallery n musée d'art m.

art n art m.

artery n artère f.

artful adj malin, astucieux.

article n article m.

articulate vt articuler.

articulation n articulation f.

artificial adj artificiel.

artillery n artillerie f.

artisan n artisan m.

artist n artiste mf.

artistry n habileté f.

as conj comme; pendant que; aussi: — ~ for, ~ to quant à.

ascend vi monter.

ascension n ascension f.

ascent n montée f.

ascertain vt établir.

ascetic adj ascétique: — n ascète mf.

ash n (bot) frêne m; cendre f.

ashamed adj honteux.

ashore adv à terre: — to go ~ débarquer.

ashtray n cendrier m.

aside adv de côté.

ask vt demander.

asleep adj endormi: — to fall ~ s'endormir.

aspect n aspect m.

aspersion n calomnie f.

asphyxiate vt asphyxier.

asphyxiation n asphyxie f.

aspirant n aspirant m, -e f.

aspiration n aspiration f.

aspire vi aspirer, désirer.

aspirin n aspirine f.

assail vt assaillir, attaquer.

assailant n assaillant.

assassin n assassin m.

assassinate vt assassiner.

assault n assaut m: — vt agresser.

assemble vt assembler: — vi s'assembler.

assembly n assemblée f.

assent n assentiment m: — vi donner son assentiment.

assert vt soutenir; affirmer.

assertion n assertion f.

assess vt évaluer.

assessment n évaluation f.

assets npl biens mpl.

assign vt assigner.

assignment n allocation f.

assimilate vt assimiler.

assist vt assister, aider.

assistance n assistance, aide f.

assistant n aide mf.

associate vt associer: — adj associé: — n associé m, -e f.

association n association f.

assortment n assortiment m.

assume vt assumer; supposer.

assumption n supposition f.

assurance n assurance f.

assure vt assurer.

asthma n asthme m.

asthmatic adj asthmatique.

astonish vt surprendre.

astonishment n surprise.

astound vt ébahir.

astrologer n astrologue mf.

astrology n astrologie f.

astronomer n astronome mf.

astronomy n astronomie f.

astute adj malin.

asylum n asile, refuge m.

at prep à; en.

atheist n athée mf.

athlete n athlète mf.

athletic adj athlétique.

atlas n atlas m.

atmosphere n atmosphère f.

atom n atome m.

atomic adj atomique.

atrocious adj atroce.

atrocity n atrocité, énormité f.

attach vt joindre.

attachment n attachement m.

attack vt attaquer: — n attaque f.

attacker n attaquant m, -e f.

attain vt atteindre, obtenir.

attempt vt essayer: — n essai m, tentative f.

attend vt servir; assister à.

attendance n service m; assistance f.

attention n attention f; soin m.
attentive adj attentif:—**~ly** adv attentivement.
attic n grenier m.
attitude n attitude f.
attract vt attirer.
attraction n attraction f; attrait m.
attractive adj attrayant.
attribute vt attribuer:—n attribut m.
auction n vente aux enchères f.
audacious adj audacieux.
audacity n audace, témérité f.
audible adj audible.
audience n audience f.
audit n audit m:—vt vérifier.
auditor n auditeur m, -trice f.
augment vt vi augmenter.
August n août m.
aunt n tante f.
auspicious adj favorable, propice.
austere adj austère, sévère.
authentic adj authentique
authenticity n authenticité f.
author n auteur m.
authorisation n autorisation f.
authorise vt autoriser.
authoritarian adj autoritaire.
authority n autorité f.

autograph n autographe m.
automatic adj automatique.
autonomy n autonomie f.
autopsy n autopsie f.
autumn n automne m.
auxiliary adj auxiliaire.
available adj disponible.
avalanche n avalanche f.
avarice n avarice f.
avenge vt venger.
avenue n avenue f.
average n moyenne f, moyen terme m.
aversion n aversion f, dégoût m.
avert vt détourner, écarter.
avoid vt éviter; échapper à.
await vt attendre.
awake vt réveiller:—vi se réveiller:—adj éveillé.
award vt attribuer:—n prix m; décision f.
aware adj conscient; au courant.
awareness n conscience f.
away adv absent; loin.
awe n peur, crainte f.
awful adj horrible, terrible.
awkward adj gauche, maladroit
axe n hache f.
axis n axe m.
axle n axe m.

B

babble vi bavarder, babiller.
babe, baby n bébé m; nourrisson m.
babyhood n petite enfance f.
babyish adj enfantin; puéril.
bachelor n célibataire m.
back n dos m:—adv en arrière, à l'arrière:—vt soutenir.

backbone n colonne vertébrale.
backdate vt antidater.
backer n partisan m, -e f.
background n fond m.
backpack n sac à dos m.
back payment n rappel de salaire m.
backside n derrière m.

backward *adj* rétrograde:—*adv* en arrière.

bacon *n* lard *m*.

bad *adj* mauvais, de mauvaise qualité; méchant:—**~ly** *adv* mal.

badge *n* insigne *m*, badge *m*.

badness *n* mauvaise qualité *f*; méchanceté *f*.

baffle *vt* déconcerter, confondre.

bag *n* sac *m*; valise *f*.

baggage *n* bagages *mpl*; équipement *m*.

bait *vt* appâter:—*n* appât *m*.

bake *vt* faire cuire au four.

bakery *n* boulangerie *f*.

baker *n* boulanger *m*, -ère *f*.

baking *n* cuisson *f*; fournée *f*.

balance *n* balance *f*; équilibre *m*:—*vt* équilibrer.

balcony *n* balcon *m*.

bald *adj* chauve.

baldness *n* calvitie *f*.

ball *n* balle *f*; boule *f*; ballon *m*.

ballad *n* ballade *f*.

ballerina *n* ballerine *f*.

ballet *n* ballet *m*.

balloon *n* aérostat *m*.

ballot *n* scrutin *m*; vote *m*:—*vi* voter au scrutin secret.

balm, balsam *n* baume *m*.

bamboo *n* bambou *m*.

ban *n* interdiction *f*:—*vt* interdire.

banal *adj* banal.

banana *n* banane *f*.

band *n* bande *f*; orchestre *m*.

bandage *n* bande *f*, bandage *m*:—*vt* bander.

bang *n* claquement *m*, détonation *f*:—*vt* frapper violemment; claquer.

bangle *n* bracelet *m*.

banish *vt* bannir.

banishment *n* bannissement *m*.

bank *n* rive *f*; banque *f*; banc *m*.

banker *n* banquier *m*, -ière *f*.

banknote *n* billet de banque *m*.

bankrupt *adj* failli:—*n* failli *m*.

bankruptcy *n* banqueroute, faillite *f*.

banquet *n* banquet *m*.

baptise *vt* baptiser.

baptism *n* baptême *m*.

bar *n* bar *m*; barre *f*; obstacle *m*:—*vt* interdire; exclure.

barbarian *n* barbare *mf*:—*adj* barbare, cruel.

barbarity *n* barbarie, atrocité *f*.

barbecue *n* barbecue *m*.

barber *n* coiffeur (pour hommes) *m*.

bare *adj* nu; pur:—*vt* dénuder, découvrir.

barefoot(ed) *adj* aux pieds nus.

barely *adv* à peine, tout juste.

bareness *n* nudité *f*.

bargain *n* affaire *f*; contrat:—*vi* conclure un marché.

bark *n* écorce *f*; aboiement *m*:—*vi* aboyer.

barn *n* grange *f*; étable *f*.

barometer *n* baromètre *m*.

barracks *npl* caserne *f*.

barrage *n* barrage *m*.

barrel *n* tonneau, fût *m*.

barren *adj* stérile, infertile.

barricade *n* barricade *f*:—*vt* barricader.

barrier *n* barrière *f*; obstacle *m*.

barring *adv* excepté, sauf.

bartender *n* barman *m*.

barter *vi* faire du troc:—*vt* troquer, échanger.

base *n* base *f*; partie inférieure *f*:—*vt* fonder sur:—*adj* vil, abject.

basement *n* sous-sol *m*.

baseness *n* bassesse, vilenie *f*.

bashful *adj* timide, modeste.

basic *adj* fondamental, de base.

basin *n* cuvette *f*; lavabo *m*.

basis n base f; fondement m.

basket n panier m, corbeille f.

bass n (mus) contrebasse f.

bastard n, adj bâtard m.

baste vt arroser.

bat n chauve-souris f.

batch n fournée f.

bath n bain m.

bathe vt (vi) (se) baigner.

bathing suit n maillot de bain m.

bathroom n salle de bain f.

baths npl piscine f.

bathtub n baignoire f.

batter vt battre: — n pâte à frire f.

battery n pile, batterie f.

battle n bataille f: — vi se battre.

battlefield n champ de bataille m.

bawdy adj paillard.

bawl vi brailler, (fam) gueuler.

bay n baie f; laurier m.

bazaar n bazar m.

be vi être.

beach n plage f.

beacon n phare m.

bead n perle f.

beak n bec m.

beaker n gobelet m.

beam n rayon m; poutre f: — vi rayonner.

bean n haricot m.

bear n ours m.

bear vt porter, supporter.

bearable adj supportable.

beard n barbe f.

bearded adj barbu.

bearer n porteur m, -euse f.

beast n bête f; brute f.

beat vt battre: — vi battre: — n battement m; pulsation f.

beating n raclée f; battement m.

beautiful adj beau m belle f.

beautify vt embellir; décorer.

beauty n beauté f.

because conj parce que: — prép ~ of en raison de.

become vi devenir, se faire.

becoming adj convenable, seyant.

bed n lit m.

bedclothes npl couvertures et draps mpl.

bedroom n chambre f.

bedspread n dessus-de-lit m invar.

bee n abeille f.

beef n bœuf (viande) m.

beefsteak n bifteck m.

beeline n ligne droite f.

beer n bière f.

befit vt convenir à.

before adv prep avant; devant: — conj avant de, avant que.

beforehand adv à l'avance, au préalable.

beg vt mendier.

beggar n mendiant m, -e f.

begin vt vi commencer.

beginner n débutant m, -e f.

beginning n commencement.

behave vi se comporter, se conduire.

behaviour n conduite f.

behead vt décapiter.

behind prep derrière: — adv derrière, par-derrière, en arrière.

behold vt voir; contempler.

being n existence f; être m.

belated adj tardif.

belch vi éructer: — n éructation f, rot m.

belie vt démentir, tromper.

belief n foi, croyance f.

believable adj croyable.

believe vt croire: — vi penser, croire.

believer n croyant m, -e f.

belittle vt rabaisser.

bell n cloche f.

belligerent adj belligérant.

bellow vi beugler, mugir.

belly n ventre m.

belong vi appartenir à.

beloved adj chéri, bien-aimé.

below adv en dessous, en bas:—prep sous, au-dessous de.

belt n ceinture f.

bench n banc m.

bend vt courber:—vi se courber:—n courbe f.

beneath adv au-dessous:—prep sous, au-dessous de.

benefactor n bienfaiteur m, -trice f.

beneficent adj bienfaisant.

beneficial adj profitable, salutaire, utile.

beneficiary n bénéficiaire mf.

benefit n profit m; bienfait m:—vi bénéficier.

benevolence n bienveillance f.

benevolent adj bienveillant.

benign adj bienveillant, doux.

bequeath vt léguer à.

bequest n legs m.

bereavement n perte f; deuil m.

beret n béret m.

berserk adj fou furieux.

beseech vt supplier, implorer.

beset vt assaillir.

beside(s) prep à côté de; excepté:—adv de plus, en outre.

besiege vt assiéger.

best adj le meilleur, la meilleure:—adv le mieux:—n le meilleur, le mieux m.

bestial adj bestial, brutal.

bestiality n bestialité, brutalité f.

bestow vt accorder, conférer.

bet n pari m:—vt parier.

betray vt trahir.

betrayal n trahison f.

better adj adv meilleur, mieux:—vt améliorer.

between prep entre;* adv au milieu.

beverage n boisson f.

bewilder vt déconcerter.

bewilderment n perplexité f.

beyond prep au-delà de:—adv au-delà, plus loin.

bias n préjugé m; inclination f.

Bible n Bible f.

bibliography n bibliographie f.

bicycle n bicyclette f.

bid vt ordonner; offrir:—n offre, tentative f.

bide vt attendre, supporter.

biennial adj biennal, bisannuel.

big adj grand, gros; important.

bigness n grandeur, grosseur f.

bigot n fanatique mf.

bigoted adj fanatique.

bike n vélo m.

bikini n bikini m.

bilingual adj bilingue.

bill n bec (d'oiseau) m; addition f; billet m.

billet n logement m.

billion n mil milliard m.

bin n coffre m.

bind vt attacher; lier.

biochemistry n biochimie f.

binoculars npl jumelles f pl.

biographer n biographe mf.

biography n biographie f.

biological adj biologique.

biology n biologie f.

bird n oiseau m.

birth n naissance f.

birth certificate n extrait de naissance m.

birth control n limitation des naissances f.

birthday n anniversaire m.

biscuit n biscuit m.

bishop n évêque m.

bit n morceau m; peu m.

bite vt mordre: —n morsure f.

bitter adj amer, âpre; acerbe.

bitterness n amertume f.

bizarre adj étrange, bizarre.

black adj noir, obscur: —n noir m.

blackboard n tableau (noir) m.

blacken vt noircir, ternir.

blackleg n jaune m.

blackmail n chantage m: —vt faire chanter.

blackness n noirceur f.

blacksmith n forgeron m.

bladder n vessie f.

blade n lame f.

blame vt blâmer: —n faute f.

blameless adj irréprochable.

blanch vt blanchir.

bland adj affable, suave.

blank adj blanc; vide: —n blanc m.

blanket n couverture f.

blare vi retentir.

blaspheme vt blasphémer.

blasphemy n blasphème m.

blast n souffle d'air m; explosion f: —vt faire sauter.

blatant adj flagrant.

blaze n flamme f: —vi flamber.

bleach vt blanchir.

bleak adj morne, lugubre.

bleakness n froid m; austérité f.

bleat n bêlement m: —vi bêler.

bleed vi, vt saigner.

bleeding n saignement m.

blemish vt gâter: —n tache f.

blend vt mélanger.

bless vt bénir.

blessing n bénédiction f; bienfait m.

blight vt détruire.

blind adj aveugle: —vt aveugler; éblouir

blindly adv à l'aveuglette, aveuglément.

blindness n cécité f.

blink vi clignoter.

bliss n bonheur extrême m.

blissful adj heureux; béat.

blister n ampoule f.

blizzard n tempête de neige f.

bloated adj gonflé.

blob n goutte, tache f.

bloc n bloc m.

block n bloc m; pâté de maisons m: — ~ (up) vt bloquer.

blockade n blocus m: —vt bloquer.

blog n blogue m.

blond adj blond: —n blond m, -e f.

blood n sang m.

blood donor n donneur(-euse) de sang m(f).

blood group n groupe sanguin m.

bloodiness n (fig) cruauté f.

blood pressure n pression artérielle f.

bloodstream n système sanguin m.

bloodthirsty adj sanguinaire.

blood transfusion n transfusion sanguine f.

blood vessel n vaisseau sanguin m.

bloody adj sanglant, ensanglanté.

blossom n fleur f.

blot vt tacher; sécher: —n tache f.

blouse n chemisier m.

blow vi souffler; sonner: —vt souffler: —n coup m.

blubber n blanc de baleine m: —vi pleurnicher.

blue adj bleu.

blueprint n (fig) projet m.

bluff n esbrouffe f: —vt faire de l'esbrouffe.

bluish adj bleuâtre.

blunder n gaffe f: —vi faire une gaffe.

blunt adj émoussé: —vt émousser.

blur n tache f: —vt tacher.

blush n rougeur f: —vi rougir.

board n planche f; table f; conseil m: —vt monter à bord de.

boarder n pensionnaire mf.

boarding house n internat m; pension (de famille) f.

boast vi se vanter: —n vantardise f.

boastful adj vantard.

boat n bateau m; canot mf.

boating n canotage m.

bobsleigh n bobsleigh m.

bodily adj adv physique(ment).

body n corps m; cadavre m.

bodywork n (auto) carrosserie f.

bog n marécage m.

bogus adj faux.

boil vi bouillir: —n furoncle m.

boiler n casserole f; chaudière f.

boisterous adj bruyant; turbulent.

bold adj audacieux.

boldness n audace f.

bolt n verrou m: —vt verrouiller.

bomb n bombe f.

bombard vt bombarder.

bombardment n bombardement m.

bond n lien m; engagement m.

bone n os m: —vt désosser.

bonnet n bonnet m.

bonus n prime f.

bony adj osseux.

boo vt huer.

book n livre m.

bookcase n bibliothèque f.

bookkeeper n comptable mf.

bookkeeping n comptabilité f.

bookseller n libraire mf.

bookstore n librairie f.

bookworm n rat de bibliothèque m.

boom n essor m.

boot n botte f; coffre m.

booth n cabine f; baraque f.

border n bord m; frontière f: —vt border, avoisiner.

bore vt forer; ennuyer: —n perceuse f; raseur m.

boredom n ennui m.

boring adj ennuyeux.

born adj né.

borrow vt emprunter.

borrower n emprunteur m, -euse f.

bosom n sein m, poitrine f.

boss n chef m; patron(ne) m(f).

botanic(al) adj botanique.

botany n botanique f.

botch vt cochonner.

both pron tou(te)s les deux, l'un(e) et l'autre: —adj les deux.

bother vt ennuyer.

bottle n bouteille f.

bottleneck n embouteillage m.

bottle-opener n ouvre-bouteille m invar.

bottom n fond m: —adj du bas; dernier.

bough n branche f; rameau m.

bounce vi rebondir; bondir.

bound n limite f; saut m: —vi bondir: —adj à destination de.

boundary n limite f; frontière f.

bourgeois adj bourgeois.

bout n attaque f; combat m.

bow vi se courber: —n salut m.

bow n arc m; nœud m.

bowels npl entrailles fpl.

bowl n bol m; boule f.

bowling n boules fpl.

bow tie n nœud papillon m.

box n boîte, caisse f; loge f: —vt mettre en boîte: —vi boxer.

boxer n boxeur m.

box office n guichet m.

boy n garçon m.

boycott vt boycotter: —n boycottage m.

boyfriend n petit ami m.

bra *n* soutien-gorge *m*.

bracelet *n* bracelet *m*

bracket *n* tranche *f*; parenthèse *f*; crochet *m*.

brag *n* fanfaronnade *f*. — *vi* fanfaronner.

braid *n* tresse *f*. — *vt* tresser.

brain *n* cerveau *m*; tête *f*.

brainwave *n* idée lumineuse *f*.

brainy *adj* intelligent.

brake *n* frein *m*. — *vi* freiner.

brake light *n* feu de stop *m*.

branch *n* branche *f*. — *vi* se ramifier.

brand *n* marque *f*.

brandy *n* cognac *m*.

brash *adj* grossier; impertinent.

brat *n* môme, gosse *mf*.

brave *adj* courageux, brave.

bravery *n* bravoure *f*; courage *m*.

brawl *n* bagarre, rixe *f*. — *vi* se bagarrer.

breach *n* brèche *f*; violation *f*.

bread *n* pain *m*: — **brown** ~ pain bis *m*.

breadth *n* largeur *f*.

break *vt* casser; briser: — *vi* se casser: — *n* cassure, rupture *f*; interruption *f*.

breakdown *n* panne *f*; dépression nerveuse *f*.

breakfast *n* petit déjeuner *m*. — *vi* déjeuner.

breast *n* poitrine *f*, sein *m*.

breaststroke *n* brasse *f*.

breath *n* haleine *f*; respiration *f*.

breathe *vt vi* respirer; exhaler.

breathtaking *adj* stupéfiant.

breed *n* race, espèce *f*. — *vt* élever: — *vi* se reproduire.

breeder *n* éleveur *m*, -euse *f*.

breeze *n* brise *f*.

brevity *n* brièveté *f*; concision *f*.

brew *vt* brasser.

brewer *n* brasseur *m*.

brewery *n* brasserie *f*.

bribe *n* pot-de-vin *m*: — *vt* soudoyer.

brick *n* brique *f*.

bricklayer *n* maçon *m*.

bride *n* mariée *f*.

bridegroom *n* marié *m*.

bridge *n* pont *m*.

bridle *n* bride *f*; frein *m*.

brief *adj* bref, concis: — *n* résumé *m*.

briefcase *n* serviette *f*.

bright *adj* clair, brillant.

brighten *vt* faire briller: — *vi* s'éclairer.

brilliance *n* éclat *m*.

brilliant *adj* éclatant; génial.

bring *vt* apporter; amener.

brisk *adj* vif, rapide, frais.

bristle *n* poil *m*: — *vi* se hérisser.

brittle *adj* cassant, fragile.

broad *adj* large.

broadcast *n* émission *f*: — *vt vi* diffuser.

broaden *vt* élargir: — *vi* s'élargir.

broadness *n* largeur *f*.

broccoli *n* brocoli *m*.

brochure *n* brochure *f*, dépliant *m*.

broken *adj* cassé; interrompu.

broker *n* courtier *m*.

bronze *n* bronze *m*.

brooch *n* broche *f*.

brood *vi* couver; ruminer *f*.

broom *n* genêt *m*; balai *m*.

brother *n* frère *m*.

brother-in-law *n* beau-frère *m*.

brow *n* sourcil *m*; front *m*.

brown *adj* marron; brun: — *n* marron *m*: — *vt* brunir.

browse *vt* brouter: — *vi* paître.

bruise *n* bleu, ecchymose *f*.

brush *n* brosse *f*; pinceau *m*.

brutal *adj* brutal.

brutality *n* brutalité *f*.

brute *n* brute *f*. — *adj* bestial.

bubble *n* bulle *f*: — *vi* bouillonner; pétiller.

bucket n seau m.

buckle n boucle f: —vt boucler: —vi se déformer.

budge vi bouger, remuer.

budget n budget m.

buffet n buffet m: —vt gifler.

bug n punaise f.

build vt construire, bâtir.

builder n constructeur m.

building n bâtiment m; immeuble, édifice m.

bulb n bulbe m; oignon m.

bulge vi se renfler: —n renflement m.

bulk n masse f; volume m.

bulky adj volumineux.

bull n taureau m.

bullet n balle f.

bulletproof adj pare-balles, blindé.

bullion n or en barre m.

bully n tyran m: —vt tyranniser.

bump n heurt m; bosse f: —vt heurter.

bumpy adj cahoteux, bosselé.

bun n petit pain m; chignon m.

bunch n botte f; groupe m.

bundle n paquet m, liasse f: —vt empaqueter.

bungle vt bousiller.

bunk n couchette f.

buoy n (mar) bouée f.

buoyancy n flottabilité f.

buoyant adj flottable; gai, enjoué.

burden n charge f: —vt charger.

bureau n commode f; bureau m.

bureaucrat n bureaucrate mf.

burial n enterrement m; obsèques fpl.

burly adj robuste.

burn vt vi brûler: —n brûlure f.

burning adj brûlant.

burst vi éclater: —**to ~ out laughing** éclater de rire.

bury vt enterrer, inhumer.

bus n (auto)bus m.

bush n buisson, taillis m.

business n entreprise f; commerce m.

businessman n homme d'affaires m.

businesswoman n femme d'affaires f.

bus-stop n arrêt d'autobus m.

busy adj occupé; actif.

but conj mais; sauf, excepté, seulement.

butcher n boucher m, -ère f: —vt abattre, massacrer.

butchery n boucherie f, carnage m.

butter n beurre m: —vt beurrer.

butterfly n papillon m.

button n bouton m: —vt boutonner.

buy vt acheter.

buyer n acheteur m, -euse f.

buzz n bourdonnement: —vi bourdonner.

by prep à côté de, près de; par.

bypass n route de contournement f.

by-product n sous-produit m.

by-road n chemin de traverse m.

byte n (comput) octet m.

C

cabbage n chou m.

cabin n cabine f; cabane f.

cabinet n meuble de rangement m; console f.

cable n câble m.

cache n cachette f.

cackle vi caqueter, jacasser.

cafe n café m.

cafeteria n cafétéria f.

caffein(e) n caféine f.

cage n cage f:— vt mettre en cage.

cake n gâteau m.

calamity n calamité f, désastre m.

calculate vt calculer, compter.

calculation n calcul m.

calendar n calendrier m.

calf n veau m.

calibre n calibre m.

call vt appeler; convoquer:— n appel m; cri m.

calligraphy n calligraphie f.

calling n profession, vocation f.

callous adj dur; insensible.

calm n calme m:— adj calme:— vt calmer.

calorie n calorie f.

camera n caméra f.

camouflage n camouflage m.

camp n camp m:— vi camper.

campaign n campagne f.

camper n campeur m, -euse f.

camping n camping m.

campsite n camping m.

campus n campus m.

can v aux pouvoir:— n boîte de conserve f.

canal n conduit m; canal m.

cancel vt annuler.

cancer n cancer m.

candid adj candide, simple.

candidate n candidat(e) m(f).

candle n bougie f; cierge m.

candour n candeur f; sincérité f.

cane n canne f; bâton m.

cannon n canon m.

canoe n canoë m.

canon n canon m; règle f.

can opener n ouvre-boîte m.

canopy n baldaquin m.

cantankerous adj acariâtre.

canteen n cantine f.

canvas n toile f.

canvass vt sonder.

canvasser n prospecteur m, -trice f.

cap n casquette f.

capability n capacité, aptitude.

capable adj capable.

capacity n capacité; potentiel m.

cape n cap, promontoire m.

capital adj capital:— n capital m; capitale f.

capitalise vt capitaliser.

capitalist n capitaliste mf.

capital punishment n peine de mort.

capitulate vi capituler.

capitulation n capitulation f.

capricious adj capricieux.

capsize vt (mar) chavirer.

capsule n capsule f.

captain n capitaine m.

captivate vt captiver.

captivation n fascination f.

captive n captif m, -ive f, prisonnier m, -ière f.

captivity n captivité f.
capture n capture f: — vt capturer.
car n voiture f; wagon m.
caravan n caravane f.
carbohydrates npl hydrates de carbone m pl.
carcass n cadavre m.
card n carte f.
cardboard n carton m.
cardinal adj cardinal, principal: — n cardinal m.
card table n table de jeu f.
care n soin m; souci m: — vi se soucier de.
career n carrière f; cours m.
careful adj soigneux, consciencieux.
careless adj insouciant, négligent.
carelessness n négligence.
caress n caresse f: — vt caresser.
caretaker n concierge mf.
cargo n cargaison f.
caricature n caricature f: — vt caricaturer.
carnage n carnage m.
carnal adj charnel; sensuel.
carnival n carnaval m.
carnivorous adj carnivore.
carpenter n charpentier m.
carpentry n charpenterie f.
carpet n tapis m.
carriage n port m; voiture f.
carrier n porteur, transporteur m.
carrion n charogne f.
carrot n carotte f.
carry vt porter: — vi porter.
cart n charrette f.
cartel n cartel m.
cartilage n cartilage m.
cartoon n dessin animé m.
cartridge n cartouche f.
carve vt tailler, sculpter.
carving n sculpture f.

case n cas m; boîte f; étui m; enveloppe f.
cash n espèces fpl: — vt encaisser.
cashier n caissier m, -ière f.
casing n chambranle m.
casino n casino m.
cask n tonneau, fût m.
casket n cercueil m.
casserole n cocotte f.
cassette n cassette f.
cassette player magnétophone m.
cast vt jeter, lancer: — n moule m.
caste n caste f.
castigate vt punir.
castle n château m.
castrate vt castrer.
castration n castration f.
casual adj accidentel, fortuit.
cat n chat m, chatte f.
catalogue n catalogue m.
catapult n catapulte f.
cataract n cascade f; déluge m.
catastrophe n catastrophe f.
catch vt attraper, saisir: — n prise f.
catchword n slogan m.
catechism n catéchisme m.
categorical adj catégorique.
category n catégorie f.
caterer n fournisseur, traiteur m.
catering n restauration f.
caterpillar n chenille f.
cathedral n cathédrale f.
catholic adj n catholique mf.
cattle n bétail m.
cauliflower n chou-fleur m.
cause n cause f; raison f: — vt causer.
cauterise vt cautériser.
caution n prudence, précaution: — vt avertir.
cautious adj prudent, circonspect.
cavalry n cavalerie f.
cave n grotte f; caverne f.

cavern *n* caverne *f*.

cavity *n* cavité *f*.

cease *vt* cesser, arrêter.

ceaseless *adj* incessant, continuel.

cede *vt* céder.

ceiling *n* plafond *m*.

celebrate *vt* célébrer, fêter.

celebration *n* fête *f*.

celibate *adj* célibataire.

cell *n* cellule *f*.

cellar *n* cave *f*; cellier *m*.

cement *n* ciment *m*: —*vt* cimenter.

cemetery *n* cimetière *m*.

censor *n* censeur *m*.

censorship *n* censure *f*.

censure *n* censure: —*vt* censurer.

census *n* recensement *m*.

centenary *n* centenaire *m*: —*adj* centenaire.

centigrade *n* centigrade *m*.

centimetre *n* centimètre *m*.

central *adj* central.

centralise *vt* centraliser.

centre *n* centre *m*: —*vt* centrer.

century *n* siècle *m*.

cereal *n* céréal *f*.

ceremonial *adj n* cérémonial *m*; rituel *m*.

ceremony *n* cérémonie *f*.

certain *adj* certain, sûr.

certainty *n* certitude *f*.

certificate *n* certificat, acte *m*.

certification *n* authentification *f*.

certify *vt* certifier, assurer.

cessation *n* cessation *f*.

chafe *vt* irriter; frotter.

chagrin *n* dépit *m*.

chain *n* chaîne *f*: —*vt* enchaîner.

chair *n* chaise *f*: —*vt* présider.

chairman *n* président *m*.

chalk *n* craie *f*.

challenge *n* défi *m*: —*vt* défier.

chamber *n* pièce *f*; chambre *f*.

champagne *n* champagne *m*.

champion *n* champion *m*, -ionne *f*: —*vt* défendre.

championship *n* championnat *m*.

chance *n* hasard *m*.

chancellor *n* chancelier *m*.

change *vt* changer: —*vi* changer, se transformer: —*n* modification *f*; change *m*.

changeable *adj* changeant.

channel *n* canal *m*: —*vt* canaliser.

chant *n* chant *m*.

chaotic *adj* chaotique.

chapel *n* chapelle *f*.

chapter *n* chapitre *m*.

character *n* caractère *m*; personnage *m*.

characteristic *adj* caractéristique.

charcoal *n* charbon de bois *m*.

charge *vt* charger; accuser: —*n* fardeau *m*; accusation *f*.

chargeable *adj* passible.

charitable *adj* caritatif.

charity *n* charité, bienfaisance *f*.

charm *n* charme *m*: —*vt* charmer.

chart *n* carte (marine) *f*; diagramme *m*.

charter *n* charte *f*; privilège *m*: —*vt* affréter.

chase *vt* poursuivre: —*n* chasse *f*.

chaste *adj* chaste; pur.

chastise *vt* châtier, punir.

chastisement *n* châtiment *m*.

chastity *n* chasteté, pureté *f*.

chat *vi* causer: —*n* bavardage *m*.

chatter *vi* jacasser.

chauffeur *n* chauffeur *m*.

chauvinist *n* chauvin *m*, -e *f*.

cheap *adj* bon marché.

cheapen *vt* baisser le prix de.

cheat *vt* tromper, frauder: —*n* tricheur *m*, -euse *f*.

check *vt* vérifier; contrôler; réprimer,

enrayer; stopper; enregistrer: —*n* contrôle *m*.

checkup *n* bilan de santé *m*.

cheek *n* joue *f*.

cheer *n* gaieté *f*; applaudissement *m*: —*vt* réconforter.

cheerful *adj* gai, enjoué, joyeux.

cheerfulness *n* gaieté *f*; bonne humeur *f*.

cheese *n* fromage *m*.

chef *n* chef (de cuisine) *m*.

chemist *n* chimiste *mf*; pharmacien *m*, -ienne *f*.

chemistry *n* chimie *f*.

cheque *n* chèque *m*.

cherish *vt* chérir, aimer.

chess *n* échecs *mpl*.

chest *n* poitrine *f*.

chew *vt* mâcher, mastiquer.

chick *n* poussin *m*.

chicken *n* poulet *m*.

chief *adj* principal, en chef: —*n* chef *m*.

chieftain *n* chef *m*.

child *n* enfant *m*.

childbirth *n* accouchement *m*.

childhood *n* enfance *f*.

childish *adj* enfantin.

children *npl* de **child**, enfants *mpl*.

chill *n* froid *m*: —*vt* refroidir.

chilly *adj* froid, très frais.

chimney *n* cheminée *f*.

chin *n* menton *m*.

chip *vt* ébrécher: —*n* fragment, éclat *m*; frite *f*.

chisel *n* ciseau *m*: —*vt* ciseler.

chivalrous *adj* chevaleresque.

chocolate *n* chocolat *m*.

choice *n* choix *m*, préférence.

choir *n* chœur *m*.

choke *vt* étrangler; étouffer.

choose *vt* choisir, élire.

chop *vt* trancher, hacher: —*n* côtelette *f*.

chore *n* corvée *f*; travail routinier *m*.

chorus *n* chœur *m*.

christen *vt* baptiser.

christening *n* baptême *m*.

Christian *adj n* chrétien *m*, -ne *f*.

Christmas *n* Noël *f*.

Christmas Eve *n* veille de Noël *f*.

chronic *adj* chronique.

chronicle *n* chronique *f*.

chronicler *n* chroniqueur *m*.

chronological *adj* chronologique

chronology *n* chronologie *f*.

chuckle *vi* rire, glousser.

chum *n* copain *m*, copine *f*.

church *n* église *f*.

cider *n* cidre *m*.

cigar *n* cigare *m*.

cigarette *n* cigarette *f*.

cinder *n* cendre *f*.

cinema *n* cinéma *m*.

circle *n* cercle *m*; groupe *m*: —*vt* encercler.

circuit *n* circuit *m*; tour *m*; tournée *f*.

circular *adj* circulaire: —*n* circulaire *f*.

circulate *vi* circuler.

circulation *n* circulation *f*.

circumference *n* circonférence *f*.

circumnavigation *n* circumnavigation *f*.

circumspect *adj* circonspect.

circumspection *n* circonspection *f*.

circumstance *n* circonstance, situation *f*.

circumvent *vt* circonvenir.

circus *n* cirque *m*.

citation *n* citation *f*.

cite *vt* citer.

citizen *n* citoyen *m*, -enne *f*.

city *n* ville *f*.

civic *adj* civique.

civil *adj* civil, courtois.

civilian *n* civil *m*, -e *f*.

civilisation *n* civilisation *f*.

civilise *vt* civiliser.

claim *vt* revendiquer, réclamer: — *n* demande *f*; réclamation *f*.

claimant *n* demandeur *m*.

clamour *n* clameur *f*.

clamp *n* attache *f*. — *vt* serrer.

clandestine *adj* clandestin.

clap *vt vi* applaudir.

clapping *n* applaudissements *mpl*.

clarification *n* clarification *f*.

clarify *vt* clarifier, éclaircir.

clarity *n* clarté *f*.

clash *vi* se heurter.

clasp *n* fermoir *m*; boucle *f*.

class *n* classe *f*; catégorie *f*. — *vt* classer.

classic(al) *adj* classique.

classification *n* classification *f*.

classify *vt* classifier.

classroom *n* salle de classe *f*.

clatter *vi* résonner; cliqueter.

claw *n* griffe *f*; serre *f*.

clean *adj* propre; net: — *vt* nettoyer.

cleaning *n* nettoyage *m*.

cleanliness *n* propreté, pureté *f*.

cleanse *vt* nettoyer.

clear *adj* clair; net: — *vt* clarifier.

cleft *n* fissure, crevasse *f*.

clemency *n* clémence *f*.

clement *adj* clément.

clergy *n* clergé *m*.

clergyman *n* ecclésiastique *m*.

clerical *adj* clérical.

clerk *n* employé *m*.

clever *adj* intelligent; habile.

click *vt* claquer.

client *n* client *m*, -e *f*.

cliff *n* falaise *f*.

climate *n* climat *m*.

climatic *adj* climatique.

climax *n* apogée *m*.

climb *vt vi* grimper, escalader.

climber *n* alpiniste *mf*.

cling *vi* s'accrocher (à).

clinic *n* clinique *f*.

clip *vt* couper: — *n* clip *m*.

cloak *n* cape *f*: — *vt* masquer.

cloakroom *n* vestiaire *m*.

clock *n* horloge *f*.

clog *n* sabot *m*: — *vi* se boucher.

close *vt* fermer: — *n* fin *f*; conclusion *f*: — *adj* proche: — *adv* de près.

closeness *n* proximité *f*.

closure *n* fermeture *f*; clôture *f*.

cloth *n* tissu *m*; toile *f*.

clothe *vt* habiller, vêtir.

clothes *npl* vêtements *mpl*.

cloud *n* nuage *m*; nuée *f*.

cloudiness *n* nébulosité *f*.

cloudy *adj* nuageux.

clover *n* trèfle *m*.

clown *n* clown *m*.

club *n* matraque *f*; club *m*.

clue *n* indice *m*, indication *f*.

clumsiness *n* gaucherie *f*.

clumsy *adj* gauche, maladroit.

cluster *n* grappe *f*: — *vt* grouper.

clutch *n* prise *f*; embrayage *m*: — *vt* empoigner.

coach *n* autocar *m*; wagon *m*; entraîneur *m*: — *vt* entraîner.

coal *n* charbon *m*.

coalesce *vi* s'unir.

coalition *n* coalition *f*.

coarse *adj* rude; grossier.

coast *n* côte *f*.

coastal *adj* côtier.

coastguard *n* gendarmerie maritime *f*.

coastline *n* littoral *m*.

coat *n* manteau *m*; couche *f*: — *vt* enduire.

coating *n* revêtement *m*.

coax *vt* cajôler.
cobweb *n* toile d'araignée *f*.
cock *n* coq *m*.
cockpit *n* cabine de pilotage *f*.
cocoa *n* cacao *m*.
coconut *n* noix de coco *f*.
cocoon *n* cocon *m*.
cod *n* morue *f*.
code *n* code *m*.
coercion *n* coercition.
coexistence *n* coexistence *f*.
coffee *n* café *m*.
coffeepot *n* cafetière *f*.
coffer *n* coffre *m*; caisse *f*.
coffin *n* cercueil *m*.
cog *n* dent d'engrenage *f*.
cogency *n* puissance, force *f*.
cogent *adj* convaincant, puissant.
cognac *n* cognac *m*.
cognisance *n* connaissance *f*; compétence *f*.
cogwheel *n* roue dentée *f*.
cohabit *vi* cohabiter.
cohabitation *n* cohabitation *f*.
cohere *vi* se tenir; être cohérent.
coherent *adj* cohérent; logique.
cohesive *adj* cohésif.
coil *n* rouleau *m*:—*vt* enrouler.
coin *n* pièce de monnaie *f*.
coincide *vi* coïncider.
coincidence *n* coïncidence *f*.
colander *n* passoire *f*.
cold *adj* froid; indifférent:—*n* froid *m*; rhume *m*.
coldness *n* froideur *f*.
collaborate *vi* collaborer.
collaboration *n* collaboration *f*.
collapse *vi* s'écrouler:—*n* écroulement.
collapsible *adj* pliant.
collar *n* col *m*.
collate *vt* collationner.

collateral *adj* concomitant:—*n* nantissement *m*.
collation *n* collation *f*.
colleague *n* collègue *mf*.
collect *vt* rassembler; collectionner.
collection *n* collection *f*.
collective *adj* collectif.
collector *n* collectionneur *m*, -euse *f*.
college *n* collège *m*.
collide *vi* se heurter.
collision *n* collision *f*, heurt *m*.
colloquial *adj* familier.
colloquialism *n* expression familière *f*.
collusion *n* collusion *f*.
colonial *adj* colonial.
colonise *vt* coloniser.
colonist *n* colon *m*.
colony *n* colonie *f*.
colour *n* couleur *f*:—*vt* colorer:—*vi* se colorer.
colourful *adj* coloré.
colouring *n* teint *m*.
column *n* colonne *f*.
columnist *n* chroniqueur *m*.
coma *n* coma *m*.
comatose *adj* comateux.
comb *n* peigne *m*:—*vt* peigner.
combat *n* combat *m*:—*vt* combattre.
combatant *n* combattant *m*, -e *f*.
combination *n* combinaison *f*.
combine *vt* combiner:—*vi* s'unir.
combustion *n* combustion *f*.
come *vi* venir:—**to ~ across, ~ upon** *vt* rencontrer par hasard:—**to ~ round, ~ to** *vi* revenir à soi.
comedian *n* comédien *m*; comique *m*.
comedy *n* comédie *f*.
comet *n* comète *f*.
comfort *n* confort *m*:—*vt* réconforter; soulager.
comfortable *adj* confortable.

comic(al) *adj* comique.
command *vt* ordonner, commander:
— *n* ordre *m*.
commander *n* commandant *m*.
commemorate *vt* commémorer.
commemoration *n* commémoration *f*.
commence *vt vi* commencer.
commencement *n* commencement *m*.
commend *vt* recommander.
commendation *n* louange *f*; recommandation *f*.
commensurate *adj* proportionné.
comment *n* commentaire *m*: — *vt* commenter.
commentary *n* commentaire *m*; observation *f*.
commentator *n* commentateur *m*, -trice *f*.
commerce *n* commerce *m*.
commercial *adj* commercial.
commiserate *vt* compatir avec.
commiseration *n* commisération, pitié *f*.
commission *n* commission *f*: — *vt* commissionner.
commit *vt* commettre; confier à; engager.
commitment *n* engagement *m*.
committee *n* comité *m*.
common *adj* commun; ordinaire.
common sense *n* bon sens *m*.
commonly *adv* communément, généralement.
commotion *n* vacarme *m*.
communicable *adj* communicable
communicate *vt* communiquer: — *vi* communiquer.
communication *n* communication *f*.
communion *n* communion *f*.
communist *n* communiste *mf*.
community *n* communauté *f*.
commutable *adj* interchangeable, permutable.

commute *vt* échanger.
compact *adj* compact, serré.
compact disc *n* disque compact *m*.
companion *n* compagnon *m*, compagne *f*.
company *n* compagnie; société *f*.
comparable *adj* comparable.
comparative *adj* comparatif.
compare *vt* comparer.
comparison *n* comparaison *f*.
compartment *n* compartiment *m*.
compass *n* boussole *f*.
compassion *n* compassion *f*.
compassionate *adj* compatissant.
compatibility *n* compatibilité *f*.
compatible *adj* compatible.
compatriot *n* compatriote *mf*.
compel *vt* contraindre, obliger, forcer.
compensate *vt* compenser.
compensation *n* compensation *f*.
compete *vi* rivaliser (avec).
competence *n* compétence *f*; aptitude *f*.
competent *adj* compétent.
competition *n* compétition *f*; concurrence *f*.
competitive *adj* concurrentiel, compétitif.
competitor *n* concurrent *m*, -e *f*.
complacency *n* suffisance *f*.
complacent *adj* suffisant.
complain *vi* se plaindre.
complaint *n* plainte *f*; réclamation *f*.
complement *n* complément *m*.
complementary *adj* complémentaire.
complete *adj* complet; achevé: — *vt* achever.
completion *n* achèvement *m*.
complex *adj* complexe.
complexion *n* teint *m*; aspect *m*.
complexity *n* complexité *f*.
compliance *n* conformité *f*; soumission *f*.
complicate *vt* compliquer.
complication *n* complication *f*.

complicity *n* complicité *f*.

compliment *n* compliment *m*: — *vt* complimenter.

comply *vi* se conformer.

component *adj* composant.

compose *vt* composer.

composer *n* compositeur *m*, -trice *f*.

composition *n* composition *f*.

composure *n* maîtrise de soi *f*.

compound *vt* composer: — *adj* *n* composé *m*.

comprehend *vt* comprendre.

comprehensible *adj* compréhensible.

comprehension *n* compréhension *f*.

comprehensive *adj* global; compréhensif.

compress *vt* comprimer.

comprise *vt* comprendre, embrasser.

compromise *n* compromis *m*: — *vt* compromettre.

compulsion *n* compulsion *f*.

compulsory *adj* obligatoire.

computer *n* ordinateur *m*.

computerise *vt* traiter par ordinateur, informatiser.

computer science *n* informatique *f*.

comrade *n* camarade *mf*.

comradeship *n* camaraderie *f*.

conceal *vt* cacher.

concealment *n* dissimulation *f*.

concede *vt* concéder, accorder.

conceit *n* vanité *f*.

conceive *vt* *vi* concevoir.

concentrate *vt* concentrer.

concentration *n* concentration *f*.

concept *n* concept *m*.

conception *n* conception *f*.

concern *vt* concerner: — *n* affaire *f*; souci *m*.

concerning *prep* en ce qui concerne, concernant.

concert *n* concert *m*.

concession *n* concession *f*.

conciliate *vt* concilier.

conciliation *n* conciliation *f*.

concise *adj* concis, succinct.

conclude *vt* conclure.

conclusion *n* conclusion.

conclusive *adj* décisif, concluant.

concoct *vt* confectionner.

concord *n* entente, harmonie *f*.

concordance *n* accord *m*.

concrete *n* béton *m*: — *vt* bétonner.

concur *vi* coïncider; s'entendre.

concurrence *n* consentement *m*.

concussion *n* commotion *f*.

condemn *vt* condamner.

condemnation *n* condamnation *f*.

condensation *n* condensation *f*.

condense *vt* condenser.

condescend *vi* condescendre.

condescension *n* condescendance *f*.

condition *vt* conditionner: — *n* condition, situation *f*; état *m*.

conditional *adj* conditionnel.

condolences *npl* condoléances *fpl*.

condom *n* préservatif *m*.

conduct *n* conduite *f*.: — *vt* conduire.

conduit *n* conduit *m*; tuyau *m*.

cone *n* cône *m*.

confectioner *n* confiseur *m*, -euse *f*.

confectionery *n* confiserie *f*.

confer *vt* *vi* conférer.

conference *n* conférence *f*.

confess *vt* confesser: — *vi* se confesser.

confession *n* confession *f*.

confidant *n* confident *m*, -e *f*.

confide *vt* confier: — ~ **in** se confier à.

confidence *n* confiance *f*; assurance *f*.

confident *adj* confiant, sûr (de soi).

confidential *adj* confidentiel.

confine *vt* limiter.

confinement *n* détention *f*; alitement *m*.

confirm *vt* confirmer; ratifier.

confirmation *n* confirmation *f*.

confiscate *vt* confisquer.

confiscation *n* confiscation *f*.

conflict *n* conflit *m*; lutte *f*.

conflicting *adj* contradictoire.

conform *vi* se conformer (à).

conformity *n* conformité *f*.

confront *vt* confronter.

confrontation *n* confrontation *f*.

confuse *vt* confondre.

confusion *n* confusion *f*; désordre *m*.

congeal *vi* se congeler.

congenial *adj* sympathique.

congenital *adj* congénital.

congestion *n* congestion *f*.

congratulate *vt* complimenter, féliciter.

congratulations *npl* félicitations *fpl*.

congregate *vt* rassembler, réunir.

congregation *n* assemblée *f*.

congress *n* congrès *m*; conférence *f*.

congruity *n* congruence *f*.

congruous *adj* congru, approprié.

conifer *n* conifère *m*.

conjecture *n* conjecture.

conjugal *adj* conjugal.

conjunction *n* conjonction *f*.

conjuncture *n* conjoncture *f*.

connect *vt* relier, joindre.

connection *n* liaison, connexion *f*.

connoisseur *n* connaisseur *m*, -euse *f*.

conquer *vt* conquérir.

conqueror *n* conquérant *m*.

conquest *n* conquête *f*.

conscience *n* conscience *f*.

conscientious *adj* consciencieux.

conscious *adj* conscient.

consciousness *n* conscience *f*.

consecrate *vt* consacrer.

consecration *n* consécration *f*.

consecutive *adj* consécutif.

consensus *n* consensus *m*.

consent *n* consentement:—*vi* consentir.

consequence *n* conséquence *f*; importance *f*.

consequent *adj* consécutif.

conservation *n* conservation *f*.

conservative *adj* conservateur.

conserve *vt* conserver:—*n* conserve *f*.

consider *vt* considérer.

considerable *adj* considérable.

considerate *adj* prévenant, attentionné.

consideration *n* considération *f*.

consign *vt* confier, remettre.

consignment *n* expédition *f*.

consist *vi* consister (en).

consistency *n* consistance *f*.

consistent *adj* constant; cohérent.

consolation *n* consolation *f*; réconfort *m*.

console *vt* consoler.

consolidate *vt* consolider.

consolidation *n* consolidation *f*.

conspicuous *adj* voyant, manifeste.

conspiracy *n* conspiration *f*.

conspire *vi* conspirer.

constancy *n* constance *f*.

constant *adj* constant.

constellation *n* constellation *f*.

consternation *n* consternation *f*.

constitute *vt* constituer; établir.

constitution *n* constitution *f*.

constitutional *adj* constitutionnel.

constrain *vt* contraindre.

constraint *n* contrainte *f*.

constrict *vt* serrer; gêner.

construct *vt* construire, bâtir.

construction *n* construction *f*.

consulate *n* consulat *m*.

consult *vt* consulter.

consultation *n* consultation.

consume *vt* consommer.

consumer n consommateur m, -trice f.
consumerism n consumérisme m.
consummate vt consommer: —adj accompli.
consummation n consommation f.
consumption n consommation f.
contact n contact m.
contagious adj contagieux.
contain vt contenir.
container n récipient m.
contaminate vt contaminer.
contamination n contamination f.
contemplate vt contempler.
contemplation n contemplation f.
contemporary adj contemporain.
contempt n mépris, dédain m.
contemptible adj méprisable.
contemptuous adj méprisant.
contend vi combattre.
content adj content, satisfait: —vt contenter, satisfaire: —n contentement m.
contention n querelle, altercation f.
contentment n contentement m, satisfaction f.
contest vt contester, discuter: —n concours m.
contestant n concurrent m, -e f.
context n contexte m.
continent n continent m.
continental adj continental.
contingency n contingence f.
contingent n contingent m: —adj contingent.
continual adj continuel.
continuation n continuation.
continue vt vi continuer.
continuous adj continu.
contort vt tordre, déformer.
contortion n contorsion f.
contour n contour m.

contraception n contraception f.
contraceptive n contraceptif m: —adj contraceptif.
contract vt contracter: —n contrat m.
contradict vt contredire.
contradiction n contradiction f.
contradictory adj contradictoire.
contraption n gadget, bidule (fam) m.
contrary adj contraire: —n contraire m.
contrast n contraste m: —vt contraster.
contravention n infraction f.
contribute vt contribuer.
contribution n contribution f.
contrite adj contrit, repentant.
contrivance n dispositif m; invention f.
control n contrôle m; maîtrise f: —vt maîtriser; contrôler.
controversial adj polémique.
controversy n polémique f.
contusion n contusion f.
conurbation n conurbation f.
convalescence n convalescence f.
convalescent adj convalescent.
convene vt convoquer.
convenience n commodité, convenance f.
convenient adj commode, pratique
convention n convention f.
conventional adj conventionnel.
converge vi converger.
convergence n convergence f.
convergent adj convergent.
conversant adj au courant; compétent.
conversation n conversation f.
converse vi converser.
conversion n conversion; transformation f.
convert vt convertir: —n converti m, -e f.
convey vt transporter.
conveyance n transport m; cession f.
convict n détenu m, -e f.

conviction n condamnation f; conviction f.

convince vt convaincre, persuader.

convivial adj jovial.

conviviality n jovialité f.

convoke vt convoquer.

convoy n convoi m.

convulse vt ébranler.

convulsion n convulsion f; bouleversement m.

convulsive adj convulsif.

cook n cuisinier m, -ière f: — vt cuire.

cooker n cuisinière f.

cookery n cuisine f.

cool adj frais: — n fraîcheur f: — vt rafraîchir.

coolness n fraîcheur f; sang-froid m.

cooperate vi coopérer.

cooperation n coopération f.

cooperative adj coopératif.

coordinate vt coordonner.

coordination n coordination f.

cope vi se débrouiller.

copious adj copieux.

copy n copie f: — vt copier.

copyright n droit d'auteur m.

coral n corail m.

cord n corde f, cordon m.

cordial adj cordial, chaleureux.

core n trognon m; noyau, centre, cœur m.

cork n bouchon m: — vt boucher.

corkscrew n tire-bouchon m.

corn n maïs m; grain m; blé m.

corner n coin m; angle m.

cornerstone n pierre angulaire f.

corollary n corollaire f.

coronation n couronnement m.

coroner n coroner m.

corporate adj en commun; d'entreprise.

corporation n corporation f; société par actions f.

corps n corps m.

corpse n cadavre m.

corpulent adj corpulent.

correct vt corriger; rectifier: — adj correct.

correction n correction f; rectification f.

corrective adj correcteur, correctif: — n correcteur m.

correctness n correction f.

correlation n corrélation f.

correlative adj corrélatif.

correspond vi correspondre.

correspondence n correspondance f.

correspondent adj correspondant: — n correspondant m, -e f.

corridor n couloir, corridor m.

corroborate vt corroborer.

corrode vt corroder.

corrosion n corrosion f.

corrosive adj n corrosif m.

corrupt vt corrompre: — adj corrompu.

corruption n corruption f; dépravation f.

cosmetic adj n cosmétique m.

cosmic adj cosmique.

cosmopolitan adj cosmopolite.

cost n prix, coût m: — vi coûter.

costly adj coûteux, cher.

costume n costume m.

cottage n cottage m.

cotton n coton m.

cotton wool n coton hydrophile m.

couch n canapé, divan m.

cough n toux f: — vi tousser.

council n conseil m.

counsel n conseil m; avocat m.

counsellor n conseiller m, -ère f.

count vt compter: — n compte m.

countenance n visage m.

counter n comptoir m; jeton m.

counteract vt contrecarrer.

counterbalance vt contrebalancer.

counterfeit vt contrefaire:—adj faux.

counterpart n contrepartie f.

countersign vt contresigner.

countrified adj rustique; campagnard.

country n pays m; patrie f:—adj rustique; campagnard.

countryman n campagnard m; compatriote m.

county n comté m.

couple n couple m:—vt unir, associer.

coupon n coupon m.

courage n courage m.

courageous adj courageux.

courier n messager m; guide m.

course n cours m; route f; chemin m:—of ~ bien sûr.

court n cour f; tribunal m:—vt courtiser. adj courtois.

courtesy n courtoisie f.

courthouse n palais de justice m.

courtroom n salle de tribunal f.

cousin n cousin m, -e f.

cover n couverture f:—vt (re)couvrir.

covert adj voilé; caché.

cover-up n dissimulation f.

covet vt convoiter.

cow n vache f.

coward n lâche mf.

cowardice n lâcheté f.

cowboy n cowboy m.

coy adj timide; coquet; évasif.

coyness n timidité f; modestie f.

crab n crabe m.

crack n craquement m; fente f:—vt fêler:—vi se fêler; craquer.

crackle vi crépiter, pétiller.

cradle n berceau m:—vt bercer.

craft n habileté f; barque f.

craftsman n artisan m.

crafty adj astucieux, rusé.

cram vt bourrer:—vi s'entasser.

cramp n crampe f:—vt entraver.

crane n grue f.

crash vi s'écraser:—n fracas m; collision f.

crate n caisse f; cageot m.

crater n cratère m.

crawl vi ramper.

crayon n crayon m.

craze n manie f, engouement m.

craziness n folie f.

crazy adj fou.

creak vi grincer, craquer.

cream n crème f:—adj crème.

crease n pli m:—vt froisser.

create vt créer; causer.

creation n création f.

creature n créature f.

credence n croyance; créance f.

credibility n crédibilité f.

credible adj crédible.

credit n crédit m; honneur m.

creditable adj estimable, honorable.

credit card n carte de crédit f.

creep vi ramper.

cremate vt incinérer.

cremation n incinération, crémation f.

crematorium n crématoire m.

crest n crête f.

crevice n fissure, lézarde f.

crew n bande, équipe f; équipage m.

crib n berceau m; mangeoire f.

crime n crime m; délit m.

criminal adj criminel:—n criminel m, -elle f.

cripple n, adj invalide mf:—vt paralyser.

crisis n crise f.

criterion n critère m.

critic n critique m.

critic(al) adj critique.

criticise vt critiquer.

criticism n critique f.

croak vi coasser, croasser.

crockery n poterie f.

crocodile n crocodile m.

crook n (fam) escroc m.

crop n culture f; récolte f.

cross n croix f; croisement m:—adj fâché:—vt traverser, croiser.

crossbreed n hybride m.

crossing n traversée f; passage pour piétons m.

cross-reference n renvoi m, référence f.

crossroad n carrefour m.

crouch vi s'accroupir, se tapir.

crow n corbeau m.

crowd n foule f; monde m; vi s'entasser.

crown n couronne f:—vt couronner.

crucial adj crucial.

crucifix n crucifix m.

crude adj brut, grossier.

cruel adj cruel.

cruelty n cruauté f.

crumb n miette f.

crumble vt émietter; effriter:—vi s'émietter.

crunch vt croquer.

crush vt écraser; opprimer:—n cohue f.

crust n croûte f.

crutch n béquille f.

crux n cœur m.

cry vt vi crier; pleurer:—n cri m; sanglot m.

crystal n cristal m.

crystalline adj cristallin; pur.

crystallise vi se cristalliser.

cube n cube m.

cuddle vt embrasser.

cuff n manchette f.

culinary adj culinaire.

culminate vi culminer.

culpable adj coupable.

culprit n coupable mf.

cult n culte m.

cultivate vt cultiver.

cultivation n culture f.

culture n culture f.

cumbersome adj encombrant.

cumulative adj cumulatif.

cunning adj astucieux, rusé.

cup n tasse, coupe f.

cupboard n placard m.

curb n frein m:—vt freiner, juguler.

cure n remède m; cure f:—vt guérir.

curiosity n curiosité f.

curious adj curieux.

curl n boucle de cheveux f:—vt boucler.

curly adj frisé, bouclé.

currency n monnaie f; cours m.

current adj courant; actuel:—n courant m.

current affairs npl actualité f.

curse vt maudire.

curt adj succinct; sec.

curtain n rideau m.

curve vt courber:—n courbe f.

cushion n coussin m.

custodian n gardien m, -ienne f.

custom n coutume f, usage m.

customary adj habituel, coutumier.

customer n client m, -e f.

customs npl douane f.

customs officer n douanier m.

cut vt découper; couper:—n coup m; coupure f.

cutlery n couverts mpl.

cutting n coupure f.

cycle n cycle m; bicyclette f:—vi aller à bicyclette.

cycling n cyclisme m.

cyclist n cycliste mf.

cylinder n cylindre m; rouleau m.

cynic(al) adj cynique:—n cynique mf.

D

dad(dy) n papa m.

daily adj quotidien:—adv quotidiennement.

daintiness n élégance f; délicatesse f.

dainty adj délicat; élégant.

dairy n laiterie f.

dam n barrage m:—vt endiguer.

damage n dommage m; tort m:—vt endommager.

damnation n damnation f.

damp adj humide:—vt humidifier.

dampen vt humidifier.

dance n danse f; soirée dansante f:—vi, vt danser.

dancer n danseur m, -euse f.

danger n danger m.

dangerous adj dangereux.

dangle vi pendre.

dare vi oser:—vt défier.

daring n audace f:—adj audacieux.

dark adj sombre, obscur:—n obscurité f; ignorance f.

darken vt assombrir:—vi s'assombrir.

darkness n obscurité f.

darling n, adj chéri m, -e f.

dart n dard m.

dash vi se dépêcher.

data n données fpl.

data processing n traitement de données m.

date n date f; rendez-vous m.

dated adj démodé.

daughter n fille f:—~ in-law belle-fille f.

dawn n aube f.

day n jour m, journée f:—~ by ~ de jour en jour.

daylight n lumière du jour.

daze vt étourdir.

dazzle vt éblouir.

dead adj mortl.

deaden vt amortir.

deadline n date limite f.

deadlock n impasse f.

deadly adj mortel.

deaf adj sourd.

deafen vt assourdir.

deafness n surdité f.

deal n accord m; marché m:—a great ~ beaucoup:—vt distribuer.

dealer n commerçant m; trafiquant m.

dear adj ~ly adv cher.

dearness n cherté f.

death n mort f.

death certificate n acte de décès m.

death penalty n peine de mort f.

debar vt exclure.

debase vt dégrader.

debasement n dégradation f.

debatable adj discutable.

debate n débat m:—vt discuter; examiner.

debilitate vt débiliter.

debit n débit m:—vt débiter.

debt n dette f:—get into ~ s'endetter.

debtor n débiteur m, -trice f.

decade n décennie f.

decadence n décadence f.

decaffeinated adj décaféiné.

decay vi décliner; pourrir:—n pourrissement m.

deceased adj décédé.

deceit n tromperie f.

deceive *vt* tromper.

December *n* décembre *m.*

decency *n* décence *f*; pudeur *f.*

decent *adj* décent; bien, bon.

decide *vt* decider: — *vi* se décider.

decided *adj* décidé.

decimate *vt* décimer.

decipher *vt* déchiffrer.

decision *n* décision, détermination *f.*

decisive *adj* décisif.

deck *n* pont *m*: — *vt* orner.

declaration *n* déclaration *f.*

declare *vt* déclarer.

decode *vt* décoder.

decor *n* décor *m*; décoration *f.*

decorate *vt* décorer, orner.

decoration *n* décoration *f.*

decorative *adj* décoratif.

decoy *n* leurre *m.*

decrease *vt* diminuer: — *n* diminution *f.*

decree *n* décret *m*: — *vt* décréter; ordonner.

decrepit *adj* décrépit.

dedicate *vt* dédier; consacrer.

dedication *n* dédicace *f*; consacration *f.*

deduce *vt* déduire, conclure.

deduct *vt* déduire, soustraire.

deed *n* action *f*; exploit *m.*

deep *adj* profond.

deepen *vt* approfondir.

deepness *n* profondeur *f.*

default *n* défaut *m*: — *vi* manquer à ses engagements.

defeat *n* défaite *f*: — *vt* vaincre; frustrer.

defect *n* défaut *m.*

defective *adj* défectueux.

defend *vt* défendre; protéger.

defendant *n* accusé *m*, -e *f.*

defense *n* défense *f*; protection *f.*

defensive *adj* défensif.

defer *vt* déférer.

deference *n* déférence *f.*

defiance *n* défi *m.*

deficiency *n* défaut *m*; manque *m.*

deficient *adj* insuffisant.

define *vt* définir.

definite *adj* sûr; précis.

definition *n* définition *f.*

definitive *adj* définitif.

deflect *vt* dévier.

deform *vt* déformer.

deformity *n* déformité *f.*

defraud *vt* frauder.

deft *adj* habile.

degenerate *vi* dégénérer: — *adj* dégénéré.

degeneration *n* dégénération *f.*

degradation *n* dégradation *f.*

degrade *vt* dégrader.

degree *n* degré *m*; diplôme *m.*

dejected *adj* découragé.

dejection *n* découragement *m.*

delay *vt* retarder: — *n* retard *m.*

delegate *vt* déléguer: — *n* délégué *m*, -e *f.*

delegation *n* délégation *f.*

delete *vt* effacer.

deliberate *vt* examiner: — *adj* délibéré.

deliberation *n* délibération *f.*

delicacy *n* délicatesse *f.*

delicate *adj* délicat.

delicious *adj* délicieux.

delight *n* délice *m*: — *vt* enchanter.

delighted *adj* enchanté.

delightful *adj* charmant.

delinquency *n* délinquance *f.*

delinquent *n* délinquant *m*, -e *f.*

delirious *adj* délirant.

deliver *vt* livrer; délivrer.

delivery *n* livraison *f.*

delude *vt* tromper.

delusion *n* tromperie *f*; illusion *f.*

demand *n* demande *f*: — *vt* exiger; réclamer.

demanding *adj* exigeant.

demean *vi* s'abaisser.

demeanour *n* conduite *f*.

democracy *n* démocratie *f*.

democratic *adj* démocratique.

demolish *vt* démolir.

demolition *n* démolition *f*.

demonstrate *vt* démontrer, prouver: —*vi* manifester.

demonstration *n* démonstration *f*.

demonstrator *n* manifestant *m*, -e *f*.

demoralisation *n* démoralisation *f*.

demoralise *vt* démoraliser.

den *n* antre *m*.

denial *n* dénégation *f*.

denims *npl* jean *m*.

denomination *n* valeur *f*; dénomination *f*.

denote *vt* dénoter, indiquer.

denounce *vt* dénoncer.

dense *adj* dense, épais.

dentist *n* dentiste *mf*.

dentistry *n* dentisterie *f*.

denture *n* dentier *m*.

denunciation *n* dénonciation *f*.

deny *vt* nier.

deodorant *n* déodorant *m*.

depart *vi* partir.

department *n* département *m*; service *m*.

department store *n* grand magasin *m*.

departure *n* départ *m*.

depend *vi* dépendre.

dependable *adj* fiable; sûr.

dependent *adj* dépendant.

depict *vt* dépeindre, décrire.

deplorable *adj* déplorable.

deplore *vt* déplorer, lamenter.

depopulated *adj* dépeuplé.

deport *vt* déporter.

deportation *n* déportation *f*.

deportment *n* comportement *m*.

deposit *vt* déposer: —*n* dépôt *m*; caution *f*.

deposition *n* déposition *f*.

depot *n* dépôt *m*.

depreciate *vi* se déprécier.

depreciation *n* dépréciation *f*.

depress *vt* déprimer.

depression *n* dépression *f*.

deprivation *n* privation *f*.

deprive *vt* priver.

depth *n* profondeur *f*.

deputation *n* députation *f*.

depute *vt* députer, déléguer.

deputy *n* député *m*.

deranged *adj* dérangé.

derelict *adj* abandonné.

deride *vt* se moquer de.

derision *n* dérision *f*.

derivative *n* dérivé *m*.

derive *vt vi* dériver.

descend *vi* descendre.

descendant *n* descendant *m*, -e *f*.

descent *n* descente *f*.

describe *vt* décrire.

description *n* description *f*.

descriptive *adj* descriptif.

desert *n* désert *m*: —*adj* désert.

desert *vt* abandonner; déserter: —*n* mérite *m*.

desertion *n* désertion *f*.

deserve *vt* mériter.

design *vt* concevoir; dessiner: —*n* dessein *m*.

designate *vt* désigner.

desirable *adj* désirable.

desire *n* désir *m*: —*vt* désirer.

desist *vi* abandonner.

desk *n* bureau *m*.

desolate *adj* désert, désolé.

despair *n* désespoir *m*: —*vi* se désespérer.

desperate *adj* désespéré.

desperation *n* désespoir *m*.

despicable *adj* méprisable.

despise *vt* mépriser.
despite *prep* malgré.
despondency *n* abattement *m.*
despondent *adj* abattu.
dessert *n* dessert *m.*
destination *n* destination *f.*
destine *vt* destiner.
destiny *n* destin, sort *m.*
destitute *adj* indigent.
destitution *n* indigence *f.*
destroy *vt* détruire.
destruction *n* destruction *f.*
detach *vt* séparer, détacher.
detachable *adj* détachable.
detail *n* détail *m:—in ~* en détail:—*vt* détailler.
detain *vt* retenir; détenir.
detect *vt* détecter.
detection *n* détection *f;* découverte *f.*
detective *n* détective *m.*
detention *n* détention *f.*
deteriorate *vt* détériorer.
deterioration *n* détérioration *f.*
determination *n* détermination *f.*
determine *vt* déterminer, décider.
detest *vt* détester.
detestable *adj* détestable.
detour *n* déviation *f.*
detriment *n* détriment *m.*
devaluation *n* dévaluation *f.*
devaluate *vt* dévaster.
devastation *n* dévastation *f.*
develop *vt* développer.
development *n* développement *m.*
deviate *vi* dévier.
deviation *n* déviation *f.*
device *n* mécanisme *m.*
devil *n* diable, démon *m.*
devise *vt* inventer; concevoir.
devoid *adj* dépourvu.
devote *vt* consacrer.

devoted *adj* dévoué.
devotion *n* dévotion *f.*
devour *vt* dévorer.
dew *n* rosée *f.*
dexterity *n* dextérité *f.*
diagnosis *n* (*med*) diagnostic *m.*
diagram *n* diagramme *m.*
dialect *n* dialecte *m.*
dialogue *n* dialogue *m.*
diamond *n* diamant *m.*
diary *n* journal *m.*
dictate *vt* dicter:—*n* ordre *m.*
dictionary *n* dictionnaire *m.*
die *vi* mourir.
diet *n* diète *f;* régime *m:—vi* être au régime.
differ *vi* différer.
difference *n* différence *f.*
different *adj* différent.
difficult *adj* difficile.
difficulty *n* difficulté *f.*
dig *vt* creuser.
digest *vt* digérer.
digestion *n* digestion *f.*
digestive *adj* digestif.
digit *n* chiffre *m.*
digital *adj* digital.
dignified *adj* digne.
dignity *n* dignité *f.*
digression *n* digression *f.*
dilemma *n* dilemme *m.*
diligence *n* assiduité *f.*
diligent *adj* assidu.
dilute *vt* diluer.
dim *adj* indistinct; faible; sombre.
dimension *n* dimension *f.*
diminish *vt vi* diminuer.
diminutive *n* diminutif *m.*
din *n* vacarme *m.*
dine *vi* dîner.
dinner *n* dîner *m.*

dint n: — **by** ~ **of** à force de.

dip vt tremper.

diploma n diplôme m.

diplomat n diplomate m.

diplomatic adj diplomatique.

dire adj atroce, affreux.

direct adj direct: — vt diriger.

direction n direction f; instruction f.

director n directeur m, -trice f.

directory n annuaire m.

dirt n saleté f.

dirty adj sale.

disability n incapacité f; infirmité f.

disabled adj infirme.

disadvantage n désavantage m: — vt désavantager.

disagree vi ne pas être d'accord.

disagreeable adj désagréable.

disagreement n désaccord m.

disallow vt rejeter.

disappear vi disparaître.

disappearance n disparition f.

disappoint vt décevoir.

disappointment n déception f.

disapproval n désapprobation f.

disapprove vt désapprouver.

disarm vt désarmer.

disaster n désastre m.

disastrous adj désastreux.

disbelief n incrédulité f.

discard vt jeter.

discern vt discerner, percevoir.

discerning adj perspicace.

disciple n disciple m.

discipline n discipline f: — vt discipliner.

disclose vt révéler.

disclosure n révélation f.

disco n discothèque f.

discomfort n incommodité f.

disconnect vt débrancher.

disconsolate adj inconsolable.

discontent n mécontentement m: — adj mécontent.

discontented adj mécontent.

discontinue vt interrompre.

discord n discorde f.

discount n escompte m: — vt escompter.

discourage vt décourager.

discouragement n découragement m.

discourse n discours m.

discourteous adj discourtois.

discover vt découvrir.

discovery n découverte f.

discredit vt discréditer.

discreet adj discret.

discrepancy n contradiction f.

discretion n discrétion f.

discretionary adj discrétionnaire.

discriminate vt distinguer; discriminer.

discrimination n discrimination f.

discuss vt discuter.

discussion n discussion f.

disdain vt dédaigner: — n dédain, mépris m.

disdainful adj dédaigneux.

disease n maladie f.

disembark vt vi débarquer.

disenchant vt désenchanter.

disenchanted adj désenchanté.

disengage vt dégager.

disfigure vt défigurer.

disgrace n honte f; scandale m: — vt déshonorer.

disgraceful adj honteux.

disguise vt déguiser: — n déguisement m.

disgust n dégoût m: — vt dégoûter.

dish n plat m; assiette f.

dishearten vt démoraliser.

dishonest adj malhonnête.

dishonesty n malhonnêteté f.

disillusion vt désillusionner.

disillusioned adj désillusionné.

disinfect *vt* désinfecter.
disinfectant *n* désinfectant *m*.
disinherit *vt* déshériter.
disintegrate *vi* se désintégrer.
disinterested *adj* désintéressé.
disk *n* disque *m*; disquette *f*.
dislike *n* aversion *f*: —*vt* ne pas aimer.
dislocate *vt* disloquer.
dislocation *n* dislocation *f*.
dislodge *vt* déloger.
disloyal *adj* déloyal.
dismantle *vt* démonter.
dismay *n* consternation *f*.
dismiss *vt* renvoyer; écarter.
dismissal *n* renvoi *m*; rejet *m*.
disobedience *n* désobéissance *f*.
disobedient *adj* désobéissant.
disobey *vt* désobéir.
disorder *n* désordre *m*.
disorderly *adj* en désordre, confus.
disorganization *n* désorganisation *f*.
disparage *vt* dénigrer.
disparity *n* disparité *f*.
dispatch *vt* envoyer: —*n* envoi *m*; dépêche *f*.
dispel *vt* dissiper.
dispensary *n* dispensaire *m*.
dispense *vt* dispenser; distribuer.
disperse *vt* disperser.
displace *vt* déplacer.
display *vt* exposer: —*n* exposition *f*.
displeased *adj* mécontent.
displeasure *n* mécontentement *m*.
dispose *vt* disposer.
disposition *n* disposition *f*.
disprove *vt* réfuter.
dispute *n* dispute *f*; controverse *f*: —*vt* mettre en cause.
disqualify *vt* rendre incapable.
dissatisfaction *n* mécontentement *m*.
dissatisfied *adj* mécontent.

disseminate *vt* disséminer.
dissension *n* dissension *f*.
dissent *n* dissension *f*.
dissertation *n* thèse *f*.
dissident *n* dissident *m*, -e *f*.
dissimilar *adj* dissemblable.
dissimilarity *n* dissemblance *f*.
dissipate *vt* dissiper.
dissipation *n* dissipation *f*.
dissolution *n* dissolution *f*.
dissolve *vt* dissoudre.
dissonance *n* dissonance *f*.
dissuade *vt* dissuader.
distance *n* distance *f*.
distant *adj* distant.
distaste *n* dégoût *m*.
distasteful *adj* désagréable.
distil *vt* distiller.
distinct *adj* distinct.
distinction *n* distinction *f*.
distinctive *adj* distinctif.
distinguish *vt* distinguer; discerner.
distort *vt* déformer.
distortion *n* distortion *f*.
distract *vt* distraire.
distracted *adj* distrait.
distraction *n* distraction *f*; confusion *f*.
distress *n* souffrance *f*: —*vt* désoler.
distribute *vt* distribuer, répartir.
distribution *n* distribution *f*.
district *n* district *m*.
disturb *vt* déranger.
disturbance *n* dérangement *m*; trouble *m*.
disturbed *adj* troublé.
disturbing *adj* troublant.
disuse *n* désuétude *f*.
disused *adj* abandonné.
ditch *n* fossé *m*.
dive *vi* plonger.
diver *n* plongeur *m*, -euse *f*.

diverge *vi* diverger.

divergent *adj* divergent.

diverse *adj* divers, différent.

diversion *n* diversion *f.*

diversity *n* diversité *f.*

divert *vt* dévier; divertir.

divide *vt* diviser: — *vi* se diviser.

divine *adj* divin.

divinity *n* divinité *f.*

divisible *adj* divisible.

division *n* division *f.*

divorce *n* divorce *m:* — *vi* divorcer.

divorced *adj* divorcé.

divulge *vt* divulguer.

dizziness *n* vertige *m.*

dizzy *adj* pris de vertige.

do *vt* faire.

docile *adj* docile.

dock *n* dock *m.*

do-it-yourself *n* bricolage *m.*

doctor *n* docteur *m.*

doctrine *n* doctrine *f.*

document *n* document *m.*

documentary *adj* documentaire.

dodge *vt* esquiver.

dog *n* chien *m.*

dogmatic *adj* dogmatique.

doll *n* poupée *f.*

dolphin *n* dauphin *m.*

dome *n* dôme *m.*

domestic *adj* domestique.

domesticate *vt* domestiquer.

domesticity *n* domesticité *f.*

domicile *n* domicile *m.*

dominate *vi* dominer.

domination *n* domination *f.*

donate *vt* donner, faire don de.

donation *n* donation *f.*

donkey *n* âne *m.*

donor *n* donneur *m;* donateur *m.*

door *n* porte *f.*

doorway *n* entrée *f.*

dormant *adj* latent; dormant.

dormitory *n* dortoir *m.*

dosage *n* dose *f;* dosage *m.*

dose *n* dose *f:* — *vt* doser.

dossier *n* dossier *m.*

dot *n* point *m.*

double *adj* double: — *vt* doubler: — *n* double *m.*

double room *n* chambre pour deux *f.*

double-dealing *n* duplicité *f.*

doubt *n* doute *m:* — *vt* douter de.

doubtful *adj* douteux.

douse *vt* éteindre.

dove *n* colombe *f.*

down *n* duvet *m:* — *prep* en bas: — **upside ~** à l'envers.

down-to-earth *adj* pratique; terre à terre.

downfall *n* ruine *f.*

downhearted *adj* découragé.

downhill *adv* en descendant, dans la descente.

downstairs *adv* en bas.

dowry *n* dot *f.*

doze *vi* somnoler.

dozen *n* douzaine *f.*

drab *adj* gris; morne.

drag *vt* tirer: — *n* drague *f;* ennui *m.*

drain *vt* drainer; vider: — *n* tuyau d'écoulement *m.*

drama *n* drame *m.*

dramatic *adj* dramatique.

dramatist *n* dramaturge *mf.*

draught *n* courant d'air *m.*

draw *vt* tirer; dessiner.

drawback *n* désavantage.

drawer *n* tiroir *m.*

drawing *n* dessin *m.*

drawing room *n* salon *m.*

dread *n* terreur *f:* — *vt* redouter.

dreadful *adj* horrible.

dream *n* rêve *m*:—*vi*, *vt* rêver.
dreary *adj* triste, morne.
dress *vi* s'habiller:—*n* robe *f*.
dressing *n* pansement *m*; sauce *f*.
dressy *adj* élégant.
drift *vi* aller à la dérive.
drill *n* perceuse *f*, *vt* percer.
drink *vt vi* boire:—*n* boisson *f*.
drinker *n* buveur *m*, -euse *f*.
drip *vi* goutter:—*n* goutte *f*.
drive *vt vi* conduire.
driver *n* conducteur *m*, -trice *f*; chauffeur *m*.
driving licence *n* permis *m* de conduire.
drizzle *vi* pleuvasser.
drop *n* goutte *f*:—*vt* laisser tomber.
drought *n* sécheresse *f*.
drown *vt* noyer:—*vi* se noyer.
drowsiness *n* somnolence *f*.
drug *n* drogue *f*:—*vt* droguer.
drum *n* tambour *m*:—*vi* jouer du tambour.
drunk *adj* ivre.
drunken *adj* ivre.
drunkenness *n* ivresse *f*.
dry *adj* sec:—*vt* faire sécher:—*vi* sécher.

dryness *n* sécheresse *f*.
dual *adj* double.
dub *adj* doubler.
due *adj* dû, *f* due *n* droit *m*.
duel *n* duel *m*.
dull *adj* terne; insipide.
duly *adv* dûment.
dumb *adj* muet.
dump *n* tas *m*:—*vt* jeter.
duplicate *vt* dupliquer.
duplicity *n* duplicité *f*.
durability *n* durabilité *f*.
durable *adj* durable.
duration *n* durée *f*.
during *prep* pendant.
dusk *n* crépuscule *m*.
dust *n* poussière *f*:—*vt* épousseter.
dutiful *adj* obéissant, soumis.
duty *n* devoir *m*; obligation *f*.
dwarf *n* nain *m*, naine *f*:—*vt* rapetisser.
dwell *vi* habiter, vivre.
dwelling *n* habitation *f*; domicile *m*.
dye *vt* teindre:—*n* teinture *f*.
dying *p*, *adj* mourant.
dynamic *adj* dynamique.
dynasty *n* dynastie *f*.

E

each *pn* chacun:—~ **other** les un(e)s les autres.
eager *adj* enthousiaste.
eagerness *n* enthousiasme *m*.
eagle *n* aigle *m*.
ear *n* oreille *f*; ouïe *f*.
early *adj* premier:—*adv* tôt.
earn *vt* gagner.

earnest *adj* sérieux
earth *n* terre *f*:—*vt* brancher à la terre.
earthquake *n* tremblement de terre *m*.
ease *n* aise *f*; facilité *f*.
easiness *n* facilité *f*.
east *n* est *m*; orient *m*.
Easter *n* Pâques *fpl*.
eastern *adj* de l'est, oriental.

easy *adj* facile.

eat *vt vi* manger.

ebb *n* reflux *m*:—*vi* refluer.

eccentric *adj* excentrique.

eccentricity *n* excentricité *f*.

echo *n* écho *m*:—*vi* résonner.

eclipse *n* éclipse *f*:—*vt* éclipser.

ecology *n* écologie *f*.

economic *adj* économique

economist *n* économiste *mf*.

economise *vt* économiser.

economy *n* économie *f*.

ecstasy *n* extase *f*.

ecstatic *adj* extatique.

edge *n* fil *m*; pointe *f*.

edible *adj* mangeable.

edifice *n* édifice *m*.

edit *vt* diriger; rédiger.

edition *n* édition *f*.

editor *n* rédacteur *m*, -trice *f*.

educate *vt* éduquer; instruire.

education *n* éducation *f*.

efface *vt* effacer.

effect *n* effet *mf*:—~**s** *npl* biens *mpl*: —*vt* effectuer.

effective *adj* efficace; effectif.

effectiveness *n* efficacité *f*.

effectual *adj* efficace.

effeminate *adj* efféminé.

effervescence *n* effervescence *f*.

efficiency *n* efficacité *f*.

efficient *adj* efficace.

effort *n* effort *m*.

egg *n* œuf *m*.

ego(t)ist *n* égoïste *mf*.

ego(t)istical *adj* égoïste.

eight *adj n* huit *m*.

eighteen *adj n* dix-huit *m*.

eighteenth *adj n* dix-huitième *mf*.

eighth *adj n* huitième *mf*.

eightieth *adj n* quatre-vingtième *mf*.

eighty *adj n* quatre-vingt.

either *pn* n'importe lequel/laquelle: —*conj* ou, soit.

eject *vt* éjecter, expulser.

ejection *n* éjection, expulsion *f*.

elaborate *vt* élaborer:—*adj* élaboré.

elapse *vi* passer.

elastic *adj* élastique.

elbow *n* coude *m*.

elder *adj* aîné.

eldest *adj* aîné.

elect *vt* élire; choisir.

election *n* élection *f*; choix *m*.

electoral *adj* électoral.

electorate *n* électorat *m*.

electric(al) *adj* électrique.

electrician *n* électricien *m*.

electricity *n* électricité *f*.

electrify *vt* électriser.

electronic *adj* électronique.

elegance *n* élégance *f*.

elegant *adj* élégant.

element *n* élément *m*.

elementary *adj* élémentaire.

elephant *n* éléphant *m*.

elevate *vt* élever, hausser.

elevation *n* élévation *f*; hauteur *f*.

eleven *adj n* onze *m*.

eleventh *adj n* onzième *mf*.

eligibility *n* éligibilité *f*.

eligible *adj* éligible.

eliminate *vt* éliminer.

elocution *n* élocution *f*.

eloquence *n* éloquence *f*.

eloquent *adj* éloquent.

else *pn* autre.

elsewhere *adv* ailleurs.

elude *vt* éluder; éviter.

emaciated *adj* émacié.

email, e-mail *n* courriel *m*.

emancipate *vt* émanciper.

emancipation *n* émancipation *f*.

embargo *n* embargo *m*.

embark *vt* embarquer.

embarkation *n* embarcation *f*.

embarrass *vt* embarrasser.

embarrassment *n* embarras *m*.

embassy *n* ambassade *f*.

emblem *n* emblème *m*.

embody *vt* incorporer; incarner.

embrace *vt* étreindre; comprendre.

embryo *n* embryon *m*.

emerald *n* émeraude *f*.

emerge *vi* émerger; apparaître.

emergency *n* urgence *f*.

emergency exit *n* sortie de secours *f*.

emigrate *vi* émigrer.

emigration *n* émigration *f*.

emission *n* émission *f*.

emit *vt* émettre.

emotion *n* émotion *f*.

emotional *adj* émotionnel.

emphasise *vt* souligner, accentuer.

emphatic *adj* emphatique.

empire *n* empire *m*.

employ *vt* employer.

employee *n* employé *m*, -e *f*.

employer *n* employeur *m*.

employment *n* emploi, travail *m*.

emptiness *n* vide *m*.

empty *adj* vide; vain: — *vt* vider.

emulate *vt* imiter.

enable *vt* permettre.

enamour *vt* s'éprendre de.

encamp *vi* camper.

encampment *n* campement *m*.

encase *vt* entourer.

enchant *vt* enchanter.

enchantment *n* enchantement *m*.

encircle *vt* encercler.

enclose *vt* entourer.

enclosure *n* clôture *f*.

encompass *vt* comprendre.

encounter *n* rencontre *f*: — *vt* rencontrer.

encourage *vt* encourager.

encouragement *n* encouragement *m*.

encyclopedia *n* encyclopédie *f*.

end *n* fin *f*; extrémité *f*: — **to the ~ that** afin que: — *vt vi* terminer.

endanger *vt* mettre en danger.

endeavour *vi* s'efforcer: — *n* effort *m*.

endorse *vt* endosser; approuver.

endorsement *n* endos *m*; approbation *f*.

endurable *adj* supportable.

endurance *n* endurance *f*.

endure *vt* supporter: — *vi* durer.

enemy *n* ennemi *mf*.

energetic *adj* énergique.

energy *n* énergie, force *f*.

enfeeble *vt* affaiblir.

enfold *vt* envelopper.

enforce *vt* mettre en vigueur.

engage *vt* aborder.

engaged *adj* fiancé; occupé.

engagement *n* engagement *m*.

engender *vt* engendrer.

engine *n* moteur *m*; locomotive *f*.

engineer *n* ingénieur *m*; mécanicien *m*.

engineering *n* ingénierie *f*.

enigma *n* énigme *f*.

enjoy *vr*: — **to ~ oneself** s'amuser.

enjoyable *adj* agréable; amusant.

enjoyment *n* plaisir *m*; jouissance *f*.

enlarge *vt* agrandir; étendre.

enlargement *n* agrandissement *m*.

enlist *vt* recruter.

enliven *vt* animer; égayer.

enmity *n* inimitié *f*; haine *f*.

enormous *adj* énorme.

enough *adv* suffisamment; assez: — *n* assez *m*.

enrich *vt* enrichir; orner.

enrichment *n* enrichissement *m*.

enrol vt enrôler; inscrire.

ensue vi s'ensuivre.

ensure vt assurer.

entail vt impliquer, entraîner.

enter vt entrer dans; inscrire.

enterprise n entreprise f.

enterprising adj entreprenant.

entertain vt divertir.

entertaining adj divertissant, amusant.

enthusiasm n enthousiasme m.

enthusiast n enthousiaste mf.

enthusiastic adj enthousiaste.

entire adj entier, complet.

entitle vt intituler.

entity n entité f.

entrance n entrée f; admission f.

entrant n participant m, -e f.

entreat vt implorer.

entrust vt confier.

entry n entrée f.

enumerate vt énumérer.

envelop vt envelopper.

envelope n enveloppe f.

envious adj envieux.

environment n environnement m.

environmental adj relatif à l'environnement.

envisage vt envisager.

envy n envie f:—vt envier.

epidemic adj épidémique:—n épidémie f.

episode n épisode m.

epitomise vt incarner; résumer.

equable adj uniforme.

equal adj égal; semblable:—n égal m, -e f:—vt égaler.

equalise vt égaliser.

equality n égalité f.

equanimity n équanimité f.

equate vt égaliser.

equator n équateur m.

equilibrium n équilibre m.

equip vt équiper.

equipment n équipement m.

equivalent adj n équivalent m.

equivocal adj équivoque.

equivocate vt équivoquer.

era n ère f.

eradicate vt supprimer.

eradication n suppression f.

erase vt effacer.

eraser n gomme f.

erect vt ériger:—adj droit, debout.

erode vt éroder; ronger.

erotic adj érotique.

err vi se tromper.

errand n message m.

erratic adj changeant; irrégulier.

erroneous adj erroné.

error n erreur f.

erudite adj érudit.

eruption n éruption f.

escalate vi monter en flèche.

escape vt éviter:—vi s'évader, s'échapper:—n évasion.

escort n escorte f:—vt escorter.

especial adj spécial.

essay n essai m.

essence n essence f.

essential n essentiel m:—adj essentiel.

establish vt établir.

establishment n établissement m.

estate n état m; biens mpl.

esteem vt estimer:—n estime f.

esthetic adj esthétique f.

estimate vt estimer; évaluer.

estimation n estimation.

estuary n estuaire m.

eternal adj éternel.

eternity n éternité f.

ethical adj éthique.

ethics npl éthique f.

ethnic adj ethnique.

etiquette n étiquette f.

evacuate vt évacuer.

evacuation n évacuation f.

evade vt éviter; échapper à.

evaluate vt évaluer.

evaporate vi s'évaporer.

evaporation n évaporation f.

evasion n dérobade f.

evasive adj évasif.

eve n veille f.

even adj pair:—adv même:—vt égaliser.

evening n soir m, soirée f.

evenness n égalité f; impartialité f.

event n événement m.

eventual adj final:—~ly adv finalement, en fin de comptes.

eventuality n éventualité f.

ever adv toujours; jamais.

everlasting adj éternel.

every adj chacun, chacune:—~where partout:—~thing tout:—~one, ~body tout le monde.

evict vt expulser.

eviction n expulsion f.

evidence n évidence f.

evident adj évident.

evil adj malveillant:—n mal m.

evocative adj évocateur.

evoke vt évoquer.

evolution n évolution f.

evolve vi évoluer.

exacerbate vt exacerber.

exact adj exact:—vt exiger.

exacting adj exigeant.

exaction n exaction f; extorsion f.

exactness n exactitude f.

exaggerate vt exagérer.

exaggeration n exagération f.

exalt vt exalter; élever.

examination n examen m.

examine vt examiner.

example n exemple m.

exasperate vt exaspérer.

exasperation n exaspération f.

excavate vt excaver, creuser.

excavation n excavation f.

exceed vt excéder, dépasser.

excel vt surpasser; vi exceller.

excellence n excellence f.

excellent adj excellent.

except vt excepter:—~(ing) prep excepté, à l'exception de.

exception n exception f.

exceptional adj exceptionnel.

excess n excès m.

excessive adj excessif.

exchange vt échanger:—n échange m.

exchange rate n taux de change m.

excise n impôt m.

excitable adj excitable.

excite vt exciter; animer.

excited adj animé, enthousiaste.

excitement n animation f.

exciting adj passionnant; stimulant.

exclaim vi s'exclamer.

exclamation n exclamation f.

exclude vt exclure.

exclusion n exclusion f; exception f.

exclusive adj exclusif.

excommunicate vt excommunier.

exculpate vt disculper; justifier.

excursion n excursion f; digression f.

excusable adj excusable.

excuse vt excuser:—n excuse f.

execute vt exécuter.

execution n exécution f.

executive adj exécutif.

exemplary adj exemplaire.

exemplify vt exemplifier.

exempt adj exempt.

exemption n exemption f.

exercise n exercice m:—vt exercer.

exert vt employer, exercer.

exertion n effort m.

exhale vt exhaler.

exhaust n vt épuiser.

exhaustion n épuisement m.

exhaustive adj exhaustif.

exhibit vt exhiber.

exhibition n exposition, présentation f.

exhilarating adj stimulant.

exhilaration n joie f; stimulation f.

exhume vt exhumer, déterrer.

exile n exil m:—vt exiler, déporter.

exist vi exister.

existence n existence f.

existent adj existant.

exit n sortie f:—vi sortir.

exonerate vt disculper.

exoneration n disculpation f.

exorbitant adj exorbitant, excessif.

exotic adj exotique.

expand vt étendre.

expanse n étendue f.

expansion n expansion f.

expect vt attendre; espérer.

expectancy n attente f; espoir m.

expectation n expectative f; attente f.

expediency n convenance f; opportunité f.

expedient adj opportun.

expedite vt accélérer; expédier.

expedition n expédition f.

expel vt expulser.

expend vt dépenser; utiliser.

expense n dépense f; coût m.

expensive adj cher; coûteux.

experience n expérience f; pratique f:—vt ressentir; connaître.

experienced adj expérimenté.

experiment n expérience f:—vi expérimenter.

experimental adj expérimental.

expert adj expert.

expertise n habileté f.

explain vt expliquer.

explanation n explication f.

explanatory adj explicatif.

explicit adj explicite.

explode vt faire exploser:—vi exploser.

exploit vt exploiter:—n exploit m.

exploitation n exploitation f.

exploration n exploration f.

explore vt explorer; sonder.

explorer n explorateur m, -trice f.

explosion n explosion f.

explosive adj n explosif m.

export vt exporter.

exportation n exportation f.

exporter n exportateur m, -trice f.

expose vt exposer; dévoiler.

exposition n exposition f.

exposure n exposition f; temps de pose m.

expound vt exposer; interpréter.

express vt exprimer:—adj exprès:—n exprès m; (rail) rapide m.

expression n expression f.

expressive adj expressif.

expropriate vt exproprier.

expulsion n expulsion f.

exquisite adj exquis.

extemporise vi improviser.

extend vt étendre:—vi s'étendre.

extension n extension f.

extensive adj étendu.

extent n extension f.

extenuate vt atténuer.

exterior adj n extérieur m.

exterminate vt exterminer.

external adj externe.

extinct adj disparu; éteint.

extinction n extinction f.

extinguish vt éteindre.

extinguisher n extincteur m.

extort vt extorquer.

extortion n extorsion f.

extra adv particulièrement; n supplément m.

extract vt extraire:—n extrait m.

extraction n extraction f; origine f.

extraneous adj superflu; sans rapport.

extraordinary adj extraordinaire.

extravagance n extravagance f.

extravagant adj extravagant.

extreme adj extrême.

extremist adj n extrémiste mf.

extricate vt extirper, démêler.

extrovert adj n extraverti m, -e f.

exuberance n exubérance f.

exuberant adj exubérant.

eye n œil m:—vt regarder; lorgner.

eyebrow n sourcil m.

eyelash n cil m.

eyelid n paupière f.

eyesight n vue f.

F

fabric n tissu m.

fabricate vt fabriquer; inventer.

fabrication n fabrication f.

fabulous adj fabuleux.

face n visage m; mine f; apparence f:—vt faire face à.

facet n facette f.

facile adj facile.

facilitate vt faciliter.

facility n facilité f; équipement m.

facing n revers m:—prep en face de.

fact n fait m; réalité f:—**in ~** en fait.

factory n usine f.

factual adj factuel.

faculty n faculté f.

fail vt échouer à; omettre:—vi échouer; faiblir; manquer.

failure n faillite f; manquement m.

faint vi s'évanouir, défaillir:—n évanouissement m:—adj faible.

fair adj beau; blond; équitable; considérable:—n foire f.

fairness n beauté f; justice f.

fair play n fair-play.

faith n foi f; croyance f; fidélité f.

faithful adj fidèle, loyal.

fake n falsification f:—adj faux:—vt falsifier.

fall vi tomber; baisser:—n chute f; automne m.

fallacy n erreur f; tromperie f.

fallibility n faillibilité f.

fallible adj faillible.

false adj faux.

false alarm n fausse alerte f.

falsify vt falsifier.

falter vi vaciller.

fame n réputation f; renommée f.

familiar adj familier.

familiarise vt familiariser.

familiarity n familiarité f.

family n famille f.

famine n famine f.

famous adj célèbre, fameux.

fan n éventail m; ventilateur m:—vt éventer.

fancy n caprice m:—vt avoir envie de; s'imaginer.

fantastic adj fantastique; excentrique.

fantasy n fantaisie f.

far *adv* loin: — *adj* lointain, éloigné.

fare *n* prix (du voyage) *m*; tarif *m*; régime alimentaire *m*.

farewell *n* adieu *m*.

farm *n* ferme *f*: — *vt* cultiver.

farmer *n* fermier *m*; agriculteur *m*.

farming *n* agriculture *f*.

fascinate *vt* fasciner, captiver.

fascination *n* fascination *f*; charme *m*.

fashion *n* manière, façon *f*; mode *f*: — *vt* façonner.

fashionable *adj* à la mode; chic.

fast *vi* jeûner: — *n* jeûne *m*: — *adj* rapide: — *adv* rapidement.

fasten *vt* attacher; fixer.

fast food *n* restauration rapide *f*.

fat *adj* gros, gras: — *n* graisse *f*.

fatal *adj* mortel.

fatality *n* fatalité *f*.

fate *n* destin, sort *m*.

father *n* père *m*.

fatherhood *n* paternité *f*.

fatigue *n* fatigue *f*: — *vt* fatiguer.

fatuous *adj* imbécile.

fault *n* défaut *m*, faute *f*; délit *m*.

faulty *adj* défectueux.

favour *n* faveur *f*: — *vt* favoriser.

favourable *adj* favorable.

favourite *n* favori *m*: — *adj* favori.

fax *n* fax *m*: — *vt* envoyer par fax.

fear *vt* craindre: — *n* crainte *f*.

fearful *adj* effrayant; craintif.

fearless *adj* intrépide, courageux.

feasibility *n* faisabilité *f*.

feasible *adj* faisable.

feast *n* banquet *m*; fête *f*.

feat *n* exploit *m*; prouesse *f*.

feather *n* plume *f*.

feature *n* trait *m*: — *vi* figurer.

February *n* février *m*.

fed-up *adj*: — **to be** ~ en avoir marre.

fee *n* honoraires *mpl*.

feeble *adj* faible, frêle.

feebleness *n* faiblesse *f*.

feed *vt* nourrir: — *vi* manger; se nourrir.

feel *vt* sentir; toucher: — *n* sensation *f*.

feeling *n* sensation *f*; sentiment *m*.

feign *vt* feindre, simuler.

fellow *n* homme, type *m*.

female *n* femelle *f*: — *adj* femelle.

feminine *adj* féminin.

feminist *n* féministe *mf*.

fence *n* barrière *f*; clôture *f*.

ferment *n* agitation *f*: — *vi* fermenter.

ferocious *adj* féroce.

ferocity *n* férocité *f*.

ferry *n* bac *m*; ferry *m*: — *vt* transporter.

fertile *adj* fertile, fécond.

fertility *n* fertilité, fécondité *f*.

fervent *adj* fervent; ardent.

fervour *n* ferveur *f*.

festival *n* fête *f*; festival *m*.

festive *adj* de fête.

fetch *vt* aller chercher.

fetching *adj* charmant, séduisant.

feud *n* rivalité *f*.

fever *n* fièvre *f*.

feverish *adj* fiévreux.

few *adj* peu: — **a** ~ quelques.

fibre *n* fibre *f*.

fickle *adj* volage, inconstant.

fiction *n* fiction *f*; invention *f*.

fictional *adj* fictif.

fictitious *adj* fictif, imaginaire.

fidelity *n* fidélité, loyauté *f*.

fidget *vi* s'agiter, remuer.

fidgety *adj* agité, remuant.

field *n* champ *m*; domaine *m*.

fiend *n* démon *m*.

fiendish *adj* diabolique.

fierce *adj* féroce; acharné.

fierceness *n* férocité, fureur *f*.

fifteen *adj n* quinze *m*.

fifteenth *adj n* quinzième *mf*.

fifth *adj n* cinquième *mf*.

fiftieth *adj n* cinquantième *mf*.

fifty *adj n* cinquante *m*.

fight *vt vi* combattre; lutter: —*n* combat *m*.

fighter *n* combattant *m*.

figure *n* figure *f*; image *f*; chiffre *m*.

file *n* file *f*; liste *f*; dossier *m*; fichier *m*: —*vt* enregistrer; classer.

fill *vt* remplir.

fillet *n* filet *m*.

film *n* pellicule *f*; film *f*: —*vt* filmer: —*vi* s'embuer.

filter *n* filtre *m*: —*vt* filtrer.

filth *n* immondice, ordure *f*.

filthy *adj* crasseux, dégoûtant.

fin *n* nageoire *f*.

final *adj* dernier; définitif.

finalise *vt* parachever.

finance *n* finance *f*.

financial *adj* financier.

financier *n* financier *m*.

find *vt* trouver: —*n* trouvaille *f*.

findings *npl* résultats *mpl*.

fine *adj* fin; pur; délicat: —*n* amende *f*.

finesse *n* finesse, subtilité *f*.

finger *n* doigt *m*: —*vt* manier.

fingernail *n* ongle *m*.

finish *vt* finir, terminer.

fir (tree) *n* sapin *m*

fire engine *n* voiture de pompiers *f*.

fire extinguisher *n* extincteur *m*.

fire *n* feu *m*; incendie *m*: —*vt* incendier: —*vi* s'enflammer.

fire station *n* caserne de pompiers *f*.

firearm *n* arme à feu *f*.

fireman *n* pompier *m*.

fireplace *n* cheminée *f*, foyer *m*.

fireproof *adj* ignifugé.

fireworks *npl* feu d'artifice *m*.

firm *adj* ferme: —*n* (*com*) compagnie *f*.

firmness *n* fermeté *f*; résolution *f*.

first *adj* premier: —*adv* premièrement.

first aid *n* premiers secours *mpl*.

first name *n* prénom *m*.

first-class *adj* de première classe.

first-hand *adj* de première main.

first-rate *adj* de première qualité.

fish *n* poisson *m*: —*vi* pêcher.

fisherman *n* pêcheur *m*.

fishing *n* pêche *f*.

fissure *n* fissure, crevasse *f*.

fist *n* poing *m*.

fit *n* accès *m*: —*adj* en forme; capable: —*vt* adapter: —*vi* (bien) aller.

fitness *n* forme physique *f*.

fitting *adj* qui convient, approprié: —*n* accessoire *ml*.

five *adj n* cinq *m*.

fix *vt* fixer, établir.

fixation *n* obsession *f*.

fixed *adj* fixe.

fizz(le) *vi* pétiller.

fizzy *adj* gazeux.

flabby *adj* mou, *f* molle, flasque.

flag *n* drapeau *m*: —*vi* s'affaiblir.

flagrant *adj* flagrant.

flair *n* flair *m*; talent *m*.

flake *n* flocon *m*: —*vi* s'effriter.

flamboyant *adj* flamboyant.

flame *n* flamme *f*, ardeur *f*.

flammable *adj* inflammable.

flank *n* flanc *m*.

flap *n* battement *m*; rabat *m*.

flare *vi* luire, briller: —*n* flamme *f*.

flash *n* éclat *m*: —*vt* allumer.

flask *n* flasque *f*; flacon *m*.

flat *adj* plat; insipide.

flatten *vt* aplanir; aplatir.

flatter *vt* flatter.

flattery n flatterie f.

flaunt vt étaler, afficher.

flavour n saveur m: — vt assaisonner.

flaw n défaut m; imperfection f.

fleck n petite tache f; particule f.

flee vt fuir de: — vi s'enfuir.

fleece n toison f.

fleet n flotte f; parc m.

fleeting adj fugace, fugitif.

flesh n chair f.

flex n cordon m: — vt fléchir.

flexibility n flexibilité f.

flexible adj flexible, souple.

flicker vi vaciller; trembloter.

flier n aviateur m, -trice f.

flight n vol m; fuite f; volée f.

flight attendant n steward m, hôtesse de l'air f.

flimsy adj léger; fragile.

flinch vi sourciller.

fling vt lancer, jeter.

flip vt lancer.

flippant adj désinvolte, cavalier.

flipper n nageoire f.

flirt vi flirter: — n charmeur m, -euse f.

flirtation n flirt f.

float vt faire flotter: — vi flotter: — n flotteur m; char (de carnaval) m.

flock n troupeau m; foule f: — vi affluer.

flood n inondation f; déluge m: — vt inonder.

floodlight n projecteur m.

floor n sol m; plancher m; étage m: — vt parqueter.

flop n four, fiasco m.

floppy adj lâche: — n disquette f.

flora n flore f.

floral adj floral.

florid adj fleuri.

florist n fleuriste mf.

flounder n flet m: — vi patauger.

flour n farine f.

flourish vi fleurir; prospérer.

flourishing adj florissant.

flout vt mépriser.

flow vi couler; circuler: — n flux m; écoulement m; flot m.

flower n fleur f: — vi fleurir.

flowery adj fleuri.

fluctuate vi fluctuer.

fluctuation n fluctuation f.

fluency n aisance f.

fluent adj coulant; facile.

fluff n peluche f.

fluid adj n fluide m.

fluke n veine f.

flurry n rafale f; agitation f.

flush vi rougir: — n rougeur f; éclat m.

flushed adj rouge.

fluster vt énerver.

flute n flûte f.

flutter vi voleter; s'agiter.

fly vt piloter: — vi voler; fuir: — n mouche f; braguette f.

flying n aviation f.

foam n écume f: — vi écumer.

foamy adj écumeux.

focus n foyer m; centre m.

foe n ennemi m, -e f.

fog n brouillard m.

foggy adj brumeux.

fold n pli m: — vt plier.

folder n chemise f; dépliant m.

folding adj pliant.

foliage n feuillage m.

folio n folio m.

folk n gens mpl.

folklore n folklore m.

follow vt suivre: — vi suivre, s'ensuivre.

follower n partisan m, -e f; adhérent m, -e f.

folly n folie, extravagance f.

fond adj affectueux: — **to be ~ of** aimer.

fondle *vt* caresser.

fondness *n* prédilection *f*; affection *f*.

food *n* nourriture *f*.

food processor *n* robot *m*.

foodstuffs *npl* denrées alimentaires *fpl*.

fool *n* imbécile *mf*:—*vt* duper.

foolhardy *adj* téméraire.

foolish *adj* idiot, insensé.

foolproof *adj* infaillible.

foolscap *n* papier ministre *m*.

foot *n* pied *m*.

football *n* football *m*; ballon de football *m*.

footballer *n* footballeur *m*, -euse *f*.

footbridge *n* passerelle *f*.

footnote *n* note (de bas de page) *f*.

footpath *n* sentier *m*.

footprint *n* empreinte (de pas) *f*.

footstep *n* pas *m*.

for *prep* pour; en raison de; pendant: —*conj* car:—**as ~ me** quant à moi.

foray *n* incursion *f*.

forbid *vt* interdire, défendre.

forbidding *adj* menaçant; sévère.

force *n* force *f*; puissance:—*vt* forcer, contraindre.

forceful *adj* énergique.

forceps *n* forceps *m*.

forcible *adj* énergique, vigoureux.

forearm *n* avant-bras *m*.

foreboding *n* pressentiment *m*.

forecast *vt* prévoir:—*n* prévision *f*.

forefinger *n* index *m*.

foregone *adj* passé; anticipé.

foreground *n* premier plan *m*.

forehead *n* front *m*.

foreign *adj* étranger.

foreigner *n* étranger *m*, -ère *f*.

foreman *n* contremaître *m*.

foremost *adj* principal.

forensic *adj* judiciaire.

forerunner *n* précurseur *m*.

foresee *vt* prévoir.

foresight *n* prévoyance *f*; prescience *f*.

forest *n* forêt *f*.

foretaste *n* avant-goût *m*.

foretell *vt* prédire.

forever *adv* toujours; un temps infini.

forewarn *vt* prévenir à l'avance.

foreword *n* préface *f*.

forfeit *n* amende *f*:—*vt* perdre.

forge *n* forge *f*:—*vt* forger.

forger *n* faussaire *mf*.

forgery *n* contrefaçon *f*.

forget *vt vi* oublier.

forgetful *adj* étourdi; négligent.

forgive *vt* pardonner.

forgiveness *n* pardon *m*.

fork *n* fourchette *f*; fourche *f*:—*vi* bifurquer.

forked *adj* fourchu.

form *n* forme *f*; formalité *f*; moule *m*:—*vt* former.

formal *adj* formel.

formality *n* formalité *f*.

format *n* format *m*:—*vt* formater.

formation *n* formation *f*.

formative *adj* formateur *m*, -trice *f*.

former *adj* précédent, ancien:—**~ly** *adv* autrefois, jadis.

formula *n* formule *f*.

forsake *vt* abandonner, renoncer à.

fort *n* fort *m*.

forthcoming *adj* prochain; sociable.

forthwith *adv* immédiatement, tout de suite.

fortieth *adj n* quarantième *mf*.

fortification *n* fortification *f*.

fortify *vt* fortifier, renforcer.

fortnight *n* quinze jours *mpl*:—*adj* **~ly** bimensuel:—*adv* **~ly** tous les quinze jours.

fortuitous *adj* fortuit; imprévu.

fortunate adj chanceux.

fortune n chance f; sort m; fortune f.

forty adj n quarante m.

forward adj avancé; précoce; présomptueux: — ~(s) adv en avant:—vt transmettre.

forwardness n précocité f.

fossil n fossile m.

foster vt élever.

foster child n enfant adoptif m.

foul adj infect:—vt polluer.

found vt fonder, créer; établir.

foundation n foundation f; fondement m.

foundry n fonderie f.

fountain n fontaine f.

four adj n quatre m.

fourfold adj quadruple.

fourteen adj n quatorze m.

fourteenth adj n quatorzième mf.

fourth adj n quatrième mf:—n quart m.

fowl n volaille f.

fox n renard f.

foyer n vestibule m.

fracas n rixe f.

fraction n fraction f.

fracture n fracture f:—vt fracturer.

fragile adj fragile.

fragility n fragilité f.

fragment n fragment m.

fragmentary adj fragmentaire.

fragrance n parfum m.

fragrant adj parfumé, odorant.

frail adj frêle, fragile.

frailty n fragilité f; faiblesse f.

frame n charpente f; cadre m:—vt encadrer.

franchise n droit de vote m; franchise f.

frank adj franc, direct.

frankness n franchise f.

frantic adj frénétique.

fraternal adv fraternel.

fraternise vi fraterniser.

fratricide n fratricide mf.

fraud n fraude, tromperie f.

fraudulent adj frauduleux.

free adj libre; autonome; gratuit; dégagé: —vt affranchir; libérer; débarrasser.

freedom n liberté f.

freelance adj indépendant:—adv en indépendant.

freely adv librement; libéralement.

freewheel vi rouler au point mort.

free will n libre arbitre m.

freeze vi geler:—vt congeler; geler.

freezer n congélateur m.

freezing adj gelé.

freight n cargaison f; fret m.

freighter n affréteur m.

French fries npl frites fpl.

French window n porte-fenêtre f.

frenzied adj fou, frénétique.

frenzy n frénésie f; folie f.

frequency n fréquence f.

frequent adj fréquent:—vt fréquenter.

fresco n fresque f.

fresh adj frais; nouveau, récent.

freshen vt rafraîchir:—vi se rafraîchir.

freshly adv récemment.

freshness n fraîcheur f.

freshwater adj d'eau douce.

fret vi s'agiter, se tracasser.

friction n friction f.

Friday n vendredi m:—**Good ~** Vendredi Saint m.

friend n ami m, -e f.

friendliness n amitié, bienveillance f.

friendly adj amical.

friendship n amitié f.

fright n peur, frayeur f.

frighten vt effrayer.

frightened adj effrayé, apeuré.

frightful adj épouvantable.

frigid adj glacé; frigide.

fringe n frange f.

frisk vt fouiller.

frivolity n frivolité f.

frivolous adj frivole.

fro adv: — **to go to and ~** aller et venir.

frock n robe f.

frog n grenouille f.

frolic vi folâtrer.

from prep de; depuis; à partir de.

front n avant, devant m; front m: — adj de devant; premier.

front door n porte d'entrée f.

frontier n frontière f.

front-wheel drive n (auto) traction avant f.

frost n gel m; gelée f: — vt geler.

frostbite n engelure f.

frostbitten adj gelé.

frosty adj glacial; givré.

froth n écume f: — vi écumer.

frothy adj mousseux, écumeux.

frown vt froncer les sourcils.

frozen adj gelé.

frugal adj frugal; économique.

fruit n fruit m.

fruiterer n fruitier m, -ière f.

fruitful adj fécond, fertile; fructueux.

fruition n réalisation f.

fruitless adj stérile.

frustrate vt contrecarrer; annuler.

frustrated adj frustré.

frustration n frustration f.

fry vt frire.

frying pan n poêle f.

fudge n caramel m.

fuel n combustible, carburant m.

fuel tank n réservoir à carburant m.

fugitive adj n fugitif m, -ive f.

fulfil vt accomplir; réaliser.

fulfilment n accomplissement m.

full adj plein, rempli; complet: — adv pleinement, entièrement.

full moon n pleine lune f.

fullness n plénitude f; abondance f.

full-time adj à plein temps.

fully adv pleinement, entièrement.

fumble vi farfouiller.

fume vi rager, fumer.

fumigate vt fumiger.

fun n amusement m: — **to have ~** (bien) s'amuser.

function n fonction f.

functional adj fonctionnel.

fund n fonds m: — vt financer.

fundamental adj fondamental.

funeral service n office des morts m.

funeral n enterrement m.

funnel n entonnoir m; cheminée f.

funny adj amusant; curieux.

fur n fourrure f.

furious adj furieux; déchaîné.

furnace n fourneau m; chaudière f.

furnish vt meubler; fournir.

furniture n meubles mpl.

furrow n sillon m: — vt sillonner.

furry adj à poil.

further adj supplémentaire; plus lointain: — adv plus loin; en outre; de plus: — vt favoriser; promouvoir.

further education n formation continue f.

furthermore adv de plus.

furtive adj furtif; secret.

fury n fureur f; colère f.

fuse vi fondre, sauter: — n fusible m; amorce f.

fuse box n boîte à fusibles f.

fusion n fusion f.

fuss n tapage m.

fussy adj tatillon, chipoteur.

futile adj futile, vain.

futility n futilité f.

future adj futur: — n futur m; avenir m.

fuzzy adj flou, confus.

G

gabble *vi* baragouiner: — *n* charabia *m*.
gadget *n* gadget *m*.
gaiety *n* gaieté *f*.
gain *n* gain *m*; bénéfice *m*: — *vt* gagner.
gait *n* démarche *f*; maintien *m*.
galaxy *n* galaxie *f*.
gale *n* grand vent *m*.
gallant *adj* galant.
gallery *n* galerie *f*.
gallop *n* galop *m*: — *vi* galoper.
galore *adv* en abondance.
galvanise *vt* galvaniser.
gamble *vi* jouer; spéculer: — *n* risque *m*; pari *m*.
gambler *n* joueur *m*, -euse *f*.
gambling *n* jeu *m*.
game *n* jeu *m*; divertissement *m*: — *vi* jouer.
gang *n* gang *m*, bande *f*.
gangway *n* passerelle *f*.
gap *n* vide *m*; écart *m*.
garage *n* garage *m*.
garbage *n* ordures *fpl*.
garbage can *n* poubelle *f*.
garden *n* jardin *m*.
gardener *n* jardinier *m*, -ière *f*.
gardening *n* jardinage *m*.
garlic *n* ail *m*.
garment *n* vêtement *m*.
garnish *vt* garnir: — *n* garniture *f*.
garret *n* mansarde *f*.
garrulous *adj* locace, bavard.
garter *n* jarretelle *f*.
gas *n* gaz *m*; essence *f*.
gas cylinder *n* bouteille de gaz *f*.
gaseous *adj* gazeux.

gash *n* entaille *f*: — *vt* entailler.
gasoline *n* essence *f*.
gasp *vi* haleter.
gas station *n* poste d'essence *m*.
gassy *adj* gazeux.
gastronomic *adj* gastronomique.
gate *n* porte *f*; portail *m*.
gather *vt* rassembler; ramasser: — *vi* se rassembler.
gaudy *adj* criard.
gauge *n* calibre *m*: — *vt* calibrer.
gaunt *adj n* maigre *mf*.
gay *adj* gai; vif.
gaze *vi* contempler: — *n* regard *m*.
gear *n* équipement *m*, matériel *m*; vitesse *f*.
gearbox *n* boîte de vitesses *f*.
gem *n* pierre précieuse *f*; perle *f*.
gender *n* genre *m*.
gene *n* gène *m*.
genealogical *adj* généalogique.
genealogy *n* généalogie *f*.
general *adj* général: — **in ~** en général: — *n* général *m*.
generalisation *n* généralisation *f*.
generalise *vt* généraliser.
generation *n* génération *f*.
generator *n* générateur *m*.
generosity *n* générosité, libéralité *f*.
generous *adj* généreux.
genial *adj* bienveillant; doux.
genitals *npl* organes génitaux *mpl*.
genius *n* génie *m*.
gentle *adj* doux, *f* douce, modéré.
gentleman *n* gentleman *m*.
gentleness *n* douceur *f*.

162

genuine *adj* authentique; sincère.

genus *n* genre *m*.

geographer *n* géographe *mf*.

geography *n* géographie *f*.

geologist *n* géologue *mf*.

geology *n* géologie *f*.

geometry *n* géométrie *f*.

germinate *vi* germer.

gesticulate *vi* gesticuler.

gesture *n* geste *m*.

get *vt* avoir; obtenir:—*vi* devenir.

geyser *n* geyser *m*; chauffe-eau *m invar*.

ghost *n* fantôme, spectre *m*.

giant *n* géant *m*, -e *f*.

gibe *vi* se moquer:—*n* moquerie *f*.

giddiness *n* vertige *m*.

giddy *adj* vertigineux.

gift *n* cadeau *m*.

gifted *adj* talentueux; doué.

gigantic *adj* gigantesque.

gild *vt* dorer.

gills *pl* branchies *fpl*.

ginger *n* gingembre *m*.

ginger-haired *adj* roux, *f* rousse.

girl *n* fille *f*.

girlfriend *n* amie *f*; petite amie *f*.

gist *n* essence *f*.

give *vt* donner; remettre.

gizzard *n* gésier *m*.

glacial *adj* glacial.

glacier *n* glacier *m*.

glad *adj* joyeux, content.

gladden *vt* réjouir.

glamour *n* attrait *m*, séduction *f*.

glamorous *adj* attrayant, séduisant.

glance *vi* jeter un coup d'œil.

glare *n* éclat *m*:—*vi* éblouir.

glass *n* verre *m*:—~**es** *pl* lunettes *fpl*.

glaze *vt* vitrer.

gleam *n* rayon *m*.

glee *n* joie *f*; exultation *f*.

glide *vi* glisser; planer.

glimmer *n* lueur *f*:—*vi* luire.

glimpse *n* aperçu *m*:—*vt* entrevoir.

glint *vi* briller, scintiller.

glitter *vi* luire, briller.

global *adj* global; mondial.

globe *n* globe *m*; sphère *f*.

gloom *n* obscurité *f*; mélancolie.

gloomy *adj* sombre, mélancolique.

glorious *adj* glorieux, illustre.

glory *n* gloire, célébrité *f*.

glove *n* gant *m*.

glow *vi* rougeoyer:—*n* rougeoiment *m*.

glue *n* colle *f*:—*vt* coller.

glum *adj* abattu, triste.

glutton *n* glouton *m*, -onne *f*.

gnome *n* gnome *m*.

go *vi* aller:—~ **away** s'en aller.

goal *n* but, objectif *m*.

gobble *vt* engloutir.

God *n* Dieu *m*.

godfather *n* parrain *m*.

godlike *adj* divin.

godmother *n* marraine *f*.

gold *n* or *m*.

golden *adj* doré; d'or.

goldsmith *n* orfèvre *m*.

golf *n* golf *m*.

golfer *n* golfeur *m*, -euse *f*.

gong *n* gong *m*.

good *adj* bon; valable:—*n* bien *m*:—~**s** *pl* biens *mpl*.

goodbye! *excl* au revoir!

good-looking *adj* beau.

goodness *n* bonté *f*, qualité *f*.

goodwill *n* bienveillance *f*.

goose *n* oie *f*.

gorge *n* gorge *f*:—*vt* engloutir, avaler.

gorgeous *adj* merveilleux.

gory *adj* sanglant.

gossip *n* potins *mpl*:—*vi* potiner.

govern *vt* gouverner, diriger.
government *n* gouvernement *m*.
governor *n* gouverneur *m*.
gown *n* toge *f*; robe *f*.
grab *vt* saisir.
grace *n* grâce *f*:—*vt* honorer.
graceful *adj* gracieux.
gradation *n* gradation *f*.
grade *n* grade *m*.
gradual *adj* graduel.
graduate *vi* obtenir son diplôme.
graft *n* greffe *f*:—*vt* greffer.
grain *n* grain *m*.
grammar *n* grammaire *f*.
grammatical *adj* grammatical.
grand *adj* grandiose; magnifique.
grandchild *n* petit-fils *m*; petite-fille *f*:—
  grandchildren *pl* petits-enfants *m pl*.
grandad *n* pépé *m*.
granddaughter *n* petite-fille *f*.
grandeur *n* grandeur *f*; pompe *f*.
grandfather *n* grand-père *m*.
grandma *n* mémé *f*.
grandmother *n* grand-mère *f*.
grandparents *npl* grands-parents *mpl*.
grandson *n* petit-fils *m*.
grandstand *n* tribune *f*.
granny *n* mémé *f*.
grant *vt* accorder:—*n* bourse *f*.
granulate *vt* granuler.
granule *n* granule *m*.
grape *n* raisin *m*.
grapefruit *n* pamplemousse *m*.
graph *n* graphe, graphique *m*.
graphic(al) *adj* graphique.
grasp *vt* saisir, empoigner; comprendre.
grass *n* herbe *f*.
grasshopper *n* sauterelle *f*.
grassy *adj* herbeux.
grate *n* grille *f*:—*vt* râper:—*vi* grincer.
grateful *adj* reconnaissant.

gratification *n* satisfaction *f*.
gratify *vt* satisfaire.
gratifying *adj* réjouissant.
gratis *adv* gratis, gratuitement.
gratitude *n* gratitude, reconnaissance *f*.
gratuitous *adj* gratuit; volontaire.
gratuity *n* gratification *f*.
grave *n* tombe *f*:—*adj* grave.
graveyard *n* cimetière *m*.
gravity *n* gravité *f*.
gravy *n* jus de viande *m*; sauce *f*.
graze *vt* paître:—*vi* paître.
grease *n* graisse *f*:—*vt* graisser.
great *adj* grand; important.
greatness *n* grandeur *f*; importance *f*.
greed *n* avidité *f*; gloutonnerie *f*.
greedy *adj* avide; glouton.
green *adj* vert:—*n* vert *m*; verdure *f*.
greenery *n* verdure *f*.
greenhouse *n* serre *f*.
greenish *adj* verdâtre.
greet *vt* saluer; accueillir.
greeting *n* salutation *f*; accueil *m*.
grey *adj* gris:—*n* gris *m*.
greyish *adj* grisâtre; grisonnant.
grid *n* grille *f*; réseau *m*.
grief *n* chagrin *m*, douleur.
grievance *n* grief *m*; doléance *f*.
grieve *vt* peiner:—*vi* se chagriner.
grievous *adj* douloureux; grave.
grill *n* gril *m*:—*vt* faire griller.
grim *adj* peu engageant.
grimace *n* grimace *f*; moue *f*.
grime *n* saleté *f*.
grind *vt* moudre.
grip *n* prise *f*; poignée *f*:—*vt* saisir, agripper.
groan *vi* gémir; grogner:—*n* gémisse-
  ment *m*.
grocer *n* épicier *m*, -ière *f*.
groom *n* valet *m*; marié *m*:—*vt* panser;
  préparer.

groove n rainure f.
grope vt chercher à tâtons: — vi tâtonner.
gross adj gros; grossier.
grotesque adj grotesque.
ground n terre f, sol m; terrain: — vt fonder.
ground floor n rez-de-chaussée m.
groundless adj sans fondement.
group n groupe m: — vt regrouper.
grove n bosquet m.
grovel vi se traîner; ramper.
grow vt cultiver: — vi pousser.
grower n cultivateur m, -trice f.
growl vi grogner.
growth n croissance f.
grudge n rancune f.
gruelling adj difficile, pénible.
gruesome adj horrible.
grumble vi grogner; grommeler.
guarantee n garantie f: — vt garantir.
guard n garde f: — vt garder.
guardian n tuteur m, -trice f.
guardianship n tutelle f.
guess vt deviner: — vi deviner: — n conjecture f.
guest n invité m, invitée f.
guidance n guidage m; direction f.
guide vt guider, diriger: — n guide m.
guidebook n guide m.

guild n association f; corporation f.
guile n astuce f.
guilt n culpabilité f.
guilty adj coupable.
guise n apparence f.
guitar n guitare f.
gullibility n crédulité f.
gullible adj crédule.
gulp n gorgée f: — vi, vt avaler.
gum n gomme f: — vt coller.
gun n pistolet m; fusil m.
gunpowder n poudre à canon f.
gunshot n coup de feu m.
gurgle vi gargouiller.
gush vi jaillir; bouillonner: — n jaillissement m.
gust n rafale f; bouffée f.
gusto n plaisir m, délectation f.
gusty adj venteux.
gut n intestin m: — vt vider.
gutter n gouttière f; caniveau m.
guy n mec, type m.
guzzle vt bouffer, engloutir.
gymnasium n gymnase m.
gymnast n gymnaste mf.
gymnastic adj gymnastique: — ~s npl gymnastique f.
gynecologist n gynécologue mf.
gypsy n gitan m, -e f.

H

habit n habitude f.
habitable adj habitable.
habitat n habitat m.
habitual adj habituel.
haemorrhage n hémorragie f.
haggard adj décharné hagard.

haggle vi marchander.
hail n grêle f: — vt saluer: — vi grêler.
hair n cheveu m; poil m.
haircut n coupe de cheveux f.
hairless adj chauve; sans poils.
hairstyle n coiffure f.

hairy *adj* chevelu; poilu.

hale *adj* vigoureux.

half *n* moitié *f*: — *adj* demi: — *adv* à moitié.

half-hearted *adj* peu enthousiaste.

half-hour *n* demi-heure *f*.

half-moon *n* demi-lune *f*.

halfway *adv* à mi-chemin.

hall *n* vestibule *m*.

hallow *vt* consacrer, sanctifier.

hallucination *n* hallucination *f*.

halt *vi* s'arrêter: — *n* arrêt *m*; halte *f*.

ham *n* jambon *m*.

hammer *n* marteau *m*: — *vt* marteler.

hammock *n* hamac *m*.

hamper *n* panier *m*: — *vt* entraver.

hand *n* main *f*: — *vt* donner, passer.

handbag *n* sac à main *m*.

handbrake *n* frein à main *m*.

handful *n* poignée *f*.

handicap *n* handicap *m*.

handicapped *adj* handicapé.

handkerchief *n* mouchoir *m*.

handle *n* manche *m*: — *vt* manier.

handlebars *npl* guidon *m*.

handrail *n* garde-fou *m*.

handsome *adj* beau.

handwriting *n* écriture *f*.

hang *vt* accrocher; pendre: — *vi* pendre.

hangover *n* gueule de bois *f*.

haphazard *adj* fortuit.

hapless *adj* malheureux.

happen *vi* se passer.

happening *n* événement *m*.

happily *adv* heureusement.

happiness *n* bonheur *m*.

happy *adj* heureux.

harass *vt* harceler.

harbour *n* port *m*: — *vt* héberger.

hard *adj* dur; pénible; sévère.

harden *vt vi* durcir.

hardiness *n* robustesse *f*.

hardly *adv* à peine: — ~ **ever** presque jamais.

hardness *n* dureté *f*; difficulté *f*.

hard-up *adj* fauché.

hardy *adj* fort, robuste.

hare *n* lièvre *m*.

harm *n* mal *m*; tort *m*: — *vt* nuire à.

harmful *adj* nuisible.

harmonious *adj* harmonieux.

harmony *n* harmonie *f*.

harp *n* harpe *f*.

harsh *adj* dur; austère; rude.

harshness *n* aspérité, dureté *f*; austérité *f*.

harvest *n* moisson *f*: — *vt* moissonner.

harvester *n* moissonneur *m*, -euse *f*.

haste *n* hâte *f*.

hasten *vt* accélérer: — *vi* se dépêcher.

hasty *adj* hâtif; irréfléchi.

hat *n* chapeau *m*.

hatch *vt* couver; faire éclore: — *n* écoutille *f*.

hatchet *n* hachette *f*.

hate *n* haine *f*: — *vt* haïr, détester.

hatred *n* haine *f*.

haughtiness *n* orgueil *m*.

haughty *adj* orgueilleux.

haul *vt* tirer: — *n* prise *f*.

haunt *vt* hanter: — *n* repaire *m*.

have *vt* avoir; posséder.

haversack *n* sac à dos *m*.

havoc *n* ravages *mpl*.

hay *n* foin *m*.

hay fever *n* rhume des foins *m*.

hazard *n* risque, danger *m*: — *vt* risquer.

hazardous *adj* risqué, dangereux.

haze *n* brume *f*.

hazelnut *n* noisette *f*.

hazy *adj* brumeux.

he *pn* il.

head *n* tête *f*; chef *m*: — *vt* conduire.

headache *n* mal de tête *m*.
headland *n* promontoire *m*.
headlight *n* phare *m*.
headline *n* titre *m*.
headlong *adv* à toute allure.
headstrong *adj* têtu.
headwaiter *n* maître d'hôtel *m*.
heady *adj* capiteux.
heal *vt vi* guérir.
health *n* santé *f*.
healthiness *n* bonne santé *f*.
healthy *adj* en bonne santé; sain.
heap *n* tas *m*:—*vt* entasser.
hear *vt* entendre; écouter:—*vi* entendre.
hearing *n* ouïe *f*.
heart *n* cœur *m*.
heart failure *n* arrêt cardiaque *m*.
hearth *n* foyer *m*.
heartless *adj* cruel.
hearty *adj* cordial.
heat *n* chaleur *f*:—*vt* chauffer.
heater *n* radiateur *m*.
heathen *n* païen *m*, païenne *f*.
heating *n* chauffage *m*.
heatwave *n* onde de chaleur *f*.
heave *vt* lever; tirer.
heaven *n* ciel *m*.
heaviness *n* lourdeur *f*.
heavy *adj* lourd, pesant.
hectic *adj* agité.
hedge *n* haie *f*.
hedgehog *n* hérisson *m*.
heed *vt* tenir compte de:—*n* attention *f*.
heedless *adj* inattentif, étourdi.
heel *n* talon *m*.
hefty *adj* fort; gros.
height *n* hauteur *f*; altitude *f*.
heighten *vt* rehausser.
heinous *adj* atroce.
heir *n* héritier *m*.
helicopter *n* hélicoptère *m*.

hell *n* enfer *m*.
helmet *n* casque *m*.
help *vt* aider, secourir:—*n* aide *f*; secours *m*.
helper *n* aide *mf*.
helpful *adj* utile.
helpless *adj* impuissant.
hemisphere *n* hémisphère *m*.
hen *n* poule *f*.
henceforward *adv* dorénavant.
hen-house *n* poulailler *m*.
hepatitis *n* hépatite *f*.
her *pn* son, sa, ses; elle; la; lui.
herb *n* herbe *f*.
herbalist *n* herboriste *mf*.
herd *n* troupeau *m*.
here *adv* ici.
hereby *adv* par la présente.
hereditary *adj* héréditaire.
heredity *n* hérédité *f*.
heritage *n* patrimoine, héritage *m*.
hermit *n* ermite *m*.
hernia *n* hernie *f*.
hero *n* héros *m*.
heroic *adj* héroïque.
hers *pn* le sien, la sienne, le(s) sien(ne)s, à elle.
herself *pn* elle-même.
hesitate *vi* hésiter.
hesitation *n* hésitation *f*.
heterogeneous *adj* hétérogène.
heterosexual *adj n* hétérosexuel *m*, -elle *f*.
hiatus *n* (*gr*) hiatus *m*.
hiccup *n* hoquet *m*:—*vi* avoir le hoquet.
hide *vt* cacher:—*n* cuir *m*; peau *f*.
hideaway *n* cachette *f*.
hideous *adj* hideux; horrible.
hierarchy *n* hiérarchie *f*.
hi-fi *n* hi-fi *f invar*.
high *adj* haut; élevé.

highlight *n* point fort *m*.

highness *n* hauteur *f*; altesse *f*.

hike *vi* faire une randonnée.

hilarious *adj* hilarant; hilare.

hill *n* colline *f*.

hillside *n* coteau *m*.

hilly *adj* montagneux.

him *pn* lui; le.

himself *pn* lui-même; soi.

hinder *vt* gêner, entraver.

hindrance *n* gêne *f*, obstacle *m*.

hindsight *n*: — **with ~** rétrospectivement.

hint *n* allusion *f*: — *vt* insinuer; suggérer.

hip *n* hanche *f*.

hire *vt* louer: — *n* location *f*.

his *poss adj* son, sa, ses; *poss pn* le sien, la sienne, les sien(ne)s; à lui.

hiss *vt vi* siffler.

historian *n* historien *m*, -ienne *f*.

historic(al) *adj* historique.

history *n* histoire *f*.

hit *vt* frapper; atteindre.

hitch-hike *vi* faire du stop.

hoard *n* stock *m*; trésor caché *m*: — *vt* accumuler.

hoarse *adj* rauque.

hoarseness *n* voix rauque *f*.

hobby *n* passe-temps *m invar*.

hoist *vt* hisser: — *n* grue *f*.

hold *vt* tenir; détenir: — *n* prise *f*; pouvoir *m*.

holder *n* détenteur *m*, -trice *f*.

holdup *n* hold-up *m*.

hole *n* trou *m*.

holiday *n* jour de congé *m*: — **~s** *pl* vacances *fpl*.

hollow *adj* creux: — *n* creux *m*: — *vt* creuser.

holocaust *n* holocauste *m*.

holy *adj* saint; bénit.

homage *n* hommage *m*.

home *n* maison *f*; domicile *m*.

homeless *adj* sans abri.

homely *adj* simple.

homesick *adj* nostalgique.

homesickness *n* nostalgie *f*.

homework *n* devoirs *mpl*.

homicide *n* homicide *m*; homicide *mf*.

homogeneous *adj* homogène.

homosexual *adj n* homosexuel *m*, -elle *f*.

honest *adj* honnête.

honesty *n* honnêteté *f*.

honey *n* miel *m*.

honor *n* honneur *m*: — *vt* honorer.

honorable *adj* honorable.

honorary *adj* honoraire.

hood *n* capot *m*; capuche *f*.

hoof *n* sabot *m*.

hook *n* crochet *m*; hameçon *m*: — *vt* accrocher.

hoop *n* cerceau *m*.

hooter *n* sirène *f*.

hop *n* saut *m*: — *vi* sauter.

hope *n* espoir *m*, espérance *f*: — *vi* espérer.

hopeful *adj* plein d'espoir; prometteur.

horizon *n* horizon *m*.

horizontal *adj* horizontal.

hormone *n* hormone *f*.

horn *n* corne *f*.

horoscope *n* horoscope *m*.

horrible *adj* horrible.

horrific *adj* horrible, affreux.

horrify *vt* horrifier.

horror *n* horreur *f*.

hors d'œuvre *n* hors-d'œuvre *m invar*.

horse *n* cheval *m*.

horseback *adv*: — **on ~** à cheval.

horseman *n* cavalier *m*.

horsepower *n* cheval-vapeur *m*; puissance en chevaux *f*.

horseshoe *n* fer à cheval *m*.

horticulture *n* horticulture *f*.
horticulturist *n* horticulteur *m*, -trice *f*.
hospitable *adj* hospitalier.
hospital *n* hôpital *m*.
hospitality *n* hospitalité *f*.
host *n* hôte *m*; hostie *f*.
hostage *n* otage *m*.
hostess *n* hôtesse *f*.
hostile *adj* hostile.
hostility *n* hostilité *f*.
hot *adj* chaud; épicé.
hotel *n* hôtel *m*.
hotelier *n* hôtelier *m*, -ière *f*.
hotheaded *adj* exalté.
hotplate *n* plaque chauffante *f*.
hour *n* heure *f*.
hour-glass *n* sablier *m*.
hourly *adv* toutes les heures.
house *n* maison *f*; maisonnée *f*: — *vt* loger.
houseboat *n* péniche *f*.
household *n* famille *f*, ménage *m*.
householder *n* propriétaire *mf*; chef de famille *m*.
housekeeper *n* gouvernante *f*.
housewife *n* ménagère *f*.
housework *n* travaux ménagers *mpl*.
housing *n* logement *m*.
hovel *n* taudis *m*.
hover *vi* planer.
how *adv* comme; comment: — ~ **do you do!** enchanté.
however *adv* de quelque manière que; cependant, néanmoins.
howl *vi* hurler: — *n* hurlement *m*.
hub *n* centre *m*; moyeu *m*.
hue *n* teinte *f*; nuance *f*.
hug *vt* étreindre: — *n* étreinte *f*.
huge *adj* énorme.
hull *n* (*mar*) coque *f*.
hum *vi* chantonner.
human *adj* humain.

humane *adj* humain.
humanise *vt* humaniser.
humanist *n* humaniste *mf*.
humanity *n* humanité *f*.
humble *adj* humble: — *vt* humilier.
humdrum *adj* monotone.
humid *adj* humide.
humiliate *vt* humilier.
humiliation *n* humiliation *f*.
humility *n* humilité *f*.
humorous *adj* humoristique.
humour *n* sens de l'humour *m*, humour *m*.
hump *n* bosse *f*.
hundred *adj* cent: — *n* centaine *f*.
hundredth *adj* centième.
hunger *n* faim *f*: — *vi* avoir faim.
hungry *adj* affamé.
hunt *vt* chasser: — *n* chasse *f*.
hunter *n* chasseur *m*.
hurdle *n* haie *f*.
hurl *vt* jeter.
hurricane *n* ouragan *m*.
hurry *vt* presser: — *vi* se presser: — *n* hâte *f*.
hurt *vt* faire mal à; blesser: — *n* mal *m*.
hurtful *adj* blessant.
husband *n* mari *m*.
hut *n* cabane, hutte *f*.
hydrant *n* bouche d'incendie *f*.
hydraulic *adj* hydraulique.
hydroelectric *adj* hydroélectrique.
hygiene *n* hygiène *f*.
hygienic *adj* hygiénique.
hypochondriac *adj n* hypocondriaque *mf*.
hypocrisy *n* hypocrisie *f*.
hypocritical *adj* hypocrite.
hypothesis *n* hypothèse *f*.
hypothetical *adj* hypothétique.
hysterical *adj* hystérique.
hysterics *npl* hystérie *f*.

I

I *pn* je, j'; moi
ice *n* glace *f*:—*vt* glacer.
ice cream *n* glace *f*.
ice rink *n* patinoire *f*.
ice skating *n* patinage sur glace *m*.
icon *n* icône *f*.
icy *adj* glacé.
idea *n* idée *f*.
ideal *adj* idéal.
identical *adj* identique.
identification *n* identification *f*.
identify *vt* identifier.
identity *n* identité *f*.
idiot *n* imbécile *mf*.
idiotic *adj* idiot, bête.
idle *adj* désœuvré; au repos.
idleness *n* paresse *f*.
idler *n* paresseux *m*, -euse *f*.
idol *n* idole *f*.
idolise *vt* idôlatrer.
idyllic *adj* idyllique.
if *conj* si:—~ **not** sinon.
ignite *vt* allumer, enflammer.
ignoble *adj* ignoble; bas.
ignominious *adj* ignominieux.
ignorance *n* ignorance *f*.
ignorant *adj* ignorant.
ignore *vt* ne pas tenir compte de.
ill *adj* malade:—*n* mal *m*.
illegal *adj* illégal.
illegality *n* illégalité *f*.
illegible *adj* illisible.
illegitimacy *n* illégitimité *f*.
illegitimate *adj* illégitime.
illicit *adj* illicite.
illiterate *adj* analphabète.

illness *n* maladie *f*.
illogical *adj* illogique.
illuminate *vt* illuminer.
illusion *n* illusion *f*.
illusory *adj* illusoire.
illustrate *vt* illustrer.
illustration *n* illustration *f*.
illustrious *adj* illustre.
image *n* image *f*.
imaginary *adj* imaginaire.
imagination *n* imagination *f*.
imagine *vt* imaginer.
imbecile *adj* imbécile, idiot.
imitate *vt* imiter.
imitation *n* imitation *f*.
immaterial *adj* insignifiant.
immeasurable *adj* incommensurable.
immediate *adj* immédiat.
immense *adj* immense.
immigrant *n* immigrant *m*, -e *f*.
immigration *n* immigration *f*.
imminent *adj* imminent.
immobile *adj* immobile.
immobility *n* immobilité *f*.
immoderate *adj* immodéré.
immoral *adj* immoral.
immorality *n* immoralité *f*.
immortal *adj* immortel.
immune *adj* immunisé.
immunise *vt* immuniser.
immutable *adj* immuable.
impact *n* impact *m*.
impalpable *adj* impalpable.
impart *vt* communiquer.
impartial *adj* impartial.
impartiality *n* impartialité *f*.

impassive *adj* impassible.

impatience *n* impatience *f*.

impatient *adj* impatient.

impeccable *adj* impeccable.

impede *vt* empêcher; entraver.

impending *adj* imminent.

impenetrable *adj* impénétrable.

imperceptible *adj* imperceptible.

imperfect *adj* imparfait.

imperfection *n* imperfection *f*; défaut *m*.

impermeable *adj* imperméable.

impersonal *adj* impersonel.

impertinence *n* impertinence *f*.

impertinent *adj* impertinent.

impetuosity *n* impétuosité *f*.

impetuous *adj* impétueux.

implement *n* outil *m*; ustensile *m*.

implicate *vt* impliquer.

implication *n* implication *f*.

implicit *adj* implicite.

implore *vt* supplier.

imply *vt* supposer.

impolite *adj* impoli.

import *vt* importer: — *n* importation *f*.

importance *n* importance *f*.

important *adj* important.

impose *vt* imposer.

imposition *n* imposition *f*.

impossibility *n* impossibilité *f*.

impossible *adj* impossible.

impostor *n* imposteur *m*.

impotence *n* impotence *f*.

impotent *adj* impotent.

impoverish *vt* appauvrir.

impoverishment *n* appauvrissement *m*.

impracticable *adj* impraticable.

imprecise *adj* imprécis.

impress *vt* impressionner.

impression *n* impression *f*; édition *f*.

impressionable *adj* impressionnable.

impressive *adj* impressionnant.

imprint *n* empreinte *f*: — *vt* imprimer.

imprison *vt* emprisonner.

imprisonment *n* emprisonnement *m*.

improbability *n* improbabilité *f*.

improbable *adj* improbable.

improper *adj* indécent; impropre.

improve *vt* améliorer: — *vi* s'améliorer.

improvement *n* amélioration *f*.

improvise *vt* improviser.

imprudent *adj* imprudent.

impudent *adj* impudent.

impulse *n* impulsion *f*.

impulsive *adj* impulsif.

impunity *n* impunité *f*.

in *prep* dans; en.

inability *n* incapacité *f*.

inaccurate *adj* inexact.

inactive *adj* inactif.

inadequate *adj* inadéquat.

inadmissible *adj* inadmissible.

inane *adj* inepte.

inanimate *adj* inanimé.

inapplicable *adj* inapplicable.

inaudible *adj* inaudible.

incalculable *adj* incalculable.

incapable *adj* incapable.

incapacitate *vt* mettre dans l'incapacité.

incapacity *n* incapacité *f*.

incarcerate *vt* incarcérer.

incautious *adj* imprudent.

incentive *n* prime, aide *f*

inception *n* commencement *m*.

incessant *adj* incessant, continuel.

incidence *n* fréquence *f*.

incident *n* incident *m*.

incidental *adj* fortuit.

incisive *adj* incisif.

incite *vt* inciter, encourager.

inclination *n* inclination, propension *f*.

incline *vt* incliner: — *vi* s'incliner.

include *vt* inclure, comprendre.

including *prep* inclus, y compris.
incoherence *n* incohérence *f.*
incoherent *adj* incohérent.
income *n* revenu *m*; recettes *fpl.*
incomparable *adj* incomparable.
incompetence *n* incompétence *f.*
incompetent *adj* incompétent.
incomplete *adj* incomplet.
incomprehensible *adj* incompréhensible.
inconceivable *adj* inconcevable.
incongruity *n* incongruité *f.*
incongruous *adj* incongru.
inconsiderate *adj* inconsidéré.
inconsistent *adj* inconsistant.
inconspicuous *adj* discret.
incontrovertible *adj* incontestable.
inconvenience *n* inconvénient:—*vt* incommoder.
inconvenient *adj* incommode.
incorporate *vt* incorporer:—*vi* s'incorporer.
incorporation *n* incorporation *f.*
incorrect *adj* incorrect.
increase *vt vi* augmenter:—*n* augmentation *f.*
increasing *adj* croissant.
incredible *adj* incroyable.
incredulous *adj* incrédule.
incriminate *vt* incriminer.
incur *vt* encourir.
incurable *adj* incurable.
incursion *n* incursion *f.*
indebted *adj* endetté; redevable.
indecent *adj* indécent.
indecision *n* indécision, irrésolution *f.*
indecisive *adj* indécis, irrésolu.
indefatigable *adj* infatigable.
indefinite *adj* indéfini.
indemnify *vt* indemniser.
indemnity *n* indemnité *f.*
independence *n* indépendance *f.*

independent *adj* indépendant.
indeterminate *adj* indéterminé.
index *n* indice *m.*
indicate *vt* indiquer.
indication *n* indication *f*; indice *m.*
indifference *n* indifférence *f.*
indifferent *adj* indifférent.
indigenous *adj* indigène.
indigent *adj* indigent.
indigestion *n* indigestion *f.*
indignant *adj* indigné.
indignation *n* indignation *f.*
indirect *adj* indirect.
indiscreet *adj* indiscret.
indiscretion *n* indiscrétion *f.*
indispensable *adj* indispensable.
indisputable *adj* indiscutable.
indistinct *adj* indistinct.
indistinguishable *adj* indistinctible.
individual *adj* individuel:—*n* individu *m.*
individuality *n* individualité *f.*
indolence *n* indolence *f.*
indolent *adj* indolent.
indoors *adv* à l'intérieur.
induce *vt* persuader; provoquer.
inducement *n* encouragement *m*; incitation *f.*
indulge *vt* céder à; *vi* se permettre.
indulgent *adj* indulgent.
industrial *adj* industriel.
industrialise *vt* industrialiser.
industrious *adj* travailleur.
industry *n* industrie *f.*
inebriated *vt* ivre.
inedible *adj* non comestible.
inefficiency *n* inefficacité *f.*
inefficient *adj* inefficace.
ineligible *adj* inéligible.
inept *adj* inepte; déplacé.
inequality *n* inégalité *f.*
inertia *n* inertie *f.*

inestimable *adj* inestimable.

inevitable *adj* inévitable.

inexhaustible *adj* inépuisable.

inexpedient *adj* imprudent, inopportun.

inexpensive *adj* bon marché.

inexplicable *adj* inexplicable.

infallible *adj* infaillible.

infamous *adj* vil, infâme.

infancy *n* enfance *f*.

infant *n* bébé *m*; enfant *mf*.

infantile *adj* infantile.

infatuated *adj* fou.

infatuation *n* folie *f*; obsession *f*.

infect *vt* infecter.

infectious *adj* infectieux.

infer *vt* inférer.

inference *n* inférence *f*.

inferior *adj* inférieur.

inferiority *n* infériorité *f*.

infernal *adj* infernal.

infest *vt* infester.

infidelity *n* infidélité *f*.

infiltrate *vi* s'infiltrer.

infinite *adj* infini.

infinity *n* infini *m*; infinité *f*.

infirm *adj* infirme.

infirmity *n* infirmité *f*.

inflame *vt* enflammer:—*vi* s'enflammer.

inflammation *n* inflammation *f*.

inflatable *adj* gonflable.

inflate *vt* gonfler.

inflation *n* inflation *f*.

inflict *vt* infliger.

influence *n* influence *f*:—*vt* influencer.

influential *adj* influent.

influenza *n* grippe *f*.

inform *vt* informer.

informal *adj* informel.

informality *n* simplicité *f*.

information *n* information *f*.

infrequent *adj* rare.

infringe *vt* enfreindre.

infringement *n* infraction *f*.

infuriate *vt* rendre furieux.

ingenious *adj* ingénieux.

ingenuity *n* ingéniosité *f*.

ingenuous *adj* ingénu.

inglorious *adj* honteux.

ingot *n* lingot *m*.

ingratitude *n* ingratitude *f*.

ingredient *n* ingrédient *m*.

inhabit *vt vi* habiter.

inhabitable *adj* habitable.

inhabitant *n* habitant *m*, -e *f*.

inhale *vt* inhaler.

inherit *vt* hériter.

inheritance *n* héritage *m*.

inhibit *vt* inhiber.

inhibition *n* inhibition *f*.

inhospitable *adj* inhospitalier.

inhuman *adj* inhumain.

inhumanity *n* inhumanité.

inimical *adj* hostile, ennemi.

inimitable *adj* inimitable.

initial *adj* initial:—*n* initiale *f*.

initiate *vt* commencer; initier.

initiation *n* initiation *f*.

initiative *n* initiative *f*.

inject *vt* injecter.

injection *n* injection *f*.

injunction *n* injonction *f*.

injure *vt* blesser.

injury *n* blessure *f*; tort *m*.

injustice *n* injustice *f*.

ink *n* encre *f*.

inlet *n* entrée *f*; bras de mer *m*.

inn *n* auberge *f*; hôtel *m*.

innate *adj* inné.

inner *adj* intérieur.

innkeeper *n* aubergiste *mf*.

innocence *n* innocence *f*.

innocent *adj* innocent.

innocuous *adj* inoffensif.

innovate *vt* innover.

innuendo *n* allusion *f*; insinuation *f*.

innumerable *adj* innombrable.

inoculate *vt* inoculer.

inoffensive *adj* inoffensif.

inopportune *adj* inopportun.

inquest *n* enquête *f*.

inquire *vt vi* demander.

inquiry *n* enquête *f*.

inquisition *n* investigation *f*.

inquisitive *adj* curieux.

insane *adj* fou, *f* folle.

insanity *n* folie *f*.

insatiable *adj* insatiable.

inscribe *vt* inscrire.

inscription *n* inscription *f*.

inscrutable *adj* impénétrable.

insect *n* insecte *m*.

insecure *adj* peu assuré.

insecurity *n* insécurité *f*.

insemination *n* insémination *f*.

insensible *adj* inconscient.

insensitive *adj* insensible.

inseparable *adj* inséparable.

insert *vt* introduire, insérer.

insertion *n* insertion *f*.

inside *n* intérieur *m*: —*adv* à l'intérieur.

inside out *adv* à l'envers.

insidious *adj* insidieux.

insight *n* perspicacité *f*.

insignificant *adj* insignifiant.

insinuate *vt* insinuer.

insinuation *n* insinuation *f*.

insipid *adj* insipide.

insist *vi* insister.

insistence *n* insistance *f*.

insistent *adj* insistant.

insolence *n* insolence *f*.

insolent *adj* insolent.

inspect *vt* examiner, inspecter.

inspection *n* inspection *f*.

inspector *n* inspecteur *m*, -trice *f*.

instability *n* instabilité *f*.

instal *vt* installer.

installation *n* installation *f*.

instalment *n* installation *f*.

instance *n* exemple *m*.

instant *adj* instantané: —*n* instant.

instead (of) *pr* au lieu.

instigate *vt* inciter; susciter.

instinct *n* instinct *m*.

instinctive *adj* instinctif.

institute *vt* instituer.

institution *n* institution *f*.

instruct *vt* instruire.

instrument *n* instrument *m*.

insufficiency *n* insuffisance *f*.

insufficient *adj* insuffisant.

insular *adj* insulaire.

insulate *vt* isoler.

insulation *n* isolation *f*.

insult *vt* insulter: —*n* insulte *f*.

insurance *n* (*com*) assurance *f*.

insure *vt* assurer.

intact *adj* intact.

integrate *vt* intégrer.

integration *n* intégration *f*.

integrity *n* intégrité *f*.

intellect *n* intellect *m*.

intellectual *adj* intellectuel.

intelligence *n* intelligence *f*.

intelligent *adj* intelligent.

intelligible *adj* intelligible.

intend *vt* avoir l'intention de.

intense *adj* intense.

intensify *vt* intensifier.

intensity *n* intensité *f*.

intensive *adj* intensif.

intention *n* intention *f*, dessein *m*.

intentional *adj* intentionnel: —**~ly** *adv* à dessein, intentionnellement.

intercede *vi* intercéder.

intercept *vt* intercepter.

interest *vt* intéresser:—*n* intérêt *m*.

interesting *adj* intéressant.

interfere *vi* s'ingérer.

interior *adj* intérieur.

interlock *vi* s'entremêler.

interlude *n* intermède *m*.

intermediary *n* intermédiaire *mf*.

intermediate *adj* intermédiaire.

interminable *adj* interminable.

intermingle *vt* entremêler:—*vi* s'entremêler.

intermittent *adj* intermittent.

intern *n* interne *mf*.

internal *adj* intérieur; interne.

international *adj* international.

internet, Internet *n* Internet *m*.

interpret *vt* interpréter.

interpretation *n* interprétation *f*.

interpreter *n* interprète *mf*.

interrogate *vt* interroger.

interrogation *n* interrogatoire *m*.

interrupt *vt* interrompre.

interruption *n* interruption *f*.

intersect *vi* se croiser.

intersection *n* croisement *m*.

intertwine *vt* entrelacer.

interval *n* intervalle *m*; mi-temps *f*.

intervene *vi* intervenir.

intervention *n* intervention *f*.

interview *n* entrevue *f*; interview *f*.

interviewer *n* interviewer *m*.

intestine *n* intestin *m*.

intimacy *n* intimité *f*.

intimate *adj* intime *vt* insinuer.

intimidate *vt* intimider.

into *prep* dans, en.

intolerable *adj* intolérable.

intolerant *adj* intolérant.

intonation *n* intonation *f*.

intoxicate *vt* enivrer.

intoxication *n* ivresse *f*.

intricacy *n* complexité *f*.

intricate *adj* complexe.

intrigue *n* intrigue *f*:—*vi* intriguer.

intriguing *adj* intrigant.

intrinsic *adj* intrinsèque.

introduce *vt* introduire.

introduction *n* introduction *f*.

introvert *n* introverti *m*, -ie *f*.

intruder *n* intrus *m*, -e *f*.

intuition *n* intuition *f*.

intuitive *adj* intuitif.

inundate *vt* inonder.

invade *vt* envahir.

invader *n* envahisseur *m*, -euse *f*.

invalid *n* invalide *mf*.

invalidate *vt* invalider.

invaluable *adj* inappréciable.

invasion *n* invasion *f*.

invent *vt* inventer.

invention *n* invention *f*.

inventor *n* inventeur *m*, -trice *f*.

investigation *n* investigation *f*.

investigator *n* investigateur *m*, -trice *f*.

invincible *adj* invincible.

inviolable *adj* inviolable.

invisible *adj* invisible.

invitation *n* invitation *f*.

invite *vt* inviter.

invoice *n* facture *f*.

invoke *vt* invoquer.

involuntary *adj* involontaire.

involve *vt* impliquer, entraîner.

involvement *n* implication *f*.

irascible *adj* irascible.

irate *adj* irrité.

iron *n* fer *m*:—*adj* de fer.

ironic *adj* ironique.

irony *n* ironie *f*.

irrational *adj* irrationnel.

irreconcilable *adj* irréconciliable.
irregular *adj* irrégulier.
irregularity *n* irrégularité *f.*
irreparable *adj* irréparable.
irreplaceable *adj* irremplaçable.
irresistible *adj* irrésistible.
irresponsible *adj* irresponsable.
irreverence *n* irrévérence *f.*
irrigate *vt* irriguer.
irrigation *n* irrigation *f.*
irritability *n* irritabilité *f.*
irritable *adj* irritable.
irritate *vt* irriter.
irritation *n* irritation *f.*
island *n* île *f.*

isle *n* île *f.*
isolate *vt* isoler.
isolation *n* isolement *m.*
issue *n* sujet *m*, question *f:—vt* publier.
it *pn* il, elle; le, la; cela, ça, ce, c'.
itch *n* démangeaison *f:—vi* avoir des démangeaisons.
item *n* article *m.*
itinerant *adj* itinérant.
itinerary *n* itinéraire *m.*
its *pn* son, sa, ses.
itself *pn* lui-même, elle-même.
ivory *n* ivoire *m.*
ivy *n* lierre *m.*

J

jabber *vi* bafouiller.
jack *n* cric *m*; valet *m.*
jacket *n* veste *f*; couverture *f.*
jackpot *n* gros lot *m.*
jagged *adj* dentelé.
jail *n* prison *f.*
jailer *n* geôlier *m*, -ière *f.*
jam *n* confiture *f*, embouteillage *m.*
January *n* janvier *m.*
jar *vi* (*mus*) détonner:—*n* pot *m.*
jargon *n* jargon *m.*
jaw *n* mâchoire *f.*
jazz *n* jazz *m.*
jealous *adj* jaloux.
jealousy *n* jalousie *f.*
jeans *npl* jean *m.*
jeer *vi* railler:—*n* raillerie.
jelly *n* gelée *f.*
jeopardise *vt* mettre en péril.
jerk *n* secousse *f.*

jersey *n* jersey *m.*
jest *n* blague.
jester *n* bouffon *m.*
jet *n* avion à réaction *m*; jet *m.*
jettison *vt* se défaire de.
jewel *n* bijou *m.*
jewellery *n* bijouterie *f.*
Jewish *adj* juif.
jibe *n* raillerie, moquerie *f.*
jigsaw *n* puzzle *m.*
jinx *n* porte-malheur *m invar.*
job *n* travail *m.*
jockey *n* jockey *m.*
jocular *adj* joyeux; facétieux.
jog *vi* faire du jogging.
join *vt* joindre, unir.
joint *n* articulation *f:—adj* commun.
joke *n* blague:—*vi* blaguer.
joker *n* blagueur *m*, -euse *f.*
jolly *adj* gai, joyeux.

jostle vt bousculer.
journal n revue f.
journalism n journalisme m.
journalist n journaliste mf.
journey n voyage m:—vi voyager.
joy n joie f.
joyful adj joyeux.
jubilation n jubilation f.
jubilee n jubilé m.
Judaism n judaïsme m.
judge n juge m:—vt juger.
judgment n jugement m.
judicious adj judicieux.
judo n judo m.
jug n cruche f.
juggle vi jongler.
juice n jus m; suc m.

juicy adj juteux.
July n juillet m.
jumble vt mélanger:—n mélange m.
jump vi sauter:—n saut m.
June n juin m.
jungle n jungle f.
junior adj plus jeune.
jurisdiction n juridiction f.
juror n juré m.
jury n jury m.
just adj juste:—adv justement, exactement.
justice n justice f.
justification n justification f.
justify vt justifier.
juvenile adj juvénile.
juxtaposition n juxtaposition f.

K

kaleidoscope n kaléidoscope m.
kangaroo n kangourou m.
keen adj enthousiaste; vif.
keenness n enthousiasme m.
keep vt garder, conserver.
kernel n amande f; noyau m.
kettle n bouilloire f.
key n clé, clef f; (mus) ton m; touche f.
keyboard n clavier m.
key ring n porte-clefs m invar.
keystone n clef de voûte f.
kick vi (vt) donner un coup de pied (à).
kidnap vt kidnapper.
kidney n rein m; rognon m.
killer n assassin m.
killing n assassinat m.
kiln n four m.
kilo n kilo m.

kilogram n kilogramme m.
kilometre n kilomètre m.
kin n parents mpl.
kind adj gentil:—n genre m.
kindle vt allumer:—vi s'allumer.
kindliness n gentillesse, bonté f.
kindly adj bon, bienveillant.
kindness n bonté f.
king n roi m.
kingdom n royaume m.
kiss n baiser m:—vt embrasser.
kit n équipement m.
kitchen n cuisine f.
kitten n chaton m.
knack n don, chic m.
knead vt pétrir.
knee n genou m.
kneel vi s'agenouiller.

knife n couteau m.
knight n chevalier m.
knit vt vi tricoter.
knob n bouton m.
knock vt vi cogner, frapper: —n coup m.
knot n nœud m: —vt nouer.

know vt vi savoir; connaître.
know-how n savoir-faire m.
knowledge n connaissances fpl.
knowledgeable adj bien informé.
knuckle n articulation f.

L

label n étiquette f.
laboratory n laboratoire m.
laborious adj laborieux.
labour n travail m: —vi travailler.
labourer n ouvrier m.
lace vt lacer.
lacerate vt lacérer.
lack vt manquer de: —vi manquer: —n manque m.
lad n garçon m.
ladder n échelle f.
lady n dame f.
lag vi se laisser distancer.
lagoon n lagune f.
lair n repaire m.
lake n lac m.
lame adj boiteux.
lament vt se lamenter sur: —n lamentation f.
lamentable adj lamentable.
lamentation n lamentation f.
lamp n lampe f.
lance n lance f: —vt inciser.
lancet n bistouri m.
land n pays m; terre f: —vi atterrir.
landlord n propriétaire m.
landmark n point de repère m.
landscape n paysage m.
landslide n glissement de terrain m.
lane n allée, ruelle f; file f.

language n langue f; langage m.
languish vi languir.
lantern n lanterne f.
lapel n revers m.
lapse n laps m; défaillance f: —vi expirer.
larder n garde-manger m invar.
large adj grand: —**at** ~ en liberté.
larva n larve f.
lascivious adj lascif.
lash n coup de fouet m: —vt fouetter.
last adj dernier: —vi durer.
last-minute adj de dernière minute.
late adj en retard; défunt: —adv tard: —~ly adv récemment.
latent adj latent.
lateral ad latérale.
lather n mousse f.
latitude n latitude f.
laudable adj louable.
laugh vi rire: —**to** ~ **at** vt rire de: —n rire m.
laughter n rires mpl.
launch vt lancer: —vi se lancer.
laundry n lessive f.
lava n lave f.
lavatory n toilettes fpl.
lavish adj prodigue: —vt prodiguer.
law n loi f; droit m.
lawful adj légal; légitime.

lawmaker n législateur m, -trice f.
lawn n pelouse f, gazon m.
lawyer n avocat m; notaire m.
lax adj relâché.
laxative n laxatif m.
lay vt mettre; pondre.
layer n couche f.
laziness n paresse f.
lazy adj paresseux.
lead n plomb m:—vt vi conduire, mener.
leader n chef m.
leadership n direction f.
leading adj principal; premier.
leaf n feuille f.
leaflet n feuillet m.
league n ligue f; lieue f.
leak n fuite f:—vi (mar) faire eau.
lean vi s'appuyer:—adj maigre.
leap vi sauter:—n saut m.
learn vt vi apprendre.
learning n érudition f.
lease n bail m:—vt louer.
leash n laisse f.
least adj moindre:—**at** ~ au moins.
leather n cuir m.
leave n permission f; congé m:—vt laisser.
lecture n conférence f:—vi faire une conférence.
lecturer n conférencier m, -ière f.
leeway n liberté d'action f.
left adj gauche.
left-handed adj gaucher.
left-luggage office n consigne f.
leftovers npl restes mpl.
leg n jambe f; patte f.
legal adj légal, légitime.
legalise vt légaliser.
legality n légalité, légitimité f.
legend n légende f.
legendary adj légendaire.

legible adj lisible.
legion n légion f.
legislate vi, vt légiférer.
legislation n législation f.
legislative adj législatif.
legislature n corps législatif m.
legitimacy n légitimité f.
legitimate adj légitime:—vt légitimer.
leisure n loisir m:—~**ly** adj tranquille.
lemon n citron m.
lemonade n limonade f.
lend vt prêter.
length n longueur f; durée f:—**at** ~ longuement.
lengthen vt allonger:—vi s'allonger.
lengthy adj long.
lenient adj indulgent.
lens n lentille f.
leotard n justaucorps m.
lesbian n lesbienne f.
less adj moins:—adv moins.
lessen vt vi diminuer.
lesser adj moindre.
lesson n leçon f.
let vt laisser, permettre.
lethal adj mortel.
lethargic adj léthargique.
lethargy n léthargie f.
letter n lettre f.
lettering n inscription f.
lettuce n salade f.
level adj plat, égal:—n niveau m:—vt niveler.
lever n levier m.
levity n légèreté f.
liability n responsabilité f.
liable adj sujet (à); responsable.
liaise vi effectuer une liaison.
liaison n liaison f.
liar n menteur m, -euse f.
liberal adj libéral; généreux.

liberate *vt* libérer.

liberation *n* libération *f*.

liberty *n* liberté *f*.

librarian *n* bibliothécaire *mf*.

library *n* bibliothèque *f*.

licence *n* licence *f*; permis *m*.

lick *vt* lécher.

lid *n* couvercle *m*.

lie *n* mensonge *m*:—*vi* mentir; être allongé.

lieu *n*:—**in ~ of** au lieu de.

life *n* vie *f*.

life jacket *n* gilet de sauvetage *m*.

lifeless *adj* mort; sans vie.

life sentence *n* condamnation à perpétuité *f*.

life-sized *adj* grandeur nature.

lift *vt* lever.

ligament *n* ligament *m*.

light *n* lumière *f*:—*adj* léger; clair:—*vt* allumer.

lighten *vi* s'éclaircir:—*vt* éclairer; éclaircir.

lighthouse *n* (*mar*) phare *m*.

lighting *n* éclairage *m*.

lightning *n* éclair *m*.

light year *n* année-lumière *f*.

like *adj* pareil:—*adv* comme:—*vt vi* aimer.

likelihood *n* probabilité *f*.

likely *adj* probable, vraisemblable.

liken *vt* comparer.

likeness *n* ressemblance *f*.

likewise *adv* pareillement.

liking *n* goût *m*.

limb *n* membre *m*.

limit *n* limite *f*:—*vt* limiter.

limitation *n* limitation *f*; restriction *f*.

limp *vi* boiter:—*n* boitement *m*:—*adj* mou.

line *n* ligne *f*; ride *f*:—*vt* rayer; rider.

linear *adj* linéaire.

liner *n* transatlantique *m*.

linger *vi* traîner.

linguist *n* linguiste *mf*.

linguistic *adj* linguistique.

link *n* chaînon *m*:—*vt* relier.

lion *n* lion *m*.

lip *n* lèvre *f*; bord *m*.

lip-read *vi* lire sur les lèvres.

lipstick *n* rouge à lèvres *m*.

liqueur *n* liqueur *f*.

liquid *adj* liquide:—*n* liquide *m*.

liquidise *vt* liquéfier.

liquor *n* spiritueux *m*.

lisp *vi* zézayer:—*n* zézaiement *m*.

list *n* liste *f*:—*vt* faire une liste de.

listen *vi* écouter.

literal *adj* littéral.

literary *adj* littéraire.

literature *n* littérature *f*.

litigation *n* litige *m*.

litigious *adj* litigieux.

litre *n* litre *m*.

litter *n* litière *f*; ordures *fpl*:—*vt* recouvrir.

little *adj* petit:—*n* peu *m*.

live *vi* vivre; habiter:—*adj* vivant.

livelihood *n* moyens de subsistance *mpl*.

liveliness *n* vivacité *f*.

lively *adj* vif.

liver *n* foie *m*.

livid *adj* livide; furieux.

living *n* vie *f*:—*adj* vivant.

living room *n* salle de séjour *f*.

load *vt* charger:—*n* charge *f*.

loaf *n* pain *m*.

loan *n* prêt *m*.

loathe *vt* détester.

loathing *n* aversion *f*.

lobster *n* langouste *f*.

local *adj* local.

locate *vt* localiser.
location *n* situation *f*.
lock *n* serrure *f*; —*vt* fermer à clé.
locker *n* casier *m*.
lockout *n* grève patronale *f*.
locomotive *n* locomotive *f*.
lodge *vi* se loger.
lodger *n* locataire *mf*.
log *n* bûche *f*.
logic *n* logique *f*.
logical *adj* logique.
loiter *vi* s'attarder.
lollipop *n* sucette *f*.
lonely *adj* seul, solitaire.
loneliness *n* solitude *f*.
long *adj* long, *f* longue; —*vi* désirer.
longevity *n* longévité *f*.
longing *n* désir *m*.
long-range *adj* à longue portée.
long-term *adj* à long terme.
look *vi* regarder; sembler; —*n* aspect *m*; regard *m*.
loop *n* boucle *f*.
loose *adj* lâché; desserré
loosen *vt* lâcher; desserrer.
loot *vt* piller; —*n* butin *m*.
loquacious *adj* loquace.
loquacity *n* loquacité *f*.
lose *vt vi* perdre.
loss *n* perte *f*.
lot *n* sort *f*; lot *m*; —**a ~** beaucoup.
lotion *n* lotion *f*.
loud *adj* fort, bruyant.
loudspeaker *n* haut-parleur *m*.
lounge *n* salon *m*.
lovable *adj* sympathique.

love *n* amour *m*; —*vt* aimer.
loveliness *n* beauté *f*.
lovely *adj* beau.
lover *n* amant *m*.
loving *adj* affectueux.
low *adj* bas; —*vi* meugler.
lower *vt* baisser.
lowly *adj* humble.
loyal *adj* loyal, fidèle.
loyalty *n* loyauté *f*; fidélité *f*.
lucid *adj* lucide.
luck *n* chance *f*.
luckless *adj* malchanceux.
lucky *adj* chanceux.
lucrative *adj* lucratif.
ludicrous *adj* absurde.
luggage *n* bagages *mpl*.
lukewarm *adj* tiède.
lull *vt* bercer; —*n* répit *m*.
luminous *adj* lumineux.
lump *n* bosse *f*; grosseur *f*.
lunch *n* déjeuner *m*.
lungs *npl* poumons *mpl*.
lure *n* leurre *m*; attrait *m*; —*vt* séduire, attirer.
lurk *vi* se cacher.
lush *adj* luxuriant.
lust *n* luxure *f*; —*vi* désirer.
lustre *n* lustre *m*.
luxuriance *n* luxuriance *f*.
luxuriant *adj* luxuriant.
luxurious *adj* luxueux.
luxury *n* luxe *m*.
lyrical *adj* lyrique.
lyrics *npl* paroles *fpl*.

M

macerate *vt* macérer.
machination *n* machination *f*.
machine *n* machine *f*.
machinery *n* machinerie *f*; mécanisme *m*.
mad *adj* fou, *f* folle; insensé.
madam *n* madame *f*.
madden *vt* rendre fou; rendre furieux.
madman *n* fou *m*.
madness *n* folie *f*.
magazine *n* magazine *m*, revue *f*; magasin *m*.
magic *n* magie *f*.—*adj* magique.
magnanimous *adj* magnanime.
magnet *n* aimant *m*.
magnetic *adj* magnétique.
magnetism *n* magnétisme *m*.
magnificence *n* magnificence *f*.
magnificent *ad* magnifique.
magnify *vt* grossir; exagérer.
magnitude *n* magnitude *f*.
maid *n* bonne *f*.
mail *n* courrier *m*.
mail train *n* (*rail*) train-poste *m*.
maim *vt* mutiler.
main *adj* principal; essentiel:—**in the ~** en général.
mainland *n* continent *m*.
main line *n* (*rail*) grande ligne *f*.
main street *n* rue principale *f*.
maintain *vt* maintenir; soutenir.
maintenance *n* entretien *m*.
majestic *adj* majestueux.
majesty *n* majesté *f*.
major *adj* majeur.
majority *n* majorité *f*.
make *vt* faire *n* marque *f*.

make-up *n* maquillage *m*.
malady *n* maladie *f*.
malaise *n* malaise *m*.
malaria *n* malaria *f*.
malcontent *adj n* mécontent *m*, -e *f*.
male *adj* mâle; masculin:—*n* mâle *m*.
malevolence *n* malveillance *f*.
malevolent *adj* malveillant.
malice *n* malice *f*.
malicious *adj* méchant.
malign *adj* nocif:—*vt* calomnier.
malleable *adj* malléable.
malnutrition *n* malnutrition *f*.
malpractice *n* négligence *f*.
maltreat *vt* maltraiter.
mammal *n* mammifère *m*.
man *n* homme *m*.
manage *vt* diriger; réussir:—*vi* réussir.
management *n* direction *f*.
manager *n* directeur *m*.
managing director *n* directeur général *m*.
mandate *n* mandat *m*.
mandatory *adj* obligatoire.
manhandle *vt* maltraiter; manutentionner.
maniac *n* maniaque *mf*.
manic *adj* maniaque.
manifest *adj* manifeste:—*vt* manifester.
manifestation *n* manifestation *f*.
manipulate *vt* manipuler.
manipulation *n* manipulation *f*.
mankind *n* humanité *f*.
manliness *n* virilité *f*.
manly *adj* viril.
man-made *n* artificiel.
manner *n* manière *f*.

manoeuvre *n* manœuvre *f*.

manual *adj n* manuel *m*.

manufacture *n* fabrication *f*.

manufacturer *n* fabricant *m*.

manuscript *n* manuscrit *m*.

many *adj* beaucoup de: — **how ~?** combien?

map *n* carte *f*; plan *m*.

mar *vt* gâter, gâcher.

marble *n* marbre *m*: — *adj* marbré.

March *n* mars *m*.

march *n* marche *f*: — *vi* marcher.

margarine *n* margarine *f*.

margin *n* marge *f*; bord *m*.

marginal *adj* marginal.

marine *adj* marin.

maritime *adj* maritime.

mark *n* marque *f*; signe *m*: — *vt* marquer.

marker *n* marque *f*; marqueur *m*.

market *n* marché *m*.

marketable *adj* vendable.

marmalade *n* confiture d'oranges *f*.

marriage *n* mariage *m*.

marriageable *adj* mariable.

married *adj* marié; conjugal.

marry *vi* se marier.

marsh *n* marécage *m*.

marshy *adj* marécageux.

martial *adj* martial.

martyr *n* martyr *m*, -e *f*.

marvel *n* merveille *f*: — *vi* s'émerveiller.

marvellous *adj* merveilleux.

masculine *adj* masculin, viril.

mask *n* masque *m*: — *vt* masquer.

mason *n* maçon *m*.

mass *n* masse *f*; messe *f*; multitude *f*.

massacre *n* massacre *m*: — *vt* massacrer.

massage *n* massage *m*.

massive *adj* énorme.

mast *n* mât *m*.

master *n* maître *m*: — *vt* maîtriser.

mastermind *vt* diriger.

mastery *n* maîtrise *f*.

match *n* allumette *f*: — *vt* égaler.

matchless *adj* incomparable, sans pareil.

mate *n* camarade *mf*: — *vt* accoupler.

material *adj* matériel.

maternal *adj* maternel.

maternity hospital *n* maternité *f*.

mathematical *adj* mathématique.

mathematics *npl* mathématiques *fpl*.

matrimonial *adj* matrimonial.

matted *adj* emmêlé.

matter *n* matière, substance *f*: — *vi* importer.

mattress *n* matelas *m*.

mature *adj* mûr: — *vi* mûrir.

maturity *n* maturité *f*.

maximum *n* maximum *m*.

may *v aux* pouvoir: — **~be** peut-être.

May *n* mai *m*.

mayor *n* maire *m*.

maze *n* labyrinthe *m*.

me *pn* moi; me.

meadow *n* prairie *f*, pré *m*.

meagre *adj* pauvre.

meal *n* repas *m*.

mean *adj* avare, mesquin; moyen: — **~s** *npl* moyens *mpl*: — *vt vi* signifier.

meander *vi* serpenter.

meaning *n* sens *m*.

meanness *n* avarice, mesquinerie *f*.

meantime *adv* pendant ce temps-là.

measure *n* mesure *f*: — *vt* mesurer.

measurement *n* mesure *f*.

meat *n* viande *f*.

mechanic *n* mécanicien *m*.

mechanical *adj* mécanique.

mechanism *n* mécanisme *m*.

medal *n* médaille *f*.

media *npl* média *mpl*.

mediate *vi* agir en tant que médiateur.

mediator n médiateur m, -trice f.

medical adj médical.

medicinal adj médicinal.

medicine n médecine f.

mediocre adj médiocre.

meditate vi méditer.

meditation n méditation f.

meditative adj méditatif.

Mediterranean adj méditerranéen.

medium n milieu m; médium m:—adj moyen.

medium wave n ondes moyennes fpl.

meek adj doux.

meekness n douceur f.

meet vt rencontrer:—vi se rencontrer.

meeting n réunion f; congrès m.

melancholy n mélancolie f:—adj mélancolique.

mellow adj mûr; doux:—vi mûrir.

melody n mélodie f.

melon n melon m.

melt vt faire fondre:—vi fondre.

member n membre m.

memorable adj mémorable.

memorandum n mémorandum m.

memorise vt mémoriser.

memory n mémoire f; souvenir m.

menace n menace f.

mend vt réparer; raccommoder.

menial adj vil.

menstruation n menstruation f.

mental adj mental.

mentality n mentalité f.

mention n mention f:—vt mentionner.

menu n menu m.

mercantile adj commercial.

mercenary adj n mercenaire m.

merchandise n marchandise f.

merchant n négociant m, -e f.

merciful adj miséricordieux.

mercy n pitié f.

mere adj simple.

merge vt vi fusionner.

merger n fusion f.

merit n mérite m:—vt mériter.

merry adj joyeux.

mesh n maille f.

mesmerise vt hypnotiser.

mess n désordre m; confusion f.

message n message m.

messenger n messager m, -ère f.

metal n métal m.

metallic adj métallique.

meteorological adj météorologique.

meteorology n météorologie f.

meter n compteur m; mètre m.

method n méthode f.

methodical adj, ~ly adv méthodique(ment).

metropolitan adj métropolitain.

mew vi miauler.

microphone n microphone m.

microscope n microscope m.

mid adj demi; mi-.

midday n midi m.

middle adj moyen; du milieu:—n milieu m.

middling adj moyen.

midnight n minuit m.

midway adv à mi-chemin.

midwife n sage-femme f.

might n force f.

mighty adj fort, puissant.

migrate vi émigrer.

migration n émigration f.

mild adj doux; modéré.

mildness n douceur f.

mile n mille m.

militant adj militant.

militate vi militer.

milk n lait m:—vt traire.

milky adj laiteux.

mill n moulin m: — vt moudre.

millimetre n millimètre m.

million n million m.

millionaire n millionaire mf.

millionth adj n millionième mf.

mime n mime m.

mimic vt mimer.

mimicry n mimique f.

mince vt hacher.

mind n esprit m: — vt prendre soin de.

minded adj disposé.

mindful adj conscient; attentif.

mine pn le mien, la mienne, les mien(ne)s; à moi: — n mine f.

miner n mineur m.

mineral adj n minéral m.

mingle vt mêler.

miniature n miniature f.

minimise vt minimiser.

minimum n minimum m.

minister n ministre m: — vt servir.

ministry n ministère m.

minor adj mineur: — n mineur m, -e f.

minority n minorité f.

minus adv moins.

minute adj minuscule.

minute n minute f.

miracle n miracle m.

miraculous adj miraculeux.

mirage n mirage m.

mirror n miroir m.

misadventure n mésaventure f.

misbehave vi se conduire mal.

misbehaviour n mauvaise conduite f.

miscarriage n fausse couche f.

miscellaneous adj divers, varié.

miscellany n mélange, assortiment m.

mischief n mal, tort m.

mischievous adj mauvais; espiègle.

misconception n méprise f.

misconduct n mauvaise conduite f.

misdeed n méfait m.

misdemeanour n délit m.

miser n avare mf.

miserable adj malheureux.

misery n malheur m; misère f.

misfortune n infortune f.

misgovern vt mal gouverner.

mishap n mésaventure f.

misjudge vt méjuger.

mislead vt induire en erreur.

misogynist n misogyne mf.

misprint n coquille f.

Miss n Mlle, Mademoiselle f.

miss vt rater; s'ennuyer de.

missing adj perdu; absent.

mission n mission f.

mist n brouillard m.

mistake vt confondre: — vi se tromper: — n erreur f.

Mister n Monsieur m.

mistress n maîtresse f.

mistrust vt se méfier de: — n méfiance f.

misty adj brumeux.

misunderstanding n malentendu m.

misuse vt faire un mauvais usage de.

mitigate vt atténuer.

mitigation n atténuation f.

mix vt mélanger.

mixed adj mélangé; mixte.

mixture n mélange m.

moan n gémissement m: — vi gémir.

moat n fossé m.

mob n foule f; masse f.

mobile adj mobile.

mobilise vt mobiliser.

mobility n mobilité f.

mock vt se moquer de.

mockery n moquerie f.

mode n mode m.

model n modèle m: — vt modeler.

moderate adj modéré: — vt modérer.

moderation *n* modération *f*.

modern *adj* moderne.

modernise *vt* moderniser.

modest *adj* modeste.

modesty *n* modestie *f*.

modification *n* modification *f*.

modify *vt* modifier.

moist *adj* humide.

moisten *vt* humidifier.

moisture *n* humidité *f*.

molest *vt* importuner.

molten *adj* fondu.

moment *n* moment *m*.

momentary *adj* momentané.

monastery *n* monastère *m*.

monastic *adj* monastique.

Monday *n* lundi *m*.

monetary *adj* monétaire.

money *n* argent *m*; pièce de monnaie *f*.

monk *n* moine *m*.

monkey *n* singe *m*.

monopolise *vt* monopoliser.

monopoly *n* monopole *m*.

monotonous *adj* monotone.

monotony *n* monotonie *f*.

monster *n* monstre *m*.

monstrous *adj* monstrueux.

month *n* mois *m*.

monthly *adj* mensuel; *adv* mensuellement.

mood *n* humeur *f*.

moon *n* lune *f*.

moonlight *n* clair de lune *m*.

moped *n* vélomoteur *m*.

moral *adj* moral: — ~s *npl* moralité *f*.

morale *n* moral *m*.

morality *n* moralité *f*.

morbid *adj* morbide.

more *adj adv* plus: — ~ and ~ de plus en plus.

moreover *adv* de plus, en outre.

morning *n* matin *m*: — **good** ~ bonjour.

morsel *n* bouchée *f*; morceau *m*.

mortal *adj* mortel: — *n* mortel *m*, -elle *f*.

mortality *n* mortalité *f*.

mortgage *n* hypothèque *f*: — *vt* hypothéquer.

mortuary *n* morgue *f*.

mosque *n* mosquée *f*.

most *adj pn* la plupart de: — ~**ly** *adv* surtout, essentiellement.

mother *n* mère *f*.

motherhood *n* maternité *f*.

mother-in-law *n* belle-mère *f*.

motherly *adj* maternel.

mother tongue *n* langue maternelle *f*.

motif *n* motif *m*.

motion *n* mouvement *m*.

motionless *adj* immobile.

motivated *adj* motivé.

motive *n* motif *m*.

motor *n* moteur *m*.

motorbike *n* moto *f*.

motor vehicle *n* automobile *f*.

motto *n* devise *f*.

mould *n* moule *m*: — *vt* mouler.

mound *n* monticule *m*.

mount *n* mont *m*: — *vt* gravir.

mountain *n* montagne *f*.

mountaineer *n* alpiniste *mf*.

mountainous *adj* montagneux.

mourn *vt* pleurer.

mourning *n* deuil *m*.

mouse *n* (*pl* mice) souris *f*; (*comput*) souris *f*.

moustache *n* moustache *f*.

mouth *n* bouche *f*; embouchure *f*.

mouthful *n* bouchée *f*.

movable *adj* mobile.

move *vt* déplacer: — *vi* bouger: — *n* mouvement *m*.

movement *n* mouvement *m*.

moving *adj* touchant, émouvant.

mow *vt* tondre.
Mrs *n* Mme, Madame *f.*
much *adj pn* beaucoup:—*adv* beaucoup,
très.
mud *n* boue *f.*
muddy *adj* boueux.
multiple *adj* multiple.
multiplication *n* multiplication *f.*
multiply *vt* multiplier.
multitude *n* multitude *f.*
mumble *vt vi* grommeler.
munch *vt* mâcher.
mundane *adj* banal.
municipal *adj* municipal.
mural *n* mural *m.*
murder *n* meurtre *m:*—*vt* assassiner.
murderer *n* assassin, meurtrier *m.*
murky *adj* obscur.
murmur *n* murmure *m:*—*vt vi* murmurer.
muscle *n* muscle *m.*

muscular *adj* musculaire.
museum *n* musée *m.*
music *n* musique *f.*
musical *adj* musical; mélodieux.
musician *n* musicien *m,* -ienne *f.*
Muslim *adj* musulman(e) *m(f)*
must *v aux* devoir.
musty *adj* moisi.
mute *adj* muet, silencieux.
mutilate *vt* mutiler.
mutilation *n* mutilation *f.*
mutter *vt vi* grommeler:—*n* grommelle-
ment *m.*
mutual *adj* mutuel, réciproque.
my *pn* mon, ma, mes.
myself *pn* moi-même.
mysterious *adj* mystérieux.
mystery *n* mystère *m.*
myth *n* mythe *m.*
mythology *n* mythologie *f.*

N

nag *vt* harceler.
nail *n* ongle *m;* clou *m:*—*vt* clouer.
naive *adj* naïf.
naked *adj* nu; dénudé; pur.
name *n* nom *m:*—*vt* nommer.
nap *n* sieste *f,* somme *m.*
nape *n* nuque *f.*
napkin *n* serviette *f.*
narrate *vt* narrer, raconter.
narrative *adj* narratif:—*n* narration *f.*
narrow *adj* étroit.
nasty *adj* méchant; mauvais.
nation *n* nation *f.*
national *adj* national.
nationalist *adj n* nationaliste *mf.*

nationality *n* nationalité *f.*
native *adj* natal:—*n* autochtone *mf.*
natural *adj* naturel.
naturalist *n* naturaliste *mf.*
nature *n* nature *f;* sorte *f.*
naughty *adj* méchant.
nausea *n* nausée.
nauseous *adj* écœurant.
navel *n* nombril *m.*
navigate *vi* naviguer.
navigation *n* navigation *f.*
navy *n* marine *f.*
near *prep* près de:—*adv* près; à côté:—
adj proche.
nearly *adv* presque.

neat *adj* soigné; net.

necessary *adj* nécessaire.

necessitate *vt* nécessiter.

necessity *n* nécessité *f*.

neck *n* cou *m*.

necklace *n* collier *m*.

need *n* besoin *m*:—*vt* avoir besoin de.

needle *n* aiguille *f*.

needy *adj* nécessiteux.

negation *n* négation *f*.

negative *adj* négatif:—*n* négative *f*.

neglect *vt* négliger:—*n* négligence *f*.

negligence *n* négligence *f*.

negligent *adj* négligent.

negotiate *vt vi* négocier.

negotiation *n* négociation *f*.

Negro *adj* noir:—*n* Noire *m*.

neighbour *n* voisin *m*, -e *f*.

neighbouring *adj* voisin.

neither *conj* ni:—*pn* aucun(e), ni l'un(e) ni l'autre.

nephew *n* neveu *m*.

nerve *n* nerf *m*; courage *m*.

nervous *adj* nerveux.

nest *n* nid *m*; nichée *f*.

net *n* filet *m*.

net curtain *n* voile *m*.

nettle *n* ortie *f*.

network *n* réseau *f*.

neutral *adj* neutre.

neutrality *n* neutralité *f*.

never *adv* jamais.

nevertheless *adv* cependant, néanmoins.

new *adj* neuf; nouveau.

newborn *adj* nouveau-né, *f* nouveau-née.

news *npl* nouvelles, informations *fpl*.

newspaper *n* journal *m*.

New Year *n* Nouvel An *m*:—~**'s Day** *n* Jour du Nouvel An *m*:—~**'s Eve** Saint-Sylvestre *f*.

next *adj* prochain:—*adv* ensuite, après.

nibble *vt* mordiller.

nice *adj* gentil, *f* gentille; agréable.

niche *n* niche *f*.

nickname *n* surnom *m*:—*vt* surnommer.

niece *n* nièce *f*.

night *n* nuit *f*:—**good ~** bonne nuit.

nightly *adv* toutes les nuits:—*adj* nocturne.

nightmare *n* cauchemar *m*.

nimble *adj* léger; agile.

nine *adj n* neuf *m*.

nineteen *adj n* dix-neuf *m*.

nineteenth *adj n* dix-neuvième *mf*.

ninetieth *adj n* quatre-vingt-dixième *mf*.

ninety *adj n* quatre-vingt-dix *m*.

ninth *adj n* neuvième *mf*.

no *adv* non:—*adj* aucun; pas de.

noble *adj* noble:—*n* noble *mf*.

nobody *pn* personne.

nocturnal *adj* nocturne.

nod *n* signe de tête *m*:—*vi* faire un signe de la tête.

noise *n* bruit *m*.

noisiness *n* bruit, tapage *m*.

nominal *adj* nominal.

nominate *vt* nommer.

nomination *n* nomination *f*.

nonchalant *adj* nonchalant.

none *pn* aucun; personne.

nonentity *n* nullité *f*.

nonetheless *adv* cependant.

nonplussed *adj* perplexe.

nonsense *n* absurdité *f*.

nonsensical *adj* absurde.

nonstop *adj* direct.

noon *n* midi *m*.

nor *conj* ni.

normal *adj* normal.

north *n* nord *m*:—*adj* du nord.

northeast *n* nord-est *m*.

northern *adj* du nord.

northwest *n* nord-ouest *m*.

nose *n* nez *m*.

nostalgia *n* nostalgie *f*.

nostril *n* narine *f*.

not *adv* pas; non.

notable *adj* notable.

note *n* note *f*; billet *m*:—*vt* noter, marquer.

notebook *n* carnet *m*.

nothing *n* rien *m*.

notice *n* notice *f*; avis *m*:—*vt* remarquer.

noticeable *adj* visible.

notify *vt* notifier.

notion *n* notion *f*; idée *f*.

notoriety *n* notoriété *f*.

notorious *adj* notoire.

nourish *vt* nourrir, alimenter.

nourishment *n* nourriture *f*, aliments *mpl*.

novel *n* roman *m*.

novelty *n* nouveauté *f*.

November *n* novembre *m*.

novice *n* novice *mf*.

now *adv* maintenant.

nowadays *adv* de nos jours.

nowhere *adv* nulle part.

nuance *n* nuance *f*.

nuclear *adj* nucléaire.

nude *adj* nu.

nudity *n* nudité *f*.

nuisance *n* ennui *m*; gêne *f*.

null *adj* nul.

numb *adj* engourdi:—*vt* engourdir.

number *n* numéro, nombre *m*:—*vt* numéroter.

numbness *n* engourdissement *m*.

numeral *n* chiffre *m*.

numerical *adj* numérique.

nurse *n* infirmière *f*:—*vt* soigner.

nursery *n* crèche *f*.

nurture *vt* élever.

nut *n* noix *f*.

nutritious *adj* nutritif.

nylon *n* nylon *m*.

O

oak *n* chêne *m*.

oar *n* rame *f*.

oath *n* serment *m*.

obedience *n* obéissance *f*.

obedient *adj* obéissant.

obese *adj* obèse.

obesity *n* obésité *f*.

obey *vt* obéir à.

object *n* objet *m*:—*vt* objecter.

objection *n* objection *f*.

objective *adj* *n* objectif *m*.

obligation *n* obligation *f*.

obligatory *adj* obligatoire.

oblige *vt* obliger.

obliging *adj* obligeant.

oblique *adj* oblique.

oblivious *adj* oublieux.

obnoxious *adj* odieux.

obscene *adj* obscène.

obscure *adj* obscur:—*vt* obscurcir.

obscurity *n* obscurité *f*.

observant *adj* observateur.

observation *n* observation *f*.

observatory *n* observatoire *m*.

observe *vt* observer.

obsess *vt* obséder.

obsessive *adj* obsédant.

obsolete *adj* désuet.

obstacle *n* obstacle *m*.

obstinate *adj* obstiné.

obstruct *vt* obstruer; entraver.

obstruction *n* obstruction *f*; encombrement *m*.

obtain *vt* obtenir.

obtainable *adj* disponible.

obvious *adj* évident.

occasion *n* occasion *f*.—*vt* occasionner.

occasional *adj* occasionnel.

occupant *n* occupant *m*, -e *f*.

occupation *n* occupation *f*; emploi *m*.

occupy *vt* occuper.

occur *vi* se produire, arriver.

occurrence *n* incident *m*.

ocean *n* océan *m*.

oceanic *adj* océanique.

October *n* octobre *m*.

odd *adj* impair; étrange.

odious *adj* odieux.

odour *n* odeur *f*; parfum *m*.

of *prep* de; à.

off *adj* éteint; fermé; annulé.

offend *vt* offenser, blesser.

offense *n* offense *f*; injure *f*.

offensive *adj* offensant.

offer *vt* offrir:—*n* offre *f*.

office *n* bureau *m*; poste *m*.

officer *n* officier *m*; fonctionnaire *mf*.

official *adj* officiel:—*n* employé *m*, -e *f*.

officiate *vi* officier.

offset *vt* compenser; décaler.

offshore *adj* côtier.

offspring *n* progéniture *f*.

oil *n* huile *f*.—*vt* huiler.

oil painting *n* peinture à l'huile *f*.

oil tanker *n* pétrolier *m*.

ointment *n* onguent *m*.

OK, okay *excl* OK, d'accord.

old *adj* vieux, *f* vieille.

old age *n* vieillesse *f*.

olive *n* olivier *m*; olive *f*.

olive oil *n* huile d'olive *f*.

omelette *n* omelette *f*.

omission *n* omission *f*; négligence *f*.

omit *vt* omettre.

on *prep* sur, dessus; en; pour:—*adj* allumé, branché.

once *adv* une fois:—~ **more** encore une fois.

one *adj* un, une.

onerous *adj* lourd; onéreux.

oneself *pn* soi-même.

one-sided *adj* partial.

onion *n* oignon *m*.

online *adj* en ligne.

onlooker *n* spectateur *m*, -trice *f*.

only *adj* seul, unique:—*adv* seulement.

onus *n* responsabilité *f*.

opaque *adj* opaque.

open *adj* ouvert; sincère, franc:—*vt* ouvrir; *vi* s'ouvrir.

opening *n* ouverture *f*.

openness *n* clareté *f*.

opera *n* opéra *m*.

operate *vi* fonctionner; opérer.

operation *n* fonctionnement *m*; opération *f*.

operator *n* opérateur *m*, -trice *f*.

opine *vt* être d'avis (que).

opinion *n* opinion *f*; jugement *m*.

opinion poll *n* sondage *m*.

opponent *n* opposant *m*, -e *f*.

opportune *adj* opportun.

opportunity *n* occasion *f*.

oppose *vt* s'opposer à.

opposing *adj* opposé.

opposite *adj* opposé:—*adv* en face:—*prep* en face de:—*n* contraire *m*.

opposition *n* opposition *f*.

oppress *vt* opprimer.
oppressive *adj* oppressif.
optimist *n* optimiste *mf*.
optimistic *adj* optimiste.
optimum *adj* optimum.
option *n* option *f*.
optional *adj* optionnel.
opulent *adj* opulent.
or *conj* ou.
oral *adj* oral, verbal.
orange *n* orange *f*.
orbit *n* orbite *f*.
orchestra *n* orchestre *m*.
ordain *vt* ordonner.
order *n* ordre *m*; commande *f*:—*vt* ordonner.
orderly *adj* ordonné; réglé.
ordinary *adj* ordinaire.
ore *n* minerai *m*.
organ *n* organe *m*.
organic *adj* organique.
organisation *n* organisation *f*.
organise *vt* organiser.
organism *n* organisme *m*.
oriental *adj* oriental.
orifice *n* orifice *m*.
origin *n* origine *f*.
original *adj* original.
originality *n* originalité *f*.
ornament *n* ornement *m*:—*vt* ornementer.
ornate *adj* ornementé.
orphan *adj n* orphelin *m*, -e *f*.
orthodox *adj* orthodoxe.
oscillate *vi* osciller.
other *pn* autre.
otherwise *adv* autrement.
ought *v aux* devoir; falloir.
our *pn* notre, *pl* nos.
ours *pn* le nôtre, la nôtre, les nôtres; à nous.

ourselves *pn pl* nous-mêmes.
out *adv* dehors; éteint.
outburst *n* explosion *f*.
outcome *n* résultat *m*.
outdo *vt* surpasser.
outdoor *adj* de plein air:—**~s** *adv* à l'extérieur.
outer *adj* extérieur.
outfit *n* tenue *f*; équipement *m*.
outgoing *adj* extroverti; sortant.
outlay *n* dépenses *fpl*, frais *mpl*.
outline *n* contour *m*; grandes lignes *fpl*.
outlook *n* perspective *f*.
output *n* rendement *m*; sortie *f*.
outrage *n* outrage *m*:—*vt* outrager.
outright *adv* absolument:—*adj* absolu.
outset *n* commencement *m*.
outside *n* surface *f*; extérieur *m*:—*adv* dehors:—*prep* en dehors de.
outstrip *vt* devancer; surpasser.
oval *n*, *adj* ovale *m*.
ovary *n* ovaire *m*.
oven *n* four *m*.
over *prep* sur, dessus; plus de; pendant:—*adj* fini.
overall *adj* total:—**~s** *npl* salopette *f*.
overbalance *vi* perdre l'équilibre.
overcast *adj* couvert.
overcharge *vt* surcharger.
overcoat *n* pardessus *m*.
overcome *vt* vaincre.
overdo *vi* exagérer.
overdraft *n* découvert *m*.
overdue *adj* en retard; arriéré.
overestimate *vt* surestimer.
overflow *vi* déborder:—*n* surplus *m*.
overhaul *vt* réviser:—*n* révision *f*.
overland *adj adv* par voie de terre.
overlap *vi* se chevaucher.
overlook *vt* donner sur; oublier; tolérer; négliger.

overnight *adv* pendant la nuit:—*adj* de nuit.

overpower *vt* dominer, écraser.

overrate *vt* surévaluer.

overrun *vt* envahir; infester; dépasser.

overseas *adv* à l'étranger; outre-mer:—*adj* étranger.

oversee *vt* inspecter, surveiller.

oversight *n* oubli *m*; erreur *f*.

oversleep *vi* se réveiller en retard.

overtake *vt* doubler.

overthrow *vt* renverser:—*n* renversement *m*.

overtime *n* heures supplémentaires *fpl*.

overturn *vt* renverser.

overwhelm *vt* écraser.

overwhelming *adj* écrasant.

overwork *vi* se surmener.

owe *vt* devoir.

owing *adj* dû:—~ **to** en raison de.

owl *n* chouette *f*.

own *adj* propre:—*vt* posséder.

owner *n* propriétaire *mf*.

ox *n* bœuf *m*.

oxygen *n* oxygène *m*.

oyster *n* huître *f*.

ozone *n* ozone *m*.

P

pace *n* pas *m*; allure *f*:—*vi* marcher.

pacific *adj* pacifique.

pacification *n* pacification *f*.

pacify *vt* pacifier.

pack *n* paquet *m*; bande *f*:—*vt* empaqueter:—*vi* faire ses valises.

package *n* paquet *m*.

packet *n* paquet *m*.

pact *n* pacte *m*.

pad *n* bloc *m*; tampon *m*; (*sl*) piaule *f*:—*vt* rembourrer.

paddle *vi* ramer:—*n* pagaie *f*.

pagan *adj n* païen *m*, païenne *f*.

page *n* page *f*; page *m*.

pail *n* seau *m*.

pain *n* douleur *f*; peine *f*:—*vt* peiner.

pained *adj* peiné.

painful *adj* douloureux; pénible.

painstaking *adj* soigneux.

paint *vt* peindre.

painter *n* peintre *m*.

painting *n* peinture *f*; tableau *m*.

pair *n* pair *m*.

palatable *adj* savoureux.

palate *n* palais *m*.

pale *adj* pâle; clair.

palette *n* palette *f*.

pallet *n* palette *f*.

pallid *adj* pâle.

palpable *adj* palpable; évident.

palpitation *n* palpitation *f*.

pamper *vt* gâter, dorloter.

pamphlet *n* pamphlet *m*; brochure *f*.

pan *n* casserole *f*; poêle *f*.

panache *n* panache *m*.

pane *n* vitre *f*.

panel *n* panneau *m*; comité *m*.

pang *n* angoisse *f*; tourment *m*.

panic *adj n* (de) panique *f*.

pant *vi* haleter.

panther *n* panthère *f*.

pantry *n* placard *m*.

pants *npl* slip *m*; pantalon *m*.
paper *n* papier *m*; journal *m*:—*adj* en papier:—*vt* tapisser.
paperweight *n* presse-papiers *m*.
par *n* équivalence *f*; pair *m*.
parachute *n* parachute *m*.
parade *n* parade *f*.
paradise *n* paradis *m*.
paradox *n* paradoxe *m*.
paragraph *n* paragraphe *m*.
parallel *adj* parallèle:—*n* parallèle *f*.
paralyse *vt* paralyser.
paralysis *n* paralysie *f*.
paramount *adj* suprême, supérieur.
paranoid *adj* paranoïaque.
parasite *n* parasite *m*.
parcel *n* paquet *m*; parcelle *f*:—*vt* empaqueter.
parch *vt* dessécher.
pardon *n* pardon *m*:—*vt* pardonner.
parent *n* père *m*; mère *f*:—**~s** parents *mpl*.
park *n* parc *m*:—*vt* garer; *vi* se garer.
parking *n* stationnement *m*.
parking lot *n* parking *m*.
parliament *n* parlement *m*.
parody *n* parodie *f*:—*vt* parodier.
parry *vt* parer.
part *n* partie *f*; part *f*; rôle (d'acteur) *m*:—*vt* séparer; diviser:—*vi* se séparer; se diviser:—**~ly** *adv* en partie.
partial *adj* partial.
participate *vi* participer (à).
participation *n* participation *f*.
particle *n* particule *f*.
particular *adj* particulier:—*n* particulier *m*; particularité *f*.
partition *n* partition, séparation *f*:—*vt* partager,
partner *n* associé *m*, -e *f*.
party *n* parti *m*; fête *f*.

pass *vt* passer; dépasser:—*vi* passer:—*n* permis *m*; passage *m*.
passage *n* passage *m*.
passenger *n* passager *m*, -ère *f*.
passer-by *n* passant *m*, -e *f*.
passion *n* passion *f*; amour *m*.
passionate *adj* passionné.
passive *adj* passif.
passport *n* passeport *m*.
past *adj* passé:—*n* passé *m*:—*prep* au-delà de; après.
paste *n* pâte *f*; colle *f*:—*vt* coller.
pastime *n* passe-temps *m invar*.
pastry *n* pâtisserie *f*.
pasture *n* pâture *f*.
patch *n* pièce *f*; terrain *m*:—*vt* rapiécer.
patent *adj* évident:—*n* brevet *m*:—*vt* faire breveter.
patentee *n* détenteur d'un brevet *m*.
paternal *adj* paternel.
paternity *n* paternité *f*.
path *n* chemin, sentier *m*.
pathetic *adj* pathétique.
patience *n* patience *f*.
patient *adj* patient:—**~ly** *adv* patiemment:—*n* patient *m*, -e *f*.
patrol *n* patrouille *f*:—*vi* patrouiller.
patron *n* protecteur *m*; client *m*, -e *f*.
patronise *vt* patronner, protéger.
pattern *n* motif *m*; modèle *m*.
pause *n* pause *f*:—*vi* faire une pause; hésiter.
pave *vt* paver; carreler.
pavement *n* trottoir *m*.
paw *n* patte *f*:—*vt* tripoter.
pay *vt* payer:—**to ~ back** *vt* rembourser:—*n* paie *f*; salaire *m*.
payable *adj* payable.
payment *n* paiement *m*.
pea *n* pois *m*.
peace *n* paix *f*.

peaceful adj paisible; pacifique.

peak n pic m; maximum m.

pear n poire f.

pearl n perle f.

peasant n paysan m, -anne f.

pebble n caillou m; galet m.

peculiar adj étrange, singulier.

peculiarity n particularité, singularité f.

pedal n pédale f:—vi pédaler.

pedestrian n piéton m, -onne f:—adj pédestre.

peel vt peler:—n peau f; pelure f.

peer n pair m.

peerless adj incomparable.

pelt n fourrure f.

pen n stylo m; plume f.

penalty n peine f; sanction f; amende f.

pencil n crayon m.

pendulum n pendule m.

penetrate vt pénétrer dans.

peninsula n péninsule f.

penitentiary n pénitencier m.

penknife n canif m.

penpal n correspondant m, -e f.

pension n pension f:—vt pensionner.

pensive adj pensif.

penultimate adj pénultième.

people n peuple m; nation f; gens mpl:—vt peupler.

pepper n poivre m:—vt poivrer.

per prep par.

per annum adv par an.

perceive vt percevoir.

percentage n pourcentage m.

perception n perception f; notion f.

perch n perche f.

percussion n percussion f.

perdition n perte, ruine f.

perennial adj perpétuel.

perfect adj parfait; idéal:—vt parfaire, perfectionner.

perfection n perfection f.

perform vt exécuter:—vi donner une représentation.

performance n exécution f; accomplissement m.

performer n exécutant m, -e f; acteur m, -trice f.

perfume n parfum m:—vt parfumer.

perhaps adv peut-être.

peril n péril, danger m.

perilous adj dangereux.

perimeter n périmètre m.

period n période f; époque f.

periodic adj périodique.

perish vi périr.

perishable adj périssable.

permanent adj permanent.

permissible adj permis.

permission n permission f.

permissive adj permissif.

permit vt permettre:—n permis m.

perpetrate vt perpétrer, commettre.

perpetual adj perpétuel.

perplex vt confondre, laisser perplexe.

persecute vt persécuter; importuner.

persecution n persécution f.

persevere vi persévérer.

persist vi persister.

persistence adj persistance f.

persistent adj persistant.

person n personne f.

personage n personnage m.

personal adv personnel.

personal computer n ordinateur individuel m.

personality n personnalité f.

personnel n personnel m.

perspective n perspective f.

perspiration n transpiration f.

perspire vi transpirer.

persuade vt persuader.

persuasion *n* persuasion *f*.

persuasive *adj* persuasif.

pertaining:—~ to *prep* relatif à.

pertinent *adj* pertinent.

perturb *vt* perturber.

peruse *vt* lire; examiner attentivement.

perverse *adj* pervers, dépravé.

pessimist *n* pessimiste *mf*.

pest *n* insecte nuisible *m*; casse-pieds (*fam*) *mf invar*.

pester *vt* importuner, fatiguer.

pestilence *n* peste *f*.

pet *n* animal domestique *m*:—*vt* gâter.

petal *n* (*bot*) pétale *m*.

petition *n* pétition *f*.

petticoat *n* jupon *m*.

pettiness *n* insignifiance *f*.

petty *adj* mesquin; insignifiant.

phantom *n* fantôme *m*.

pharmacist *n* pharmacien *m*, -ienne *f*.

pharmacy *n* pharmacie *f*.

phase *n* phase *f*.

phenomenal *adj* phénoménal.

phenomenon *n* phénomène *m*.

philosopher *n* philosophe *mf*.

philosophical *adj* philosophique.

philosophise *vi* philosopher.

philosophy *n* philosophie *f*.

phobia *n* phobie *f*.

phone *n* téléphone *m*:—*vt* téléphoner à.

phone book *n* annuaire *m*.

phone call *n* coup de téléphone *m*.

photograph *n* photo(graphie) *f*:—*vt* photographier.

photographer *n* photographe *mf*.

photography *n* photographie *f*.

phrase *n* phrase *f*:—*vt* exprimer.

phrase book *n* guide de conversation *m*.

physical *adv* physique.

physician *n* médecin *m*.

physicist *n* physicien *m*, -ienne *f*.

physiotherapy *n* physiothérapie *f*.

physique *n* physique *m*.

pianist *n* pianiste *mf*.

piano *n* piano *m*.

pick *vt* choisir; cueillir:—*n* pic *m*; choix *m*.

picnic *n* pique-nique *m*.

pictorial *adj* pictural; illustré.

picture *n* image *f*; peinture *f*:—*vt* dépeindre.

pie *n* gâteau *m*; tarte *f*; pâté en croûte *m*.

piece *n* morceau *m*; pièce *f*.

pierce *vt* percer, transpercer.

piercing *adj* perçant.

pig *n* cochon *m*.

pigeon *n* pigeon *m*.

pile *n* tas *m*; pile *f*; amas *m*:—*vt* entasser.

pilgrim *n* pèlerin *m*.

pill *n* pilule *f*.

pillar *n* pilier *m*.

pillow *n* oreiller *m*.

pilot *n* pilote *m*:—*vt* piloter; (*fig*) mener.

pin *n* épingle *f*:—*vt* épingler.

pincers *n* pinces, tenailles *fpl*.

pine *n* (*bot*) pin *m*:—*vi* languir.

pineapple *n* ananas *m*.

pink *n*, *adj* rose *m*.

pint *n* pinte *f*.

pioneer *n* pionnier *m*.

pious *adj* pieux, dévot.

pipe *n* tube, tuyau *m*; pipe *f*.

pipeline *n* canalisation *f*.

piracy *n* piraterie *f*.

pirate *n* pirate *m*.

pistol *n* pistolet *m*.

pitch *n* lancement *m*:—*vt* lancer, jeter.

pitcher *n* cruche *f*.

pitiable *adj* pitoyable.

pitiful *adj* pitoyable.

pity *n* pitié *f*:—*vt* avoir pitié de.

placard *n* affiche *f*.

placate *vt* apaiser.

place *n* endroit, lieu *m*: — *vt* placer.

placid *adj* placide, calme.

plague *n* peste *f*: — *vt* tourmenter.

plain *adj* uni; simple; évident: — *n* plaine *f*.

plait *n* pli *m*; tresse *f*: — *vt* plier.

plan *n* plan *m*: — *vt* projeter.

plane *n* avion *m*; plan *m*: — *vt* aplanir.

planet *n* planète *f*.

plank *n* planche *f*.

planner *n* planificateur *m*, -trice *f*.

plant *n* plante *f*; usine *f*: — *vt* planter.

plantation *n* plantation *f*.

plaster *n* plâtre *m*; emplâtre *m*: — *vt* plâtrer.

plastic *adj* plastique.

plate *n* assiette *f*; plaque *f*; lame *f*.

platform *n* plateforme *f*.

platter *n* écuelle *f*; plat *m*.

plausible *adj* plausible.

play *n* jeu *m*; pièce *f* de théâtre: — *vt vi* jouer.

player *n* joueur *m*, -euse *f*; acteur *m*, -trice *f*.

playful *adj* enjoué, amusé.

playwright *n* dramaturge *mf*.

plea *n* appel *m*; excuse *f*, prétexte *m*.

plead *vt* plaider; prétexter.

pleasant *adj* agréable; plaisant.

please *vt* faire plaisir à.

pleased *adj* content.

pleasure *n* plaisir *m*; gré *m*.

pledge *n* promesse *f*; gage *m*: — *vt* engager.

plentiful *adj* copieux; abondant.

plenty *n* abondance *f*.

pliable *adj* pliant; souple.

pliers *npl* tenailles *fpl*.

plot *n* complot *m*; intrigue *f*: — *vt* tracer.

plough *n* charrue *f*: — *vt* labourer.

pluck *vt* tirer; arracher: — *n* courage *m*.

plug *n* bougie *f*; prise *f*: — *vt* boucher.

plumber *n* plombier *m*.

plump *adj* rondouillet, dodu.

plunge *vi* plonger; s'élancer.

plural *adj n* pluriel *m*.

plus *prep* plus.

pneumonia *n* pneumonie *f*.

poach *vt* pocher; braconner.

poacher *n* braconnier *m*.

pocket *n* poche *f*: — *vt* empocher.

poem *n* poème *m*.

poet *n* poète *m*.

poetry *n* poésie *f*.

poignant *adj* poignant.

point *n* pointe *f*; point *m*: — *vt* pointer.

pointed *adj* pointu; acéré.

poise *n* attitude *f*; équilibre *m*.

poison *n* poison *m*: — *vt* empoisonner.

poisonous *adj* vénéneux.

poke *vt* attiser.

poker-faced *adj* au visage impassible.

pole *n* pôle *m*; mât *m*; perche *f*.

police *n* police *f*.

policeman *n* agent de police *m*.

police station *n* commissariat *m*.

policy *n* politique *f*.

polish *vt* polir; cirer: — *n* poli *m*.

polished *adj* poli; ciré; élégant.

polite *adj* poli.

politeness *n* politesse.

political *adj* politique.

politician *n* homme (femme) politique *m(f)*.

politics *npl* politique *f*.

pollute *vt* polluer.

pollution *n* pollution *f*.

polytechnic *n* école d'enseignement technique *f*.

pompous *adj* pompeux.

pond *n* mare *f*; étang *m*.

ponder vt considérer.

pony n poney m.

pool n piscine f.

poor adj pauvre; mauvais

populace n populace f.

popular adj populaire.

popularity n popularité f.

populate vi peupler.

population n population f.

porch n porche m.

pork n porc m.

port n port m.

portable adj portable, portatif.

portion n portion, part f.

portrait n portrait m.

portray vt faire le portrait de; dépeindre.

pose n posture f; pose f: — vi, vt poser.

position n position f: — vt mettre en position.

positive adj positif; réel.

possess vt posséder.

possession n possession f.

possibility n possibilité f.

possible adj possible: — ~ly adv peut-être.

post n courrier m; poste f; emploi m.

postage stamp n timbre m.

postcard n carte postale f.

poster n poster m.

posterior n postérieur m.

posthumous adj posthume.

postman n facteur m.

post office n poste f, bureau de poste m.

postpone vt remettre; différer.

posture n posture f.

pot n pot m; marmite f: — vt empoter.

potato n pomme de terre.

potent adj puissant.

potential adj potentiel.

potion n potion f.

pouch n sac m.

poultry n volaille f.

pound n livre f; livre sterling f: — vt concasser.

pour vt verser; servir: — vi couler; pleuvoir à verse.

poverty n pauvreté f.

powder n poudre f: — vt poudrer.

powdery adj poudreux.

power n pouvoir m; puissance f; force f: — vt propulser.

powerful adj puissant.

powerless adj impotent.

practicable adj praticable; faisable.

practical adj pratique.

practicality n faisabilité f.

practice n pratique f; usage m; entraînement m.

practise vt pratiquer: — vi s'exercer.

pragmatic adj pragmatique.

praise n louange f: — vt louer.

prance vi cabrioler.

prattle vi jacasser: — n jacasserie f.

prawn n crevette f.

pray vi prier.

prayer n prière f.

preach vt prêcher.

preacher n prédicateur m.

precarious adj précaire, incertain.

precaution n précaution f.

precede vt précéder.

precedent adj n précédent m.

precinct n limite f; enceinte f.

precious adj précieux.

precipitate vt précipiter: — adj précipité.

precise adj précis, exact.

precision n précision, exactitude f.

precocious adj précoce, prématuré.

preconceive vt préconcevoir.

preconception n préjugé m; idée préconçue f.

predator n prédateur m.

predecessor *n* prédécesseur *m*.

predict *vt* prédire.

predictable *adj* prévisible.

prediction *n* prédiction *f*.

predominant *adj* prédominant.

predominate *vt* prédominer.

preface *n* préface *f*.

prefer *vt* préférer.

preferable *adj* préférable.

preference *n* préférence *f*.

preferential *adj* préférentiel.

prefix *vt* préfixer.

pregnancy *n* grossesse *f*.

pregnant *adj* enceinte.

prehistoric *adj* préhistorique.

prejudice *n* préjudice *m*; préjugé *m*: — *vt* préjudicier à.

prejudiced *adj* qui a des préjugés; partial.

prejudicial *adj* préjudiciable.

preliminary *adj* préliminaire.

premature *adj* prématuré.

premeditation *n* préméditation *f*.

premises *npl* locaux *mpl*.

premium *n* prix *m*; prime *f*.

premonition *n* prémonition *f*.

preparation *n* préparation *f*.

preparatory *adj* préparatoire.

prepare *vt* préparer: — *vi* se préparer.

preposterous *adj* ridicule, absurde.

prerogative *n* prérogative *f*.

prescribe *vt* prescrire.

prescription *n* prescription *f*.

presence *n* présence *f*.

present *n* cadeau *m*: — *adj* présent; actuel: — **~ly** *adv* actuellement: — *vt* présenter.

presentable *adj* présentable.

presenter *n* présentateur *m*, -trice *f*.

preservation *n* préservation *f*.

preserve *vt* préserver: — *n* conserve *f*; confiture *f*.

preside *vi* présider; diriger.

president *n* président *m*.

press *vt* appuyer sur: — *vi* se presser: — *n* presse *f*; pressoir *m*.

pressing *adj* pressant; urgent.

pressure *n* pression *f*.

prestige *n* prestige *m*.

presumable *adj* vraisemblable.

presume *vt* présumer, supposer.

presumption *n* présomption *f*.

pretence *n* prétexte *m*; simulation *f*.

pretend *vi* prétendre; faire semblant.

pretext *n* prétexte *m*.

pretty *adj* joli, mignon.

prevail *vi* prévaloir; prédominer.

prevalent *adj* prédominant.

prevent *vt* prévenir; empêcher.

prevention *n* prévention *f*.

previous *adj* précédent; antérieur: — **~ly** *adv* auparavant.

prey *n* proie *f*.

price *n* prix *m*.

prick *vt* piquer: — *n* piqûre *f*; pointe *f*.

pride *n* orgueil *m*; vanité *f*; fierté *f*.

priest *n* prêtre *m*.

priesthood *n* sacerdoce *m*, prêtrise *f*.

primacy *n* primauté *f*.

primarily *adv* principalement, surtout.

primary *adj* primaire; principal, premier.

primate *n* primate *m*.

prime *n* (*fig*) fleur *f*; commencement *m*: — *adj* premier; principal.

prime minister *n* premier ministre *m*.

primitive *adj* primitif.

prince *n* prince *m*.

princess *n* princesse *f*.

principal *adj* principal: — *n* principal *m*.

principle *n* principe *m*.

print *vt* imprimer: — *n* impression *f*; estampe *f*.

printer *n* imprimeur *m*; imprimante *f*.

prior adj antérieur, précédent.

priority n priorité f.

prison n prison f.

prisoner n prisonnier m, -ière f.

privacy n intimité f.

private adj privé; secret; particulier:— ~**ly** adv en privé.

privilege n privilège m.

prize n prix m:—vt apprécier, évaluer.

pro prep pour.

probability n probabilité f; vraisemblance f.

probable adj probable, vraisemblable.

probation n essai m; probation f.

probationary adj d'essai.

probe n sonde f:—vt sonder.

problem n problème m.

problematical adj problématique.

procedure n procédure f.

proceed vi procéder; provenir.

process n processus m; procédé m.

procession n procession f.

proclaim vt proclamer; promulguer.

proclamation n proclamation f; décret m.

procure vt procurer.

procurement n obtention f.

prod vt pousser.

prodigious adj prodigieux.

prodigy n prodige m.

produce vt produire; créer.

producer n producteur m, -trice f.

product n produit m; œuvre f; fruit m.

production n production f; produit m.

productive adj productif.

profess vt professer; déclarer.

profession n profession f.

professional adj professionnel.

professor n professeur m.

proficiency n capacité f.

proficient adj compétent.

profile n profil m.

profit n bénéfice, profit m:—vi profiter (de).

profitability n rentabilité f.

profitable adj profitable, avantageux.

profound adj profond.

program(me) n programme m.

programmer n programmeur m, -euse f.

progress n progrès m; cours m:—vi progresser.

progression n progression f; avance f.

progressive adj progressif.

prohibit vt prohiber; défendre.

project vt projeter:—n projet m.

projection n projection f.

prolific adj prolifique, fécond.

prolong vt prolonger.

promenade n promenade f.

prominence n proéminence f.

prominent adj proéminent.

promise n promesse f:—vt promettre.

promising adj prometteur.

promote vt promouvoir.

promoter n promoteur m.

promotion n promotion f.

prompt adj prompt:—vt suggérer.

prone adj enclin (à).

pronounce vt prononcer; déclarer.

pronounced adj marqué, prononcé.

pronouncement n déclaration f.

pronunciation n prononciation f.

proof n preuve f:—adj imperméable; résistant.

prop vt soutenir:—n appui, soutien m.

propaganda n propagande f.

propel vt propulser.

propeller n hélice f.

propensity n propension, tendance f.

proper adj propre; convenable.

property n propriété f.

prophecy n prophétie f.

prophet n prophète m.

proportion n proportion f.
proportional adj proportionnel.
proposal n proposition f; offre f.
propose vt proposer.
proposition n proposition f.
proprietor n propriétaire mf.
prosecute vt poursuivre en justice.
prosecution n poursuites fpl; accusation f.
prospect n perspective f:—vt vi prospecter.
prospective adj probable; futur.
prosper vi prospérer.
prosperity n prospérité f.
prosperous adj prospère.
prostitute n prostituée f.
protagonist n protagoniste mf.
protect vt protéger; abriter.
protection n protection f.
protective adj protecteur.
protein n protéine f.
protest vi protester:—n protestation f.
Protestant n protestant m, -e f.
protester n protestataire mf.
prototype n prototype m.
proud adj fier, orgueilleux.
prove vt prouver; justifier:—vi s'avérer; se révéler.
proverb n proverbe m.
provide vt fournir.
provided conj:—~ that pourvu que.
providence n providence f.
province n province f.
provincial adj n provincial m, -e f.
provision n provision f; disposition f.
provisional adj provisoire.
provocation n provocation f.
provocative adj provocateur.
provoke vt provoquer.
prowess n prouesse f.
prowl vi rôder.

prowler n rôdeur m, -euse f.
proximity n proximité f.
prudence n prudence f.
prudent adj prudent.
pry vi espionner.
pseudonym n pseudonyme m.
psychiatric adj psychiatrique.
psychiatrist n psychiatre mf.
psychic adj psychique.
psychoanalyst n psychanaliste mf.
psychologist n psychologue mf.
psychology n psychologie f.
puberty n puberté f.
public adj public; commun:—n public m.
publication n publication f; édition f.
publicity n publicité f.
publish vt publier.
publisher n éditeur m, -trice f.
publishing n édition f.
pudding n pudding m; dessert m.
puddle n flaque d'eau f.
puff n souple m; bouffée f:—vt souffler; dégager.
pull vt tirer; arracher:—n tirage m; secousse f.
pulley n poulie f.
pulsate vi battre.
pulse n pouls m.
pulverise vt pulvériser.
pump n pompe f:—vt pomper; puiser.
punch n coup de poing m:—vt cogner.
punctual adj ponctuel, exact.
punctuate vt ponctuer.
punctuation n ponctuation f.
punish vt punir.
punishment n châtiment m, punition f; peine f.
puny adj chétif, maigrelet.
pupil n élève mf; pupille mf.
puppet n marionnette f.
puppy n chiot m.

purchase *vt* acheter: — *n* achat *m*; acquisition *f*.
purchaser *n* acheteur *m*, -euse *f*.
pure *adj* pur.
purification *n* purification *f*.
purify *vt* purifier.
purity *n* pureté *f*.
purple *adj n* pourpre, violet *m*.
purpose *n* intention *f*; but, dessein *m*: — **on ~** exprès, à dessein.
purse *n* sac à main *m*; porte-monnaie *m invar*.
pursue *vi* poursuivre; suivre.

pursuit *n* poursuite *f*; occupation *f*.
push *vt* pousser; presser: — *n* poussée *f*; impulsion *f*.
put *vt* mettre, poser.
putrid *adj* putride.
putty *n* mastic *m*.
puzzle *n* énigme *f*; casse-tête *m invar*.
puzzling *adj* curieux; inexplicable.
pyjamas *npl* pyjama *m*.
pylon *n* pylône *m*.
pyramid *n* pyramide *f*.
python *n* python *m*.

Q

quack *vi* cancaner: — *n* (*sl*) charlatan *m*.
quagmire *n* marécage *m*.
quaint *adj* désuet; bizarre.
quake *vi* trembler.
qualification *n* qualification *f*.
qualified *adj* qualifié.
qualify *vt* qualifier: — *vi* se qualifier.
quality *n* qualité *f*.
qualm *n* scrupule *m*.
quantity *n* quantité *f*.
quarantine *n* quarantaine *f*.
quarrel *n* querelle *f*: — *vi* se quereller.
quarrelsome *adj* querelleur.
quarry *n* carrière *f*.
quarter *n* quart *m*: — *vt* diviser en quatre.
quarterly *adj* trimestriel: — *adv* tous les trimestres.
quash *vt* écraser; annuler.
quay *n* quai *m*.
queen *n* reine *f*; femme *f*.
queer *adj* extrange: — *n* (*sl*) pédale *f*.
quell *vt* étouffer.
quench *vt* assouvir.

query *n* question *f*: — *vt* demander.
quest *n* recherche *f*.
question *n* question *f*: — *vt* questionner.
questionable *adj* discutable; douteux.
questioner *n* interrogateur *m*.
questionnaire *n* questionnaire *m*.
quibble *vi* chicaner.
quick *adj* rapide; vif.
quicken *vt* accélérer: — *vi* s'accélérer.
quiet *adj* calme; silencieux.
quietness *n* calme *m*, tranquillité *f*; silence *m*.
quip *n* sarcasme *m*: — *vt* railler.
quit *vt* arrêter de: — *vi* abandonner.
quite *adv* assez; complètement, absolument.
quiver *vi* trembler.
quiz *n* concours *m*; examen *m*: — *vt* interroger.
quota *n* quota *m*.
quotation *n* citation *f*.
quote *vt* citer.

R

rabbit *n* lapin *m*.

rabble *n* cohue *f*.

rabies *n* rage *f*.

race *n* course *f*; race *f*: —*vi* courir; foncer.

racial *adj* racial: —**~ist** *adj n* raciste *mf*.

rack *n* casier *m*; étagère *f*.

racket *n* vacarme *m*; raquette *f*.

radiant *adj* rayonnant, radieux.

radiate *vt vi* rayonner, irradier.

radiation *n* irradiation *f*.

radiator *n* radiateur *m*.

radical *adj* radical.

radio *n* radio *f*.

radioactive *adj* radioactif.

raft *n* radeau.

rag *n* lambeau *m*, loque *f*.

rage *n* rage *f*; fureur *f*: —*vi* faire rage.

ragged *adj* déguenillé.

raging *adj* furieux, enragé.

raid *n* raid *m*: —*vt* faire un raid sur.

rail *n* rambarde *f*; (*rail*) rail, chemin de fer *m*.

railway *n* chemin de fer *m*.

rain *n* pluie *f*: —*vi* pleuvoir.

rainbow *n* arc-en-ciel *m*.

rainy *adj* pluvieux.

raise *vt* lever, soulever.

raisin *n* raisin sec *m*.

rally *vt* (*mil*) rallier: —*vi* se rallier.

ramble *vi* errer; faire une randonnée.

ramp *n* rampe *f*.

ramshackle *adj* délabré.

rancid *adj* rance.

rancour *n* rancœur *f*.

random *adj* fortuit, fait au hasard.

range *vt* ranger: —*vi* s'étendre: —*n* rangée *f*; chaîne *f*; fourneau de cuisine *m*.

rank *n* rang *m*, classe *f*, grade *m*.

ransack *vt* saccager, piller.

ransom *n* rançon *f*.

rape *n* viol *m*: —*vt* violer.

rapid *adj* rapide.

rapidity *n* rapidité *f*.

rapist *n* violeur *m*.

rapt *adj* extasié; absorbé.

rapture *n* ravissement *m*; extase *f*.

rare *adj* rare.

rarity *n* rareté *f*.

rash *adj* imprudent: —*n* éruption (cutanée) *f*.

rashness *n* imprudence *f*.

rat *n* rat *m*.

rate *n* taux, prix *m*; vitesse *f*: —*vt* estimer, évaluer.

rather *adv* plutôt.

ratification *n* ratification *f*.

ratify *vt* ratifier.

ration *n* ration *f*.

rational *adj* rationnel.

rattle *vi* s'entrechoquer: —*n* hochet *m*; cliquetis *m*.

ravage *vt* ravager: —*n* ravage *m*.

rave *vi* délirer.

ravenous *adj* vorace.

ravine *n* ravin *m*.

raw *adj* cru; brut.

rawness *n* crudité *f*; inexpérience *f*.

ray *n* rayon *m*.

raze *vt* raser.

razor *n* rasoir *m*.

reach *vt* atteindre: — *vi* porter: — *n* portée *f*.

react *vi* réagir.

reaction *n* réaction *f*.

read *vt vi* lire.

reader *n* lecteur *m*, -trice *f*.

readily *adv* volontiers.

readiness *n* bonne volonté *f*.

reading *n* lecture *f*.

readjust *vt* réajuster.

ready *adj* prêt; enclin.

real *adj* réel, vrai.

realisation *n* réalisation *f*.

realise *vt* se rendre compte de; réaliser.

reality *n* réalité *f*.

reappear *vi* réapparaître.

rear *n* arrière *m*; derrière *m*: — *vt* élever.

reason *n* raison *f*; cause *f*: — *vt vi* raisonner.

reasonable *adj* raisonnable.

reasoning *n* raisonnement *m*.

reassure *vt* rassurer.

rebel *n* rebelle *mf*: — *vi* se rebeller.

rebellion *n* rébellion *f*.

rebound *vi* rebondir.

rebuild *vt* reconstruire.

rebuke *vt* réprimander: — *n* réprimande *f*.

recall *vt* (se) rappeler.

recapture *n* reprise *f*.

recede *vi* reculer.

receipt *n* reçu *m*; réception *f*.

receivable *adj* recevable.

receive *vt* recevoir; accueillir.

recent *adj* récent, neuf.

receptacle *n* récipient *m*.

reception *n* réception *f*.

recession *n* récession *f*.

recipe *n* recette *f*.

recipient *n* destinataire *mf*.

reciprocal *adj* ~**ly** *adv* réciproque(ment).

recital *n* récit *m*.

recite *vt* réciter.

reckless *adj* téméraire.

reckon *vt* compter: — *vi* calculer.

reclaim *vt* assainir; récupérer.

recline *vt* reposer: — *vi* être allongé.

recognise *vt* reconnaître.

recognition *n* reconnaissance *f*.

recoil *vi* reculer.

recollect *vt* se rappeler.

recollection *n* souvenir *m*.

recommend *vt* recommander.

recompense *n* récompense *f*: — *vt* récompenser.

reconcile *vt* réconcilier.

reconciliation *n* réconciliation *f*.

reconsider *vt* reconsidérer.

record *vt* enregistrer: — *n* rapport *m*, registre *m*; disque *m*; record *m*.

recount *vt* raconter.

recourse *n* recours *m*.

recover *vt* retrouver: — *vi* se remettre.

recovery *n* guérison *f*; reprise *f*.

recreation *n* détente *f*; récréation *f*.

recriminate *vi* récriminer.

recrimination *n* récrimination *f*.

recruit *vt* recruter: — *n* (*mil*) recrue *f*.

rectangle *n* rectangle *m*.

rectification *n* rectification *f*.

rectify *vt* rectifier.

recumbent *adj* couché, étendu.

recur *vi* se reproduire.

recurrence *n* répétition *f*.

recurrent *adj* répétitif.

red *adj* rouge: — *n* rouge *m*.

redden *vt vi* rougir.

redeem *vt* racheter, rembourser.

redemption *n* rachat *m*.

redness *n* rougeur, rousseur *f*.

redouble *vt vi* redoubler.

redress *vt* réparer; redresser.

reduce vt réduire; diminuer.

reduction n réduction f; baisse f.

redundancy n licenciement m.

redundant adj superflu.

reel n bobine f; dévidoir m:—vi chanceler.

re-enter vt rentrer.

re-establish vt rétablir; réhabiliter.

refer vt se référer à:—vi se référer.

referee n arbitre m.

reference n référence f.

refine vt raffiner, affiner.

refinement n raffinement m.

reflect vt réfléchir, refléter:—vi réfléchir.

reflection n réflexion, pensée f.

reform vt réformer:—vi se réformer.

reform n réforme f.

reformer n réformateur m, -trice f.

refrain vi:—~ **from** s'abstenir de.

refresh vt rafraîchir.

refrigerator n glacière f; réfrigérateur m.

refuge n refuge, asile m.

refugee n réfugié m, -e f.

refund vt rembourser:—n remboursement m.

refusal n refus m.

refuse vt refuser:—n déchets mpl.

regain vt recouvrer.

regal adj royal.

regard vt regarder:—n considération f.

regardless adv quand même.

regenerate vt régénérer.

regeneration n régénération f.

regime n régime m.

region n région f.

register n registre m:—vt enregistrer.

registration n enregistrement m.

regressive adj régressif.

regret n regret m:—vt regretter.

regular adj régulier:—n habitué m, -e f.

regularity n régularité f.

regulate vt régler.

regulation n règlement m.

rehabilitate vt réhabiliter.

rehabilitation n réhabilitation f.

reimburse vt rembourser.

reimbursement n remboursement m.

reinforce vt renforcer.

reiterate vt réitérer.

reiteration n réitération f.

reject vt rejeter.

rejection n refus m.

rejoice vt réjouir:—vi se réjouir.

relapse vi retomber:—n rechute f.

relate vt relater:—vi se rapporter.

relation n rapport m; parent m.

relationship n lien de parenté m; relation f; rapport m.

relative adj relatif:—n parent m, -e f.

relax vt relâcher:—vi se relâcher.

relaxation n relâchement m; détente f.

relay n relais m:—vt retransmettre.

release vt libérer:—n libération f.

relevant adj pertinent.

reliable adj fiable.

reliance n confiance f.

relief n soulagement m; secours m.

relieve vt soulager, alléger.

religion n religion f.

religious adj religieux.

relinquish vt abandonner.

reluctant adj peu disposé.

rely vi compter sur.

remain vi rester, demeurer.

remainder n reste, restant m.

remark n remarque:—vt (faire) remarquer.

remarkable adj remarquable, notable.

remedy n remède m:—vt remédier à.

remember vt se souvenir de.

remind vt rappeler.

reminiscence *n* réminiscence *f.*
remit *vt* remettre, pardonner.
remnant *n* reste, restant *m.*
remonstrate *vi* protester.
remote *adj* lointain, éloigné.
remoteness *n* éloignement *m*; isolement *m.*
removable *adj* amovible.
removal *n* suppression *f.*
remove *vt* enlever.
remunerate *vt* rémunérer.
render *vt* rendre, remettre.
renew *vt* renouveler.
renewal *n* renouvellement *m.*
renounce *vt* renoncer à.
renovate *vt* rénover.
renown *n* renommée *f*; célébrité *f.*
rent *n* loyer *m*: — *vt* louer.
renunciation *n* renonciation *f.*
reorganisation *n* réorganisation *f.*
reorganise *vt* réorganiser.
repair *vt* réparer: — *n* réparation *f.*
repatriate *vt* rapatrier.
repay *vt* rembourser.
repayment *n* remboursement *m.*
repeal *vt* abroger: — *n* abrogation.
repeat *vt* répéter.
repel *vt* repousser, rebuter.
repent *vi* se repentir.
repetition *n* répétition *f.*
replace *vt* replacer.
replenish *vt* remplir de nouveau.
replete *adj* rempli.
reply *n* réponse *f*: — *vi* répondre.
report *vt* rapporter: — *n* rapport *m*; compte rendu *m.*
reporter *n* journaliste *mf.*
reprehend *vt* condamner.
reprehensible *adj* répréhensible.
represent *vt* représenter.
representation *n* représentation *f.*

representative *adj* représentatif: — *n* représentant(e) *m(f).*
repress *vt* réprimer, contenir.
repression *n* répression *f.*
reprieve *n* sursis *m.*
reprimand *vt* réprimander.
reprisal *n* représailles *fpl.*
reproach *n* reproche: — *vt* reprocher.
reproduce *vt* reproduire.
reproduction *n* reproduction *f.*
republic *n* république *f.*
republican *adj n* républicain *m*, -e *f.*
repudiate *vt* renier.
repulse *vt* repousser.
repulsion *n* répulsion *f.*
repulsive *adj* répulsif.
reputation *n* réputation *f.*
request *n* requête *f*: — *vt* demander.
require *vt* demander, nécessiter.
requirement *n* besoin *m*; exigence *f.*
requisite *adj* nécessaire, indispensable.
rescue *vt* sauver, secourir: — *n* secours *m.*
research *vt* faire de la recherche: — *n* recherche *f.*
resemblance *n* ressemblance *f.*
resemble *vt* ressembler à.
resent *vt* être contrarié.
resentment *n* ressentiment *m.*
reservation *n* réservation *f.*
reserve *vt* réserver: — *n* réserve *f.*
reside *vi* résider.
residence *n* résidence *f.*
resident *n* résident *m*, -e *f.*
resign *vt* démissionner de: — *vi* démissionner.
resignation *n* démission *f.*
resist *vt* résister, s'opposer.
resistance *n* résistance *f.*
resolute *adj* résolu.
resolution *n* résolution *f.*
resolve *vt* resoudre: — *vi* (se) résoudre.

resort *vi* recourir: — *n* lieu de vacances *m*.

resource *n* ressource *f*.

respect *n* respect *m*; égard *m*: — *vt* respecter.

respectability *n* respectabilité *f*.

respectable *adj* respectable.

respectful *adj* respectueux.

respecting *prep* en ce qui concerne.

respective *adj* respectif.

respond *vi* répondre.

response *n* réponse.

responsibility *n* responsabilité *f*.

responsible *adj* responsable.

rest *n* repos *m*; reste, restant *m*: — *vi* se reposer.

restitution *n* restitution *f*.

restive *adj* rétif, récalcitrant.

restoration *n* restauration *f*.

restore *vt* restaurer.

restrain *vt* retenir.

restrict *vt* restreindre.

restriction *n* restriction *f*.

restrictive *adj* restrictif.

result *n* résultat *m*.

resume *vt* reprendre; résumer.

resuscitate *vt* réanimer.

retail *vt* détailler: — *n* vente au détail *f*.

retain *vt* retenir, conserver.

retaliate *vi* se venger.

reticence *n* réticence *f*.

retire *vt* retirer: — *vi* se retirer.

retired *adj* retraité.

retirement *n* isolement *m*.

retort *vt* rétorquer: — *n* réplique *f*.

retrace *vt* retracer.

retreat *vi* se retirer.

retribution *n* récompense *f*.

retrieve *vt* récupérer, recouvrer.

return *vt* rendre: — *n* retour *m*.

reunion *n* réunion *f*.

reunite *vt* réunir: — *vi* se réunir.

reveal *vt* révéler.

revelation *n* révélation *f*.

revenge *vt* venger: — *n* vengeance *f*.

revengeful *adj* vindicatif.

revenue *n* revenu *m*; rente *f*.

reverberate *vt* réverbérer: — *vi* résonner.

reverberation *n* réverbération *f*.

reversal *n* renversement *m*.

reverse *vt* renverser: — *vi* faire marche arrière: — *n* inverse *m*.

reversible *adj* réversible.

reversion *n* retour *m*; réversion *f*.

revert *vi* revenir; retourner.

review *vt* revoir: — *n* revue *f*; examen *m*.

revise *vt* réviser.

revision *n* révision *f*.

revival *n* reprise *f*; renouveau *m*.

revive *vt* ranimer.

revoke *vt* révoquer.

revolt *vi* se révolter: — *n* révolte *f*.

revolution *n* révolution *f*.

revolutionary *adj n* révolutionnaire *mf*.

revolve *vt* (re)tourner: — *vi* tourner.

revue *n* revue *f*.

reward *n* récompense *f*: — *vt* récompenser.

rhetorical *adj* rhétorique.

rheumatic *adj* rhumatisant.

rheumatism *n* rhumatisme *m*.

rhyme *n* rime *f*: — *vi* rimer.

rhythm *n* rythme *m*.

rhythmical *adj* rythmique.

rib *n* côte *f*.

ribbon *n* ruban *m*.

rice *n* riz *m*.

rich *adj* riche; somptueux.

richness *n* richesse *f*; abondance *f*.

rid *vt* débarrasser.

riddle *n* crible *m*: — *vt* cribler.

ride *vi* monter (à cheval); aller (en voiture).

ridge *n* arête, crête *f*.

ridicule *n* ridicule *m*: — *vt* ridiculiser.

ridiculous *adj* ~**ly** *adv* ridicule.

rifle *n* fusil *m*.

rig *vt* équiper; truquer: — *n* plate-forme de forage *f*.

right *adj* droit, bien: — ~**!** bien!, bon!; à juste titre: — *n* droit *m*; droite *f*.

righteous *adj* droit, vertueux.

rigid *adj* rigide; sévère.

rigorous *adj* rigoureux.

rigour *n* rigueur *f*; sévérité *f*.

rim *n* bord *m*, monture *f*.

ring *n* anneau, cercle, rond *m*: — *vt* sonner: — *vi* sonner, retentir.

rink *n* (*also* **ice** ~) patinoire *f*.

rinse *vt* rincer.

riot *n* émeute *f*.

riotous *adj* séditieux; dissolu.

rip *vt* déchirer.

ripe *adj* mûr.

ripen *vt vi* mûrir.

ripple *n* ondulation *f*, ride *f*.

rise *vi* se lever; monter: — *n* hausse *f*; augmentation *f*.

rising *n* insurrection *f*.

risk *n* risque: — *vt* risquer.

risky *adj* risqué.

rite *n* rite *m*.

ritual *adj n* rituel *m*.

rival *adj* rival: — *n* rival *m*, -e *f*: — *vt* rivaliser avec.

rivalry *n* rivalité *f*.

river *n* rivière *f*.

road *n* route *f*.

roam *vt* errer dans: — *vi* errer.

roar *vi* rugir: — *n* rugissement *m*.

roast *vt* rôtir; griller.

rob *vt* voler.

robber *n* voleur *m*, -euse *f*.

robbery *n* vol *m*.

robust *adj* robuste.

robustness *n* robustesse *f*.

rock *n* roche *f*: — *vt* bercer; balancer.

rocket *n* fusée *f*.

rocking chair *n* fauteuil à bascule *m*.

rocky *adj* rocheux.

rodent *n* rongeur *m*.

rogue *n* coquin, polisson *m*; gredin *m*.

roll *vt* rouler: — *vi* (se) rouler: — *n* roulement *m*; rouleau *m*.

roller *n* rouleau, cylindre *m*.

romance *n* romance *f*; roman *m*.

romantic *adj* romantique.

roof *n* toit *m*; voûte *f*: — *vt* couvrir.

room *n* pièce, salle *f*; espace *m*.

root *n* racine *f*; origine *f*.

rope *n* corde *f*; cordage *m*.

rose *n* rose *f*.

rosemary *n* (*bot*) romarin *m*.

rot *vi* pourrir: — *n* pourriture *f*.

rotate *vt* faire tourner: — *vi* tourner.

rotation *n* rotation *f*.

rotund *adj* rond, replet.

rouge *n* rouge (à joues) *m*.

rough *adj* accidenté, rugueux; rude.

roughness *n* rugosité *f*, rudesse *f*.

round *adj* rond, circulaire: — *n* cercle *m*; rond *m*; tour *m*; tournée *f*: — *adv* autour de; environ: — *vt* arrondir.

roundness *n* rondeur *f*.

rouse *vt* réveiller; exciter.

rout *n* déroute *f*.

route *n* itinéraire *m*; route *f*.

routine *adj* habituel: — *n* routine *f*.

rove *vi* vagabonder.

row *n* querelle *f*.

row *n* rangée, file *f*.

royal *adj* royal; princier.

royalty *n* royauté *f*; droits d'auteur *mpl*.

rub *vt* frotter; irriter: — *n* frottement *m*.

rubber *n* caoutchouc *m*.

rubbish *n* détritus *mpl*; ordures *fpl*.

rudder *n* gouvernail *m*.

ruddiness *n* teint vif *m*, rougeur *f*.

rude *adj* impoli, rude.

rudeness *n* impolitesse *f*; rudesse *f*.

ruffle *vt* ébouriffer, déranger.

rug *n* tapis *m*.

rugged *adj* accidenté, déchiqueté.

ruin *n* ruine *f*;—*vt* ruiner.

ruinous *adj* ruineux.

rule *n* règle *f*; règlement *m*:—*vt* gouverner, dominer.

rumble *vi* gronder, tonner.

ruminate *vt* ruminer.

rummage *vi* fouiller.

rumour *n* rumeur *f*.

run *vt* diriger:—*vi* courir.

rung *n* barreau, échelon *m*.

runner *n* coureur *m*.

runway *n* piste de décollage *f*.

rupture *n* rupture *f*:—*vt* rompre:—*vi* se rompre.

ruse *n* ruse *f*, stratagème *m*.

rush *n* ruée *f*; hâte *f*:—*vi* se précipiter.

rust *n* rouille *f*:—*vi* se rouiller.

rustic *adj* rustique:—*n* paysan, rustaud *m*.

rustle *vi* bruire:—*vt* faire bruire; froisser.

rusty *adj* rouillé; roux.

ruthless *adj* cruel, impitoyable.

rye *n* seigle *m*.

S

sabotage *n* sabotage *m*.

sachet *n* sachet *m*.

sack *n* sac *m*

sacrament *n* sacrement *m*.

sacred *adj* saint, sacré.

sacrifice *n* sacrifice *m*:—*vt* sacrifier.

sacrilege *n* sacrilège *m*.

sad *adj* triste, déprimé.

sadden *vt* attrister.

saddle *n* selle *f*; col *m*:—*vt* seller.

sadness *n* tristesse *f*.

safe *adj* sûr; en sécurité:—*n* coffre-fort *m*.

safeguard *n* sauvegarde *f*:—*vt* sauvegarder.

safety *n* sécurité *f*; sûreté *f*.

sage *n* sage *m*:—*adj* sage.

sail *n* voile *f*:—*vt* piloter:—*vi* aller à la voile.

sailing *n* navigation *f*.

sailor *n* marin *m*.

saint *n* saint *m*, -e *f*.

sake *n* bien *m*, égard *m*.

salad *n* salade *f*.

salary *n* salaire *m*.

sale *n* vente *f*; solde *m*.

salesman *n* vendeur *m*.

saliva *n* salive *f*.

salmon *n* saumon *m*.

saloon *n* bar *m*.

salt *n* sel *m*:—*vt* saler.

salt cellar *n* salière *f*.

salubrious *adj* salubre, sain.

salubrity *n* salubrité *f*.

salutary *adj* salutaire.

salute *vt* saluer:—*n* salut *m*.

salvation *n* salut *m*.

same *adj* même, identique.

sameness *n* identité *f*.

sample *n* échantillon *m*:—*vt* goûter.

sanatorium *n* sanatorium *m*.
sanctify *vt* sanctifier.
sanction *n* sanction *f*.—*vt* sanctionner.
sanctuary *n* sanctuaire *m*; asile *m*.
sand *n* sable *m*:—*vt* sabler.
sandal *n* sandale *f*.
sandwich *n* sandwich *m*.
sandy *adj* sablonneux, sableux.
sane *adj* sain.
sanguine *adj* sanguin.
sanity *n* santé mentale, raison *f*.
sapling *n* jeune arbre *m*.
sarcasm *n* sarcasme *m*.
sarcastic *adj* sarcastique.
sardine *n* sardine *f*.
satchel *n* cartable *m*.
satellite *n* satellite *m*.
sate *vt* rassasier, assouvir.
satin *n* satin *m*:—*adj* en *ou* de satin.
satire *n* satire *f*.
satirical *adj* satirique.
satisfaction *n* satisfaction *f*.
satisfactory *adj* satisfaisant.
satisfy *vt* satisfaire.
saturate *vt* saturer.
Saturday *n* samedi *m*.
sauce *n* sauce *f*; assaisonnement *m*.
saucepan *n* casserole *f*.
saucer *n* soucoupe *f*.
saunter *vi* flâner, se balader.
sausage *n* saucisse *f*.
savage *adj* sauvage:—*n* sauvage *mf*.
savagery *n* sauvagerie, barbarie *f*.
save *vt* sauver; économiser:—*adv* sauf, à l'exception de.
saving *prep* sauf, à l'exception de: —*n* sauvetage *m*.
savings bank *n* caisse d'épargne *f*.
savour *n* saveur *f*:—*vt* savourer.
saw *n* scie *f*:—*vt* scier.
say *vt* dire.

saying *n* dicton, proverbe *m*.
scaffolding *n* échafaudage *m*.
scald *vt* échauder:—*n* brûlure *f*.
scale *n* balance *f*; échelle *f*:—*vt* escalader.
scan *vt* scruter; explorer; scander.
scandal *n* scandale *m*; infamie *f*.
scandalise *vt* scandaliser.
scandalous *adj* scandaleux.
scant *adj* rare, insuffisant.
scantiness *n* insuffisance, pauvreté *f*.
scapegoat *n* bouc émissaire *m*.
scar *n* cicatrice *f*.
scarce *adj* rare.
scare *vt* effrayer:—*n* peur; panique *f*.
scarf *n* écharpe *f*.
scarlet *n* écarlate *f*:—*adj* écarlate.
scatter *vt* éparpiller; disperser.
scene *n* scène *f*; lieu *m*.
scenery *n* vue *f*; décor (de théâtre) *m*.
scenic *adj* scénique.
scent *n* parfum *m*, odeur *f*:—*vt* parfumer.
sceptic *n* sceptique *mf*.
sceptic(al) *adj* sceptique.
schedule *n* horaire *m*; programme *m*.
scheme *n* projet, plan *m*; schéma *m*: —*vt* machiner:—*vi* intriguer.
scholar *n* élève *mf*; érudit *m*, -e *f*.
school *n* école *f*:—*vt* instruire.
schoolboy *n* écolier, élève *m*.
schoolgirl *n* écolière, élève *f*.
schoolteacher *n* instituteur/trice *mf*; professeur *mf*.
science *n* science *f*.
scientific *adj* scientifique.
scientist *n* scientifique *mf*.
scintillate *vi* scintiller, étinceler.
scissors *npl* ciseaux *mpl*.
scoff *vi* se moquer.
scold *vt* réprimander:—*vi* grogner.
scope *n* portée, envergure *f*.

scorch vt brûler:—vi se brûler.

score n score m; marque f; entaille f:
—vt marquer.

scorn vt mépriser:—n mépris m.

scornful adj dédaigneux.

scoundrel n vaurien m.

scour vt récurer, frotter.

scout n (mil) éclaireur m, -euse f, guetteur m.

scowl vi se renfrogner.

scramble vi grimper; se battre, se disputer:—n bousculade f.

scrap n bout m; bagarre f; ferraille f.

scrape vt vi racler, gratter:—vt érafler.

scratch vt griffer, égratigner:—n égratignure f.

scream vi hurler:—n hurlement m.

screen n écran m; paravent m:—vt abriter; sélectionner.

screw n vis f:—vt visser.

screwdriver n tournevis m.

scribble vt gribouiller:—n gribouillage m.

script n scénario m; script m.

Scripture n Ecriture sainte f.

scroll n rouleau (de papier ou parchemin) m, * vi (comput) défiler.

scrub vt récurer; annuler:—n broussailles fpl.

scruple n scrupule m.

scrupulous adj scrupuleux.

scuffle n rixe f:—vi se bagarrer.

sculptor n sculpteur m, -trice f.

sculpture n sculpture f.

scum n écume f; crasse f.

sea n mer f:—adj marin.

seafood n fruits de mer mpl.

seagull n mouette f.

seal n sceau m; phoque m:—vt sceller.

seamy adj sordide.

search vt fouiller; inspecter:—n fouille f; recherche f.

seashore n bord de mer m.

seasickness n mal de mer m.

season n saison f.

seasonable adj opportun, à propos.

seasoning n assaisonnement m.

seat n siège m; place f:—vt (faire) asseoir.

seaweed n algue f.

seclude vt éloigner, isoler.

seclusion n solitude f; isolement m.

second adj deuxième:—n second m; seconde f.

secondary adj secondaire.

secrecy n secret m; discrétion f.

secret adj n secret m.

secretary n secrétaire mf.

secretive adj secret, dissimulé.

section n section f.

sector n secteur m.

secular adj séculaire.

secure adj sûr; en sûreté:—vt assurer.

security n sécurité f; sûreté f.

sedative n sédatif m.

sediment n sédiment m; lie f.

sedition n sédition f.

seduce vt séduire.

seduction n séduction f.

seductive adj séduisant.

see vt voir, remarquer.

seed n graine f:—vi monter en graine.

seek vt chercher; demander.

seem vi paraître, sembler.

seemliness n bienséance f.

seemly adj convenable, bienséant.

seesaw n bascule f:—vi osciller.

segment n segment m.

seize vt saisir.

seizure n saisie f.

seldom adv rarement, peu souvent.

select vt sélectionner.

selection n sélection f.

self n soi-même: — **the ~** le moi: — *pref* auto-.

self-confident *adj* sûr de soi.

self-defence n autodéfense f.

self-employed *adj* indépendant.

self-interest n intérêt personnel m.

selfish *adj* égoïste.

selfishness n égoïsme m.

self-portrait n autoportrait m.

self-respect n respect de soi m.

self-service *adj* libre-service.

self-styled *adj* soi-disant.

self-sufficient *adj* autosuffisant.

self-taught *adj* autodidacte.

sell *vt* vendre: — *vi* se vendre.

seller n vendeur m, -euse f.

semblance n semblant m.

semicircle n demi-cercle m.

senate n sénat m.

senator n sénateur m, -trice f.

send *vt* envoyer.

senile *adj* sénile.

senility n sénilité f.

senior n aîné m, -e f: — *adj* aîné.

seniority n ancienneté f.

sensation n sensation f.

sense n sens m; sensation f.

senseless *adj* insensé.

sensible *adj* sensé; sensible.

sensibly *adj* raisonnablement.

sensitive *adj* sensible.

sensual *adj* sensuel.

sensuality n sensualité f.

sentence n phrase f; condamnation f.

sentiment n sentiment m.

sentimental *adj* sentimental.

sentinel n sentinelle f.

separable *adj* séparable.

separate *vt* séparer: — *vi* se séparer: — *adj* séparé.

separation n séparation f.

September n septembre m.

sepulchre n sépulcre m.

sequel n conséquence f; suite f.

sequence n ordre m, série f.

serenade n sérénade f: — *vt* jouer une sérénade pour.

serene *adj* serein.

serenity n sérénité f.

sergeant n sergent m.

serial *adj* de/en série: — n feuilleton m.

series n série f.

serious *adj* sérieux, grave.

sermon n sermon m.

serpent n serpent m.

servant n domestique mf.

serve *vt* servir; desservir: — *vi* servir; être utile.

service n service m; entretien m: — *vt* entretenir.

serviceable *adj* utilisable; pratique.

servile *adj* servile.

servitude n servitude f.

session n séance, session f.

set *vt* mettre, poser: — n jeu m; ensemble m: — *adj* fixe, figé.

setting n disposition f; cadre m; monture f: — **~ of the sun** coucher du soleil m.

settle *vt* poser, installer: — *vi* se poser; s'installer.

settlement n règlement m; établissement m.

seven *adj* n sept m.

seventeen *adj* n dix-sept m.

seventeenth *adj* n dix-septième mf.

seventh *adj* n septième mf.

seventieth *adj* n soixante-dixième mf.

seventy *adj* n soixante-dix m.

several *adj* pn plusieurs.

severe *adj* sévère, rigoureux.

severity n sévérité f.

sew *vt vi* coudre.

sewer n égout m.

sex n sexe m.

sexist adj n sexiste mf.

sexual adj sexuel.

shabby adj miteux.

shade n ombre f; nuance f: — vt ombrager.

shadow n ombre f.

shady adj ombreux, ombragé.

shaft n fût m; (tech) arbre m; rayon m.

shake vt secouer: — vi trembler: — n secousse f.

shallow adj peu profond, superficiel.

sham vt feindre: — n imposture f.

shame n honte f: — vt déshonorer.

shamefaced adj honteux, confus.

shameful adj honteux; scandaleux.

shampoo n shampooing m.

shape vt former; façonner: — vi prendre forme: — n forme f.

shapely adj bien proportionné.

share n part, portion f: — vt partager.

shark n requin m.

sharp adj aigu, acéré.

sharpen vt aiguiser, affûter.

sharpness n acuité f; aigreur f.

shatter vt fracasser.

shave vi se raser.

shaver n rasoir électrique m.

shaving n rasage m.

shawl n châle m.

she pn elle.

sheaf n gerbe f; liasse f.

shear vt tondre.

shed n hangar m; cabane f.

sheep n mouton m.

sheer adj pur; abrupt: — adv abruptement.

sheet n drap m; plaque f.

shelf n étagère f.

shell n coquille f; écorce f: — vt écosser, décortiquer; bombarder.

shelter n abri m: — vt abriter: — vi s'abriter.

shepherd n berger m.

sheriff n shérif m.

shield n bouclier m: — vt protéger.

shift vi changer; se déplacer: — vt changer, bouger: — n changement m.

shine vi briller.

shining adj resplendissant.

ship n bateau m; navire m: — vt embarquer.

shipment n cargaison f.

shipwreck n naufrage m.

shirt n chemise f.

shiver vi frissonner.

shock n choc m; coup m: — vt bouleverser; choquer.

shoe n chaussure f.

shoemaker n cordonnier m.

shoot vt tirer: — vi pousser: — n pousse f.

shooting n fusillade f; tir m.

shop n magasin m; atelier m.

shopper n acheteur m, -euse f.

shore n rivage, bord m.

short adj court, bref.

shortcoming n insuffisance f.

shorten vt raccourcir; abréger.

short-sighted adj myope.

shortwave n ondes courtes fpl.

shot n coup m; décharge f.

shotgun n fusil de chasse m.

shoulder n épaule f; accotement m.

shout vt vi crier: — n cri m.

shove vt vi pousser: — n poussée f.

shovel n pelle f: — vt pelleter.

show vt montrer: — vi se voir: — n exposition f.

shower n averse f; douche f.

showy adj voyant, ostentatoire.

shred n lambeau m: — vt mettre en lambeaux.

shrewd *adj* astucieux; perspicace.

shriek *vt vi* hurler:—*n* hurlement *m*.

shrill *adj* aigu, strident.

shrimp *n* crevette *f*.

shrink *vi* rétrécir.

shrivel *vi* se ratatiner.

shroud *n* voile *m*; linceul *m*.

shudder *vi* frissonner:—*n* frisson *m*.

shun *vt* fuir, éviter.

shut *vt* fermer; *vi* (se) fermer.

shutter *n* volet *m*.

shy *adj* timide; réservé.

shyness *n* timidité *f*.

sick *adj* malade; écœuré.

sicken *vt* rendre malade.

sickly *adj* maladif.

sickness *n* maladie *f*.

side *n* côté *m*; parti *m*:—*adj* latéral.

sideboard *n* buffet *m*.

sidelong *adj* oblique.

siege *n* (*mil*) siège *m*.

sieve *n* tamis *m*:—*vt* tamiser.

sift *vt* tamiser.

sigh *vi* soupirer:—*n* soupir *m*.

sight *n* vue *f*; spectacle *m*.

sightseeing *n* tourisme *m*.

sign *n* signe *m*, indication *f*:—*vt* signer.

signal *n* signal *m*.

signature *n* signature *f*.

significance *n* importance *f*.

significant *adj* considérable.

signify *vt* signifier.

silence *n* silence *m*.

silent *adj* silencieux.

silicon chip *n* puce de silicium *f*.

silk *n* soie *f*.

silken *adj* soyeux.

sill *n* rebord *m*; seuil *m*.

silliness *n* bêtise, niaiserie *f*.

silly *adj* bête, stupide.

silver *n* argent *m*:—*adj* en argent.

silvery *adj* argenté.

similar *adj* semblable; similaire.

similarity *n* ressemblance *f*.

simile *n* comparaison *f*.

simmer *vi* cuire à feux doux, mijoter.

simper *vi* minauder:—*n* sourire affecté *m*.

simple *adj* simple; naïf.

simplicity *n* simplicité *f*.

simplification *n* simplification *f*.

simplify *vt* simplifier.

simulate *vt* simuler, feindre.

simultaneous *adj* simultané.

sin *n* péché *m*:—*vi* pécher.

since *adv prep* depuis:—*conj* depuis que; puisque.

sincere *adj* sincère; réel, vrai:—**~ly** *adv* sincère(ment).

sincerity *n* sincérité *f*.

sinew *n* tendon *m*; nerf *m*.

sing *vt vi* chanter.

singe *vt* roussir.

singer *n* chanteur *m*, -euse *f*.

single *adj* seul, unique; célibataire.

singly *adv* séparément.

singular *adj* singulier.

singularity *n* singularité *f*.

sinister *adj* sinistre.

sink *vi* couler:—*n* évier *m*.

sinner *n* pécheur *m*, pécheresse *f*.

sinuous *adj* sinueux.

sir *n* monsieur *m*.

sister *n* sœur *f*.

sister-in-law *n* belle-sœur *f*.

sit *vi* s'asseoir.

site *n* emplacement *m*; site *m*.

sitting *n* séance, réunion *f*.

sitting room *n* salle de séjour *f*.

situation *n* situation *f*.

six *adj n* six *m*.

sixteen *adj n* seize *m*.

sixteenth *adj n* seizième *mf*.

sixth *adj n* sixième *mf*.

sixtieth *adj n* soixantième *mf*.

sixty *adj n* soixante *m*.

size *n* taille, grandeur *f*.

sizeable *adj* assez grand.

skate *n* patin *m*:—*vi* patiner.

skating rink *n* patinoire *f*.

skeleton *n* squelette *m*.

sketch *n* croquis *m*.

skewer *n* broche *f*; brochette *f*:—*vt* embrocher.

ski *n* ski *m*:—*vi* skier.

skid *n* dérapage *m*:—*vi* déraper.

skier *n* skieur *m*, -euse *f*.

skiing *n* ski *m*.

skill *n* habileté, adresse *f*.

skilful *adj* adroit, habile.

skim *vt* écrémer; effleurer.

skin *n* peau *f*:—*vt* écorcher.

skinny *adj* maigre, efflanqué.

skip *vi* sautiller.

skirmish *n* escarmouche *f*.

skirt *n* jupe *f*; bordure *f*:—*vt* contourner.

skulk *vi* rôder furtivement.

skull *n* crâne *m*.

sky *n* ciel *m*.

skylight *n* lucarne *f*.

skyscraper *n* gratte-ciel *m invar*.

slab *n* dalle *f*.

slack *adj* lâche, négligent.

slack(en) *vt* relâcher:—*vi* se relâcher.

slackness *n* ralentissement *m*.

slam *vt* claquer violemment.

slander *vt* calomnier:—*n* calomnie *f*.

slanderous *adj* calomnieux.

slang *n* argot *m*.

slant *vi* pencher:—*n* inclinaison *f*.

slap *n* gifle *f*:—*vt* gifler.

slaughter *n* carnage, massacre *m*:—*vt* abattre.

slave *n* esclave *mf*.

slavery *n* esclavage *m*.

slay *vt* tuer.

sleazy *adj* louche.

sledge *n* traîneau *m*.

sleep *vi* dormir:—*n* sommeil *m*.

sleeper *n* dormeur *m*, -euse *f*.

sleepiness *n* envie de dormir *f*.

sleepwalking *n* somnambulisme *m*.

sleepy *adj* qui a envie de dormir; endormi.

sleet *n* neige fondue *f*.

sleeve *n* manche *f*.

slender *adj* svelte, mince.

slenderness *n* sveltesse *f*, minceur *f*.

slice *n* tranche *f*; spatule *f*:—*vt* couper.

slide *vi* glisser:—*n* glissade *f*; diapositive *f*.

slight *adj* léger, mince:—*n* affront *m*.

slightness *n* fragilité *f*; insignifiance *f*.

slim *adj* mince:—*vi* maigrir.

slimming *n* amaigrissement *m*.

sling *n* écharpe *f*:—*vt* lancer.

slip *vi* (se) glisser:—*vt* glisser:—*n* glissade *f*; faux pas *m*.

slipper *n* pantoufle *f*.

slippery *adj* glissant.

slit *vt* fendre, inciser.

slogan *n* slogan *m*.

slope *n* inclinaison *f*; pente *f*:—*vt* incliner.

sloth *n* paresse *f*.

slovenliness *n* manque de soin *m*.

slovenly *adj* négligé, débraillé.

slow *adj* lent; lourd.

slowness *n* lenteur, lourdeur *f*.

sluggish *adj* paresseux; léthargique.

slum *n* taudis *m*.

slump *n* récession *f*.

slur *vt* dénigrer; mal articuler:—*n* calomnie *f*.

slush n neige fondante f.

sly adj rusé.

slyness n ruse, finesse f.

smack n claque f: — vt donner une claque à.

small adj petit, menu.

smallness n petitesse f.

smart adj élégant; astucieux: — vi brûler.

smartness n astuce, vivacité, finesse f.

smash vt casser, briser, se fracasser: — n fracas m.

smear vt enduire; salir.

smell vt vi sentir: — n odorat m; odeur f.

smelt vt fondre.

smile vi sourire: — n sourire m.

smite vt frapper.

smith n forgeron m.

smoke n fumée f: — vt vi fumer.

smoker n fumeur m, -euse f.

smoky adj enfumé; qui fume.

smooth adj lisse, uni: — vt lisser; adoucir.

smoothness n douceur f; aspect lisse m.

smother vt étouffer.

smudge vt salir: — n tache f.

smuggle vt passer en contrebande.

smuggler n contrebandier m, -ière f.

snack n collation f.

snail n escargot m.

snake n serpent m.

snap vt casser net: — claquer: — n claquement m.

snare n piège m; collet m.

snatch vt saisir.

sneer vi ricaner.

sneeze vi éternuer.

sniff vt renifler.

snivel n pleurnicherie f: — vi pleurnicher.

snob n snob mf.

snobbish adj snob.

snooze n petit somme m.

snore vi ronfler.

snow n neige f: — vi neiger.

snowman n bonhomme de neige m.

snowplough n chasse-neige m invar.

snowy adj neigeux; enneigé.

snub vt repousser, rejeter.

snug adj confortable, douillet.

so adv si, tellement, aussi; ainsi.

soak vi tremper: — vt faire tremper.

soap n savon m: — vt savonner.

soar vi monter en flèche.

sob n sanglot m: — vi sangloter.

sober adj sobre; sérieux.

sobriety n sobriété f.

sociability n sociabilité f.

sociable adj sociable.

social adj social, sociable.

socialist n socialiste mf.

social worker n assistant(e) social(e) m(f).

society n société f; compagnie f.

sociologist n sociologue mf.

sock n chaussette f.

socket n prise de courant f.

sofa n sofa m.

soft adj doux, moelleux.

soften vt (r)amollir, adoucir.

softness n douceur f, mollesse f.

software n logiciel m.

soil vt salir: — n sol m; terre f.

solace vt consoler: — n consolation f.

solar adj solaire.

solder vt souder: — n soudure f.

soldier n soldat m.

sole n plante du pied f: — adj seul, unique.

solemn adj solennel.

solemnity n solennité f.

solicit vt solliciter.

solicitor n notaire m.

solicitude n sollicitude f.

solid adj solide, compact: — n solide m.

solidify vt solidifier.

solidity n solidité f.
solitary adj solitaire, retiré.
solitude n solitude f.
solstice n solstice m.
soluble adj soluble.
solution n solution f.
solve vt résoudre.
solvency n solvabilité f.
solvent adj solvable.
some adj du, de la, de l', des; quelques; quelconque; certain(e)s; quelque.
somebody pn quelqu'un.
somehow adv d'une façon ou d'une autre.
something pn quelque chose.
sometimes adv quelquefois, parfois.
somewhat adv quelque peu.
somewhere adv quelque part.
somnolence n somnolence f.
somnolent adj somnolent.
son n fils m.
song n chanson f.
son-in-law n gendre m.
sonorous adj sonore.
soon adv bientôt.
sooner adv plus tôt; plutôt.
soot n suie f.
soothe vt calmer.
sophisticate vt sophistiquer.
sophisticated adj sophistiqué.
soporific adj soporifique.
sordid adj sordide, sale.
sore n plaie f.—adj douloureux, sensible.
sorrow n peine f.—vi se lamenter.
sorrowful adj triste, affligé.
sorry adj désolé; déplorable.
sort n sorte f; genre m.—vt classer; trier.
soul n âme f.
sound adj sain; valide;—n son m; bruit m.—vt sonner (de).

soundness n santé f; solidité f.
soup n soupe f.
sour adj aigre, acide.
source n source f; origine f.
souvenir n souvenir m.
south n sud m.
southern adj du sud, sud, méridional.
southward(s) adv vers le sud.
sovereign adj n souverain m, -e f.
sovereignty n souveraineté f.
sow vt semer.
space n espace m; intervalle m:—vt espacer.
spacious adj spacieux.
spade n bêche f.
span n envergure f.—vt enjamber.
spare vt vi épargner; ménager:—adj de trop; de réserve.
sparing adj limité, modéré.
spark n étincelle f.
sparkle n scintillement m:—vi étinceler.
sparse adj clairsemé.
spasm n spasme m.
spatter vt éclabousser.
speak vt parler; dire.
speaker n interlocuteur m, -trice f; orateur m.
spear n lance f.
special adj spécial.
speciality n spécialité f.
species n espèce f.
specific adj spécifique.
specification n spécification f.
specify vt spécifier.
specimen n spécimen m.
spectacle n spectacle m.
spectator n spectateur m, -trice f.
spectre n spectre m.
speculate vi spéculer.
speculation n spéculation f.
speculative adj spéculatif, méditatif.

speech *n* parole *f*; discours *m*.
speed *n* vitesse *f*; rapidité *f*.
speediness *n* promptitude, célérité *f*.
speed limit *n* limitation de vitesse *f*.
speedy *adj* rapide, prompt.
spell *n* charme *m*; période *f*: — *vt* écrire.
spelling *n* ortographe *f*.
spend *vt* dépenser; passer.
sphere *n* sphère *f*.
spherical *adj* sphérique.
spice *n* épice *f*: — *vt* épicer.
spicy *adj* épicé.
spider *n* araignée *f*.
spike *n* clou *m*: — *vt* clouter.
spill *vt* répandre: — *vi* se répandre.
spin *vt* filer: — *vi* tourner: — *n* tournoiement *m*.
spinal *adj* spinal.
spine *n* colonne vertébrale.
spire *n* flèche *f*; aiguille *f*.
spirit *n* esprit *m*; âme *f*; caractère *m*.
spirited *adj* vif, fougueux.
spiritless *adj* sans entrain, abattu.
spiritual *adj* spirituel.
spirituality *n* spiritualité *f*.
spit *n* crachat *m*: — *vt vi* cracher.
spite *n* dépit *m*: — **in ~ of** malgré.
spiteful *adj* rancunier.
splash *vt* éclabousser: — *n* éclaboussure *f*.
splendid *adj* splendide.
splendour *n* splendeur *f*.
splinter *n* éclat *m*: — *vt* (*vi*) (se) fendre en éclats.
split *n* fente *f*: — *vt* fendre.
spoil *vt* abîmer.
spokesman *n* porte-parole *m invar*.
sponge *n* éponge *f*.
sponsor *n* parrain *m*.
sponsorship *n* parrainage *m*.
spontaneity *n* spontanéité *f*.

spontaneous *adj* spontané.
spoon *n* cuiller *f*.
sporadic(al) *adj* sporadique.
sport *n* sport *m*; jeu *m*.
sportsman *n* sportif *m*.
sportswoman *n* sportive *f*.
spot *n* tache *f*; endroit *m*: — *vt* apercevoir.
spotless *adj* impeccable.
spouse *n* époux *m*; épouse *f*.
spout *vi* jaillir: — *vt* faire jaillir: — *n* bec *m*.
sprain *n* entorse *f*.
spray *n* spray *m*; pulvérisation *f*.
spread *vt* étendre: — *vi* s'étendre: — *n* diffusion *f*.
spreadsheet *n* feuille de calcul *m*.
spring *vi* bondir: — *n* printemps *m*; saut *m*.
sprinkle *vt* arroser.
sprout *n* pousse *f*.
spruce *adj* net, impeccable.
spur *n* éperon *m*; stimulant *m*: — *vt* éperonner; stimuler.
spurn *vt* repousser avec mépris.
sputter *vi* bafouiller.
spy *n* espion *m*, -onne *f*: — *vt* espionner.
squabble *vi* se quereller: — *n* querelle *f*.
squad *n* équipe *f*.
squadron *n* escadron *m*.
squalid *adj* misérable, sordide.
squalor *n* saleté *f*; misère *f*.
square *adj* carré: — *n* carré *m*; place *f*.
squash *vt* écraser.
squat *vi* s'accroupir.
squeak *vi* grincer, crier.
squeal *vi* couiner.
squeeze *vt* presser, tordre.
squint *vi* loucher: — *n* strabisme.
squirt *vt* faire gicler: — *n* giclée *f*.
stab *vt* poignarder.
stability *n* stabilité.

stable n écurie f: —adj stable.

stack n pile f: —vt empiler.

staff n personnel m; bâton m.

stage n étape f; scène f.

stagger vi vaciller.

stagnation n stagnation f.

stagnate vi stagner.

stain vt tacher: —n tache f.

stair n marche f.

stairs n escalier m.

stake n pieu m: —vt marquer.

stale adj rance.

stalk n tige f.

stall n stalle f; étalage m: —vt caler.

stamina n résistance f.

stammer vi bégayer: —n bégaiement m.

stamp vt trépigner; timbrer: —n timbre m; estampille f.

stand vi être debout: —vt supporter: —n position, prise de position f; étalage m.

standard n étendard m; norme f: —adj normal.

standing n importance f; rang m.

standstill n arrêt m.

staple n agrafe f: —adj principal, de base.

star n étoile f.

starch n amidon m.

stare vi: —**to ~ at** regarder fixement.

starry adj étoilé.

start vi,vt commencer: —n début m.

starter n starter, démarreur m.

startle vt faire sursauter.

starvation n inanition, faim f.

starve vi mourir de faim.

state n état m; condition f: —vt déclarer.

stately adj majestueux, imposant.

statement n déclaration f.

statesman n homme d'Etat m.

static adj statique.

station n station f; (rail) gare f: —vt placer.

stationary adj stationnaire.

stationery n papeterie f.

statistical adj statistique.

statue n statue f.

stature n stature, taille f.

statute n statut m; loi f.

stay n séjour m: —vi rester.

steadfast adj ferme, résolu.

steadiness n fermeté f.

steady adj stable: —vt affermir.

steak n bifteck m; steak m.

steal vt vi voler.

stealthy adj furtif.

steam n vapeur f: —vt cuire à la vapeur.

steam engine n locomotive à vapeur f.

steel n acier m: —adj d'acier.

steep adj abrupt: —vt tremper.

steepness n raideur f.

steer vt diriger.

steering wheel n volant m.

stem n tige f.

stenographer n sténographe mf.

stenography n sténographie f.

step n pas m, marche f: —vi faire un pas.

stepbrother n demi-frère m.

stepsister n demi-sœur f.

stereotype vt stéréotyper.

sterile adj stérile.

sterility n stérilité f.

sterling adj de bon aloi, veritable.

stern adj sévère, rigide.

stew n ragoût m.

steward n intendant m.

stewardess n hôtesse de l'air f.

stick n bâton m: —vt coller.

sticky adj collant, poisseux.

stiff adj raide, rigide.

stiffen vt raidir: —vi se raidir.

stiffness n raideur f.

stifle vt étouffer.

stifling adj suffocant.

stigmatise *vt* stigmatiser.

still *vt* calmer: — *adj* calme: — *adv* encore; toujours.

stillness *n* calme *m*.

stimulate *vt* stimuler.

stimulus *n* stimulant *m*.

sting *vt* piquer; piqûre *f*.

stinginess *n* mesquinerie *f*.

stingy *adj* mesquin.

stink *vi* puer: — *n* puanteur *f*.

stipulate *vt* stipuler.

stipulation *n* stipulation *f*.

stir *vt* remuer; agiter.

stitch *vt* coudre: — *n* point *m*.

stock *n* réserve *f*; provision *f*: — *vt* approvisionner.

stockbroker *n* agent de change *m*.

stock exchange *n* Bourse *f*.

stocking *n* bas *m*.

stoical *adj* stoïque.

stomach *n* estomac *m*.

stone *n* pierre *f*: — *adj* de pierre: — *vt* empierrer.

stony *adj* pierreux.

stool *n* tabouret *m*.

stoop *vi* se pencher.

stop *vt* arrêter: — *vi* s'arrêter: — *n* arrêt *m*.

stoppage *n* obstruction *f*.

storage *n* emmagasinage *m*.

store *n* provision *f*: — *vt* emmagasiner.

stork *n* cigogne *f*.

storm *n* tempête *f*, orage *m*.

stormy *adj* orageux.

story *n* histoire *f*; récit *m*.

stout *adj* corpulent, robuste.

stoutness *n* corpulence *f*.

stove *n* cuisinière *f*.

stow *vt* arrimer.

straight *adj* droit; direct: — *adv* droit; directement.

straightaway *adv* immédiatement.

straighten *vt* redresser.

strain *vt* tendre: — *n* tension *f*; effort *m*.

strait *n* détroit *m*.

strand *n* rive *f*.

strange *adj* inconnu; étrange.

strangeness *n* étrangeté *f*.

stranger *n* inconnu(e) *m(f)*, étranger *m*, -ère *f*.

strangle *vt* étrangler.

strap *n* lanière *f*.

stratagem *n* stratagème *m*.

strategic *adj* stratégique *m*.

strategy *n* stratégie *f*.

straw *n* paille *f*.

strawberry *n* fraise *f*.

stray *vi* s'égarer: — *adj* perdu; errant.

streak *n* raie *f*.

stream *n* ruisseau *m*: — *vi* ruisseler.

street *n* rue *f*.

strength *n* force, puissance *f*.

strengthen *vt* fortifier.

stress *n* pression *f*; stress *m*: — *vt* souligner.

stretch *vt* étendre: — *vi* s'étendre: — *n* extension *f*; étendue *f*.

stretcher *n* brancard *m*.

strew *vt* éparpiller.

strict *adj* strict, rigoureux.

strictness *n* sévérité *f*.

stride *n* grand pas *m*.

strife *n* conflit *m*, lutte *f*.

strike *vt* frapper: — *n* coup *m*; grève *f*.

striker *n* gréviste *mf*.

striking *adj* frappant; saisissant.

string *n* ficelle *f*; corde *f*.

stringent *adj* rigoureux.

strip *vi* se déshabiller: — *n* bande *f*; langue *f*.

stripe *n* raie *f*: — *vt* rayer.

strive *vi* s'efforcer.

stroke *n* coup *m*; caresse *f*: — *vt* caresser.

stroll vi flâner.

strong adj fort, vigoureux.

strongbox n coffre-fort m.

structure n structure f; construction f.

struggle vi lutter:—n lutte f.

strut vi se pavaner.

stubborn adj entêté, obstiné.

stubbornness n entêtement m.

stud n clou m; crampon m.

student n, adj étudiant m, -e f.

studio n studio, atelier m.

studious adj studieux.

study n étude f:—vt étudier.

stuff n matière f; étoffe f:—vt (rem) bourrer.

stuffing n rembourrage m.

stumble vi trébucher:—n trébuchement m.

stump n souche f; moignon m.

stun vt étourdir.

stunt n cascade f:—vt empêcher de croître.

stupefy vt stupéfier.

stupendous adj prodigieux.

stupid adj stupide.

stupidity n stupidité f.

stupor n stupeur f.

sturdiness n force, robustesse f.

sturdy adj robuste; hardi.

stutter vi bégayer.

style n style m:—vt appeler; dessiner.

stylish adj élégant.

suave adj suave.

subdivide vt subdiviser.

subdue vt assujettir.

subject adj soumis; sujet à:—n sujet m; thème m:—vt soumettre.

subjection n sujétion f.

subjugate vt subjuguer.

subjugation n subjugation f.

sublimate vt sublimer.

sublime adj sublime.

sublimity n sublimité f.

submarine adj n sous-marin m.

submerge vt submerger.

submersion n submersion f.

submission n soumission f.

submissive adj soumis.

submit vt soumettre:—vi se soumettre.

subordinate adj subalterne:—vt subordonner.

subscribe vi souscrire:—vt signer.

subscriber n souscripteur m, -trice f.

subscription n souscription f.

subsequent adj ~ly adv ultérieur (-ement).

subside vi s'affaisser.

subsidence n affaissement m.

subsidiary adj subsidiaire.

subsidise vt subventionner.

subsidy n subvention f.

subsist vi subsister; exister.

subsistence n subsistance f.

substance n substance f; fond m.

substantial adj substantiel.

substantiate vt justifier.

substitute vt substituer.

substitution n substitution f.

subterranean adj souterrain.

subtitle n sous-titre m.

subtle adj subtile.

subtlety n subtilité f.

subtract vt soustraire.

suburb n banlieue f.

suburban adj de banlieue.

subversive adj subversif.

subvert vt subvertir.

succeed vi réussir:—vt succéder à, suivre.

success n succès m.

successful adj couronné de succès.

succession n succession f.

successive *adj* successif.

successor *n* successeur *m*.

succinct *adj* succinct.

succumb *vi* succomber.

such *adj* tel, pareil.

suck *vt vi* sucer.

suckle *vt* allaiter.

sudden *adj* soudain.

suddenness *n* soudaineté *f*.

sue *vt* poursuivre en justice.

suffer *vi* souffrir.

suffering *n* souffrance *f*; douleur *f*.

suffice *vi* suffire, être suffisant.

sufficient *adj* suffisant.

suffocate *vt vi* étouffer.

suffocation *n* suffocation *f*.

sugar *n* sucre *m*: —*vt* sucrer.

sugary *adj* sucré.

suggest *vt* suggérer.

suggestion *n* suggestion *f*.

suicidal *adj* suicidaire.

suicide *n* suicide *m*; suicidé *m*, -e *f*.

suit *n* pétition *f*; costume *m*: —*vt* convenir à.

suitable *adj* approprié.

suitcase *n* valise *f*.

sulky *adj* boudeur, maussade.

sullen *adj* maussade; sombre.

sultry *adj* étouffant; chaud.

sum *n* somme *f*; total *m*: —**to ~ up** *vt* résumer.

summary *adj n* résumé *m*.

summer *n* été *m*.

summit *n* sommet *m*; cime *f*.

summon *vt* convoquer.

summons *n* convocation *f*.

sumptuous *adj* somptueux.

sun *n* soleil *m*.

sunbathe *vi* se faire bronzer.

sunburnt *adj* bronzé.

Sunday *n* dimanche *m*.

sundry *adj* divers, différent.

sunflower *n* tournesol *m*.

sunny *adj* ensoleillé.

sunrise *n* lever du soleil *m*.

sunset *n* coucher du soleil *m*.

sunshade *n* parasol *m*.

sunshine *n* ensoleillement *m*.

sunstroke *n* insolation *f*.

suntan *n* bronzage *m*.

super *adj* (*fam*) sensationnel.

superb *adj* superbe.

supercilious *adj* hautain.

superficial *adj* superficiel.

superfluity *n* superfluité *f*.

superfluous *adj* superflu.

superior *adj n* supérieur *m*, -e *f*.

superiority *n* supériorité *f*.

superlative *adj n* superlatif *m*.

supermarket *n* supermarché *m*.

supernatural *adj* surnaturel.

supersede *vt* remplacer.

supersonic *adj* supersonique.

superstition *n* superstition *f*.

superstitious *adj* superstitieux.

supervene *vi* survenir.

supervise *vt* superviser.

supervision *n* surveillance *f*.

supervisor *n* surveillant *m*, -e *f*.

supper *n* dîner *m*.

supplant *vt* supplanter.

supple *adj* souple.

supplement *n* supplément *m*.

supplementary *adj* supplémentaire.

suppleness *n* souplesse *f*.

supplicate *vt* supplier.

supplication *n* supplication *f*.

supplier *n* fournisseur *m*.

supply *vt* fournir: —*n* approvisionnement *m*; provision *f*.

support *vt* soutenir: —*n* appui *m*.

supporter *n* partisan *m*.

suppose *vt vi* supposer.

supposition *n* supposition *f.*

suppress *vt* supprimer.

suppression *n* suppression *f.*

supremacy *n* suprématie *f.*

supreme *adj* suprême.

surcharge *vt* surcharger:—*n* surtaxe *f.*

sure *adj* sûr, certain:—**~ly** *adv* sûrement.

sureness *n* certitude, sûreté *f.*

surf *n* (*mar*) ressac *m.*

surface *n* surface *f.*:—*vi* remonter à la surface.

surfboard *n* planche (de surf) *f.*

surge *n* vague, montée *f.*

surgeon *n* chirurgien *m.*

surgery *n* chirurgie *m.*

surgical *adj* chirurgical.

surly *adj* revêche, bourru.

surmise *vt* conjecturer:—*n* conjecture *f.*

surmount *vt* surmonter.

surname *n* nom de famille *m.*

surpass *vt* surpasser.

surplus *n* excédent *m*:—*adj* en surplus.

surprise *vt* surprendre:—*n* surprise *f.*

surrender *vi* se rendre:—*n* reddition *f.*

surreptitious *adj* subreptice.

surrogate *n* substitut *m.*

surround *vt* entourer.

survey *vt* examiner:—*n* enquête *f.*

survive *vi* survivre:—*vt* survivre à.

survivor *n* survivant *m*, -e *f.*

susceptibility *n* sensibilité *f.*

susceptible *adj* sensible.

suspect *vt* soupçonner:—*n* suspect *m*, -e *f.*

suspend *vt* suspendre.

suspense *n* incertitude *f*; suspense *m.*

suspicion *n* soupçon *m.*

suspicious *adj* soupçonneux.

sustain *vt* soutenir.

sustenance *n* (moyens de) subsistance *f.*

swagger *vi* plastronner.

swallow *vt* avaler.

swap *vt* échanger:—*n* échange *m.*

swarm *n* essaim *m*:—*vi* fourmiller.

swathe *vt* emmailloter:—*n* bande *f.*

sway *vi* se balancer, osciller:—*n* balancement *m*; emprise.

swear *vt* jurer:—*vi* jurer.

sweat *n* sueur *f*:—*vi* suer.

sweep *vt* balayer.

sweet *adj* doux, agréable; suave:—*n* bonbon *m.*

sweeten *vt* sucrer; adoucir.

sweetener *n* édulcorant *m.*

sweetness *n* goût sucré *m*, douceur *f.*

swell *vi* gonfler:—*n* houle *f.*

swelling *n* gonflement *m.*

swerve *vt* dévier.

swift *adj* rapide.

swiftness *n* rapidité, promptitude *f.*

swim *vi* nager:—*n* baignade *f.*

swimming *n* natation *f.*

swimming pool *n* piscine *f.*

swimsuit *n* maillot de bain *m.*

swindle *vt* escroquer.

swing *vi* se balancer:—*vt* balancer: —*n* balancement *m.*

swirl *n* tourbillon.

switch *n* interrupteur *m*:—*vt* changer de:—**to ~ off** éteindre:—**to ~ on** allumer.

swivel *vt* faire pivoter.

swoon *vi* s'évanouir:—*n* évanouissement *m.*

swoop *vi* fondre sur.

sword *n* épée *f.*

sycophant *n* sycophante *mf.*

syllabic *adj* syllabique.

syllable *n* syllabe *f.*

syllabus *n* programme d'un cours *m.*

symbol *n* symbole *m*.

symbolic(al) *adj* symbolique.

symbolise *vt* symboliser.

symmetrical *adj* symétrique.

symmetry *n* symétrie *f*.

sympathetic *adj* compatissant.

sympathise *vi* compatir.

sympathy *n* compassion *f*.

symphony *n* symphonie *f*.

symptom *n* symptôme *m*.

synagogue *n* synagogue *f*.

syndrome *n* syndrome *m*.

synonym *n* synonyme *m*.

synonymous *adj* synonyme.

synopsis *n* synopsis *f*; résumé *m*.

syntax *n* syntaxe *f*.

synthesis *n* synthèse *f*.

syringe *n* seringue *f*.

system *n* système *m*.

systematic *adj* systématique.

T

table *n* table *f*:—*vt* mettre en forme de tableau.

tablecloth *n* nappe *f*.

tablet *n* tablette *f*; comprimé *m*.

tacit *adj* tacite.

taciturn *adj* taciturne.

tack *n* broquette *f*:—*vt* clouer.

tackle *n* attirail, équipement.

tact *n* tact *m*.

tactics *npl* tactique *f*.

tag *n* ferret *m*:—*vt* ferrer.

tail *n* queue *f*.

tailor *n* tailleur *m*.

tailoring *n* métier de tailleur *m*.

taint *vt* infecter.

tainted *adj* infecté.

take *vt* prendre.

takeoff *n* décollage *m*.

takeover *n* prise de possession *f*.

takings *npl* recette *f*.

talc *n* talc *m*.

talent *n* talent *m*.

talented *adj* talentueux.

talk *vi* parler; causer:—*n* conversation *f*.

talkative *adj* loquace.

tall *adj* grand, élevé.

tally *vi* correspondre.

tame *adj* apprivoisé:—*vt* apprivoiser.

tamper *vi* toucher à.

tan *vt vi* bronzer:—*n* bronzage *m*.

tangible *adj* tangible.

tangle *vt* enchevêtrer.

tank *n* réservoir *m*.

tanker *n* pétrolier *m*.

tantrum *n* accès de colère *m*.

tap *vt* taper doucement:—*n* petite tape *f*; robinet *m*.

tape *n* ruban *m*:—*vt* enregistrer.

tape recorder *n* magnétophone *m*.

target *n* cible *f*.

tariff *n* tarif *m*.

tarnish *vt* ternir.

tart *n* tarte, tartelette *f*.

task *n* tâche *f*.

taste *n* goût *m*; saveur *f*:—*vt* déguster.

tasteful *adj* de bon goût.

tasty *adj* savoureux.

tattoo *n* tatouage *m*:—*vt* tatouer.

taunt *vt* railler:—*n* raillerie *f*.

taut *adj* tendu.

tawdry *adj* tapageur.

tax *n* impôt *m*:—*vt* imposer.

taxable *adj* imposable.
taxation *n* imposition *f*.
taxi *n* taxi *m*.
tax payer *n* contribuable *mf*.
tea *n* thé *m*.
teach *vt* enseigner.
teacher *n* professeur *m*.
teaching *n* enseignement *m*.
team *n* équipe *f*.
teapot *n* théière *f*.
tear *vt* déchirer.
tear *n* larme *f*.
tearful *adj* larmoyant.
tease *vt* taquiner.
teaspoon *n* petite cuiller *f*.
technical *adj* technique.
technician *n* technicien *m*, -ienne *f*.
technique *n* technique *f*.
technological *adj* technologique.
technology *n* technologie *f*.
tedious *adj* ennuyeux.
tedium *n* ennui, manque d'intérêt *m*.
teenage *adj* adolescent: — **~r** *n* adolescent(e) *m(f)*.
teethe *vi* faire ses premières dents.
telegram *n* télégramme *m*.
telegraph *n* télégraphe *m*.
telepathy *n* télépathie *f*.
telephone *n* téléphone *m*.
telephone directory *n* annuaire *m*.
telephone number *n* numéro de téléphone *m*.
telescope *n* télescope *m*.
telescopic *adj* télescopique.
televise *vt* téléviser.
television *n* télévision *f*.
television set *n* téléviseur.
tell *vt* dire; raconter.
temper *vt* tempérer: — *n* colère *f*.
temperament *n* tempérament *m*.
temperate *adj* tempéré.

temperature *n* température *f*.
tempest *n* tempête *f*.
temple *n* temple *m*; tempe *f*.
temporary *adj* temporaire.
tempt *vt* tenter.
temptation *n* tentation *f*.
ten *adj n* dix *m*.
tenacious *adj* tenance.
tenacity *n* ténacité *f*.
tenant *n* locataire *mf*.
tend *vt* garder.
tendency *n* tendance *f*.
tender *adj* tendre: — *n* offre *f*: — *vt* offrir.
tendon *n* tendon *m*.
tennis *n* tennis *m*.
tenor *n* (*mus*) ténor *m*; sens *m*.
tense *adj* tendu: — *n* (*gr*) temps *m*.
tension *n* tension *f*.
tent *n* tente *f*.
tentative *adj* timide, hésitant.
tenth *adj n* dixième *mf*.
tenuous *adj* ténu.
tepid *adj* tiède.
term *n* terme *m*: — *vt* appeler.
terminal *adj* terminal: — *n* aérogare *f*; terminal *m*.
terminate *vt* terminer.
termination *n* fin, conclusion *f*.
terrace *n* terrace *f*.
terrain *n* terrain *m*.
terrestrial *adj* terrestre.
terrible *adj* terrible.
terrific *adj* terrifiant.
terrify *vt* terrifier.
territorial *adj* territorial.
territory *n* territoire *m*.
terror *n* terreur *f*.
terrorise *vt* terroriser.
terrorist *n* terroriste *mf*.
terse *adj* concis, net.
test *n* essai *m*: — *vt* essayer.

testify *vt* témoigner.

testimony *n* témoignage *m*.

test tube *n* éprouvette *f*.

tether *vt* attacher.

text *n* texte *m*.

textual *adj* textuel.

texture *n* texture *f*.

than *adv* que; de.

thank *vt* remercier.

thankful *adj* reconnaissant.

thanks *npl* remerciement(s) *m(pl)*.

that *pn* cela, ça, ce; qui, que; celui-là:—*conj* que.

thatch *n* chaume *m*.

thaw *n* dégel *m*:—*vi* dégeler.

the *art* le, la, l', les.

theatre *n* théâtre *m*.

theatrical *adj* théâtral.

theft *n* vol *m*.

their *poss adj* leur(s).

theirs *poss pn* le leur; la leur; les leurs.

them *pn* les; leur.

theme *n* thème *m*.

themselves *pn pl* eux-mêmes *mpl*, elles-mêmes *fpl*; se.

then *adv* alors; ensuite:—*conj* donc; en ce cas.

theological *adj* théologique.

theology *n* théologie *f*.

theorem *n* théorème *m*.

theoretic(al) *adj* théorique.

theory *n* théorie *f*.

therapist *n* thérapeute *mf*.

therapy *n* thérapie *f*.

there *adv* y, là.

thereafter *adv* par la suite; après.

therefore *adv* donc, par conséquent.

thermal *adj* thermal.

thermometer *n* thermomètre *m*.

these *pn pl* ceux-ci, celles-ci.

they *pn pl* ils, elles.

thick *adj* épais, gros.

thicken *vi* (s')épaissir.

thickness *n* épaisseur *f*.

thickset *adj* trapu.

thief *n* voleur *m*, -euse *f*.

thigh *n* cuisse *f*.

thin *adj* mince, fin.

thing *n* chose *f*; objet *m*; truc *m*.

think *vi vt* penser:—~ **over** *vt* réfléchir à.

thinker *n* penseur *m*, -euse *f*.

thinking *n* pensée *f*; réflexion *f*.

third *adj* troisième:—*n* troisième *mf*; tiers *m*.

thirst *n* soif *f*.

thirsty *adj* assoiffé.

thirteen *adj n* treize *m*.

thirteenth *adj n* treizième *mf*.

thirtieth *adj n* trentième *mf*.

thirty *adj n* trente *m*.

this *adj* ce, cet, cette, ces:—*pn* ceci, ce.

thistle *n* chardon *m*.

thorn *n* épine *f*.

thorough *adj* consciencieux, approfondi:—~**ly** *adv* minutieusement, à fond.

thoroughfare *n* rue, artère *f*.

those *pn pl* ceux-là, celles-la:—*adj* ces, ces… là.

though *conj* bien que:—*adv* pourtant.

thought *n* pensée, réflexion *f*.

thoughtful *adj* pensif.

thoughtless *adj* étourdi; irréfléchi.

thousand *adj n* mille *m*.

thousandth *adj n* millième *mf*.

thrash *vt* battre.

thread *n* fil *m*.

threat *n* menace *f*.

threaten *vt* menacer.

three *adj n* trois *m*.

threshold *n* seuil *m*.

thrifty *adj* économe.

thrill *vt* faire frissonner: — *n* frisson *m*.

thrive *vi* prospérer.

throat *n* gorge *f*.

throb *vi* palpiter.

throne *n* trône *m*.

throng *n* foule *f*.

throttle *n* accélérateur *m*: — *vt* étrangler.

through *prep* à travers; pendant; par: — *adj* direct.

throughout *prep* partout dans: — *adv* partout.

throw *vt* jeter: — *n* jet *m*; lancement *m*.

throwaway *adj* à jeter.

thrust *vt* enfoncer: — *n* poussée *f*.

thug *n* voyou *m*.

thumb *n* pouce *m*.

thump *n* coup de poing *m*: — *vt* cogner à.

thunder *n* tonnerre *m*: — *vi* tonner.

thunderclap *n* coup de tonnerre *m*.

thunderstorm *n* orage *m*.

Thursday *n* jeudi *m*.

thus *adv* ainsi.

thwart *vt* contrecarrer.

tic *n* tic *m*.

tick *n* tic-tac *m*; instant *m*.

ticket *n* billet, ticket *m*.

ticket office *n* guichet *m*.

tickle *vt* chatouiller.

tidal wave *n* raz-de-marée *m*.

tide *n* marée *f*.

tidy *adj* rangé, en ordre.

tie *vt* attacher: — *n* attache *f*; lacet *m*.

tier *n* gradin *m*; étage *m*.

tiger *n* tigre *m*.

tight *adj* raide, tendu.

tighten *vt* (re)serrer, tendre.

tile *n* tuile *f*; carreau *m*.

till *n* caisse *f*: — *vt* labourer.

tilt *vt* pencher: — *vi* s'incliner.

timber *n* bois de construction *m*.

time *n* temps *m*; période *f*; heure *f*: — *vt* fixer; chronométrer.

time lag *n* décalage *m*.

timeless *adj* éternel.

timely *adj* opportun.

time zone *n* fuseau horaire *m*.

timid *adj* timide.

timidity *n* timidité *f*.

tin *n* étain *m*; boîte (de conserve) *f*.

tinge *n* teinte *f*.

tingle *vi* picoter.

tinkle *vi* tinter.

tint *n* teinte *f*: — *vt* teinter.

tinted *adj* teinté; fumé.

tiny *adj* minuscule.

tip *n* pointe *f*, bout *m*; pourboire *m*: — *vt* donner un pourboire à.

tirade *n* diatribe *f*.

tire *vt* fatiguer: — *vi* se fatiguer.

tireless *adj* infatigable.

tiresome *adj* ennuyeux, fatigant.

tissue *n* tissu *m*.

titbit *n* friandise *f*.

titillate *vt* titiller.

title *n* titre *m*.

titular *adj* titulaire.

to *prep* à; vers; en.

toast *vt* (faire) griller: — *n* toast *m*.

toaster *n* grille-pain *m invar*.

tobacco *n* tabac *m*.

toboggan *n* toboggan *m*.

today *adv* aujourd'hui.

toe *n* orteil *m*; pointe *f*.

together *adv* ensemble.

toil *vi* travailler dur: — *n* labeur *m*; peine *f*.

toilet *n* toilette *f*; toilettes *fpl*: — *adj* de toilette.

toilet paper *n* papier hygiénique *m*.

toiletries *npl* articles de toilette *mpl*.

token *n* signe *m*; marque *f*; jeton *m*.

tolerable *adj* tolérable.

tolerant *adj* tolérant.

tolerate *vt* tolérer.

toll *n* péage *m*:—*vi* sonner.

tomato *n* tomate *f*.

tomb *n* tombeau *m*; tombe *f*.

tombstone *n* pierre tombale *f*.

tomorrow *adv n* demain *m*.

ton *n* tonne *f*.

tone *n* ton *m*; tonalité *f*:—*vi* s'harmoniser.

tongs *npl* pinces *fpl*.

tongue *n* langue *f*.

tonight *adv n* ce soir (*m*).

too *adv* aussi; trop.

tool *n* outil *m*; ustensile *m*.

tooth *n* dent *f*.

toothache *n* rage de dents *f*.

toothbrush *n* brosse à dents *f*.

toothpaste *n* dentifrice *m*.

top *n* sommet *m*; haut *m*; tête *f*; dessus *m*:—*adj* du haut:—*vt* dépasser.

topic *n* sujet *m*.

topical *adj* d'actualité.

topmost *adj* le plus haut.

topographic(al) *adj* topographique.

topography *n* topographie *f*.

topple *vt* renverser:—*vi* basculer.

torch *n* torche *f*.

torment *vt* tourmenter:—*n* tourment *m*.

tornado *n* tornade *f*.

torrent *n* torrent *m*.

tortuous *adj* tortueux, sinueux.

torture *n* torture *f*:—*vt* torturer.

toss *vt* lancer, secouer.

total *adj* total, global.

totality *n* totalité *f*.

totter *vi* chanceler.

touch *vt* toucher; contact *m*; touche *f*.

touchdown *n* atterrissage *m*; but *m*.

touching *adj* touchant.

tough *adj* dur; pénible.

toughen *vt* durcir.

tour *n* voyage *m*; visite *f*.

tourism *n* tourisme *m*.

tourist *n* touriste *mf*.

tournament *n* tournoi *m*.

tow *n* remorquage *m*:—*vt* remorquer.

toward(s) *prep* vers.

towel *n* serviette *f*.

tower *n* tour *f*.

town *n* ville *f*.

town hall *n* mairie *f*.

towrope *n* câble de remorquage *m*.

toy *n* jouet *m*.

trace *n* trace, piste *f*:—*vt* tracer.

track *n* trace *f*; empreinte *f*.

tract *n* étendue; brochure *f*.

traction *n* traction *f*.

trade *n* commerce *m*; métier *m*:—*vi* commercer.

trademark *n* marque de fabrique *f*.

trader *n* négociant *m*, -e *f*.

trade(s) union *n* syndicat *m*.

trade unionist *n* syndicaliste *mf*.

trading *n* commerce *m*:—*adj* commercial.

tradition *n* tradition *f*.

traditional *adj* traditionnel.

traffic *n* circulation *f*; négoce *m*.

traffic jam *n* embouteillage *m*.

tragedy *n* tragédie *f*.

tragic *adj* tragique.

trail *vt* traîner:—*n* traînée *f*.

train *vt* entraîner:—*n* train *m*.

trainer *n* entraîneur *m*.

training *n* entraînement *m*.

trait *n* trait *m*.

traitor *n* traître *m*.

tramp *n* clochard *m*, -e *f*:—*vt* piétiner.

trance *n* transe *f*; extase *f*.

tranquil *adj* tranquille.

transact *vt* traiter.

transaction *n* transaction *f*.
transcend *vt* transcender.
transcription *n* transcription *f*.
transfer *vt* transférer: — *n* transfert *m*.
transform *vt* transformer.
transfusion *n* transfusion *f*.
transition *n* transition *f*.
transitional *adj* de transition.
translate *vt* traduire.
translation *n* traduction *f*.
translator *n* traducteur *m*, -trice *f*.
transmission *n* transmision *f*.
transmit *vt* transmettre.
transparency *n* transparence *f*.
transparent *adj* transparent.
transplant *vt* transplanter.
transport *vt* transporter: — *n* transport *m*.
trap *n* piège *m*: — *vt* prendre au piège.
travel *vi* voyager: — *n* voyage *m*.
traveller *n* voyageur *m*, -euse *f*.
traveller's cheque *n* chèque de voyage *m*.
travesty *n* parodie *f*.
tray *n* plateau *m*.
treacherous *adj* traître.
treachery *n* traîtrise *f*.
tread *vi* marcher: — *n* pas *m*.
treason *n* trahison *f*.
treasure *n* trésor *m*.
treasurer *n* trésorier *m*, -ière *f*.
treat *vt* traiter: — *n* cadeau *m*.
treatment *n* traitement *m*.
treaty *n* traité *m*.
treble *adj* triple: — *vt vi* tripler.
tree *n* arbre *m*.
trek *n* randonnée *f*; étape *f*.
tremble *vi* trembler.
tremendous *adj* terrible; formidable.
trend *n* tendance *f*; mode *f*.
trespass *vt* transgresser.
trial *n* procès *m*; essai *m*.

triangle *n* triangle *m*.
tribal *adj* tribal.
tribe *n* tribu *f*.
tribunal *n* tribunal *m*.
tributary *adj n* tributaire *m*.
trick *n* ruse, astuce *f*: — *vt* attraper.
tricky *adj* délicat; difficile.
trifle *n* bagatelle, vétille *f*.
trifling *adj* futile, insignifiant.
trigger *n* détente *f*.
trim *adj* net, soigné: — *vt* arranger.
trip *vi* trébucher: — *n* faux pas *m*; voyage *m*.
triple *adj* triple: — *vt vi* tripler.
trite *adj* banal; usé.
triumph *n* triomphe *m*: — *vi* triompher.
triumphant *adj* triomphant.
trivia *npl* futilités *fpl*.
trivial *adj* insignifiant.
triviality *n* banalité *f*.
troop *n* bande *f*.
tropical *adj* tropical.
trouble *vt* affliger: — *n* problème *m*; ennui *m*.
troublesome *adj* pénible.
trousers *npl* pantalon *m*.
trout *n* truite *f*.
truck *n* camion *m*; wagon *m*.
truck driver *n* routier *m*.
truculent *adj* brutal, agressif.
true *adj* vrai, véritable.
trump *n* atout *m*.
trumpet *n* trompette *f*.
trunk *n* malle *f*.
trust *n* confiance *f*: — *vt* confier à.
trustworthy *adj* digne de confiance.
trusty *adj* fidèle, loyal.
truth *n* vérité *f*.
truthful *adj* véridique.
truthfulness *n* véracité *f*.
try *vt* essayer: — *n* tentative *f*; essai *m*.

tub n cuve f, bac m.
tube n tube m.
tuck n pli m:—vt mettre.
Tuesday n mardi m.
tug vt remorquer:—n remorqueur m.
tuition n cours, enseignement m.
tulip n tulipe f.
tumble vi tomber:—n chute f.
tumbler n verre m.
tumultuous adj tumultueux.
tune n air m; accord m.
tuneful adj mélodieux, harmonieux.
tunnel n tunnel m.
turbulence n turbulence.
turbulent adj turbulent.
turf n gazon m.
turkey n dinde f.
turmoil n agitation f; trouble m.
turn vtr (se) tourner; vt monter:—n tour m; tournure.
turning n embranchement m.
turnover n chiffre d'affaires m.
turnstile n tourniquet m.
turquoise n turquoise f.
turtle n tortue marine f.

tusk n défense f.
tutor n professeur particulier m.
tweezers npl pince à épiler f.
twelfth adj n douzième mf.
twelve adj n douze m.
twentieth adj n vingtième mf.
twenty adj n vingt m.
twice adv deux fois.
twilight n crépuscule m.
twin n jumeau m, -elle f.
twine vi s'enrouler.
twinkle vi scintiller.
twirl vi tournoyer.
twist vt tordre, tortiller.
twitch n tic m.
two adj n deux m.
twofold adj double:—adv au double.
tycoon n magnat m.
type n type m:—vi taper à la machine.
typeface n œil de caractère m.
typewriter n machine à écrire f.
typical adj typique.
tyrannical adj tyrannique.
tyrant n tyran m.
tyre n pneu m.

U

ugliness n laideur f.
ugly adj laid.
ulcer n ulcère m.
ulterior adj ultérieur.
ultimate adj final:—~ly adv finalement; à la fin.
ultimatum n ultimatum m.
umbrella n parapluie m.
umpire n arbitre m.
unable adj incapable.
unaccomplished adj inaccompli.

unaccountable adj inexplicable.
unaccustomed adj inaccoutumé.
unacknowledged adj non reconnu.
unadulterated adj pur; sans mélange.
unaltered adj inchangé.
unanimity n unanimité f.
unanimous adj unanime.
unanswerable adj incontestable.
unapproachable adj inaccessible.
unarmed adj désarmé.
unattached adj indépendant; libre.

unattainable *adj* inaccessible.

unavoidable *adj* inévitable.

unaware *adj* ignorant; inconscient.

unbalanced *adj* déséquilibré.

unbearable *adj* insupportable.

unbelievable *adj* incroyable.

unbiased *adj* impartial.

unbreakable *adj* incassable.

unbroken *adj* intact; ininterrompu.

unbutton *vt* déboutonner.

unceasing *adj* incessant.

uncertain *adj* incertain.

uncertainty *n* incertitude *f*.

unchangeable *adj* immuable.

uncharitable *adj* peu charitable.

uncivil *adj* impoli, grossier.

uncivilised *adj* non civilisé.

uncle *n* oncle *m*.

uncomfortable *adj* inconfortable.

uncommon *adj* rare, extraordinaire.

uncompromising *adj* intransigeant.

unconcerned *adj* indifférent.

unconditional *adj* inconditionnel, absolu.

unconscious *adj* inconscient.

uncork *vt* déboucher.

uncouth *adj* grossier.

uncover *vt* découvrir.

uncultivated *adj* inculte.

undecided *adj* indécis.

undeniable *adj* indéniable.

under *prep* sous; dessous:—*adv* au-dessous.

underclothing *n* sous-vêtements *mpl*.

undercover *adj* secret, clandestin.

underdeveloped *adj* sous-développé.

underestimate *vt* sous-estimer.

undergo *vt* subir.

undergraduate *n* étudiant(e) en licence *m(f)*.

undergrowth *n* brouissailles *fpl*.

underhand *adj* secret, clandestin.

underline *vt* souligner.

underneath *adv* (en) dessous:—*prep* sous, au-dessous de.

underpaid *adj* sous-payé.

underprivileged *adj* défavorisé.

underside *n* dessous *m*.

understand *vt* comprendre.

understandable *adj* compréhensible.

understanding *n* compréhension:—*adj* compréhensif.

undertake *vt* entreprendre.

undertaking *n* entreprise *f*.

undervalue *vt* sous-estimer.

underwater *adj* sous-marin:—*adv* sous l'eau.

underwear *n* sous-vêtements *mpl*.

underwrite *vt* souscrire à.

undeserved *adj* immérité.

undetermined *adj* indéterminé.

undisciplined *adj* indiscipliné.

undisputed *adj* incontesté.

undivided *adj* indivisé, entier.

undo *vt* défaire; détruire.

undoing *n* ruine *f*.

undoubted *adj* ~**ly** *adv* indubitable-(ment).

undress *vi* se déshabiller.

undue *adj* excessif.

unduly *adv* trop, excessivement.

uneasy *adj* inquiet; gêné.

uneducated *adj* sans instruction.

unemployed *adj* au chômage.

unemployment *n* chômage *m*.

unending *adj* interminable.

unequal *adj* inégal.

unequalled *adj* inégalé.

uneven *adj* inégal; impair.

unexpected *adj* inattendu.

unfailing *adj* infaillible, certain.

unfair *adj* injuste.

unfaithful *adj* infidèle.

unfashionable *adj* démodé.
unfasten *vt* détacher, défaire.
unfavourable *adj* défavorable.
unfeeling *adj* insensible.
unfinished *adj* inachevé.
unfit *adj* inapte; impropre.
unfold *vt* déplier.
unforeseen *adj* imprévu.
unforgettable *adj* inoubliable.
unfortunate *adj* malheureux.
unfounded *adj* sans fondement.
unfriendly *adj* inamical.
ungrateful *adj* ingrat.
unhappiness *n* tristesse *f*.
unhappy *adj* malheureux.
unhealthy *adj* malsain.
unheeding *adj* insouciant.
unhook *vt* décrocher.
unhurt *adj* indemne.
uniform *adj* uniforme.
uniformity *adj* uniformité *f*.
unify *vt* unifier.
unimaginable *adj* inimaginable.
uninhabitable *adj* inhabitable.
uninhabited *adj* inhabité, désert.
uninjured *adj* indemne.
unintelligible *adj* inintelligible.
unintentional *adj* involontaire.
uninterested *adj* indifférent.
uninterrupted *adj* ininterrompu.
union *n* union *f*; syndicat *m*.
unique *adj* unique, exceptionnel.
unison *n* unisson *m*.
unit *n* unité *f*.
unite *vt* unir:—*vi* s'unir.
unity *n* unité, harmonie *f*, accord *m*.
universal *adv* universel.
universe *n* univers *m*.
university *n* université *f*.
unjust *adj* injuste.
unknown *adj* inconnu.

unlawful *adj* illégal.
unlawfulness *n* illégalité *f*.
unleash *vt* lâcher.
unless *conj* à moins que/de, sauf.
unlicensed *adj* illicite.
unlikely *adj* improbable.
unlikelihood *n* improbabilité *f*.
unlimited *adj* illimité.
unload *vt* décharger.
unlucky *adj* malchanceux.
unmask *vt* démasquer.
unmerited *adj* immérité.
unmistakable *adj* indubitable
unmoved *adj* insensible, impassible.
unnecessary *adj* inutile, superflu.
unnoticed *adj* inaperçu.
unobserved *adj* inaperçu.
unoccupied *adj* inoccupé.
unoffending *adj* inoffensif.
unpack *vt* défaire.
unparalleled *adj* incomparable; sans pareil.
unpleasant *adj* désagréable.
unpopular *adj* impopulaire.
unprecedented *adj* sans précédent.
unpredictable *adj* imprévisible.
unprejudiced *adj* impartial.
unprofitable *adj* inutile; peu rentable.
unpublished *adj* inédit.
unqualified *adj* non qualifié; sans réserve.
unquestionable *adj* incontestable, indiscutable.
unreal *adj* irréel.
unreasonable *adv* déraisonnable.
unrelated *adj* sans rapport.
unrelenting *adj* implacable.
unreserved *adj* sans réserve; franc.
unrest *n* agitation *f*; troubles *mpl*.
unripe *adj* vert, pas mûr.
unroll *vt* dérouler.

unsafe *adj* dangereux, peu sûr.

unsatisfactory *adj* peu satisfaisant.

unscrew *vt* dévisser.

unseasonable *adj* hors de saison, inopportun.

unseemly *adj* inconvenant.

unsettle *vt* perturber.

unsociable *adj* insociable.

unspeakable *adj* ineffable.

unstable *adj* instable.

unsteady *adj* instable.

untamed *adj* sauvage.

untapped *adj* non exploité.

untenable *adj* insoutenable.

unthinkable *adj* inconcevable.

untidiness *n* désordre *m*.

untidy *adj* en désordre.

untie *vt* dénouer, défaire.

until *prep* jusqu'à:—*conj* jusqu'à ce que.

untimely *adj* intempestif.

untold *adj* jamais révélé; indicible.

untouched *adj* intact.

untroubled *adj* tranquille, paisible.

untrue *adj* faux.

untrustworthy *adj* indigne de confiance.

unused *adj* neuf, inutilisé.

unusual *adj* inhabituel, exceptionnel:— **~ly** *adv* exceptionnellement.

unveil *vt* dévoiler.

unwelcome *adj* importun.

unwell *adj* indisposé.

unwilling *adj* peu disposé:— **~ly** *adv* de mauvaise grâce.

unwind *vt* dérouler:—*vi* se détendre.

unwise *adj* imprudent.

unwitting *adj* involontaire.

unworkable *adj* impraticable.

unworthy *adj* indigne.

up *adv* en haut, en l'air; levé:—*prep* au haut de; vers.

upbringing *n* éducation *f*.

update *vt* mettre à jour.

upheaval *n* bouleversement *m*.

uphold *vt* soutenir.

upholstery *n* tapisserie *f*.

upkeep *n* entretien *m*.

upon *prep* sur.

upper *adj* supérieur; (plus) élevé.

uppermost *adj* le plus haut, le plus élevé:— **to be ~** prédominer.

upright *adj* droit; honnête.

uprising *n* soulèvement *m*.

uproar *n* tumulte, vacarme *m*.

uproot *vt* déraciner.

upset *vt* renverser; déranger, bouleverser:—*n* désordre *m*; bouleversement *m*:—*adj* vexé; bouleversé.

upshot *n* résultat *m*; aboutissement *m*.

upside-down *adv* sens dessus dessous.

upstairs *adv* en haut (d'un escalier).

up-to-date *adj* à jour.

upturn *n* amélioration *f*.

urban *adj* urbain.

urbane *adj* courtois.

urchin *n* oursin *m*.

urge *vt* pousser:—*n* impulsion *f*.

urgency *n* urgence *f*.

urgent *adj* urgent.

urinate *vi* uriner.

urn *n* urne *f*.

us *pn* nous.

usage *n* traitement *m*; usage *m*.

use *n* usage *m*; emploi *m*:—*vt* utiliser.

used *adj* usagé.

useful *adj* utile.

usefulness *n* utilité *f*.

useless *adj* inutile.

uselessness *n* inutilité *f*.

usher *n* huissier *m*; placeur *m*.

usual *adj* habituel, courant.

usurp *vt* usurper.

utensil *n* ustensile *m*.

uterus *n* utérus *m*.
utility *n* utilité *f*.
utmost *adj* extrême.

utter *adj* complet; total: — *vt* prononcer.
utterly *adv* complètement.

U

vacancy *n* chambre libre *f*.
vacant *adj* vacant.
vacate *vt* quitter.
vacation *n* vacances *fpl*.
vaccinate *vt* vacciner.
vacuum *n* vide *m*.
vague *adj* vague.
vain *adj* vain.
valiant *adj* courageux.
valid *adj* valide.
valley *n* vallée *f*.
valuable *adj* précieux, de valeur.
value *n* valeur *f*: — *vt* évaluer.
valve *n* soupape *f*.
van *n* camionnette *f*.
vandalise *vt* saccager.
vanish *vi* disparaître.
vanity *n* vanité *f*.
vanquish *vt* vaincre.
vantage point *n* position avantageuse *f*.
vapour *n* vapeur *f*.
variable *adj* variable; changeant.
variation *n* variation *f*.
variety *n* variété *f*.
various *adj* divers, différent.
vary *vt vi* varier: — *vi* changer.
vase *n* vase *m*.
vast *adj* vaste; immense.
vault *n* voûte *f*: — *vi* sauter.
vegetable *adj* végétal: — *n* légume *m*.
vegetarian *n* végétarien *m*, -ienne *f*.
vegetate *vi* végéter.

vegetation *n* végétation *f*.
vehemence *n* véhémence.
vehement *adj* véhément.
vehicle *n* véhicule *m*.
veil *n* voile *m*.
vein *n* veine *f*; nervure *f*.
velocity *n* vitesse *f*.
velvet *n* velours *m*.
vendor *n* vendeur *m*.
venerate *vt* vénérer.
veneration *n* vénération *f*.
vengeance *n* vengeance *f*.
venom *n* venin *m*.
venomous *adj* vénéneux.
ventilate *vt* aérer.
ventilation *n* ventilation, aération *f*.
venture *n* entreprise *f*: — *vi* s'aventurer.
verb *n* (*gr*) verbe *m*.
verbal *adj* verbal, oral.
verification *n* vérification *f*.
verify *vt* vérifier.
versatile *adj* versatile.
verse *n* vers *m*.
version *n* version *f*.
versus *prep* contre.
vertical *adj* vertical.
vertigo *n* vertige *m*.
very *adv* très, fort, bien.
vessel *n* récipient *m*; navire *m*.
veteran *adj n* vétéran *m*.
veterinarian *n* vétérinaire *mf*.
veterinary *adj* vétérinaire.

veto *n* véto *m*.

vex *vt* contrarier.

vexed *adj* contrarié.

via *prep* via, par.

viaduct *n* viaduc *m*.

vibrate *vi* vibrer.

vibration *n* vibration *f*.

vice *n* vice *m*; défaut *m*.

vicinity *n* voisinage *m*.

vicious *adj* méchant.

victim *n* victime *f*.

victor *n* vainqueur *m*.

victory *n* victoire *f*.

video *n* vidéo *f*; vidéocassette *f*.

viewer *n* téléspectateur *m*, -trice *f*.

vie *vi* rivaliser.

view *n* vue *f*:—*vt* voir; examiner.

vigil *n* veille *f*; vigile *f*.

vigilance *n* vigilance *f*.

vigilant *adj* vigilant.

vigorous *adj* vigoureux.

vigour *n* vigueur *f*.

vile *adj* vil.

village *n* village *m*.

vindicate *vt* venger.

vindication *n* défense *f*.

vindictive *adj* vindicatif.

vine *n* vigne *f*.

vinegar *n* vinaigre *m*.

vineyard *n* vignoble *m*.

violate *vt* violer.

violation *n* violation *f*.

violence *n* violence *f*.

violent *adj* violent.

violin *n* (*mus*) violon *m*.

virgin *n*, *adj* vierge *f*.

virile *adj* viril.

virility *n* virilité *f*.

virtual *adj* vrai, virtuel.

virtue *n* vertu *f*.

virtuous *adj* virtueux.

virulent *adj* virulent.

visa *n* visa *m*.

vis-a-vis *prep* vis-à-vis.

visibility *n* visibilité *f*.

visible *adj* visible.

vision *n* vision *f*; vue *f*.

visit *vt* visiter:—*n* visite *f*.

visitor *n* visiteur *m*, -euse *f*.

visual *adj* visuel.

visualise *vt* s'imaginer.

vital *adj* vital; essentiel.

vitality *n* vitalité *f*.

vitamin *n* vitamine *f*.

vivacious *adj* vif.

vivid *adj* vif; vivant.

vocabulary *n* vocabulaire *m*.

vocal *adj* oral.

vocation *n* vocation *f*.

voice *n* voix *f*:—*vt* exprimer.

void *adj* vide:—*n* vide *m*.

volatile *adj* volatile.

volcano *n* volcan *m*.

volition *n* volonté *f*.

voltage *n* voltage *m*.

voluble *adj* volubile.

volume *n* volume *m*.

voluntary *adj* volontaire.

volunteer *n* volontaire *mf*.

voluptuous *adj* voluptueux.

vomit *vt vi* vomir.

voracious *adj* vorace.

vote *n* vote *m*; voix *f*:—*vt* voter.

voter *n* électeur *m*, -trice *f*.

voucher *n* bon *m*.

vow *n* vœu *m*:—*vt* jurer.

voyage *n* traversée *f*.

vulgar *adj* vulgaire; grossier.

vulnerable *adj* vulnérable.

W

wade *vi* patauger.

wafer *n* gaufrette *f*; plaque *f*.

wag *vt vi* remuer.

wage *n* salaire *m*.

wager *n* pari *m*: — *vt* parier.

wages *npl* salaire *m*.

waggon *n* chariot *m*; (*rail*) wagon *m*.

wail *n* gémissement *m*: — *vi* gémir.

waist *n* taille *f*.

wait *vi* attendre: — *n* attente *f*.

waiter *n* garçon *m*; serveur *m*.

waive *vt* renoncer à.

wake *vi* se réveiller: — *vt* réveiller.

walk *vi* marcher: — *vt* parcourir: — *n* promenade *f*.

walker *n* marcheur *m*, -euse *f*.

walking stick *n* canne *f*.

wall *n* mur *m*; paroi *f*.

wallet *n* portefeuille *m*.

wallow *vi* se vautrer.

wallpaper *n* papier peint *m*.

walnut *n* noix *f*; noyer *m*.

wander *vi* errer.

wane *vi* décroître.

want *vt* vouloir: — *vi* manquer: — *n* besoin *m*.

wanton *adj* lascif.

war *n* guerre *f*.

wardrobe *n* garde-robe *f*.

warehouse *n* entrepôt *m*.

wariness *n* circonspection *f*.

warm *adj* chaud; chaleureux: — *vt* réchauffer.

warm-hearted *adj* affectueux.

warmth *n* chaleur *f*.

warn *vt* prévenir.

warning *n* avertissement *m*.

warp *vi* se voiler: — *vt* voiler.

warrant *n* garantie *f*; mandat *m*.

warrior *n* guerrier *m*, -ière *f*.

wary *adj* prudent, circonspect.

wash *vt* laver: — *vi* se laver.

washbowl *n* lavabo *m*.

washing *n* lessive *f*.

washing machine *n* machine à laver *f*.

washing-up *n* vaisselle *f*.

wasp *n* abeille *f*.

wastage *n* gaspillage *m*.

waste *vt* gaspiller: — *n* gaspillage *m*.

wasteful *adj* gaspilleur.

watch *n* montre *f*: — *vt* regarder.

watchful *adj* vigilant.

water *n* eau *f*: — *vt* arroser.

water closet *n* W.C. *mpl*.

watercolour *n* aquarelle *f*.

waterfall *n* cascade *f*.

watering-can *n* arrosoir *m*.

watermark *n* filigrane *m*.

watershed *n* moment critique *m*.

watertight *adj* étanche.

wave *n* vague: — *vi* faire signe de la main.

waver *vi* vaciller, osciller.

wavy *adj* ondulé.

wax *n* cire *f*.

way *n* chemin *m*; voie.

wayward *adj* capricieux.

we *pn* nous.

weak *adj* faible.

weaken *vt* affaiblir.

weakness *n* faiblesse *f*.

wealth *n* richesse *f*.

wealthy *adj* riche.

weapon n arme f.

wear vt porter; user:—vi s'user:—n usage m.

weariness n lassitude f.

weary adj las.

weather n temps m:—~ **forecast** n prévisions météorologiques fpl.

weave vt tisser.

web n toile f.

website n site Web m.

wed vi se marier.

wedding n mariage m; noces fpl.

wedding ring n alliance f.

wedge n cale f:—vt caler.

Wednesday n mercredi m.

weed n mauvaise herbe f:—vt désherber.

week n semaine f.

weekday n jour de semaine m.

weekend n week-end m, fin de semaine f.

weekly adj de la semaine, hebdomadaire.

weep vt vi pleurer.

weigh vt vi peser.

weight n poids m.

weighty adj lourd; important.

welcome adj opportun:—~! bienvenue!:—n accueil m:—vt accueillir.

welfare n bien-être m.

well n puits m:—adj bien, bon:—adv bien.

well-being n bien-être m.

well-bred adj bien élevé.

well-deserved adj bien mérité.

well-known adj connu, célèbre.

well-off adj aisé, dans l'aisance.

west n ouest, Occident m:—adj ouest, de/à l'ouest:—adv vers/à l'ouest.

westerly, western adj (d')ouest.

wet adj humide:—n humidité f:—vt mouiller.

whale n baleine f.

wharf n quai m.

what pn qu'est-ce qui,(qu'est-ce) que, quoi; que, qui; ce qui, ce que; quel(le), que:—adj quel(s), quelle(s):—excl quoi! comment!

whatever pn quoi que; n'importe quoi.

wheat n blé m.

wheel n roue f:—rouler.

wheelbarrow n brouette f.

wheelchair n fauteuil roulant m.

when adv conj quand.

whenever adv quand; chaque fois que.

where adv où:—conj où.

whereas conj tandis que; attendu que.

whereby pn par lequel (laquelle).

wherever adv où que.

whereupon conj sur quoi.

whether conj si.

which pn lequel; celui que, celui qui; ce qui, ce que; quoi, ce dont:—adj quel(s), quelle(s).

while n moment m:—conj pendant que; alors que; quoique.

whim n caprice m.

whimsical adj capricieux.

whip n fouet m:—vt fouetter.

whirl vi tourbillonner.

whirlpool n tourbillon m.

whirlwind n tornade f.

whisper vi chuchoter:—n chuchotement m.

whistle vi siffler:—n sifflement m.

white adj blanc:—n blanc m.

whiten vt vi blanchir.

whiteness n blancheur f.

who pn qui.

whoever pn quiconque, quel(le) que soit.

whole adj tout, entier:—n tout m; ensemble m.

wholesale n vente en gros f.

wholesome adj sain, salubre.

wholly adv complètement.

whom *pn* qui; que.

why *n* pourquoi *m*:—*conj* pourquoi.

wicked *adj* méchant, mauvais.

wickedness *n* méchanceté.

wide *adj* large, ample.

widen *vt* élargir, agrandir.

widow *n* veuve *f*.

widower *n* veuf *m*.

width *n* largeur *f*.

wield *vt* manier, brandir.

wife *n* femme *f*; épouse *f*.

wild *adj* sauvage, féroce.

wild life *n* faune *f*.

wilful *adj* délibéré.

wilfulness *n* obstination *f*.

will *n* volonté *f*; testament *m*.

willing *adj* prêt, disposé:—~**ly** *adv* volontiers.

willpower *n* volonté *f*.

wily *adj* astucieux.

win *vt* gagner.

wind *n* vent *m*; souffle *m*.

wind *vt* enrouler:—*vi* serpenter.

windmill *n* moulin à vent *m*.

window *n* fenêtre *f*.

window pane *n* carreau *m*.

windpipe *n* tranchée *f*.

windscreen *n* pare-brise *m invar*.

windy *adj* venteux.

wine *n* vin *m*.

wine cellar *n* cave (à vin) *f*.

wing *n* aile *f*.

wink *n* clin d'œil *m*.

winner *n* gagnant *m*, -e *f*.

winter *n* hiver *m*:—*vi* hiverner.

wintry *adj* d'hiver, hivernal.

wipe *vt* essuyer.

wire *n* fil *m*.

wireless *adj* sans fil.

wisdom *n* sagesse, prudence *f*.

wise *adj* sage, avisé.

wish *vt* souhaiter, désirer:—*n* souhait, désir *m*.

wit *n* esprit *m*, intelligence *f*.

witch *n* sorcière *f*.

with *prep* avec; à; de; contre.

withdraw *vt* retirer:—*vi* se retirer.

withdrawal *n* retrait *m*.

withhold *vt* retenir.

within *prep* à l'intérieur de:—*adv* dedans.

without *prep* sans.

withstand *vt* résister à.

witness *n* témoin *m*:—*vt* attester.

wittingly *adv* sciemment, à dessein.

witty *adj* spirituel, plein d'esprit.

woe *n* malheur *m*; affliction *f*.

woeful *adj* triste, malheureux.

wolf *n* loup *m*.

woman *n* femme *f*.

womanly *adj* féminin, de femme.

womb *n* utérus *m*.

wonder *n* merveille *f*:—*vi* s'émerveiller.

wonderful *adj* merveilleux.

woo *vt* faire la cour à.

wood *n* bois *m*.

woodcut *n* gravure sur bois *f*.

wooden *adj* de bois, en bois.

woodwork *n* menuiserie *f*.

wool *n* laine *f*.

woollen *adj* de laine.

word *n* mot *m*; parole *f*:—*vt* exprimer

wording *n* rédaction *f*.

word processing *n* traitement de texte *m*.

work *vi* travailler:—*vt* faire fonctionner; façonner:—*n* travail *m*; œuvre *f*; emploi *m*.

worker *n* travailleur *m*, -euse *f*.

workforce *n* main-d'œuvre *f*.

workshop *n* atelier *m*.

world *n* monde *m*.

worldly *adj* mondain.

worldwide *adj* mondial.

worn-out *adj* épuisé; usé.

worry *vt* inquiéter; *n* souci *m*.

worrying *adj* inquiétant.

worse *adj adv* pire.

worship *n* culte *m*; adoration *f*: — *vt* adorer.

worst *adj* le pire: — *adv* le plus mal: — *n* le pire *m*.

worth *n* valeur *f*; mérite *m*.

worthily *adv* dignement.

worthless *adj* sans valeur.

worthy *adj* digne; louable.

wound *n* blessure *f*: — *vt* blesser.

wrap *vt* envelopper.

wreath *n* couronne, guirlande *f*.

wreck *n* naufrage *m*; ruines *fpl*: — *vt* démolir.

wrench *vt* tordre: — *n* clé *f*; torsion violente *f*.

wrestle *vi* lutter.

wretched *adj* misérable.

wrinkle *n* ride *f*: — *vt* rider: — *vi* se rider.

wrist *n* poignet *m*.

wristwatch *n* montre-bracelet *f*.

write *vt* écrire; composer.

writer *n* écrivain *m*; auteur *m*.

writing *n* écriture *f*.

wrong *n* mal *m*; tort *m*: — *adj* mauvais; injuste: — *adv* mal, inexactement: — *vt* faire du tort à, léser.

wrongful *adj* injuste.

wrongly *adv* injustement.

wry *adj* ironique.

X Y Z

xenophobe *n* xénophobe *mf*.

xenophobic *adj* xénophobique.

X-ray *n* rayon X *m*.

xylophone *n* xylophone *m*.

yacht *n* yacht *m*.

yawn *vi* bâiller: — *n* bâillement *m*.

year *n* année *f*.

yearbook *n* annuaire *m*.

yearly *adj adv* annuel(lement).

yearn *vi* languir.

yeast *n* levure *f*.

yell *vi* hurler: — *n* hurlement *m*.

yellow *adj n* jaune *m*.

yes *adv* oui.

yesterday *adv n* hier *m*.

yet *conj* pourtant: — *adv* encore.

yield *vt* produire: — *vi* se rendre: — *n* production *f*.

yog(h)urt *n* yaourt *m*.

you *pn* vous; tu; te; toi.

young *adj* jeune.

youngster *n* jeune *mf*.

your *poss adj* ton, ta, tes; votre, vos.

yours *poss pn* le tien; le vôtre.

yourself *pn* toi-même; vous-même(s).

youth *n* jeunesse *f*; jeune homme *m*.

zeal *n* zèle *m*; ardeur *f*.

zealous *adj* zélé.

zenith *n* zénith *m*.

zero *n* zéro *m*.

zest *n* enthousiasme *m*.

zigzag *n* zigzag *m*.

zip *n* fermeture éclair *f*.
zodiac *n* zodiaque *m*.
zone *n* zone *f*; secteur *m*.

zoo *n* zoo *m*.
zoologist *n* zoologiste *mf*.
zoology *n* zoologie *f*.